SOUTH CAROLINA

SURVEYED BY CHARL.? BOYD D.S. 1818.

IMPROVED FOR MILLS' ATLAS:

1825.

A Goodly Heritage

History of Chester County, South Carolina

compiled by
ANNE PICKENS COLLINS

CHESTER, SOUTH CAROLINA, 1986

LIBRARY OF CONGRESS CATALOG CARD NO. 86-72258

ISBN 0-934870-16-0

MANUFACTURED IN THE UNITED STATES OF AMERICA

THE R. L. BRYAN COMPANY
COLUMBIA, SOUTH CAROLINA

DEDICATION

I dedicate this book to my mother, Iola Wilkinson Pickens who set my sails so that "the lines are fallen unto me in pleasant places; yea, I have a goodly heritage" (Ps.16:6) — and to my husband, Joel Wyman Collins who provided the pleasant places.

ANNE PICKENS COLLINS

PREFACE

Information for this *Chester County History* was compiled by me over a period of twenty years or more during which time I was a "stringer," writing features for Chester News, Rock Hill Herald, Charlotte (N.C.) Observer and The State newspapers. Material was obtained from well-documented sources and personal interviews.

In writing local history, my motive was not money, since anyone can make more of it doing almost anything else. Writing has always been the frosting on my cake and I have written primarily for my own pleasure.

Since Chester County was my space — where my husband settled me — writing about local history, people, places and events was handy grist for my mill. I wrote copiously — it takes a lot of bull to produce a filet mignon.

Something about the subject fueled my curiosity with emotion, such as affection, admiration, amusement, awe or indignation. The stimulus is what counted. No good thing has ever been written out of boredom.

So, "history — that excited and deceitful old woman," as described by Guy de Maupassant, held me in her grip. My children urged me to compile my features into a book, which I have done. If it bumps and grinds and reveals gaps and overlaps, the reason is its long incubation period.

Compiling this book has proven to be the rainbow that halos my golden years.

"None but an author knows an author's cares
   Or fancy's fondness for the child she bears" (Cowper)

I feel an indefinable excitement in the knowledge that this book will have a life of its own.

ANNE PICKENS COLLINS

CREDITS

Book Cover	Robert Emory Anderson
Original art work	Lucy Ellery Adams
Pictures	Richard Wyman Anderson
	R. Earle Steadman
Typing MSS	Debbie Glaze
	Doris Schumacher
Finances	Joel Wyman Collins, Jr.
	Dr. Andrew Pickens Collins

CONTENTS

INTRODUCTION

Chester County: A Shoot From Irish Roots

The 507 square miles of Chester County is a tree with many age rings, its limbs and trunk shaped inexorably by the winds of 250 years, but its tap root deeply embedded in local "Black Jack" soil.

Historian Daniel W. Hollis, whose family roots rest in the county says, "Much of South Carolina history was acted out in Chester County, just as much United States history was acted out in South Carolina. Both have been frontiers for most of their history."

The county and state have always possessed a unique individuality that sets them apart. They have a succinct character, a distinctly Southern style that is universally recognized. Hardy pioneer women of Chester County, as well as the men, have added their deeds of bravery, patriotic fervor and feisty independence to record exciting chapters of history. They have melded into all currents, both constructive and destructive, in the makings of America.

The trouble with too many earlier writers is that they looked back at history through rose-tinted glasses and glorified the very elements of our culture that carried the seeds of destruction. According to Historian Louis B. Wright, among them were pride, self-righteousness and overweening individualism. These qualities made it a land in which political oratory and "heated passions" flourished as luxuriantly as azaleas, dogwood and blackberry bushes.

Wright says saccharine fiction about the clinging-vine beauty and the proud and gallant cavalier ever ready to defend his or her honor in a duel under the live oaks has given an altogether distorted picture of our state and county in any period. Later fiction, called "realistic," swung to the opposite extreme and pictured the area as a miasma of bigotry and backwardness — a "Tobacco Road." This, too, is erroneous.

From early frontier days, Southerners have nourished a large capacity for unreality, an inability to think critically about themselves and their misfortunes. They were not able to see both their faults and virtues in proper perspective and perhaps still aren't.

Chester County was settled by adventurous Irish pioneers who followed well-beaten Indian trails or the "Great Waggon Road" from Pennsylvania and Virginia, or disembarked at the port of Charleston and forged their way upcountry. They were driven by discontent and determination to build a better life for themselves and their families.

W. J. Cash in *Mind of the South* says that men of position and power, men who find life bearable in their accustomed place do not embark on frail ships and cross perilous oceans to reach a dismal frontier where savages prowl and slay, and living is a grim and laborious ordeal.

Settlers who came from northern Ireland included the laborer faced with starvation, the debtor anxious to get out of jail, the apprentice reckless and eager for a fling at adventure, the peasant weary of the exactions of milord, the neurotic haunted by failure and despair, and some wealthy bourgeois smarting under the snubs of haughty aristocracy.

Chester County's ancestry fits into these categories. The hardy craving lads who thrust up from old sturdy Irish root stock came determined to make their way out and on. They craved the unaccustomed freedom of a new country, the glad relief of escape from the European straight jacket, the heady sense of bright unlimited vistas that could open up for them.

And so they came. Land lush and seemingly endless was for the taking. The new country resounded with the ringing of axes and the acrid smoke of new grounds. Fish, game and grazing for cattle were abundant as these pioneers opened up new frontiers in what was to become Chester County.

South Carolina, and consequently Chester County, was shaped by four major themes, according to Dr. Hollis: (1) presence of the Negro in large numbers and white's reaction to that number, (2) agrarianism and ruralism, with no cities until after 1880, (3) Up Country versus Low Country and resulting antagonism, and (4) the Civil War and the South's devastating defeat. These themes are woven into every facet of Chester County's history.

The County's finest hour came during the Revolutionary War. Men and women of extraordinary bravery, determination, ingenuity and sacrifice wrote a proud and immortal chapter in the Nation's fight for independence. Chester Countians' ancestors were almost to a man dedicated to the Patriot's cause. Four major battles and several skirmishes were fought in the area now encompassed by the County. Many local heroes and heroines are memoralized in books, historical markers and patriotic clubs.

The Up Country remained a frontier region until after the Revolution. With the advent of Eli Whitney's cotton gin and the back-breaking labor of the slave and the mule, the Carolinas became the greenest of pastures. Cotton fields sprawling from the Carolinas to Texas would produce the biggest cash crop the nation would ever know. Almost everybody basked in some degree of success.

The Negro slave's importation was a catalyst that changed history in many significant ways. He entered South Carolina and Chester District through the gates of toil. He was forced into the new world against his will as a "burden bearer." As early as 1720, there were 9,200 whites and 12,200 slaves in South Carolina. Negro population was increasing faster than white population and spreading, by barter and trade, all across the South.

Slavery came to be big business when rice and cotton plantations began to call for a large supply of cheap labor. The Negro slaves were conscripted to take up the burden of clearing woodlands and swamps, tending rice paddies and cultivating cotton. Thus, the slave trade was at the bottom of the rise of great commerce, economic development and prosperity in the South.

The Negro was a survivor. He was physically fitted to live and labor in the new environment. He had a superior physical endowment for the hard work at hand, and was constitutionally fitted for the climate. He came from Africa which was in the agricultural stage of civilization at this period. He was accustomed to the regular and monotonous toil necessary for plantation work and was less susceptible to fevers and hot weather than Indians and imported white bond servants from Europe.

The Negro never was — and is not now — convinced of the Anglo-Saxon ethic of the worth of labor "for its own dear sake," according to writer Asa H. Gordon. He ever tends to consider labor as some sort of narrow gate leading to happiness and fuller enjoyment. He tends to rush through his work to arrive at a good time beyond.

The slave laborer sang as he worked and gave birth to the haunting spirituals that are a unique and treasured heritage. He still sings at his work. No matter how dismal his life he found cause to laugh and to josh his fellow workers, to relax and doze in the shade, to play with his babies and enjoy his woman. Negro women well stood the test of exposure, struggle and exploitation imposed on them in those trying days of chattel slavery.

None can or will deny that the Negro made a significant contribution to South Carolina's and Chester County's economy and history.

Chester County's development was cut short by the Civil War, a war caused by a clash of life styles. Dixie self-indulgence clashed with Yankee self-denial. Because slavery was the lodestone, the mere prospect of its abolition touched of breast-beating rebellion among the slave owners. As William Stadiem wrote, they reasoned it was "far better to secede than to have their agrarian Camelot destroyed by Shylocks from the North."

Since the owners of the cotton kingdom also controlled public office and public opinion, the call to arms was answered, even in isolated upcountry pockets. Most of the prosperous planters were blithely and purposefully oblivious to the guilt of slavery. They simply could not function without it.

Chester County furnished 2428 soldiers to the Confederate Army, and for four years devoted its energies and resources with patriotic fervor. At the end it suffered a devastating economic blow in the freeing of thousands of slaves and the consequent loss of labor and means to cultivate crops for sustenance and sale. Much of its property and railroads were destroyed by war. The loss or maiming of its young men was a mortal blow from which it never has — and never will — completely recover. Reconstruction was slow and humiliating under Yankee domination and left scars slow to heal.

The South had nothing to fall back on except pride, and a hope that the cotton kingdom "someday" might be restored. It was difficult to stay proud during the horrors and indignities of Reconstruction. Several courses of action were open to them.

One was to leave the "sunken ship" of the South. Many did, including some from Chester District who migrated to the Midwest and Southwest. Another alternative many took was to stay and try to salvage as much as they could, to establish some means of livlihood, be it horseshoeing, moonshining or hanging out a lawyer's shingle. Some tried small scale farming, enlisting the freedmen as sharecroppers.

The third avenue, and one often taken, was to do nothing at all. Before the war, such occupational indolence was both respectable and feasible. Now it was a state of poverty, frustration and defeat. These "whipped" Southerners, accustomed to comfort and ease, were aimless and lost. They sat on their rotting verandas, staring at the desolation caused by Sherman and the Damnyankees, and waiting for the ill winds of fortune to blow over. The South became a charade of deposed grandeur, arrogant carpet beggars, hooded Klansmen and discombobulated blacks. Chester had its share of each.

They gradually sold their land to feed themselves or sacrificed it to greedy carpet beggars, neglect and unpaid taxes. They were left with little more than a few family heirlooms, their proud names their kin and their history which they tended to interpret in overripe terms of romanticism.

The salvation of the Upcountry was industrialization, with all its attendant ills, according to Mr. Wright. Textile mills first brought a modicum of prosperity to the region. An immense reservoir of cheap labor, including child labor, was available, and the cotton mills lured men and women from the hills and hardscrabble farms. Around each mill the management built clusters of houses, the "mill village," company-owned and controlled, where most of the employees lived. Historians have condemned such capitalistic paternalism, but it was a necessary step in industrial development of the State and County.

Chester County's first mills were built in the early 1900's in Chester and Great Falls soon after three great leaders, James Buchanan Duke, Jr., Dr. W. Gill Wylie of Chester and William

States Lee joined forces and funds to harness the Catawba River and develop hydroelectric power. Cotton mills were built in desperate and optimistic haste to use the abundance of power and bring prosperity to the stricken area.

Most of the "mill hands" lived better and had more comforts than they had ever had before. Before the days of the automobile and modern transportation they had to be in walking distance of their jobs. Colonel Elliot White Springs, a pioneer in textile progress, followed an exemplary — if paternalistic — record of providing for employees of Springs Mills in Chester, Lancaster and York counties. From recreation fields and facilities, insurance coverage and libraries to a vacation complex at Springmaid Beach, he provided for his large force of workers. On the other hand, Republic Mills, in Great Falls, under the Mebanes held an iron fist in an iron glove over its employees. Long time employee Lem W. Pittman said "you didn't 'pee' there without permission from the management."

After some abortive fits and starts Chester's mills flourished and completely dominated the local economy until the late 1970's when textile imports and automation caused mass layoffs and plant closings.

By the 1980's two major bugaboos of the South have almost disappeared, racism and the power structure made up of planters and mill owners, in a bond of white supremacy, "that managed, maneuvered and pushed around" the common people. Family farms that once covered Chester County have also almost disappeared. Farmers, Dr. Wright says, are among the most conservative and hardy specimens of the human race; only staring calamity will force them to change their ways. The boll weevil and country stores extending too much credit proved sufficiently calamitous to turn farmers to cattle raising and pine tree farming or commuting to blue collar jobs.

Economy now rests on imported industry, pulp wood, tourism and federal payments and is not as healthy as Chester Countians wish it was. In 1986 unemployment rate is one of the highest in the state. The Chamber of Commerce is working diligently to lure some of the geese that are laying golden eggs in Mecklenburg County, N.C. and the Piedmont Crescent to come to Chester County.

Tourism and industry are promoted alluringly in slick multicolored brochures, showcasing our temperate climate, our pleasant way of life, our abundance of land and water, our green forests that provide refuge for many species of game and birds.

We have never been a people to hide our light, real or imagined, under a bushel or to shrink from letting the world know of our glories. If we tend to hide our warts — what few of them we concede — who can blame us? We still like ourselves.

Chester Countians are a close knit lot and the family is still its most important institution. While forced to accept change, they cherish the past. Genealogy is moving up as one of the most popular pursuits. Many present day inhabitants and those whose roots are here are enraptly unravelling the lure of discovery, the pains and perils of wars, the arrogance of success and pathos of decline in their family histories. Some are finding much of which to be proud, others are finding "potato ancestry," the best of the lot are underground.

During World Wars I and II the long arm of Selective Service reached out for recruits. Almost all Chester County families watched their able-bodied sons and husbands don uniforms and go to far flung battle-fields to keep the world safe for democracy. Forty-three local men lost their lives in World War I, ninety-five in World War II, and an undetermined number in the Vietnam War.

Wars have written the saddest chapters of history. History teaches that the past and the present are inexorably bound up with each other; there is no such thing as wiping the slate clean, starting over, banishing the past.

William Faulkner, the Mississippi novelist, stated it best: "The past is never dead, it is not even past." In "Absolom, Absolom!" Quentin Compson, the tortured youngster trying to fathom the meaning of his past wonders if "Maybe nothing ever happens once and is finished. Maybe happen is never once but like ripples on water after the pebble sinks, the ripples moving on, spreading, the pool attached by a narrow umbilical water-cord to the next pool."

History, Quentin discovers, is a burden weighing down upon each new generation, connecting us all. We may cope with it, come to terms with it, act responsibly toward it, but we cannot wipe the slate clean, cut the umbilical water-cord.

It is our obligation to preserve it.

MONUMENT TO CATAWBAS
FORT MILL

I INDIANS

EARLIEST INHABITANTS

Down the Indians' well-trodden trading path, close behind the traders, came hordes of white settlers. First a trickle, then large numbers packed the path into a muddy wagon road. The trading path from the north through Pennsylvania and Virginia and up the rivers from Charleston opened the side doors of Carolina.

Some Germans, French Huguenots, Swiss and Highland Scots came, but the majority were Scotch-Irish Presbyterians.

The Scotch-Irish never were Irish. The term denotes a geographical heritage. The Scotch-Irish were descendants of Scots who in 1634 fled the harsh Low Country for Ireland at the suggestion of James I, the Scottish King of England. He offered them new life in northern Ireland.

Frustrated by religious and commercial restrictions, harsh rents from landlords and Irish famines of the 1720's and 1740's, the Scotch-Irish departed.

Records indicate that between 1725 and 1760, 3,000-6,000 persons left Ireland each year, nearly 300,000 altogether. Many of these, unable to pay for passage, became indentured servants in order to come. Behind them, in Ulster, villages lay empty.

James Logan, provencial secretary of Pennsylvania wrote: "It looks as if Ireland is to send all her inhabitants hither ... The common fear is that if they continue to come, they will make themselves proprietors of the province."

As early as 1732 a few Scotch-Irish settled near the mouth of Rocky Creek and began trading with the Indians. The Indians in this section were prosperous and were not bothered by the whites until after the settlements had been made in the low country for some years and settlers in larger numbers were beginning to migrate up country.

1

By that time Indians had acquired some firearms and learned to use them. When the white men came to this section he found the Indian ready to turn his own weapons against him in defense of his home and hunting grounds.

Settlers came slowly at first, probably preferring to remain near Charleston or other settlements where they could flee to the protection of the forts. In those days when there were no roads and travel was done on foot, horseback or by water, it took a man of courage to leave his settlement and push on into the wilderness among the Indians and wild beasts. But push he did, driving before him the Indians and animals, cutting trails into the forests and taming the wilderness.

It is said the early settlers suffered many and varied hardships, often existing on bread and water and the wild game they could kill. The Cherokee Indians who lived in the western part of the State gave them much trouble. The Cherokees were a large and strong tribe. They hunted in the wide area between the Broad and Catawba Rivers then fled to their mountain vastness in the Blue Ridge Mountains.

They swooped down on the colonists, scalping the men, women and children and leaving ruin and desolation in their wake. Before a rescuing party could be assembled they would be far away in the security of the mountains.

In order to protect themselves against the Indians, the settlers in what is now Chester County built two stone forts. One of these forts was built on Fishing Creek and was known as Steel's Fort. The other was built where Landsford now stands and was known as Taylor's Fort.

In 1761, a party of Indians appeared in the fishing Creek neighborhood near the homes of William and James McKenny who were away on a trip to Camden. Several of the neighbors assembled at the house of William McKenny for safety. The next morning, there being no Indians in sight or hearing, Mrs. McKenny ventured out to milk the cows. While she was milking several Indians crawled to where she was. She made no effort to escape, but agreed to go quietly to the house with them.

As they came near the house, Michael Melbery shot at and wounded the Indian that held Mrs. McKenny by the arm. She broke loose and ran toward the door, but as Ferguson opened the door to let her inside he was instantly killed and his mother mortally wounded by shots fired from the rifles of the Indians. Then the door was closed and after several of the Indians had been wounded by shots from the defenders they retired, taking Mrs. McKenny with them.

When they had taken her about half a mile from the house they tomahawked her in the back, scalped her and left her for dead. After a while she regained consciousness and crawled back home. The wound in her head never entirely healed, but she lived for many years and bore several children. One child, born three months after she was tomahawked, was still living in 1837 in Tennessee, the wife of John Steadman. John C. McFadden who held the office of clerk for many years was a great-grandson of Barbara McKenny.

On another raid on Rocky Creek made by the Indians, they killed John McDaniel and his wife and carried off his seven children, the oldest being a girl of 15 years.

These brutal acts so aroused the people that a rescuing and avenging party headed by Thomas Steel was organized and followed the Indians. They stalked them almost to the borders of the Cherokee nation and attacked them in the dead of night. They killed most of the savages, put the rest to flight and rescued the children.

It is related that Thomas Garrett of Rocky Creek killed the Indian who had tomahawked Mrs. McKenny and found her scalp in the savage's shot bag.

THE GATLIN INDIAN COLLECTION

The Claude E. Gatlin Indian collection contains more than 30,000 arrowheads, pot shards, crude instruments and tools, and other Indian artifacts collected in Chester County. The collection started by the late Mr. Gatlin in 1922, is now the prized property of the Chester County Historical Museum.

Mr. Gatlin, agent for the Seaboard Railroad in Great Falls for 48 years, retired in December, 1962. He found most of the arrowheads while hunting along the banks and bottoms of the Catawba River.

Arrowheads in this collection include small bird points used by Indian braves to kill birds and small game, and points to five inches used for bear, buffalo, wolves and other beasts of prey.

There are tomahawks, grinder rocks, axes, hatchets, nutting stones, sinkers, trade beads, bone awls, ceremonial projectile points, thumb scraper drills, celts for scraping hair from hides and arrows that were used to carry poison to its victims — all primitive and crude tools revealing the living habits of the Red Man who were the first known inhabitants of Chester County.

Catawba arrowheads and implements in the Gatlin collection are judged to be among the finest Indian artifacts east of the Mississippi.

A few pieces of broken pottery collected by Mr. Gatlin attest to the high quality and the unique finish of blending and shading of the Catawba artisans. It is readily distinguished from that of other Indian tribes.

CATAWBA INDIANS IN 1985

In 1861, able bodied Indian men joined the Confederate Army. After the war the Catawbas suffered along with the rest of the South in extreme poverty.

In the days shortly after the Civil War about 1878, Mormon missionaries came from Salt Lake City to convert the Indians. They were received warmly by the Indians and nearly the entire reservation in York and Chester Counties was converted to Mormonism. Today there is on the reservation a long, low, white stucco church, home of the Catawba Branch, Church of Jesus Christ of Latter Day Saints. It is the only church there.

Not until 1943 did South Carolina come to the aid of the Catawbas. The Memorandum of Understanding brought some relief, new land was purchased and added to the Old Reservation, and the United States Bureau of Indian Affairs gave assistance. In 1956, Chief Samuel Blue initiated a move to acquire title to tribal lands and severed all dependence upon South Carolina and the United States Government.

In 1960, the General Tribal Council voted to sell all tribal assets and distribute all proceeds among tribal members. This was done. A total of 631 persons on the tribal roll on 2 July 1960 shared in the distribution of 3,388 acres of the "new" reservation located in seven tracts east of Rock Hill, South Carolina. A total of 170 deeds were distributed. Value of the land was estimated at $190,000.

Excluded from the division were 135 acres set aside for church, school, playground, park, cemetery and other community purposes. Also, the 630-acre "old" reservation held in trust by the State of South Carolina was not dissolved. No plans have been made for the use of this land.

The Catawbas with no chief, no tribal council, and no reservation have few marks of tribal life left. Even the few artisans of the centuries-old Indian pottery are gone. The Twentieth Century has snuffed out hundreds of years of tradition. The Catawbas work in area textile mills, pay income taxes, drive pick-up trucks, attend public schools and go to football games like everybody else.

The Vanishing American has been absorbed.

ADAIR'S HISTORY OF INDIANS

James Adair's book, *History of the American Indians,* published in London in 1775, is the major source of information on life in the Indian villages.

Adair spent more than 40 years as an Indian trader, soldier and writer while living with three of the South's major tribes, the Cher-

okees in the northwest, the Catawbas in the north-central areas, and
the Chickasaws in Mississippi and in the Savannah River area.

Born in County Antrim, Ireland, Adair came to Charles Towne
in 1735. He was age 26, well educated, adventurous and unmarried.
For years he lived and traded with the Cherokees where he began
writing his book. He described in detail the Carolina Indians tribal
customs, worship and religious rites, festivals, burial rituals, medici-
nal concoctions, courting and marriage customs.

In 1743 Adair was living among the Catawbas in the Chester-
York area. He later lived with the Chicasaws in Mississippi and took
a Chicasaw wife by whom he had children. He wrote his book
between 1761-1768 while moving from village to village.

He went back to England to have his book published and spent
several years trying to find a publisher. After he succeeded he
returned to America and settled in the North Carolina mountains
where he spent the remainder of his life.

Adair's history, rare and very expensive for years, has been
reprinted by Colonial Dames of America, Tennessee chapter. After
more than 200 years, it remains a delightful and readable authority
on life in the Indian villages.

CATAWBAS AND CHEROKEES, INDIANS IN CHESTER AREA

The vast Indian hunting ground between the Broad and Catawba Rivers, where Chester County lies now, according to history,
was prized by both the Cherokees and Catawbas for the great herds
of buffalo, deer, elk and other game; (there is evidence that buffalo
were in this area as late as the 1760's). A great battle for possession of
the area took place. Hundreds of Cherokee and Catawba warriors
were slain. A truce was called, and it was decided that this hunting
ground, between the Broad and Catawba Rivers, was to be a kind of
neutral territory to be used by members of both tribes. The Broad
River was to be the dividing line and was thus named by the
Catawbas, the Eswa Huppeday — meaning Line River.

The Indian Mound on the Broad River at Turkey Creek is
evidence of the Indian antiquity of the area. There is a question as to
whether it was Cherokee, Catawba, or of some more ancient tribe in
origin. An old Cherokee Trading Path crosses the Broad River about
20 miles north of this area. This path was an upper leg of the Great
Virginia Trading Path, along which trekked traders from Virginia,
even before the founding of the Colony of South Carolina in 1670.
Some eight miles or so below, on the Broad River, is an ancient
Indian fishdam. Later this was used by early settlers as a fording area
into what is now Newberry County and the famous Dutch Fork

area. Logan, in his *History of the Upper County of South Carolina,* referring to Indian remains, mentions "a great variety of interesting relics" found throughout the Broad River Valley, including "the familiar stone implements of their warlike and domestic arts."

In early days the Catawbas had many villages but few names have come down to us. In 1728 there were sixteen villages, all on the Catawba River within a stretch of twenty miles, the most northerly of which was known as Nauvasa. In 1781 they had two called English Newton and Turkey Head, on opposite sides of the Catawba River.

The Catawba appear first in history under the name Ysa, Issa (Iswa) about 1566. In 1711-13 they assisted the Whites in their wars with the Tuscarora, and though they participated in the Yamasee uprising in 1715 peace was quickly made and the Catawba remained friends of the colonists ever after. Meanwhile they declined steadily in numbers from diseases introduced by the Whites, the use of liquor, and constant warfare with the Iroquois, Shawnee, Delaware, and other tribes. In 1738 they were decimated by smallpox and again in 1759 when the same disease destroyed nearly half of them.

A few of the Catawbas went to North Carolina, others went to the Cherokees, but most of them came back and the last of those who remained died in 1889. A few joined the "Trail of Tears" to the Choctaw Nation in what is now Oklahoma.

In 1762, remnants of the tribe settled on a tract of land 15 miles square reserved for them in South Carolina (in what is now York, Lancaster and Chester Counties). They gradually sank into relative insignificance. They sided with the colonists during the revolution. In 1826 nearly the whole of the reservation was leased to Whites, and in 1840 they sold all of it to the State of South Carolina.

Ultimately, a reservation of 800 acres was set aside for them in South Carolina and the main body has lived there ever since. Besides the two divisions of Catawba proper, the present tribe is supposed to include remnants of about 20 smaller tribes, principally Siouan.

Estimates of the number of Catawba in the area in 1600 was 5,000. About 1682 the tribe was estimated to contain 1,500 warriors and about 4,600 souls. In a steady decline, by 1775 there was estimated a total population of 400. The census of 1910 returned 124, and 1912 there were about 100, of whom 60 were attached to the reservation.

The Catawba early became recognized as the most powerful of all the Siouan peoples of Carolina. They are also the tribe which preserved its identity longest and from which the greatest amount of linquistic information has been obtained. The Catawba River and Catawba grapes get their names from the Catawba Indians.

A remarkable collection of Indian artifacts was unearthed along the banks of the Catawba River in Chester County by the late Claude Gatlin of Great Falls. Considered one of the largest and most valuable of collections, it is the property of Chester County Museum.

FUDGE ISLAND INDIAN MOUND

Fudge or Davy's Island was in the Catawba River about two miles below the old Landsford Crossing. It was reached by putting in at Buster's Landing in Fort Lawn and going upstream to the first large island. According to residents of the Fudge Community above Fort Lawn, this Indian mound is no longer existant because it was washed away in the great flood of 1916. Harry Jordan, proprietor of the Fudge Community General Store stated that the mound was located near the center of the island and was about 25 to 30 feet high. According to Mr. Jordan, there was a large buzzard's roost on top. The last anyone saw of the mound was when the rising waters reached the top, washed away the buzzard's nest and the homeless buzzard flew off into the distance.

CHESTER IN INDIAN PERIOD

L. M. Ford says that before the advent of white men, Chester's rolling hills were covered with wild pea vine from one to two feet high, while great cane breaks grew to great heights on the creek and river bottoms. The woods were made noisy by the chattering of the cat squirrels. The fox squirrels made their home in the tall pines and waxed fat on the juicy cones. Numbers of wild turkeys stalked through the forest; deer browsed and gamboled unmolested on the hillsides while the more ferocious animals such as wildcats and panthers made their homes in the swamps on the streams.

Blackbirds, wild pigeons and many varieties of song birds inhabited the forests. Ducks and geese and fish of many species abounded in the streams.

Indian settlements dotted the area. Indian wigwams were clustered about the springs.

Butler McCallum in his memoirs says:

"My grandfather, James Beldon Atkinson, once told me that when he was a lad there were yet some Catawba Indians living nearby in West Chester. He pointed to an oak tree in the yard and said that back in those days that tree was about one foot in diameter. He recalled seeing white men place small coins in the bark of the tree for Indian boys to shoot at with arrows. When the coin was hit, the Indians could claim it for good marksmanship. This took place about 125 years ago. This tree is now about five feet in diameter and is slowly dying of old age."

KING HAIGLER

The principal chief of the Catawbas and the one with the most colorful history is King Haigler (also spelled Hegler, Haggler, Hagler). He was chief of the Catawba Nation 1750-1763. He offered his services to Governor Glen of South Carolina in subduing an old enemy, the Cherokees, who inhabited the hills of upper South Carolina and often encroached on Catawba hunting grounds. Governor Glen, a forty-two year old Scottish lawyer who arrived in Charleston in 1743, virtually made a career of Indian negotiations.

The royal governor found the Catawbas "as brave fellows as any on the continent of America and our firm friends." The whites benefitted from Haigler's unwavering friendship and loyalty, and Haigler depended on Governor Glen to keep peace among white settlers, warring tribes and the Catawbas.

Haigler regularly approached the governor for gifts. Not only did he ask for corn, horses and ammunition, but also for fancy "cloathing" for his warriors and saddles for his ponies.

By 1739, Haigler sent this eloquent request to Governor Glen: "Formerly I walked fast, but now am old and unable to walk home, therefore, must beg the favor of a horse from your Excellency and as my sight is fail'd shall be obliged to you for a good gun."

Haigler's name often crops up on the pages of the South Carolina Council Journals. The Council regularly paid Catawbas for Cherokees' scalps (in the form of a bounty) and for services in tracking runaway slaves. The Catawbas were also treated to the services of doctors, gunsmiths and tavern keepers.

Governor Glen, energetic and flamboyant, served as governor for thirteen years, the longest term of any colonial governor and labored unceasingly to cement friendly relations with the red men of the frontier.

Haigler credited Governor Glen and the white men for elevating his tribe's standard of living. History records this bounty as a mixed blessing considering that the white man also brought firearms, alcohol ("fire water") and smallpox, the instruments which in less than 100 years helped to reduce the Catawba population from 6,000 to less than 1,200.

King Haigler worked for many years to secure passage of the Treaty of Augusta which set aside for the Catawbas a tract of 144,000 acres in the present counties of Lancaster, York and

Chester, South Carolina. The survey was made in 1763-64 by a Quaker, Samuel Wyly who received 1,000 lbs. out of royal funds for his work.

Haigler was ambushed and killed in 1763 by a raiding band of seven Shawnees out of Virginia who were long enemies of the Catawbas. Six bullets were fired and Haigler was killed instantly. His only companion, a slave, escaped to spread the word. Catawba drums made of deer skin stretched over clay pots spread the message. The loss of Haigler was a severe blow to the Scotch-Irish settlers who had thought themselves safe among the Catawbas.

Haigler was buried in a manner befitting royalty. His grave was 10 feet wide, 10 feet long and 10 feet deep. Buried with him were his silver-mounted rifle, gold and silver money, and other valuable personal possessions. For one month the grave was guarded by sixteen warriors. Then some Virginia gamblers got the guards drunk and pillaged the grave.

Although King Haigler was dead, his name was affixed to the survey map of the Treaty of Augusta. Its aims and intentions had been sought by him in his lifetime, and his influence prevailed even in death.

With him an era came to an end. Edward Pearson wrote of this greatest of Catawba chiefs: "They (the Catawbas) have never looked up since his death." James Mooney cited Haigler's death and said: "From this time the Catawba ceased to be of importance except in conjunction with the whites."

In Fort Mill Township a branch is named for Haigler and perpetuates his name locally. There is a memorial to Haigler atop a building at Camden. On Highway 5 in Lancaster County there is an official historical marker which reads: On the Catawba Path near here King Haigler, chief of the Catawba Nation (1750-1763) was slain on August 50, 1763, by a raiding band of northern Indian braves as he journeyed from the Waxhaw settlement on Cane Creek to a Catawba town on Twelve Mile Creek."

INDIAN CUSTOMS

White settlers found Indian civilization to be characterized by the honor given to women. A deed to the whites in 1675 is signed by "women captains" as well as by men. De Soto met an Indian queen of territory along the east bank of the Savannah. The roles assigned to women in religion, war, or social functions indicate an honorable standing. If the woman bore the burden, it was that the man might meet a sudden attack. If she tilled the fields, he endured the hardships of the hunt and the battle. Polygamy was practiced by those who could afford it, and the Indians' morality compared favorably with that of any people of a similar degree of civilization.

Great distances were traversed for war or trade. A path that led from Charleston to the Mississippi was known as the Suwali-nan, the Cheraw path, which on the tongue of the white man became the Swannonoa. The path came through the upcountry. A tribe might migrate in a few years upward of a thousand miles in search of sustenance.

Indian government was democratic. The chiefs were leaders rather than rulers, and often after the oldest and wisest had given their advice, every warrior had his part in deciding whether there should be peace or war. The lashing of passions by the war dance shows how well the Indians understood mass psychology. Making laws and enforcing authority were nebulous.

The religion of Indians was based on a belief in powers residing in animals or inanimate objects. A variety of animals were worshipped, differing as widely as the rattlesnake and rabbit. Their conception of "the Great Spirit" was apparently derived from some contact with Christianity.

Indians undeniably influenced up-country history. The constant readiness for war which their presence necessitated and the mental state of self-reliance which they helped to produce in the colonists were important parts of the latter's training for the struggle in which they were to defend their rights against the mother country. The vegetables and other products that the Indians already raised made an important contribution to the white man's comfort and wealth, and their tobacco became the economic foundation of a notable civilization.

The memory of the red men is inscribed on every part of the State in many of the most beautiful and appropriate of our geographical names. Despite his manifest faults and often bitter enmity between white and red, the dignity, the romance, the tragedy of the Indian have their part in the background of our history.

CONESTOGA WAGON 1725-1850

II EMIGRATION

WHY THE EMIGRANTS CAME

An anonymous eighteenth century author wrote that "emigration is never produced without pangs and struggles."
The pangs and struggles that drove thousands of emigrants from Ireland to the New World were two-fold. One was their burning desire for personal economic stability. They could not achieve this in the harsh mountainous region to which they had been pushed by English and Scottish settlers. These settlers, under the aegis and the beneficence of the Stuart kings, gradually took possession of the most fertile lands of Ulster, leaving generally only the mountainous regions to the native Irish.

Most of the people of this migration had been prompted to leave Scotland and England by 'poverty, scandalous lives, and adventurous seeking of better accommodation'. Ulster was nearby and land was cheap and accessible so it became their haven. This seventeenth-century stream of Scottish immigrants, a stream that at times reached flood proportions, left its mark on the character and out-look of the presbyterians of eighteenth century Ireland. To them, Ireland was a port in a storm and they held no strong emotional ties to their adopted country. Their urge and tradition of emigration were strong. To many, the survival of their presbyterian beliefs and the increasing economic distress in Ireland made their sojourn there appear as but a resting place on their journey to America, the land of promise.

The Scotch-Irish struggle for religious freedom was a force as strong as the economic as a rallying point of the people. Their quest for a free conscience and a full stomach eluded them in the homeland. The bold and adventurous were willing to go far afield and endure the crucibles of emigration in a continuing search of their green acres and their God.

This turbulent religious and economic history of Ireland in the eighteenth century determined the heights and depths of Irish emigration of that period and eventually opened the door to the settlements of the Upcountry of the Carolinas from which Chester County was eventually carved.

Scotch and Irish presbyterians for a century had suffered English repression. Although they supported and fought for causes espoused by English kings, the English government not only repeatedly failed to secure more toleration for them but also imposed on them the Test Act and other untenable laws.

This domination by the Church of England reached its apex in 1704, during the reign of Queen Anne of England, contemporaneous with the early settlement of the American Colonies. She had passed the Test Act which imposed upon the Scots an obligation quite unbearable to them. This act required the Scots living in North Ireland to swear allegiance to the established Church of England.

As a result of this edict, sixty-one of the ministers of the single province of Ulster were ejected from their churches. Four hundred of the most dedicated ministers in Scotland were ejected from their kirks and manses. In addition, they were subjected to fines, imprisonment and banishment, and some to death. The Rev. William Banks in his *Catholic Church, A Historical Discourse* says, "Yet so devoted to their ministers were many of the congregations that they wept aloud until their lamentations resembled the wild wailings of a city taken by storm."

The strength of the presbyterian bloc and the reality of the hold of the presbyterian church over the daily lives of its members had an important effect on both the attitude of the established church to toleration and on the volume of emigration. On the one hand, many were convinced that granting more freedoms to such a body would be but the prelude to a presbyterian bid for supremacy. On the other, just as coals burn more brightly when in contact with one another, so did resentment rise among the closely knit and numerically dominant presbyterian congregations in north-eastern Ireland.

If that resentment did not of itself produce emigration, it helped the waverers to make their decision and lived in many minds long after temporal hardships were forgotten. Emigration in such a community, says R. J. Dickson in *Ulster Emigration,* was likely to be as contagious as a fever in an unsanitary town. It was liable to become a local epidemic if the minister sponsored it.

Tradition has it that the Scotch-Irishman is noted for keeping the Sabbath and everything else he can lay his hands on. If so, economic conditions in Ireland were no more appealing to him than religious conditions during the century prior to the American Revolution.

A study of Scotch-Irish emigration embracing only accounts of persecution, poverty and hardship, however, would be deceptive and incomplete. The forces which induced emigration are two-fold. As well as pressure and persecution from within a country there must be some attraction from without, whether that attraction is a shining light in its own right or merely made so by the darkness of home conditions. Both of these were doubtless responsible for European emigration to America.

English Treasury records (January, 1774) throw some additional light on the influence of the attraction of America in the century by the replies of port authorities in response to an order to report to the Treasury the number of emigrants and why they emigrated. The stated reason was:

"They were informed and understood they could live much better and with more ease in the country to which they were going then they could in this country. These persons and some others who had gone to North America having wrote letters to their relations and friends in this country advising of their beneficial settlements there, and of their having purchased for a trifling sum the property of a considerable extent of lands that produce plentifully the necessaries and comforts of life have raised a spirit of emigration amongst others of the like station in the country next to madness."

Agents and advertisement, as early as 1729, were described as seeking to "entice and ensnare the unwary people of northern Ireland to seek a better land." Agents of the Brittania who, announcing the date of the vessel's departure, declared that "The ship, by the blessing of God, will then proceed on her intended voyage for the Land of Promise."

More persuasive were letters from friends and family extolling "freedom, peace and plenty to those who now wish to enjoy those blessings, as well as secure the same on the highest degree for their posterity."

When emigrants arrived in America they may have found that conditions were not what shipping advertisements and letters from friends had led them to expect. It was, however, those romantic advertisements and letters that represented, in Ireland, the actuality of American life, and their brightness attracted eyes that hardship had dimmed.

VOYAGE TO AMERICA

R. J. Dickson describes the Voyage to America. "The realities of the normal emigrant voyage need no embellishment to make it surprising that so many people emigrated. Not even lavish advertisement, unblemished by doubts but appearing side by side with accounts of disasters at sea, could conceal the danger entailed in a transatlantic voyage in an emigrant vessel. The mysteries of the deep, together with the vagaries of storms and calms over a period of weeks or months, lay ahead of all vessels.

For many, man-made hardships were added to the caprice of nature. The brutalities of ship masters, the appearance of pirates and privateers, and shortages of water and food turned emigrant ships into floating islands of despair; disease and pestilence, always a grim possibility that was all too often nurtured by overcrowding, turned them into floating lazar-houses,"

The trials of the emigrant often began before he set foot on the vessel that was to carry him to America. It was almost unusual for an emigrant vessel from the north of Ireland to sail on the advertised sailing date. Reasons given by shipping agents for the delays ranged from the lateness of the harvests to the captain's poor state of health. The most common excuse was that the delay was really a magnanimous and self-sacrificing concession to benefit intending passengers who had asked for further time in which to settle their affairs in Ireland. In some cases, the real reason was the erratic and unpredictable schedules of the ships.

Of the thirty-eight emigrant voyages between 1771-1775, it took each of these vessels an average seven weeks and four days to cross the Atlantic, the shortest voyage lasting 27 days and the longest 17 weeks.

Between 1760 and 1769, twenty-three vessels came to South Carolina and Georgia, thanks to the renewal of the bounty system which had attracted immigrants to South Carolina in the 1750's. By 1760, Indian attacks were causing "distress and consternation" in South Carolina. In order to increase the number of white inhabitants of the colony, a duty was levied on the importation of negro slaves and proceeds used to pay the passage money of protestant immigrants from Europe and to give them forty shillings to purchase tools and provisions. The head of each family was to be granted 100 acres of land, together with fifty acres for each nember of his family.

Prior to the arrival of Reverend Martin's party in 1750, some presbyterians from Octorora in eastern Pennsylvania, Virginia and North Carolina had come to South Carolina and settled on Rocky Creek. By 1755, emigrants from Ireland were coming in growing numbers, many being Covenanters.

One of the earliest Scotch-Irish settlements in the upper part of South Carolina was in what is now Chester County in the region known as Richburg. The counties of Chester, Lancaster and York were all settled about the year 1745. There was a trading post some place near Rocky Mount as early as 1732, which was continued by the British government down to the beginning of the Revolutionary War. These traders, at first, came to Rocky Mount from Charleston.

The first white man, as far as is known, who crossed the Catawba River above Rocky Mount was a man by the name of Lefeve. The river was crossed in the fall of 1732 at what was afterward called Buffalo Ford, half a mile below Thorn's Ferry. Lefeve, it seems, was on his way to the Rocky Mount trading post. He described the region as a "prairie covered with pea vines and clover haunch high, but without trees."

ERIN'S
FIRST FAMILIES

LETTERKENNY
DONEGAL

BALLYSHANNON

NORTHERN IRELAND

HICKLING
HOLLIS
HOOD
HOUSTON
LEE
LEE
LAND
MCDANIEL
MCDILL
MCCLUER
MCDANIEL
McDONALD
McCOWN
McGARITY
McGUIRT
McLURKIN
McQUISTION
MAYBEAN
MILLER
MONTGOMERY
MIDDLETON

ADAMS
BARBER
BEARD
BLAIR
BOYKIN
BRADFORD
BURNS

CAMPBELL
CHERRY
COPELAND
CULP
DICKSON
FERGUSON
GARRETT
GASTON
GIBSON
GRAY
GREGG
GILL

RAY
REALY
SCOTT
STRONG
WALKER
WILLIS
WHITE
WILLIAMS
WYLIE
WILSON

III *PIONEERS IN CAROLINA*

IRISH SETTLERS CAME IN 1750's

For more than half a century after the Lord's Proprietors planted the colony of Carolina in 1670, population did not extend further inland than thirty miles from the tide-water. But a great change came about the middle of the century. The back country began to fill in with pioneers. Neither the people nor the colonial authorities waited for treaties with the Indians for occupancy of their lands. As early as 1749, into this region of which Chester was a part, a great throng of people came and settled during the twenty-five years prior to the Revolution.

White-topped Conestoga wagons, dubbed "the vehicle of empire" formed trains southward from Pennsylvania, Virginia and North Carolina. They came by way of the Great Wagon Road from Pennsylvania through the Shanandoah Valley of Virginia. From there they followed Indian trails or made their own. Some of the settlers were men of means in the middle colonies and came to Carolina for more accessible lands and more freedom from the strictness of Quaker policies in Pennsylvania and surrounding settlements. Another throng of settlers poured in through the port of Charles Town.

J. S. Bassett in his *Life of Jackson* says the settlers sought the uplands where meadows with grass as tall as a man's head bordered a thousand creeks and brooks. Primeval nature gave way to swinging axemen; black bear left the cane breaks to domestic cattle; forests were replaced by orchards and grainfields. The skills and arts and presence of a fair-haired race announced that the white man's civilization had come to displace immemorial savagery.

In the treaty of 1753 negotiated between Governor Glen and the Cherokee Indians a fort and necessary acreage for it was provided for, with a wide wagon road to the southward from Fort

Prince George to Ninety Six. Nothing except a fort, pastures, fields, woods for the support of its garrison and the road were involved. Assumption by the whites in the following years to settle pretty much as they pleased in the Piedmont region was simply an expression of their usual determination to take good lands wherever found. They ignored, misunderstood or disregarded the terms of the treaty in staking their claims.

While a few adventurous and hardy pioneers may have ventured to establish permanent homes on the west side of the Catawba in Chester County before 1750, we are certain that they did so soon afterwards.

From both sides of the plateau on which the county seat of Chester now stands streams run into the Catawba and Broad Rivers. Rocky Creek and Fishing Creek run eastward to the Catawba. Sandy River and Turkey Creek run westward into the Broad. From official records in Secretary of State's office come the names of those who entered this area and planted their homes on Rocky Creek: John Willis, 250 acres in 1752; Frances Lee, 50 acres in 1753; George Taylor, 400 acres in 1753; Thomas Land, 400 acres in 1754; John Jacob Culp, 150 acres in 1756; Tom Luten, 50 acres in 1756; William Taylor, 200 acres in 1756; Phillip Walker, 200 acres in 1757; Ephiram Lide, 100 acres in 1757; Alexander Walker, 100 acres in 1758; Francis Henderson, 150 acres in 1758; John McFadden, 100 acres in 1756; James McCluer, 100 acres in 1760.

Settlers on Fishing Creek were John Gaston, 100 acres in 1760; Lawrence Callahan, 157 acres in 1757.

On Sandy River some pioneers of this same decade were Christian Miller, 200 acres, John Sealy, 200 acres and Samuel Wells, 100 acres.

Farther west on Turkey Creek was George Fowser, 100 acres. Nicholas Vansant was on Terrble Creek, Broad River, in 1750 when he received 500 acres. His was the earliest land grant noted.

After the Treaty of Paris terminated the Seven Years War (or Cherokee War), settlement in the upcountry took a decided upswing. These people who filtered in from the middle of the century onward until after the American Revolution were not without letters and ordinances of religion. John Fiske speaks highly of the literacy of the Scotch-Irish who were a large element among these early peoples. There were about ten per cent of Revolutionary soldiers who signed with their "marks" their indents for pay.

Pioneer life and grueling hardships of the wilderness affected the settlers, yet the decencies and proprieties of civilized life were by no means obliterated. The rude manners of the frontier forefathers were not typical of every person nor every household. Numerous families of the stretch of country from York across Chester to Fairfield maintained the amenities and signs of vigorous intelligence and gracious gentility that continue to this day.

The legacy of the Scotch-Irish is still strong and pervasive in the Chester and contiguous areas. Its tenets are conservatism, especially in finance, excellence in education and reluctance to change. Old family names peppering the area indicate how deeply and firmly our ancestors planted their roots.

The Reverend Charles Woodmason in his *Diary* flipped the other side of the coin.

REVEREND CHARLES WOODMASON

The "high living" and "gracious talks" associated with the planter aristocracy were not hallmarks of the Back Country. At the Cheraws in 1766, Reverend Charles Woodmason lambasted the monotonous diet of "pork, cornbread, Buttermilk, Clabber, and what in England is given to the Hogs and Dogs."

Woodmason, an Anglican missionary, often complained about his potential parishioners, and his critical diary is not burdened with compliments of a people who were scarcely marked by gracious manners or delicate decorum. In 1768, he reported preaching to a curious flock who had never heard a preacher before in their lives — or even heard the Lord's Prayer. In shock, he wrote, "After the Service they went out to Revelry, Drinking, Singing, Dancing and Whoring, and most of the Company was drunk before I quitted the Spott."

The tart-tongued Woodmason portrays some rather wretched conditions and uninspiring characters in his record of his own passionate combat against immorality and irreligion in general and against Baptists and Presbyterians in particular.

PATHS OF THE PIONEERS

Roads eventually cut across the old hunting grounds of the Catawba and Cherokee Indians who long blocked the development of the back country. Few white settlers ventured into Indian territory.

Many highways crisscross this land that in colonial times was made inaccessible by rivers and creeks too deep or too swift to ford.

The network of hard surface roads that has now brought villages and towns within minutes of each other makes it hard for modern travelers to realize that a different terrain isolated these same localities from each other until well into the nineteenth century.

Numerous waterways running from the highlands to the sea caused immigrants to settle along the streams instead of crossing them except for a few fords (such as Fish Dam Ford on the Broad in Chester County), and an occasional trade ferry made transit possible.

The earliest penetration of the back country was made by river boats up the navigable streams. But shoals and rapids such as the "great falls" of the Catawba ended navigation until the era of canal building that began in the late eighteenth century.

When water navigation failed, immigrants to the back country depended on pack horses or trudged on foot along ancient trails that the Indians had marked. At best, these were long, narrow and rough.

Most famous of the routes to the interior was the Cherokee Path that Indian traders and warriors had beaten long before the white man came. It roughly paralled U. S. Interstate 26 to Charleston. Another led from Charleston to the Indian settlements of the Congarees south of Columbia and from there due north to the Catawba of Chester and York Counties. A third great Indian trail crossed the Savannah River at Augusta and angled southeast to Charleston.

Many early settlers found it quicker and less expensive to follow the inland Virginia Trading Path to South Carolina, entering from North Carolina at the upper York and Lancaster County borders. Then, depending on their destination, legs of the great path were taken leading to Chester, Fairfield, Newberry, Kershaw, Sumter, Richland and other counties. Settlers bound for Newberry and Dutch Fork areas used a wagon road that crossed the Broad River at Fishdam Ford. According to legend, this ancient fish dam was built by the Catawba Indians.

A sloping row of stones from either bank of the river (still visible when water is low) drove the fish to an opening near the middle of the river where they were caught in long tapering baskets made mostly of cane. Reportedly, Indians in the river, upstream, would drive the fish toward the dam when large numbers were needed for a feast.

Fishdam Ford was downstream from the old ferry crossing on the 1825 Mills map but is just upstream from the S. C. 72 Highway bridge. This difference is due to the need of deeper water for the ferry and shallow water for the bridge. The old wagon ford was at about the same location as the present bridge.

EARLY MIGRATION

William Martin, the first Covenanting minister in South Carolina played a major role in early Chester County history. His name is mentioned prominently in nearly all accounts of Scotch-Irish settlers in the area. He was born in Londonderry County, Ireland, 16 May 1729 and "was reared in the strictest manner by Covenanter parents."

Educated at the University of Glasgow, William Martin was ordained 13 July 1757 and was placed in charge of the presbyterian "societies" centering in Ballymoney. To promote cohesiveness among the troubled presbyterians, the societies were organized and then associated themselves into corresponding meetings, and these into a General Meeting.

In the 1700's, conditions became steadily worse for presbyterians in Northern Ireland. In the spring of 1729, two presbyterian leaders, Craghead and Iredell, gave four complex reasons for emigration. They were (1) the forbidding of the erection of presbyterian meeting houses, (2) the inability of presbyterians to occupy public posts, (3) the illegality of presbyterian marriages, and (4) the prohibition of all schools other than those conducted by teachers licensed by bishops.

In 1727, a near-famine struck Ireland and the two following years were so abnormal that the awe-stricken people believed them to be either "heralds of eternity or vehicles of the wrath of God." Three years of dearth had a devastating effect on a country whose powers of resistance had already been undermined.

The woes of the presbyterians were particularly galling. Not only were they taxed to support a church not their own but most of them were either employed in some branch of the textile industry or were farmers. Business was bad in one and rents too high in the other.

Emigration agents could not have wished for a more promising field in which to work. Their artful insinuations found attentive ears among a people whose home ties were already being loosened by necessity. They were also lured by accounts sent by emigrants of previous years to their afflicted families and friends in north Ireland "inviting and encouraging them to transport themselves thither, and promising them liberty and ease as the reward of honest industry."

About this time, the Reverend William Martin received a "call" to come to South Carolina. Presbyterian tradition is that he decided to go and, following an incident of violence resulting from high rents, he preached a fiery sermon calling on all his congregation to accompany him.

Reverend Martin stated the acute problem of paying exorbitant rents, said that land would not bring in enough income to pay them, that already many were beggared and in time all would be.

He cited an incident early in 1772 where the landlords' agent came to the Beck home to collect the rent, or possibly dispossess them for failure to pay the rent. Mrs. Beck was in labor with her first child. Mr. Beck (who was a big man 6 ft. 4 in. and twenty stone, so the story goes) was so concerned about her condition that he could not be bothered and took the bailiff by the neck and threw him out of the house. Unfortunately, the man landed on his head and broke his neck. The wife and baby died. When the authorities came for Beck he could not be found.

Reverend Martin admonished his flock that more and more such incidents would occur. He said as a minister he could not stand idly by and await the violence and ruin that would come. He proposed that the congregation, under his leadership, emigrate to South Carolina where they could get free land and live as free men. The congregation, having nothing to lose by it, agreed.

Reverend Martin did go and took with him a party of some 467 families on five ships. In fact, Reverend William Martin (Kellswater) is shown as one of the agents in signing up the passengers for the Lord Dunlunce on which he sailed.

Charleston, South Carolina newspapers from midsummer 1772 to January 1773 showed arrival of five ships from North Ireland ports at the right time, furnished names of the captains and port from which they sailed. These ports were all the ones from which passengers from the Ballymoney area might logically have embarked. Four of these ships were the Lord Dunlunce, Hopewell, Pennsylvania Farmer and Free Mason. The fifth was the James and Mary which sailed from the same port as the Lord Dunlunce and passengers on it are known from several other sources to have been part of Reverend William Martin's party.

Jean Stephenson in *Scotch-Irish Migration to South Carolina* lists the probable sequence of events that followed. The James and Mary arrived at Charleston long before the rest of the ships but was detained for some time in quarantine because of smallpox having been on board. Then persons on it applied for the bounty and land. After some delay surveys were authorized and warrants and precepts prepared, dated December 11, 1772, but not issued, nor were the names of individuals entered on the Council Journal until Reverend Martin and the remaining ships arrived in port.

Information taken from advertisements in the Belfast newspaper gives the following: James and Mary: 200 tons; master, J. Workman; agents Jas. McVicker, John Moore, merchant. This vessel sailed from Larne August 25, 1772.

Lord Dunlunce: 400 tons; Master, James Gillis; agent, John

Montgomery, merchant, Reverend William Martin (Kellswater), Wm. Barklie. This ship sailed from Larne October 4, 1772 and arrived at Charlestown on December 20, 1772.

Pennsylvania Farmer: 350 tons; Master, C. Robinson; agent, John Ewing, S. Brown, merchants; later added Reverend John Logne. Sailing postponed to allow farmers to dispose of their crops; sailed from Belfast October 16, 1772.

Hopewell: 250 tons. June 16 advertised arrival in England from South Carolina; a minister urgently needed. (The "call" to Reverend Martin is believed to have been brought on the Hopewell.) Advertised Master, J. Ash; agent, Wm. Beatty, merchant; sailed from Belfast, with Capt. Martin, Master, October 19, 1772.

Free Mason: 250 tons. Master John Semple; agent, J. W. and G. Glenry, Hill Wilson, Geo. Anderson, Wm. Booth, merchants, owners. Sailed from Newry October 27, 1772.

Reverend William Martin and his party, according to David Green Stinson, expected to settle together in a colony, but found lands would not be granted in such a way as to permit it, and they had to scatter. While all were entitled to land, he continues, "Those who had means bought from old settlers." Records indicate, however, that while those with "means" may have bought improved property from earlier settlers, in a number of cases they also took up the free land to which they were entitled and improved it. If they could not remain in a group there was a tendency for each to settle where there were relatives.

Many names of earliest settlers still abound in Chester County. Some of the names vary in spelling. It should be remembered that in 1772 when surveys were officially listed in Council Journal there was no standard spelling, and names were spelled in any way that would convey the sound as heard by the person writing it.

Boundary lines were established by giving the names of adjoining property owners, branches and other physical feature.

PASSENGERS ON LORD DUNLUNCE

Persons who had lately arrived on the ship Lord Dunlunce from Ireland with Reverend Martin presented petitions for warrants of survey 6 January 1773 as listed in the South Carolina Council Journal (No. 37 pp. 15-25): Those issued in Chester area were:

Rev'd. William Martin, 400 acres on waters of Fishing Creek, bordered by Mary Gaston, John Gaston, Elesabeth Strong.

James M'Lurkam, 300 acres on Bowen Branch.

Robert Jamieson, 250 acres on waters of Rocky Creek bordered by Robert Coultor, John Casky, Thomas Huston, David Grimbs, Mary Coulter.

Andrew Agnew, 300 acres on Wateree Creek bordered by Nicholas Thompson.

David Montgomery, 350 acres on Horse Branch bordered by John Agnew, Moses Hollis.

Mary Adams, 100 acres on branches of Dry Creek, near McDaniel's land, waters of Catawba.

John Fleming, 150 acres on branch of Wateree River called Bull Run, bordered by Wm. McCaw, Wm. Coulter.

John Camble (Campbell), 300 acres on Rocky Creek bordered by James Turner, John Biggams, Wm. McGarely, Jas. Hasper.

George Cherry, 100 acres on waters of Fishing Creek.

John Mortant (Morton), 100 acres on Rocky Creek, bordered by Peter Walie (Wylie), Robert Walker, John Walker.

James Blair, 250 acres on drafts of Fishing Creek bordered by Jas. Ferguson, Thos. Martain, Wm. McFadden, Jas. Ferguson, Sr., Robert McFadden.

Robert Read, 150 acres on branch of Rocky Creek, bordered by Jas. Steart, Joshua Perry, Alexander Miller.

David McQuestion, 400 acres on small branch of Rocky Creek bordered by Wm. Matin, Jas. Burns, John Henderson, John Mills.

James McQuestion, 400 acres on small branch of Rocky Creek, bordered by John Fleming, Mary Courter, John Knox, Robert and John Walker.

Robert Walker, 100 acres on waters of Rocky Creek bordered by Philip Walker, William Harper.

William Crawford, 200 acres on branch of Wateree Creek bordered by John McGuirtz, Amuel Boyakin.

Grizell Maybean, 200 acres on branch of Rocky Creek bordered by Francis Adams, Daniel Cotney, Thomas Burns, Col. Middleton.

Elizabeth Maybean, 100 acres on south fork of Rocky Creek bordered by Wm. Stanford, Nicalas Thompson, Buckner Haigwood.

Samuel Irvine, 150 acres bordered by Wm. Archer, Wm. Stanford, Col. Middleton.

Christopher Strong, 300 acres on Rocky Creek bordered by Howy Isbel, Widow Dunseeth.

Samuel Barber, 200 acres, on waters of Rocky Creek bordered by Hugh Wilson, Co. Middleton.

Robert Bradford, 350 acres on branch of Turkey Creek, bordered by Joseph Gladney, Davidson's corner, John Ross, Michael McGarity.

John Scott, 300 acres on westside of Turkey Creek, bordered by James Cambel, Robert Cowin, Joseph Alexander, John Gilmore.

William Scott, 100 acres in Craven County on branch of Turkey Creek, bordered by Robert Cowan, John Scoat, Joseph Alexander.

Sara Rea, 100 acres in Craven County on south fork of Broad River on Gaston's branch of Turkey Creek.

Frances Rea, 200 acres in Craven County on Rocky Creek, bordered by Thomas Blair, Alexander Walker, widow Steel, Alexander Hendry, Thomas Houston.

Ninian Gregg, 250 acres on branches of Turkey Creek.

Andrew Grumbs, 100 acres on branch of Rocky Creek.

Robert Cowan, 350 acres in Craven County on Rocky Creek, bordered by Mr. Morris, Ralph Baker, John McCown, Thos. Stone, Robert McClurkan.

PASSENGERS ON HOPEWELL

James Gibson, 100 acres on south fork of Turkey Creek, bordered by Alexander Harper, Jno. Kelley, William Barrows and his own line.

Thomas Gray, 150 acres in Granville Co. on Mounting Creek, waters of Turkey Creek.

Archibald Gray, acres, in Granville Co. on Mounting Creek, the waters of Turkey Creek, bordered by Jacob Huffman, Jefferson Williams.

PENNSYLVANIA FARMER

Passengers from Ireland on the ship *Pennsylvania Farmer* (These were able to pay.)

John Smith, Sr., 250 acres in Craven Co. on branch of Rocky Creek bordered by Elisha Garrett, Matthew Grimbs, William Hood, Thomas Hickling, Jasper Roger.

David McCreight, 200 acres in Craven Co. on north side of Broad River on branch of Jackson's Creek, bordered by John Winn, Wm. McCreight, Wm. Owens.

William Willey, 350 acres in Craven Co. on head of Rocky Creek, bordered by William Willey, John Burns, John Gill, Mickel Dickson.

John Cochran, 100 acres in Craven Co., bordered by James Rogers, Samuel Houston.

On *Pennsylvania Farmer* (These were unable to pay.)

Samuel Gamble, 300 acres in Camden Dist. on branch of

Turkey Creek and waters of Broad River, bordered by Thomas Willson, vacant land.

Thomas Scott, 300 acres in Craven Co. on waters of Wateree, bordered by Jacob Gray, James M. Gill, Thomas Carter.

Henry Heerton, 200 acres (two tracts) in Craven Co. on small branch of Rocky Creek bordered by John Rowbuck, Jacob Canemore, Peter Reas, Thomas Davis. Elizabeth Steen, 100 acres in Craven Co. on branch of Rocky Creek, bordered by vacant land.

Agnes Herbeson, 100 acres in Craven Co. on small branch of Rocky Creek, bordered by Gasper Sliker, Kelly McKane, David Fairey, John Pike, vacant land.

Mary Gaston, 100 acres in Craven Co. on Fishing Creek, bordered by Hugh Gaston.

John Brown, 100 acres in Craven Co. on Rocky Creek, bordered by Robert Bailey, High Parks, William Hickling.

William Brown, 100 acres in Craven Co. on Rocky Creek, bordered by Alexander Brady, Margaret Patten, vacant land.

Andrew Grumbs, 100 acres in Craven Co. on branch of Rocky Creek, bordered by James Knox, Francis Henderson, Benjamin Mitchell, _____ Bione.

Jean Grimbs, 100 acres in Craven Co. on branch of Rocky Creek, bordered by Samuel Fulton.

Matthew Grimbs, 100 acres in Camden Dist. waters of Rocky Creek bordered by Alexander Turner, Samuel Wilson, John McDonald.

South Carolina 6 January 1773, the Governour ordered that warrants of survey be prepared for these people:

Timothy McLinto (McClintok), 500 acres in Craven Co. on waters of Fishing Creek, bordered by Jno. and Wm. Knox, Abraham Wright, Widow McClure, Wm. McClure, Widow Hannah, Widow Englis, vacant land.

Joseph Lowrey, 150 acres in Craven Co. on branch of Wateree bordered by Patrick Lowrey.

James Stinson, 200 acres in Craven Co. branch of Rocky Creek, bordered by William Hickling, James Strong, Gasper Sliker, Samuel Maxwell.

Thomas McDill, 400 acres on branch of Rocky Creek, bordered by Walter Brown, Robert Wiley, Widow Adam, _____ Matthews, William Mophet, David Chestnut.

William Stinson, 100 acres in Craven Co. on branch of Rocky Creek, bordered by "land laid out for the Dutch," Charles Dick.

Peter Wylly, 150 acres in Craven Co. on waters of Fishing Creek, bordered by William Taler, James Farginson, Robert McFadin, John Wiley, John Downy.

Rosey Wylly, 100 acres in Craven Co. on waters of Fishing Creek, bordered by Samuel Kilwell, William Farginson, John Wyly.

Charles Miller, 150 acres in Craven Co. on branch of Rocky Creek, bordered by vacant land.

Settlers who came on the *Brigantine Free Mason* and stated they were unable to pay 50 lbs. for their warrants:

Alexander Coapling, 100 acres on branch of Turkey Creek, northside of Broad River, Craven Co., bordered by William Minter, Charles Copland, John Richey.

Margaret Beard, 100 acres in Craven Co. on branch of Turkey Creek called Mill Creek, bordered by Valentine Bell, vacant land.

William Beard, 100 acres in Craven Co. north side of Broad River on Mill Creek of Turkey Creek, bordered by Balantine Bell, Market Beard, vacant land.

Charles Coapling, 100 acres in Craven Co. on branch of Turkey Creek.

(Taken from *South Carolina Gazette:* name of ship, date she arrived in South Carolina and port from which she sailed.)

EARL OF DONEGAL

On December 22, 1767, there arrived at Charleston, South Carolina, a ship called *Earl of Donegal* in charge of Duncan Ferguson, Master. On board that ship were 265 souls who had left their motherland and braved the dangers of the Atlantic Ocean in order that they might come to America to enjoy a land of liberty and freedom.

Among those passengers, who that day set foot on Carolina soil were John White and his wife, Ann Garner White of County Antrim, Ireland. They and their six children settled about three miles southeast of Chester on Chester-Great Falls highway, one-third mile west of the highway and 200 yards north of a large spring which is still in use on the J. G. L. White farm.

The land on which the Whites settled was a grant from King George III of England and this land during all these years has never been owned by anyone except members of the White family.

According to tradition, John White was killed near what was then Youngsville, now called Woodward, in Fairfield County in a skirmish with Cherokee Indians. Since that was the day before vehicles, his friends were not able to bring his body to Chester County for burial, as so his remains were interred in old Concord cemetery nearby.

Ann Garner White died in 1818 at the age of 93 and was buried in Old Purity cemetery where eight generations of Whites are buried.

THE FIGHTING IRISH

The Scotch-Irish immigrant staking out his claim in the Up-country found the bonds that had shackled and plagued him so long loosened completely. The thin distribution of the population over the vast area encompassing Craven County, the virtual absence of class distinctions and of organized law and government, the fact that at every turn a man was thrown wholly upon his own resources — all these combined to give his native individualism the widest scope of development and to spur it on to headlong growth.

His "farm" that gradually evolved into a "plantation" was an independent social unit, a self-contained and largely self-sufficient little world of its own. Thus, freed from any particular dependence on his neighbors, on his adopted country or on any form of heir-archy, the planter basked in lordly self-certainty.

These pioneers, with still vivid memories of oppression in the Old Country, had an intense distrust of, even aversion to, any exercise of authority beyond the barest essential to protect him and his property. This feeling was common to the American back-countryman in general and reached its apogee in the Scotch-Irish Carolinian. His stance — and his boast, voiced or not, was that he would knock hell out of whoever dared cross him.

This feeling perpetuated and accelerated the tendency toward violence that had grown up in the Southern backwoods as it natu-rally grows up on all frontiers. Any trespassing or violation was met promptly and head-on with fisticuffs, knife or gun play and settled by physical conflict.

Public offenses were handled the same way. When confronted by a crime that aroused his anger, the frontiersman resorted to vigilante action that often resulted in the spectacle of a body dan-gling at the end of a rope, writhing in a fire, or suffering a severe flogging.

This society of ineffective restraints and lack of social control fostered the survival of vigilante action. It not only survived but grew steadily. Long before the Civil War and long before the black man had begun to play any direct part in the pattern, the South had become peculiarly the home of lynching.

But this individualism, his bold and immediate assertion of ego, and his great stress on the inviolability of personal privilege made the Scotch-Irishman a formidable foe. He fought often hap-hazardly but with cunning and ferociousness in the Revolution. He reached his ultimate incarnation in the Confederate soldier.

W. J. Cash says of this intrepid frontiersman:

"To the end of his (military) service this soldier would not be disciplined. He slouched. He would never learn to salute in the brisk fashion so dear to the hearts of the military. His "Cap'n." and his "Gin'ral" were likely to pass his lips with a grin — were charged always with easy, unstudied familiarity. He could and did find it in himself to jeer openly and unabashed in the face of Stonewall Jackson when that austere Presbyterian captain rode along his lines. And down to the final day at Appomatox his officers knew that the way to get him to execute an order without malingering was to flatter and jest, never to command too brusquely and forthrightly. And yet — and yet — and by virtue of precisely these unsoldierly qualities, he was, as no one will care to deny, one of the world's very finest fighting men."

No people anywhere demonstrated more rigid personal integrity in dealing with their fellowmen in concern for the welfare of the weak and powerless, a real sense of obligation to those about them. This primitive uprightness was ripened, expanded and brought to fruition in a great cleanness and decency, a wholly admirable noblesse oblige, which is one of the most pleasant and unique that ever grew upon American soil.

They developed a real sense of obligation to those about them. They sought to profess and to preach good examples of conduct and principles, to offer sound advice, to extend a helping hand, and to get their fellowmen out of trouble when they got in. They still do.

In whatever colonies they settled, they fought with distinction and won honour in the conflict which was soon to result in the birth of the United States of America. Writers have not been slow to remind America of the debt which it owes to Scotch-Irish settlers. The existence of a debt would not have been acknowledged by the settlers themselves — their ardor in the Revolution was a thanksgiving to a land which had received them in their distress. The love of liberty had taken deep root in the minds of Carolinians long before it was called into action by the Revolution.

PIONEERS CHESTER COUNTY

IV REGULATORS IN THE BACK COUNTRY

EARLIEST COURTS OF JUSTICE

Through much of the history of the United States, the steady spread of settlement through one frontier after another kept carrying the population beyond the effective jurisdiction of existing governments. Again and again, Americans found themselves in places where "the writs did not run." Caught between ineffective authority at home and creating laws themselves that would involve defiance of constituted agencies of the state, the desire for order usually triumphed over respect for authority.

The people of the Upcountry under pressure of the aftermath of the Cherokee War, learned to take power into their own hands. Their efforts throw significant light on the developing attitudes toward liberty and law in the budding American nation.

When outlaws ravaged the Back Country at the end of the Indian War in the 1760's, these men of property, called Regulators, took the law into their hands; they formed bands to punish the marauders, and they petitioned the governor for redress of grievances.

Historian David Ramsay describes the organization of the Regulators: The fears and horrors caused by Cherokee hostilities in 1759 stunted the growth of the upcountry. Several flourishing settlements broke up. Some took to forts, others abandoned the country, and new settlers were afraid to move in.

After the peace of Paris in 1763, the influx of inhabitants was greater than ever. The war was ended but the consequences of it remained. Those who took up residence in the forts had nothing to do. Idleness is the parent of every vice. When they sallied out they found much property left behind by others who had quitted their homes. They took possession of it, in violation of private rights. The wrong-doers lived easily at the expense of the absentees, and acquired such vicious habits that when the war was over they despised labor and became pests of society. To steal was easier than to work.

Among all kinds of theft none was so easy in execution, so difficult in detection, and at the same time so injurious in its consequences, as horse stealing. On that useful animal the farmers depended to raise their food.

Horse stealing became common and was carried on by system and in concert with associates living remote from each other. These difficulties were increased from an inefficient system of government. If thieves were caught, they could not be brought to trial nearer than Charleston. Till the year 1770, there were no courts of justice held beyond the limits of the capital. The only legal authority in this infancy of the back country was that of "gentleman justices" appointed by the Governor. Some of these justices were sharers in the fruits of infamy.

In the year 1764, despairing of redress in legal channels, groups of "the best and most orderly inhabitants" took matters into their own hands and organized the Regulators. They were instrumental in paving the way for the circuit court law to be passed in 1769. Courts of justice nearest to Chester were in Camden. In less than two years thirty-two horse thieves were tried, convicted and punished.

It is recorded of John Mills and David Cook of Fishing Creek community:

Not long after Mills' marriage to Mary Gill, as he was returning home after dark, was fired upon by one unseen. Walking cooly into the house, he took down his gun and went out in pursuit of the enemy.

The country was infested for years after the war (Revolutionary) by gangs of horse stealers, formed into regular societies and extending from Georgia to Virginia. They had certain passwords by which to recognize each other.

Mills and David Cook, in pursuit of horses taken from the neighborhood, fell in with some of these thieves, and discovering their countersigns, introduced themselves into their corral for stolen horses and in one of the mountain passes, found the missing animals. Watching their opportunity to secure them, they made their escape and returned the horses to their neighbors.

Regulators in Craven County as listed by Richard Maxwell Brown included such prominent landholders as Thomas Frankland, John Gray, John Grigg, Moses Matthews, William Nettles, Richard Taylor, Henry Wimpey and their leader, Thomas Woodward.

Eventually the movement was dissolved, for the Regulators' chief request that courts be established in the Back Country to administer justice was granted by the passage of the Circuit Court Act of 1769.

V *REVOLUTIONARY WAR*

REVOLUTIONARY GOVERNMENT IN SOUTH CAROLINA

Pre-Revolutionary Government, constituted in 1775, was so little challenged that the British were foolish to believe, as they did, that large numbers of loyalists would rise up to support British troops on their arrival in South Carolina. Cornwallis had 8,300 troops to maintain control of South Carolina after Benjamin Lincoln's defeat at Charleston by General Clinton.

The low country planters led the Revolutionary movement in South Carolina and the upcountry population (about half the total population lived in the upcountry) distrusted the lowcountry in this and everything else the latter did. Upcountry people had counted on Royal authority to offset the power of the lowlanders, who, by failing to create counties and by malapportioning that assembly, had kept the upcountry politically impotent.

The Scotch-Irish of the upcountry were driven into rebellion by British hostility to the Presbyterian Church, by British confiscation of property, and by Clinton's requirement that instead of neutrality everyone had to declare loyalty to the crown in order to obtain full civil rights.

CHESTER COUNTY'S ROLE IN FREEDOM FIGHT

In 1980 South Carolina entered the 200th anniversary of its most important two-year period of the Revolution, for it was during this time that military actions in our state turned the tide of war. From the fall of Charleston to the British in 1780 until its ultimate return to the patriots in December of 1782, many of the pivotal battles of the Revolution were fought in this state. Four major battles and several skirmishes were fought in Chester County.

31

John H. Hill II compiled this research paper in December 1975 for the Department of History, Graduate School, University of South Carolina. Some research material was provided by Ann Davidson Marion.

In order to understand the military operations which were undertaken during the period cited, a general statement will be made of the other battles and campaigns which took place outside the Catawba frontier, which was also a name used for the upcountry encompassing Chester County. The battles in Chester County are known as: (1) Beckham's Old Field (Beckhamville), (2) Rocky Mount, (3) Fishing Creek, and (4) Fish Dam Ford.

The British made their first attack on South Carolina at Charleston on June 28, 1776 (Admiral Peter Parker's British Fleet with General Henry Clinton's army of 2,000). Colonel William Moultrie repulsed the attack with 400 men, including 22 artillerists and the 2nd South Carolina Regiment. Because of this beating by the men of South Carolina, the British withdrew and remained away from this colony for three years. This battle took place some 180 miles southeast of the village of Chester. This threat soon left the minds of the Catawba Frontier and turned back to a more pressing problem: the unfriendly Indians of the northwestern region of the state.

In the upcountry the Red Coats provided protection for the settlers. The frontier was fairly evenly split between Whigs and Tories. Between the years of 1776 and 1780 the status quo was maintained by the Scotch-Irish folk who had moved down from Pennsylvania and Virginia and settled the area in the mid 1750s.

It wasn't until the spring of 1780 when a chain of events took place to bring war to the upcountry.

With the experience of June 1776 fresh in the minds of the British High Command, they decided to change their tactics.

Florida was then a British possession. Therefore, an infiltration was begun running north through Savannah and then northwest via the Savannah River to Augusta. Soon Lt. Colonel Archibald Campbell's force had overrun the state of Georgia and the British left flank was secured.

With Georgia occupied it was time to return to the capital city of South Carolina, Charleston. American forces were required to split up and try to recover Savannah and Augusta. This left Charleston mostly undefended. In January 1780, Clinton and Cornwallis arrived at Savannah and moved to capture Charleston. On the 7th of April the British Fleet under General Clinton passed Fort Moultrie and the siege of Charleston began. On the 13th, Lt. Colonel Banastre Tarleton of the British Legion's (Green Horse) Cavalry defeated Colonel Washington at Monck's Corner. This dashing British Cavalry officer was to have a great effect on the people of the upcountry, who had been quiet up until now.

On May 12th, Charleston fell. Then on May 29th, Tarleton took over the Virginia Continentals who were retreating from the Charleston area. They had arrived too late to help, so they were withdrawing into North Carolina for safety and regrouping. These Virginians were commanded by Lt. Colonel Abraham Buford. The ensuing battle took place in the Waxhaw region of South Carolina, an area of strategic importance to the upcountry. The infantry was cut down by the British sabers. It was said that Buford sent out a flag of truce in order to reach terms with Tarleton. Buford wanted the same terms that were reached at the surrender of Charleston. While the commander was considering the matter, fighting broke out and the British brutally slaughtered the Virginia line. No quarter was given. With this single act, Tarleton was given two names, "Bloody Tarleton," "The Butcher Tarleton" and, when referring to not giving quarter in battle, it became known as "Tarleton's Quarter."

During May 1780, the British occupation of South Carolina was swift and efficient. The towns of Camden and Ninety-Six were taken over by Cornwallis. A British outpost was established at Rocky Mount in what is now southeastern Chester County.

Rocky Mount is a high point on the Catawba River which overlooks the confluence of Fishing Creek and Catawba River. At this junction the Wateree River is formed and it flows south into the Santee River. Along Fishing Creek many of the early settlers located their homes and farms. They even established two churches in the area which are still in use today. Fishing Creek Presbyterian Church and the Catholic Presbyterian Church are two of the oldest landmarks in the county.

THE BATTLE OF BECKHAM'S OLD FIELD
(Now Called Beckhamville)

John McClure, who had a farm on the Yorkville Road just north of Chester, organized a Company of Rangers (about 30 men in all) and armed them with pistols and rifles. With the occupation of Rocky Mount and the gradual rise of the Tories in the country, something had to be done to curb the British forces.

It is known in military precepts that simple guerilla warfare evolves from simple terrorism. Tarleton had supplied the terror needed to start the partisan movement in Chester. John McClure was elected Captain and took command of the Rangers and moved east toward Beckham's Old Field. This military operation was simply that British sentiment and strength were beginning to grow in the upcountry and had to be checked.

It must have been very difficult to have been a resident of the upcountry in those perilous days in May 1780. For nearly 100 years the people in the Carolinas knew only British rule. It was the Red Coats who came in to settle disputes with the warring Creeks and Cherokees, and kept the pioneers safe from their deadly raids. The people of Chester were divided and confused. What were they to do? The taking of Charleston had been bad enough, but the people of the upcountry could have lived with that. But with the massacre of Colonel Buford's men "without giving quarter" was more than they could abide. Sentiment had changed and Chester had a leader to begin the fight from within. It was, in fact, a Civil War. Families were divided, father against son, i.e., the Lacey Family.

Captain John McClure took his Rangers into the first battle of the upcountry. The Americans had not been able or willing to defend themselves up until now. Riding eastward toward Rocky Mount, the Rangers surprised about 100 Tories on Wednesday, May 24th, and with concentrated fire routed them, leaving several dead on the field.

Just 14 miles east of Rocky Mount was another British outpost at Hanging Rock. Stationed here was a troop of cavalry (Tarleton's Green Horse) under the command of Captain Christian Huck, formerly an attorney from Philadelphia. Tarleton ordered Huck to take his troops into Chester and York counties to put down the patriots' revolt. Word had spread to the British by Tory informers that the rebellious leaders were John McClure of Chester, Reverend John Simpson of Fishing Creek and William Bratton.

The British retaliatory raids began in early June. Lt. Colonel Banastre Tarleton wanted to put down for good any revolt in his outpost area. Without warning, at daybreak on Sunday, June 11th, Captain Huck's troop rode to Reverend Simpson's home on Fishing Creek and burned it to the ground. John Simpson had been one of the leaders of the attack at Beckham's Old Field. Then Huck's men rode over to Simpson's church and fired in a window, killing William Strong, who had been sitting in the church reading his Bible.

After taking vengeance on the Simpsons and killing William Strong, Captain Huck rode north on the road to Yorkville and proceeded to the York County line and destroyed Hill's (Colonel William Hill, South Carolina Militia) iron works where the Colonel cast cannon and ordnance for the patriots' forces. He burned all of the buildings and took 90 Negro captives.

He dropped back into Chester County along Fishing Creek, some six miles south of the York line, to White's Mill. Here again he burned the buildings and committed many outrages on the populace.

By this time there was no doubt what the population might

expect at the hands of the British. June 1780 was certainly the turning point in the minds of the residents of the upcountry. As in any war, both sides started to overreact to every encounter.

The British command received word that their three main detachments had advanced to Augusta, Ninety-Six and Camden unmolested. The establishment of submission and professions of loyalty to the crown were everywhere. Sir Henry Clinton felt that he had reannexed Georgia and South Carolina to the British empire. He was now determined, as his final act, to secure his conquest. On June 3rd, he issued his last proclamation. He declared to the inhabitants of South Carolina and Georgia that they were bound to the crown. He believed that he had conquered the above two (now) states and could turn over command of the area to his second in command, Lord Cornwallis. This later proved to be a fatal mistake.

On June 6th, he sailed for New York, taking with him the greater part of his army. He left Cornwallis with 4,000 British regulars with which to continue to reduce the Whigs and their revolt. The invasion had been so successful that he was lulled into a false sense of security. His faith in the Loyalist movement was much overestimated.

In July, Captain Huck plundered the Chester County plantation of Captain John McClure's mother and captured her son, James, and son-in-law, Edward Martin, and ordered that they be hanged the next day. However, Mrs. McClure's daughter, Mary, escaped and rode to General Thomas Sumter's camp at Land's Ford on the Catawba River. Colonel William Bratton and McClure rounded up 150 volunteers and rode back to Chester to the rescue. Meanwhile, Colonel Edward Lacey, Jr. found another 350 volunteers.

Lacey's father was devoted to the King and his son ordered four guards to watch him while they prepared to attack. The senior Lacey escaped, but was overtaken by the guards and tied to a bed.

Huck, meanwhile, moved into York County to Williamson's Plantation, where his force was attacked and Huck was shot off his horse and killed. The battle resulted in just one American death, but in 85 Tory deaths. James McClure and Edward Martin were rescued when the Tories fled.

THE BATTLE OF ROCKY MOUNT

The Southern Campaign was moving rapidly toward its climax. Governor Rutledge had moved his government into exile with headquarters in Salisbury, North Carolina. Because Colonel Thomas Sumter had served well with the Continental Army, Governor Rutledge appointed him Brigadier General in command of the

South Carolina Militia. Similar appointments were made to Francis Marion and Andrew Pickens. Sumter was assigned to command the upcountry between the Enoree and Catawba Rivers.

Sumter carried on raids agitating the Tories and rallying and organizing the Whigs. Cornwallis tarried in the Low Country, deploying the British, sustaining the Tories, and reorganizing the Royal government. During the fighting at Williamson's Plantation, mentioned earlier, Colonel Winn had saved the life of a Tory, and in gratitude the man had joined the Whigs. Sent out to discover Turnbull's Rocky Mount camp, he returned with information that the New York Volunteers were encamped around a large frame house situated on a high hill in the boulder-strewn triangle below the confluence of Rocky Creek and the Catawba River.

During a conference with his officers Sumter decided to attack the British outpost at Rocky Mount, as Major William R. Davie, an ardent young patriot, just graduated from Princeton with a troop of North Carolina dragoons and a few mounted riflemen, lay encamped near the Waxhaws. Sumter asked the Major to create a diversion by moving against the post at Hanging Rock. While Davie was making a brilliant feint, Sumter crossed Fishing Creek, quietly forded Rocky Creek, and on Sunday, July 30, 1780, attempted to surprise Colonel Turnbull. He failed, however, for his horsemen ran into and scattered a band of Tories, some of whom ran squawking into the bastion of Rocky Mount.

After reconnoitering the post, Sumter asked his aide to summon Turnbull. Colonel Winn prepared a formal demand for surrender:

Sir:

"I am directed by Gen'l Sumter to demand a surrender of Rocky Mount. Therefore you will surrender this place with the men, etc., under your command, which will be considered as prisoners of war."

R. Winn

Sumter dispatched an officer under a white flag to deliver his ultimatum. But George Turnbull, a Loyalist from Connecticut and one of the ablest field commanders under Cornwallis, did not frighten. He asked that hostilities cease for an hour while he studied the proposal. After the truce, he sent a defiant reply:

30 July, 1780

Sir:

"I have considered your summons and return for answer, that duty and inclination induce me to defend this place to the last extremity."

Turnbull, Colo. Command't

Upon receiving the reply, Sumter had no other alternative; he opened his attack.

Sumter and Hill were under the impression that the enemy was in a large, thin, clapboard house. Not realizing that the inner walls had been reinforced with several feet of logs, they attempted to penetrate the walls with rifle fire. After this assault failed, they developed a new plan of attack. Sumter called a council of his officers and it was decided to throw fire brands on a small house which stood nearby and which would also communicate the fire to the large house. Colonel Hill and Sergeant Jim Johnson volunteered for this mission. After two attempts they raced back to the safety of their lines.

"And here I beg leave to remark that Providence so protected us both, that neither of us lost a drop of blood," said Hill, "scarcely had we time to look back from behind the rock where our men lay, in hopes to see the fire progressing, but to our great mortification, when the great house was beginning to flame, as heavy a storm of rain fell, as hath from that time to the present, and which extinguished the flames," concluded Hill. "We were then forced to retreat under as great mortification, as ever any number of men endured."

Because of the failure of the fire, Sumter retreated North on the road to Land's Ford. When he reached Rocky Creek he had to go into bivouac due to the heavy rainfall. The creek was flooded and the troops could not cross.

Thus ended the battle of Rocky Mount. However, because of Sumter's attack, Major Davie was successful at Hanging Rock and defeated the British there.

BATTLE AT FISHING CREEK

Colonel Thomas Taylor of General Sumter's command surprised the British guard at Colonel Carey's Outpost along the Wateree River (West Bank), killed several, and captured 30 prisoners, including Colonel Carey, and a number of horses with 30 odd wagons of corn, rum, and other military supplies. Later in the day (Tuesday, August 15th) he captured 50 British regulars coming from Ninety-Six with six wagons of baggage, three hundred head of cattle, and some sheep.

Sumter, learning of Taylor's success, joined him from the Wateree Ferry. These supplies were in great demand to support the American forces. On Wednesday morning Sumter started this large convoy North along the West bank of the Wateree River enroute to the safety of Charlotte, North Carolina. Sumter could hear the heavy gunfire coming from the Battle of Camden, but had no idea of what was happening. The weather was extremely sultry and the convoy with its heavy wagons and livestock was very slow.

By midnight, they had reached Rocky Mount and found that the British had abandoned this post. He stopped the convoy for a much needed rest.

Cornwallis knew Sumter's whereabouts, but the British cavalry was exhausted by the 22-mile chase of General Gates and unable to pursue until early Thursday morning, August 17th, when he detached Tarleton with 350 men to find Sumter and harass or attack as seemed best.

Intending to cross the ford at Rocky Mount, Tarleton immediately struck out through the woods of the east bank of the Wateree. Along the way he picked up 20 Continentals from Gates' scattered army, and in the afternoon learned that Sumter was paralleling him on the west bank. When he reached the ford at twilight, he saw Sumter's camp fires on the opposite shore and immediately gave orders that all boats be secured and that no fires be lighted.

When daylight came, Sumter's force had disappeared and the British sentries reported having seen his rear guard leaving at dawn. Lt. Charles Campbell, the same who is said to have burned Sumter's house, was then sent across the river, with an advance party, to signal with a handkerchief if Sumter was holding his course up the river.

As soon as Campbell displayed the handerchief, Tarleton, having his field piece and infantry already in boats, pushed off, while the cavalry swam where it was too deep to ford. Following close on Sumter's tracks, he reached Fishing Creek at noon, but he found his troops so overcome by heat and fatigue that he weeded out half his force, and left them with the cannon. He pushed on with 100 dragoons and 60 infantry.

Five miles further on, Sumter's videttes, hidden behind some bushes, fired and killed a dragoon. That so enraged his comrades that they sabered the videttes before Tarleton could interfere or get from them news of Sumter's whereabouts.

As Tarleton came to the top of the next hill, however, he saw Sumter's men below, undisturbed by the fire of their sentries and resting on the same well-protected ground where Sumter had camped the night after his attack on Rocky Mount.

Sumter had heard the shots, but when inquired, an officer just returned from the sentries said the militia were shooting beeves. Sumter had sent men to patrol the Rocky Mount road, but it is said that they did not go far enough to see Tarleton approaching. The day was intensely hot, and Sumter having taken off his coat and boots, lay under a wagon in the shade, with his horse tied nearby.

With a shout Tarleton charged down the hill upon them.

Sumter cut loose his horse and tried to rally his men, but pandemonium reigned and the brief defense from behind wagons was soon over. Of the men in the river some were drowned and "floated down like corks of a fishing seine," while those not killed or captured fled into the bushes until clothes could be borrowed from the country people and it is said that more than one survivor reached home in petticoats.

Sumter had just barely made good his escape to Charlotte, North Carolina. This ended the debacle at Fishing Creek.

BATTLE OF FISH DAM FORD

Early in November, Sumter with 400 men moved from his camp at Stallings on Fishing Creek through the Tory country, cleared Sandy River and Mossley's Settlement, and reached Moore's Mill, five miles from the Fish Dam Ford on Broad River.

On Tuesday, November 7th, Major Wemyss of the British 63rd Regiment (Foot), while crossing the Broad River, discovered the whereabouts of Sumter and came to Cornwallis with the offer to surprise and rout him.

Cornwallis desired to capture Sumter and put an end to his harassment of the British and Tories. He approved Wemyss' plan to attack at daybreak on the 9th and gave him 40 dragoons from Tarleton's Green Horse which had been left with him.

Wemyss with these and the 63rd Foot proceeded rapidly to the mills, which he reached just after midnight. He found that Sumter had moved onto the Fish Dam Ford and encamped on low ground with his rear on the river. Wemyss immediately followed and arrived several hours ahead of the time scheduled for a daybreak attack. He feared that delay might give Sumter time to hear of the plan, so he decided to attack at once.

To make certain of capture, "an officer with five dragoons, and a guide, was appointed to attack Sumter in his tent." A Tory by the name of Sealy had been in Sumter's camp as prisoner, but had been released the day before when he claimed that he had turned Whig. It was thought afterwards by Sumter's men that he acted as guide.

Sumter's tent was pitched on the left of the Winnsboro Road at the ford, with Colonel Winn on his right along the river, and Colonel Taylor along a gully to the left of Winn. Lacey's, Bratton's and Hill's men were on the high ground in thick woods in front of the position. Twiggs, McCall, Winn and Taylor had taken extra precautions to guard against surprise that night, and were resting somewhat back from their brightly burning camp fires. Wemyss, at the head of the British dragoons, rode unexpectedly into Sumter's videttes, who fired five well aimed shots and gave the unsuspecting Major two

serious wounds, breaking an arm and his knee. His young lieutenant, not knowing that Tarleton's dragoons were to be held in reserve,
and that the 63rd as infantry should first be dismounted, led them at
a gallop into camp. The night was intensely dark, and dazzled by the
bright light of the camp fires, the British failed to secure the arms of
the Americans, while they offered the best of targets to Winn's
marksmen, who had been sleeping on their arms and were ready for
action. Immediately recovering from surprise, the Americans
opened fire and with the first volly drove back the British horses in
disorder.

The enemy party who were to secure Sumter meanwhile, led by
the guide, had reached his tent almost immediately. As Sumter
wrote Smallwood the next day, "it was with the greatest difficulty
that I escaped being cut to pieces before the pickets got in." But
quick and active Sumter was not to be captured even by seven, and
as two of the dragoons entered his marquee he ran out under the
back of his tent, leaped a fence, and hid under the river bank.

In the darkness and confusion, neither side appeared to have
known during the night who had the advantage. The Americans
dispersed, and the retreating British left their wounded commander
and 20 others, with a surgeon and a Sergeant-Major of the 63rd,
under a flag of truce at a cabin across the road.

Sumter took 25 prisoners and a "parcel of excellent horses and
arms." He lost four men killed and ten wounded. When the Americans found that even Tarleton's redoutable dragoons had abandoned the wounded young Major, they had no further doubt as to
who had won the victory. The whole back country rang with the
news, recruits poured in, and Sumter's force immediately increased
to a thousand men.

Thus ended the last battle fought in Chester County, and in a
great victory for General Sumter and his South Carolina Militia.

In 1780 and 1781, there were dozens, possibly hundreds, of
skirmishes in the upcountry of South Carolina. Probably no record
exists of many of these encounters, especially those involving a
handful of Whigs and Tories on each side.

Even though General Sumter lost more battles than he won, the
total effect on the British forces was enough to keep Lord Cornwallis
off balance and unable to secure the upcountry for the British.

The military significance of the four battles which were fought
in Chester County was primarily that it cut up the major British plan
to attack into North Carolina and secure a base of communications
for their Regular and Tory armies.

One of the important facts which has been overshadowed by
some of the major battles at Kings Mountain and Cowpens is the
demoralization caused by actions carried on in Chester and York
Counties. Without these military campaigns, Lord Cornwallis could

have carried his offensive into North Carolina as was planned. It is important to note that after Major Patrick Ferguson's defeat at Kings Mountain, Cornwallis retreated back to Winnsboro from his outpost in Charlotte, N. C. This is important because Cornwallis could find no safe place for his army in the winter of 1780-1781; that Chester County was hostile, untenable, and represented a major swing from a predominately Tory area to one where the Whig movement made major gains. By 1781 the population was firmly behind the Colonial army. On January 8, 1781 when Lt. Colonel Tarleton started his move towards Cowpens, he gave Chester County a wide berth and moved west of the Enoree River to his objective. This suggests that Cornwallis did not feel safe moving in or near Chester County.

A CHRONOLOGY

Chester County played a vital part in wresting away British control of South Carolina and helping make our country independent of the shackles of British oppression.

A total of seven battles and skirmishes were fought in this area, some are of importance. These battles were:

May 24, 1780, Battle of Old Field at Beckhamville — Captain John McLure defeated the British, under Captain Houseman.

May 26, 1780, Battle of Mobley's Meeting House — Captain John McLure defeated the British.

August 7, 1780, Battle of Hanging Rock in Lancaster County — Sumter defeated the British garrison at Hanging Rock fort.

August 1, 1780, Battle of Rocky Mount — Sumter failed to capture the fort.

August 18, 1780, Battle of Fishing Creek — Sumter was routed by Tarleton.

November 11, 1780, Battle of Fish Dam Ford — Sumter defeated British, under Col. Wemyss.

November 20, 1780, Battle of Blackstock in Union County — Sumter defeated Tarleton's British forces.

By May of 1780, South Carolina was a defeated state — or at least it was along its coast. The only thing that remained between Cornwallis and further victory in North Carolina was the conquest of upper South Carolina and forcing their British will on these frontier people.

That May, Colonel Houseman was sent into the Chester County area in an effort to bring the Scotch-Irish settlers to the side of the British. Houseman was determined to force these people to accept the will of the King, whether they liked it or not.

When he entered Beckhamville's old field, he immediately set up camp. Houseman wasted little time in drawing up circulars and having his men distribute them in the nearby settlements of Fishing Creek, Hanging Rock, Rocky Mount, and other neighboring areas.

He made it quite clear he expected everyone to pledge allegiance to the King of England or be considered a rebel. The memory of British atrocities as they swept into South Carolina was still fresh on some minds, and his request was a bitter pill to swallow.

Houseman personally went to the settlement at Fishing Creek to see Justice John Gaston, one of the most influential members of the settlement. His words were harsh and deliberate as he told the aging Gaston that he expected him, and other settlers, to pledge support to the British. Gaston, still spry and strong-willed for his 80 years, listened to the Colonel's words and shook his head in agreement. Under his breath, he cursed the officer and everything for which his red uniform stood.

Before the dust of Houseman's horse had settled as he left, Gaston sent out a call to all able-bodied men to take up arms against the British foe. The next day, Captain John McLure and 30 men showed up at Gaston's house before leaving to do battle with the British.

They stood there dressed in their home-made clothes and carrying the long squirrel rifles they had hunted food with previously. None of them were trained as soldiers but all hated the British presence on their land.

They left by the old Indian trail that led from Fishing Creek to Beckhamville, where the British were encamped. When they got there, it was dark and about 200 Tories and British troops lay sleeping, unknowing of their presence.

McLure and his men ran from the cover of the woods yelling and firing their guns at the British. Taken by surprise and confused by the situation, the soldiers fled leaving the 30 rebels victorious.

This was hardly a battle, compared to the later struggles that were necessary before South Carolina was freed of Colonial rule, but it was the beginning of resistance to a British force that had all but conquered the state.

OLD A CATHOLIC CHURCH

VI HEROES AND HEROINES OF REVOLUTIONARY WAR

MEMORIALS ERECTED IN COUNTY

Catholic Memorial Association on Wednesday, August 30, 1933, unveiled a monument to Revolutionary soldiers of Catholic Presbyterian Church. The monument was designed by ruling elder John Musco Boulware who was also an engineer. The tablet on which the names are inscribed is framed by the old granite posts of the two gates through which the dead were carried for burial.

The early settlers on Rocky Creek, for lack of roads and transportation and because of bad weather, could not get to the churchyards so used family burying places near their home sites. Mary Wylie Strange states that these family plots had many graves but few markers until the 1830s. An effort was made to locate as many as possible of these forgotten graves.

Dr. Edward Mack delivered an address at the unveiling of the monument. Unveiling ceremony was by Mary Eliza Wylie, descendant of Thomas Thorn; Margaret Dell Stevenson, descendant of George Crawford; Nellie Carolina Caldwell, descendant of David McCalla.

Accepting the monument for the Association was R. B. Caldwell, descendant of David McCalla; Taps by Banks Gladden, descendant of Captain John Steel.

REVOLUTIONARY SOLDIERS OF CATHOLIC CHURCH

Revolutionary Soldiers of Catholic Presbyterian Church honored on memorial stone that was unveiled on church grounds Wednesday, August 30, 1933:

The Rev. William Martin, Capt. Hugh Knox, Capt. Benjamin Land, William Anderson, John Bailey, James Bankhead, Joseph Barber, John Brown, Sr., John Caskey, Alexander Chestnut, Thomas Garrett, James Graham, Patrick Harbison, Robert Harper, William Hicklin, James Jamieson, John King, William Knox, John Corder, Thomas McCalla, Matthew McClurken, Hugh McDonald, William McGarity, James McKown, Moses McKown, William Nesbit, David Robinson, William Starmount, William Stinson, William Stroud, Thomas Stroud, John Stroud, Capt. John Nixon, Capt. John Steel, Samuel Adams, Robert Archer, John Bankhead, James Barber, Hugh Boyd, George Caskey, George Crawford, Samuel Chestnut, David Graham, James Harbison, William Harbison, Andrew Hemphill, Arthur Hicklin, John Johnston, James Knox, M.D., John Lee, David McCalla, John McClurken, Thomas McClurkin, William McDonald, Alexander McKown, John McKown, John McWaters, James Peden, Thomas Stanford, Thomas Steel, Andrew Stevenson, William Stroud, Jr., Hampton Stroud, Thomas Thorn, (and perhaps others).

Old Purity Presbyterian Cemetery on S. C. Hwy. 97 contains the graves of seven Revolutionary soldiers: Thomas Cabeen, John Harden, Lt. James Kennedy, Hugh Ross, Sr., John Service, Alexander Walker, and William White.

Old Stone Graveyard on S. C. Hwy. 327 contains the graves of Revolutionary soldiers: John Kenmore, Col. Robert Patton, and James Smith.

Revolutionary soldiers buried at Hopewell Associate Reformed Presbyterian Church are Robert Kilpatrick and Edward McDaniel.

REVOLUTIONARY SOLDIERS OF WHITE FAMILY OF CHESTER COUNTY

William White fought in the battles of Kings Mountain, Fishing Creek, Fishdam Ford, Blackstock and other skirmishes.

Lt. James Kennedy, husband of Margaret White Kennedy.

Alexander Walker, husband of Eleanor (Helen) White Walker.

Robert Miller, husband of Jannet White Miller. His name appears on list of those who were wounded at Kings Mountain and whose names have been inscribed on the monument erected to their memory on Kings Mountain battle field.

Robert Walker, husband of Victoria White Walker.

General Edward Lacey

General Edward Lacey of Chester District distinguished himself as a soldier during the Revolutionary War and in public service after the War. He was one of the most active partisan leaders during the dark period of the Revolutionary struggle. He freely and fearlessly gave all his energy and means to the complete overthrow of British tyranny, and to the establishment of American independence. He was in more important battles than any other officer in the State, according to biographer M. A. Moore, Sr., M.D.

Edward Lacey's life story is an absorbing and true chronicle of bravery, heroism, daring and romance, — that of a bona fide hero.

Born in Pennsylvania of an emigrant father, he ran away from home in 1755 at the age of thirteen and enlisted in a regiment opposing the French and Indians on the Ohio. Young Lacey seeing the soldiers parading the streets for the expedition against Fort DuQuesne, was seized with a lasting love for military life. Considered too young to bear arms, General Braddock employed Lacey as a pack horse rider. He was at Braddock's defeat, and continued in the army for two years until his father learned of his whereabouts and fetched him home.

At the age of sixteen, Lacey ran away again and emigrated to Chester District, South Carolina, with William Adair, (father of Governor John Adair of Kentucky) to whom he had apprenticed himself as a brick-layer, and from whom he received a good English education.

At the age of twenty-one, Edward Lacey was six feet tall, weighed 170 pounds, "with perfect symmetry of form and commanding aspect; he excelled in all athletic exercises which were the fashion of the day," Dr. Moore wrote. "His hair was black, his eyes dark, and an uncommonly handsome face, with fine address; he was a man of strong native intellect, fond of pleasure, . . . and every inch a soldier."

When about twenty-four years old, he married Jane Harper of Chester District, and settled on the headwaters of Sandy River, six miles west of Chester Court House. By her he had ten children, four of whom were born before the Revolutionary War.

Lacey's leadership and popularity influenced a British officer to offer him a large amount of gold to abandon the Rebels and join the Loyalists. Lacey indignantly spurned the offer and continued boldly to fight for liberty, organizing companies and leading them in skirmishes.

On one occasion Lacey learned that a party of Tories had assembled at the house of a Royalist named Lamb, a few miles away. Not having time to assemble his own troops, Lacey went boldly to the house and demanded a surrender which the Tories refused.

Lacey retired to a vantage point and fired on each one that showed himself. After continuing his fight this way for some time, Lacey went hurriedly to the house and advised surrender, otherwise he would not be able to keep his men under control and all the Tories would be murdered.

After a short consultation, the Tories capitulated and laid down their arms. Lacey, after rendering their guns useless, took up his own piece, and to their great chagrin and mortification, ordered them to march, that he was entirely alone. Lacey sent them to Cornwallis where they were exchanged for some of his own men who had been taken prisoners.

Lacey received a Colonel's commission in 1780, organized a Regiment of Infantry which continued in active service to the end of the war, mostly under General Thomas Sumter's command. While he was away from home, two years at one time, the Tories destroyed all his property and left his wife not even a cow to milk for her children. The only horse he owned at the close of the war was a fine little black charger that had belonged to Col. Ferguson, and on which he was killed at the battle of King's Mountain.

Tory Captain Christian Huck camped at White's Mill on Fishing Creek in Chester County with 200 British Regulars, 100 Mounted Infantry, 100 Dragoons and about 500 Tories. He was desolating the country and committing many outrages, one of which was killing a good young man by the name of Strong as he read his Bible on Sunday morning. They burned Parson Simpson's and Mrs. McLure's homes, and Col. William Hill's Iron Works (for he was casting ordnance and cannon ball for the Patriots).

Huck's conduct so incensed the people that Lacey, Bratton, McLure and others proceeded to get together all the fighting men in the neighborhood, pursued Huck's army as it moved toward Bratton's in the lower edge of York District. Although outnumbered three to one, Lacey's troops attached the British at Williamson's house, routed them completely and killed Captain Huck.

The battle, valiantly fought and won by a handful of men, led to important consequences. The defeat of Huck's army was the first repulse the British arms had met in South Carolina. It greatly revived the spirits of the Patriots and contributed much to the victory at King's Mountain two months later only twenty miles from Williamson's.

Lacey was with Sumter at the battle of Rocky Mount in Chester District which took place July 30, 1780. He was in the hard-fought battle of Hanging Rock August 7, 1780 in which the Royalists lost 269 of 278 engaged. The Patriots lost their gallant Captain John McLure of Chester District in this battle.

Lacey was an intrepid recruiter and messenger as the Patriots massed for the decisive battle of King's Mountain against Col.

Patrick Ferguson. The Patriots encircled the enemy camp on the mountain. Ferguson fell, sword in hand, and about 360 of his men were killed and 800 taken prisoners.

General Sumter, according to Dr. Moore, called on Col. Lacey (knowing him to be a dashing soldier of fine address, and likewise knowing him to have the confidence of the York and Chester Irish) to recruit troops. Lacey took with him "his facetious and witty Adjutant Jemmy Johnson, the bold Capt. Paddy McGriff, the cautious Capt. Jem Martin, and the queer and droll Sargeant Billy Wylie. All from the "Emerald Isle" . . . . a more brave and truer set of men never lived," said Dr. Moore.

In less than three days, Lacey came dashing into Sumter's camp with 150 mounted men, none the worse for an incident at Mobley's grocery on the way. The troops were treated to refreshments from a barrel of whiskey at the store that gave an additional spur to their natural bravery. When they encountered a very formidable scouting party of British Dragoons, with one accord they yelled out: "Is that the British? By Jesus, Col. Lacey, let's at them! We'll give them a clatter." Seeing he could not restrain them, Lacey determined to share their fate. A general rush ensued, helter-skelter, whopping and screaming at the top of their voices, which, no doubt magnified their appearance. The enemy prodded their mounts and fled.

Col. Lacey kept the field with his mounted Infantry. His camp and headquarters were at various times at Liberty Hill, on Turkey Creek in York District, S. C., at William's (now Wright's) Mill. He greatly annoyed the enemy by cutting off their large foraging parties. On Nov. 23, 1780, Lord Cornwallis in a letter to Col. Tarleton wrote, "Sumter's corps has been our greatest plague in this State," and, "You must dislodge Lacey from his camp at Turkey Creek so I can move up on the left hand road."

Lacey fought in the battle of Cowpens Jan. 17, 1781, where Tarleton met his worst defeat with 800 killed, wounded or taken prisoner. He was with Sumter at Friday's Fort the 19th of February 1781, at Quinby's Creek Bridge on August 15, 1781, and at Eutaw Springs on September 8, 1781.

Col. Lacey's Regiment was sent to Edisto Island where he remained until Charleston was abandoned by the British December 14, 1782.

Soon after the war, Col. Lacey was made a Brigadier General and was appointed one of the first County Court Judges in Chester District. He was sent by Chester to the General Assembly of South Carolina where he served until 1793, when he declined reelection and retired from political life.

He emigrated to the West in October, 1797 and settled permanently in Livingston County, Kentucky, where he was also a County Court Judge. He died from drowning in the backwaters of the Ohio River on March 20, 1813, at age 71.

CHESTER COUNTY HEROINES OF
THE AMERICAN REVOLUTION

Mrs. Ellett in her Women of the Revolution, Vol. 3, graphically pictures the noble daring of the women thrown "into the circle of mishap" during the Revolutionary War. Eleven in Chester District are included.

Isabella Ferguson

Isabella Barber was wooed and won by Samuel Ferguson before the fall of Charleston and the spread of the war to the upcountry. His brothers, rampant royalists, were with the royal forces at Rocky Mount, James having a colonel's commission.

Samuel and his young bride often discussed the subject of war and the difference of opinion between her brothers, Joseph and James, and his own. Samuel was never strong in argument, ... whereas Isabella was firmly indoctrinated in the Scriptures and the political creed of her people. She stood firmly on the side of freedom.

When Col. Ferguson was preparing to accompany Capt. Huck on his expedition, he left Rocky Mount one morning dressed in full and resplendent uniform, mounted on a handsome charger, and with the colors of Old England flying. Thinking to impress his sister-in-law to such an extent that she would no longer detain her husband from a chance of like splendor, he stopped by the Barber house.

Isabella was within hearing distance while the Colonel was trying to persuade her husband to join him. She could not restrain her declaration.

"I am a rebel!" she said proudly, glorying in the name. "My brothers are rebels, and the dog Trip is a rebel, too. Now, James, I had rather see you with a sheep on your back than turned out in all those fine clothes! Above all, I am told you have our minister chained by the foot like a felon! Rebel and be free! that is my creed!"

Then turning to her husband, "We have often talked it over, Samuel," she said, "and you could never justify their unhallowed practices, coming here to make slaves of us who would die first, and plundering, stealing cows and the like. Now, in the presence of the British army I tell you, if you go with them you may stay with them, for I am no longer your wife!"

Samuel was unable to withstand this determination of his beloved Isabel, so requested his brother to excuse his going at this time, to report him a true subject of the king who would do all he could at home to serve His Majesty and to try to turn the whole clan of Covenanters about.

Col. Ferguson was killed in the action at Williamson's and his forces, including two other brothers, scattered and hid in the woods. The victory proved of advantage to the wives and widows of Rocky Creek. Samuel Ferguson, when he heard the result of the expedition, the Colonel's death and the miserable situation of remaining brothers, never looked on the bonny face of Isabella without a feeling of thankfulness that he had escaped a similar fate.

Isabella exhorted him to gain the confidence of their neighbors by joining her in deeds of kindness to the defenseless and destitute, and thus deserve their good offices in return. By their joint exertions the distresses of the neighborhood were much relieved, and his brothers found advantage in adopting the same course.

At the close of the war the Ferguson brothers were almost the only loyalists permitted to remain in Chester District.

Mary McClure

Mary McClure was the mother of Capt. John McClure, a man recognized throughout the whole South as one of the master spirits of the Revolution. She was the sister of John Gaston and probably came to South Carolina about the same time and settled on the rich table lands lying on the south fork of Fishing Creek. She was one of the earliest residents of that region and suffered much from the hostile incursions of the Cherokee Indians. Because of her experiences she was called "the Cherokee heroine." She spent many days and nights in the forts where the women and children went for safety while the men were out. She was the widowed mother of seven grown children.

Mary was active in her personal exertions to serve the cause of freedom. It was owing in great part to the women of that vicinity that the men were so united and resolute, that they went forth to a man to fight the battles of the Revolution, while the women attended the farms and performed the labors both of the household and the field.

At the battle of Hanging Rock, John McClure, Mary's son, was wounded along with many others. His cousins, the four Gastons lay bleeding around him. His command sustained the largest share of the whole loss. He himself was stricken down in the bloom of life. He was borne on a bier from the battle field to Waxhaw Church then on to Charlotte where his mother came to nurse her gallant son. McClure's death was hastened by his anxiety to take the field again. On the 18th, against the surgeon's orders, he rose and walked across the room. His deep-seated wound broke inwardly and he bled to death in a few hours.

Mrs. McClure, bearing her heavy load of grief saw her other sons, Hugh and James, go to fight in the climactic battle of Kings Mountain. She set out on horseback, and alone to visit her son, Dr. Alexander McClure, who was a prisoner in Charleston.

The men of the Revolution, after the war, took pleasure in visiting "the mother of the brave captain" as they called her.

Nancy Green

Nancy Stinson Anderson Green about the year 1773 emigrated from Ireland to America among the Rev. William Martin's party. James, William and Elizabeth Stinson and their brother-in-law, William Anderson, who had married Nancy Stinson shortly before the sailing of the ship, settled on the banks of Great Rocky Creek in what is now Rossville area of Chester County.

Anderson and Nancy lived in a tent until a meeting house was built, then he built a log cabin for himself and cleared a patch on which he planted Indian corn. During the next seven years he enlarged his fields, trapped, fished, traded and became a man of substance, well to do in the world. Three children, Mary, Robert, and William were born and trained in the strict ordinances of the Covenanter religion.

But this happiness was marred by the rumors of war that penetrated even this remote section. The attack on Sullivan's Island startled many who had fancied themselves in security. John Mc-Clure of Fishing Creek, coming home, brought news of the surrender of Charleston and his own defeat at Monck's Corner. Still worse was the news from across the river, of the inhuman massacre of Buford's Troops by Tarleton's corps at the Waxhaws.

The following Sunday, the Rev. William Martin, with fiery eloquence and in his broad Scotch-Irish dialect, reminded his parishioners of the oppression they had endured in Ireland and the reasons for which they had come to America. "My hearers," he said, "talk and angry words will do no good. We must fight!" He cited many passages from Scripture to show that a people may lawfully resist wicked rulers. As he dwelt on the recent horrid tragedy, the butchery of Buford's men, cut down by British dragoons while crying for mercy, his indignation reached its height. Stretching out his hand toward Waxhaw, "Go see," he cried, "the tender mercies of Great Britain!"

To his stirring sermon the whole assembly responded. Even the women were filled with the spirit that threatened vengeance on the invaders. On his way home William Anderson was unusually silent. Nancy spoke first. "I think, William, little Lizzy and I can finish the crop and gather it in, if need be, as well as take care of the stock."

On Monday morning, William Anderson, with his wife's blessing, several sacks of provisions she had prepared, and the best saddle horse, went to join Capt. Land's troops who were drilling and getting ready to fight. He was killed in battle two months later.

Later in the war, a lone patriot on foot and needing food and a horse was befriended by Nancy Anderson after she determined he had friends and kinsmen whom she knew. His history was well known to Mrs. Anderson for she had heard it from friends. He found frequent excuses to visit the fair widow's house. One day he asked, "Would you again marry a soldier?"

"I have not thought about that; but if I ever should marry, if I think as I do now, none but a soldier would I have."

Some three or four days after this conversation, the couple on horseback rode to the house of an old friend, Justice John Gaston and were married. The newly made husband paid the fee of one dollar, all the money he possessed in the world.

Thus Nancy became Mrs. Daniel Green. She gave offence to many of her friends who had not been consulted on her hasty decision. None of them thought she had made a suitable match, and were scandalized that she had dispensed with formalities of the church such as posting the banns on three successive Sundays. It was impossible for her to comply with this requisition, there being no public religious services in those desolate war days.

Nancy did not allow their censure to make her uncomfortable since she considered herself the most competent judge in the matter. Knowing what it was to be alone and destitute, it was something to find one who could take care of her property, aid in the care of her children and defend her in case of need. Both she and her soldier had been tried in the crucible of the Revolution, and both came forth like gold refined.

Mr. and Mrs. Green found their troubles ended with the war. Prosperity attended them; they grew wealthy, but had no children to bear the name. The children of Anderson were treated by Green as his own.

Esther Gaston Walker

Esther Gaston was born in 1761 at the homestead of her parents, Justice John and Esther Waugh Gaston, on the south side of Fishing Creek at Cedar Shoals. She was eleventh of a family consisting of nine sons and three daughters. The family was strict Presbyterian and dedicated patriots in the battle for freedom.

During the darkest period of the war for the South, Esther Gaston was about eighteen years of age. Her nine brothers were fighting with the Tories. South Carolina was claimed by the British as a conquered province, the hopes of the people were prostrated. The sons of John Gaston and his nephews, McClure, Strong and Knox met as often as they could to discuss the progress and strategies of battle.

While they were talking of the disaster of Monck's Corner, from which John McClure had just escaped, a messenger brought the news that Tarleton with his cavalry had overtaken Col. Buford near the Waxhaws and slaughtered his men without mercy. The wounded had been carried to Waxhaw Church as a hospital while the tories continued to be active below Waxhaw and Fishing Creek settlements.

At this news, the young men rose with one accord, undaunted by reverse, grasped each other by the hand and voluntarily pledged themselves to suffer death rather than submit to the British.

Such were the spirits by whom Esther Gaston was surrounded. She lost no time in going to Waxhaw Church, accompanied by her married sister, Martha. The temporary hospital presented a scene of misery. The floor was strewed with wounded and dying American soldiers. Day and night the women aided the surgeon in dressing wounds, prepared food and gave comfort to those who needed it. Ignoring fatigue and exposure, they went about the neighborhoods to procure medicines and herbs, linens and supplies for the soldiers.

After Justice Gaston flatly refused Col. Houseman's command to assemble the patriots at an old field where Beckhamville now stands, to give in their names as loyal subjects of King George, and to receive British protection, the aged patriot took steps to do more than oppose his refusal. He summoned the men of the neighborhood to assemble at his home. Before midnight, thirty-three armed men were assembled and ready for any enterprise in the cause of liberty.

They took their course noiselessly along the old Indian trail down Fishing Creek, to the old field where many of the people were already gathered. Their sudden onset took by surprise the promiscuous assemblage, about two hundred in number. The enemy was defeated.

Justice Gaston was informed of the success of the battle, and judging wisely that his own safety depended on his immediate departure, he left his home, went by Waxhaw Church to share the good news with Esther and Martha and with the wounded soldiers there, then on the Mecklenburg County.

The victory at the Old Field was followed by a battle at Mobley's Meeting House and one at Brattonsville. On the night of July 30th, the American soldiers marched near the residence of Esther Gaston. She was informed, perhaps by one of her brothers, or her lover, Alexander Walker, that they were advancing against the enemy's position. By the morning she was in readiness to follow. Riding to the house of her brother, John Gaston, she enlisted her sister-in-law and they galloped down Rocky Mount road. The firing could be distinctly heard.

While these brave women were approaching the battle site, they were met by several men fleeing, with fright on their pale faces. Esther stopped the fugitives, upbraided them with their cowardice, and entreated them to return to the ranks. While they wavered she advanced and, seizing one of their guns, cried, "Give us your guns, then, and we will stand in your places!"

The most cowardly of men must have been moved at such a taunt. They wheeled and returned to the fight in company with the two heroines. During the action, Esther and Jane Gaston busied themselves diligently rendering services, dressing wounds, carrying water to allay their burning thirst. A Catawba Indian, severely wounded, was helped by them, and his last looks were turned in gratitude on those who had soothed his pain and supplied his wants.

The training Esther had received at Waxhaw enabled her to do her part skillfully. While she gave comfort to the dying, she also gave courage to the living to persevere.

In the following week, after the Battle of Hanging Rock took place, Esther Gaston went again to Waxhaw Church to nurse the wounded. Among them was her youngest brother, Joseph, a lad of sixteen, severely wounded in the face, pale as death, and exhausted from lack of blood.

Heavy cause for mourning, indeed, had the Gaston family after that fatal encounter. Three of Esther's brothers, Robert Ebenezer and David being numbered with the dead. Her cousin, John McClure was desperately wounded and died not long afterward. Another brother, Alexander Gaston, who was a lieutenant in the regular army, fell a victim of smallpox in Sumter's retreat from Wright's Bluff.

When news of the death of her sons was brought to Mrs. Gaston, it is said her words were, "I grieve for their loss, but they could not have died in a better cause."

Alexander Walker, who was in service during the whole war in the division of Col. McClure, visited and courted Esther when he obtained a leave of absence. They were married at the close of the war and settled on the north side of Fishing Creek near her parents' old homestead. Her only child, a son, was named after her father, John Gaston.

Esther continued to use the medical knowledge her practice during the war had given her. She acquired much scientific knowledge in medicine from an educated physician, Dr. McCrea, who boarded in her house. She was skillful in needlework and cutting garments. She frequently took orphan girls, most of them war orphans, exercising over them the care of a parent, teaching them in both practical and spiritual matters, then gave them in marriage to worthy young men.

Katherine Steele

Katherine Steele — nee Katherine Fisher, a native of Pennsylvania, married Thomas Steele at about age 20 years. Both belonged to the race called "The Pennsylvania Irish." They moved to South Carolina sometime in 1745.

Donald McDonald, who resided on the eastern side of the Catawba, was their first acquaintance. He had lived with the Indians for 15 to 20 years. He was first pioneer in the district. He had amassed some wealth and raised a large family.

The Steeles crossed the river near his house and fixed their residence near Fishing Creek on the west side.

Steele's was fortified as a "blockhouse" known as Steele's Fort. There was a Taylor's Fort at Landsford near a spring.

Mrs. Steele became known as "Katy of the Fort," because she was a ruler, not merely because of ownership, superior courage or firmness, but by virtue of hearty kindness and good humor. She could calm the fears of the women. They felt a sense of security in her presence. She also taught the young girls to use a rifle.

Late one night, the alarm was given that the Indians were upon them. One younger woman — Mrs. Beard, who had married an old man, bade her husband carry the child, while she bore the rifle, in readiness to use it for their defense. A young girl who lived with them was unwilling to quit the house without some of her clothes. She must "get on her blue skirt," at least. Mrs. Beard seized and dragged her from the house; exclaiming, "very fine you would look, to be sure, with your blue skirt on and your scalp off!"

One Sabbath day, while the people were at old Waxhaw Church, an Indian alarm was given. The congregation was immediately scattered, and the women fled to the "blockhouse," where they remained several days, while the men were out scouting the rough country in every direction. This proved to be a false alarm.

Sometimes, the alarms came too late for them to reach the "fort," then the women would hide in the canebreaks. Mrs. Beard, relating her own experience, said "on one occasion I indulged the impious wish that my children were dead! I lay one night, alone in a thick canebreak with my two little ones. I had them both at the breast, the older as well as the babe, to keep them from crying; I was quaking with fear that they would cry out and the Indians would find us. In the morning as soon as it was light enough to see — there lay a large rattlesnake within a few feet of me!" The mother's repining was turned to thankfulness. The child with which she was pregnant was said to have been marked with a rattlesnake. She was Mary Beard — the late Mrs. Sweet of Charleston.

Sarah McCalla

Her mother was Hannah Wayne, a first cousin of Gen. Anthony Wayne. Sarah was born in Chester County, Pennsylvania in Piqua Township. In 1775, she married Thomas McCalla of Brandy Wine, Philadelphia. In 1778, Thomas and Sarah McCalla moved from Pennsylvania to Chester District, S. C. David McCalla, brother of Thomas, had previously moved and was living with Capt. John Nixon, first house at what is now William Caldwell place. It was the place marked by the "Mulberry Tree" that the volume of the company of the 27th Regiment used to muster.

McCalla joined the Whigs in 1780 and was in every battle of the summer until the evening of August 17th when he obtained leave to visit his family. He was not at the Fishing Creek Massacre.

About this time, the British began their march from Winnsboro. They camped on the plantation of John Service in Chester District and afterwards at Turkey Creek. They were on their way to fight the Battle of Cowpens which took place on January 18th, 1781. A day or two after the Battle of Cowpens, Sarah McCalla crossed the ferry on her way back to Camden. John Adair was Captain at this time.

On January 22nd, 1781, six wagons were loaded with corn at Wade's Island, 60 miles down the Catawba for the use of Gen. Davidson's division. The whole Whig country of York, Chester and Lancaster may be said to have risen in manpower and rallied to arms. On the 24th of January, Gen. Sumter crossed the river at Landsford and received the corn and provisions from Wade's Island. He intended to cross the districts to the west, in the rear of the advancing British Army, in order to arouse the country and gather forces as he went. He intended to threaten the British Post at Ninety-Six, and go on to recover the State.

While Cornwallis marched from Services, he was met by Capt. John Mill and Capt. James Johnson. They captured two British officers, one of whom was Major McCarter. Sam Neely of Fishing Creek was sent with the flags to exchange the two officers for prisoners from Chester District. Neely failed to make exchange correctly and prisoners continued to be held in Camden until after Neely had gone to Charleston, and gotten his son Thomas off a prison ship. Capt. Mill was indignant at supposed disrespect to Gen. Sumter's cartel and sent a letter of remonstrance by Mrs. McCalla to Rawdon. She was accompanied by Mary Nixon (sister of John Adair), 11 men were released: Thomas McCalla, John Adair, Thomas Gill, William Wylie, Joseph Wade, Nicholas Bishop (80 years old) and others not named.

Joseph Wade stayed with Mr. and Mrs. McCalla, John Adair and Mrs. Nixon. He carried Adair on his back as Adair was weak from having suffered from smallpox. Wade had some provisions but had been given over a thousand lashes. These travelers spent the first night at the home of Mrs. Weatherspoon. She fed them mush and sweet milk.

Mary Nixon McCalla

Mary Nixon, daughter of Mary Adair, married Capt. John Nixon in 1774. Col. Winn advised Mrs. Nixon that the Tories were intent on getting her because her husband had fought so strongly against them, so she left home that night with her Negroes and as many articles as could be carried in a wagon and went to the Yadkins in N. C.

She married David McCalla, who has been with Nixon in camp and engaged in the hard fought battle of Eutaw together.

Two Nixon daughters were Mrs. Mary Hemphill and Mrs. McKeown.

Isabella Wylie

She was the daughter of Samuel Kelso, who in 1780 lived on North side of Fishing Creek Church yard. Isabella heard guns firing at Mr. Stroup's house. Her father and two sons were in most of the battles in 1780-1781. George, who was severely wounded, was left for dead, but crawled to a horse, mounted with difficulty, and escaped. Isabella married William Wylie, who was a prisoner at Camden, was the eldest son of Peter Wylie. His home was at Big Spring, six miles north of Chesterville. William was in the hostilities from the beginning, fought under Gen. Williamson, with Moultrie and was in the Black Springs retreat with McClure under Col. Washington in the surprise rout at Moncks Corner.

Wylie was captured on a visit home and taken to Rocky Mount. He escaped on the morning of July 12th and met up with McClure who was chasing red coats after the defeat at Brattonsville.

He also served with Capt. John Mills in Regiment under Col. Henry Hampton.

Mary Adair

Mary Adair, Chester County's gallant heroine of the Revolutionary War, was born in America. Her memory is perpetuated by the Mary Adair Chapter, Daughters of the American Revolution, of Chester. Many of her ancestors are still in the area.

In June 1934, a marker was unveiled at Catholic Presbyterian Church in southeastern Chester County stating that Mary Adair, daughter of William and Mary Moore Adair, was the granddaughter of James Moore, provincial governor of South Carolina. The marker was erected by the Mary Adair Chapter, D.A.R.

Thomas Adair, Mary's grandfather, was the sturdy pioneer who blazed his family's trail to the new world. About 1730, he and his family migrated from County Antrim, Ireland, to Chester County, Pennsylvania. They spent about 20 years in Pennsylvania then joined the Waxaw (Waxhaw) Colony of Scotch Irish settlers who migrated to South Carolina and settled in the "north counties." The date was about 1750-55.

Thomas Adair brought three of his sons to South Carolina with him. We do not know whether this was all of his family. These three brothers were founders of the most prominent families of Adairs in America. They were James, Joseph, and William, ranked in the order named.

James Adair, born in 1709, was about 21 years old when his father brought him to America. He built up and carried on an enormous trade with the Indians. He also wrote the best book ever published on the Indians. His descendants are in Arkansas and Oklahoma.

Joseph Adair was born about 1711. Most of the Adairs of South Carolina, Georgia, Alabama, and Tennessee are his descendants.

William Adair, known as William the Pioneer, the youngest son, was born in Ireland in 1719, and hence was eleven years old when his father brought him to America. He was educated in Chester County, Pennsylvania. He married Mary Moore in 1754 and secured land on Fishing Creek in Chester County, S. C. He cleared land for a farm and built a house, locating it near water as did the other pioneer settlers for better protection from the wild Indians.

William and Mary Moore Adair had six children and sent them to Charlotte, N. C. for their education. Mary Adair, born in 1756, married John Moore and raised 15 children. John, born 1757, married Catherine Palmer of Charleston, and became governor of Kentucky. William, born about 1759, married Mary Irvine. He was a lieutenant in the Revolutionary Army. James, born about 1761, was also a Revolutionary soldier. He was married and had two or three children. His descendants in Chester County have joined the D.A.R. on his war record. Alexander Adair died at the age of 16.

William Adair and his wife spent their old age in Mercer County, Kentucky, and were buried at Whitehall Cemetery in that county, along with their son, Governor John Adair.

Mary Adair remained in Chester County. She was first married to Capt. John Nixon and had two children. At the beginning of the Revolutionary War, Capt. Nixon was killed by the Tories, in 1774. Mary later married David McCalla.

An incident connected with the Revolutionary battle of Rocky

Mount reveals the kind of person Mary Adair Nixon McCalla was.

In Mrs. Ellet's "Women of the Revolution," this incident is recorded:

Even before the battle, Capt. Huck and his British troops stopped on their way at the house of Mrs. Adair on South Fishing Creek at the place where the road from Yorkville to Chester Court House now crosses that stream. They helped themselves to everything eatable on the premises. One Capt. Anderson laid a strict injunction to the old lady to bring her sons under the royal banner.

After the battle had been fought, Mrs. Adair and her husband were sent for by their sons and Col. Edward Lacy, whom they had brought up, for the purpose of sending them into North Carolina for safety.

When Mrs. Adair reached the battleground, she dismounted from her horse and passed around among her friends. Presently she came with her sons to a tent where several wounded men were lying — Capt. Anderson among them.

She said to him, "Well Captain, you ordered me last night to bring in my rebel sons. Here are two of them, and if the third had been within riding distance, he would have been here also."

The chagrined officer replied, "Yes, madam, I have seen them."

The defeat of Huck had the immediate effect of bringing the Whigs together, and in a few days a large accession of troops joined the army of General Sumter. The attack on the British at Rocky Mount was shortly followed by a complete victory over them at Hanging Rock.

Women Became Reapers

Many Chester County women made names for themselves and their families during the Revolutionary War. Much fighting was done in the county, especially in the Fishing Creek section. With their sons, brothers and husbands away doing battle, the women were left to manage the homes and farms.

The rich lands within the bounds of Fishing Creek (Presbyterian) congregation were well adapted for the growth of wheat, which was extensively cultivated by the Pennsylvania-Irish settlers.

The harvest was in June. All the men able to bear arms, with their minister John Simpson, having taken the field, none remained to gather the crop on which the livelihood of their families depended.

It was at this crisis that the young women of the neighborhood, with spirit equal to that of their gallant brothers, in the summer of 1780 formed a company of reapers for cutting and garnering the grain. Their names were Mary Gill, Margaret Gill, Ellen Gill, Isabella Kelso, Margaret Kelso, Sarah Knox, Margaret Mills, Elizabeth Mills, Mary McClure and Nancy Brown.

These young women went day after day from one farm to another and reaped the crop with the assistance of the matrons and a few old men. The only question they asked was "Is the owner out with the fighting men?" An affirmative answer was sufficient to engage them at once in the labor.

It was no small undertaking. Five or six weeks of unceasing toil being necessary to gather in the harvest through the country. It seemed that Providence smiled on the generous enterprise. There were no storms during that period to ravage the fields, and it was related for years afterwards as very remarkable, that some of the season's crops were secured several weeks after the grain was fully ripe.

Scarcely was the work accomplished, before the British and Tories were plundering everywhere and laying waste the country, determined to vanquish the spirit of resistance by distressing rebel families.

The female laborers forming this band were by no means uncouth in person or rude in manners, but might have compared with any grace of deportment, and in qualities that constitute the refinement and beauty of feminine character.

Mary Gill

Mary Gill, a heroine of the Revolution, was the daughter of Robert Gill. She was born in 1758 in the colony of Pennsylvania. Soon after her birth her father moved to South Carolina and settled on the south fork of Fishing Creek, upon which the plantation known as Lowrie place.

He was one of the early settlers and took an active part in establishing a church in the wilderness that later became Chester County. When the Revolutionary War broke out, Gill was too advanced in years to bear arms, but encouraged his sons, Thomas, Robert, Archy, John and James to do their part from the beginning of the war.

Thomas and Robert were taken prisoners and carried to Camden where Robert died in prison. Thomas was released after seven months in captivity. Archibald served to the close of the war in the State troops, and continued to have much influence and a high character in the community. He owned the celebrated fishery at the Falls of Catawba and would never tolerate the pursuit of business on Sunday. His son, Robert, was a Captain in the regular army in 1812, and at the time of his death was Attorney General of Louisiana. His daughter, Mrs. Crawford, lived all her life near Fishing Creek.

Such training and associations formed his daughter Mary's mind to the heroism displayed in time of need. On the night that Col. Nail's men under Bratton and McClure were going to Williamson's after leaving White's Mill, two of them came to Gill's house.

It was late and a very dark night. The men, anxious to catch up with Nail, had lost their way. As soon as Mary was satisfied that they were liberty men, though her father tried to dissuade her, she went with them to show a path leading out to the main road. It was so dark she was obliged to tie a white cloth upon her back so they could see to follow her along the distance of several miles.

Some years after the war one of the men named Hunter was traveling through the area and stopped for the night at the old court house at Walker's. He asked for the noble girl who had done him this service.

While Tarleton's corps encamped at White's Mill, a party of troops came to the creek where Mary and Martha were. Seeing a flock of geese nearby, the soldiers started in chase of them, cutting off the birds' heads with their broadswords. Mary picked up a stick and frightened the geese into deep water. When the men swore at her, holding their bloody swords, and saying they meant to cut off the rebels heads in like manner, she answered boldly, "If those rebels were here you would run like wild turkeys."

Mary Gill was a young woman of unusual height, build and strength and there was much dignity in her bearing. It is said that at one time the British suspected her of being a spy in female apparel and she had some trouble to convince them of their mistake.

Like most unmarried girls in the country, she had a lover who was serving in the Revolutionary Army. She expected his visits whenever he had the opportunity to come home, and looked forward to the close of the war as the time when they would be wed.

His name was John Mills, a near neighbor, of whose brave exploits she continually heard. When the enemy was driven to the low country, some of the soldiers seized the opportunity of a short furlough to lead their betrothed fair ones to the altar.

The marriage of Mary and John took place May 21, 1782. Mills had been among the first who took up arms, and early distinguished himself, being with General Sumter from the time he formed his camp at Clem's branch to the termination of his campaigns. He obtained the commission of Captain in the State troops, and might be called with propriety "Sumter's right arm." Their intimate friendship began in camp, continuing during Mills' life.

Mills kept a diary of the times of the Revolution, recording every event of the war. This volume was carefully preserved by Mrs. Mills, but when she died it came into possession of her son, and after his death was probably destroyed. Had it been saved, much of the unrecorded history of Sumter's campaigns might have been given to the public. Yet, though this was lost, tradition has preserved the remembrance of some bold acts, strange as deeds of romance.

Sarah Knox Wallace

Sarah Knox Wallace was daughter of Hugh Knox and Jennet Nesbit Knox. She was a "Gold Spoon" member and one of three original Daughters of the American Revolution in South Carolina when the Columbia Chapter was organized in 1898. Her membership was transferred to the Mary Adair Chapter of Chester when it was organized in 1900.

Revolutionary War "Gold Spoon Mother" of DAR Sallie Knox Wallace

Jane Brown Gaston

Old records state that "Joseph Gaston and Jeney Brown were married on Apprile 20th, 1790, to meet and mingal souls, and wear the joyful chain."

Jeney or Jane Brown was of the same pioneer patriot stock as her husband. Her parents, Walter and Margaret Brown came from Ireland to Mecklenburg then to Fishing Creek where she was born in 1768.

Although young at the time of the war, this daughter of a patriotic family not only bore her part in privation and suffering, but contributed her aid in doing good to the defenders of her country's rights.

She married Joseph, youngest son of Justice John Gaston and Esther Waugh Gaston of Fishing Creek. He was severely wounded at the battle of Hanging Rock on August 7, 1780, where three of his brothers, David, Ebenezer and Robert, lost their lives.

He inherited the plantation of his parents where he and Jane spent their lives. He was ruling elder in his church from youth, and was also placed in the magisterial office when very young, continuing to exercise its duties until his death. His family consisted of two sons and four daughters.

Jane Simpson Boyd

One of the chief targets of British persecution in Fishing Creek area was the Rev. John Simpson, pastor of Fishing Creek church. Mrs. Ellet says he was distinguished throughout the country for the zeal with which he promoted the cause of liberty. He was successor to the Rev. William Richardson who came as a missionary to the Waxhaws and preached in a wide area of sparsely settled frontier.

Mr. Simpson took up the work, preaching with zeal and laboring earnestly, organizing congregations in Chester, York and surrounding areas. In those days, inhabitants thought it no hardship to travel fifteen miles or more to hear preaching, sometimes on week days and in all kinds of weather. Services were held in brush arbors, log structures with split log benches, or in homes.

The Rev. John Simpson was leader of the band of heroes who had so soundly defeated the British at Old Field and Mobley's. For this reason it was determined that his punishment should be severe and speedy. A party of redcoats made its way to the church, expecting to find the pastor with his assembled congregation and intending to burn both church and people as a warning to "other disturbers of the King's peace."

Rev. Simpson on the previous Friday had shouldered his rifle and marched to the field, under the command of Capt. John McClure, who had been reared from infancy under his ministry. There he took his place in the ranks of the brave men of Chester District, encouraging them both by his counsel and his services, performing the duties of a private soldier and submitting to the rigorous discipline of the rugged camp.

While the destroyers were at the church, some of the negroes heard them declare their intention to go to Mr. Simpson's house and "burn the rascal out." They hastened to carry information to his wife, urging her to flee to safety. Mrs. Simpson looked out and saw a body of men approaching. Stopping only to gather up a set of silver spoons, a treasured gift from her mother, she took her four children, went out the back door and concealed herself in the orchard. There she watched the soldiers strip the house of valuables, take four feather beds and rip them open in the yard, take all the clothing they could wear, and set fire to the house which soon burned to the ground. They entered an outhouse which contained a valuable library and was used by Mr. Simpson as a study. This was also set afire.

As soon as the men had gone, Mrs. Simpson rushed into the burning study and carried out two aprons full of books. In doing this she was severely burned and nearly lost her life. She also gathered up enough feathers from the yard to make one bed.

Mrs. Simpson and children and a companion, Miss Neely, went to the house of a neighbor where they stayed until after her confinement which took place in four weeks. As soon as she recovered, she and her five children and Miss Neely returned to her place and took up residence in a building which had escaped destruction. She received care and assistance from the people of her husband's charge.

She continued to be harassed by enemy soldiers. At one time when she had procured some cloth and was cutting and sewing garments for the children, the tories came along and plundered all of her materials. Some of the men were dressed in Mr. Simpson's clothes, and strutting before her, tautingly asked if they were not better looking men than her husband, telling her at the same time that they would someday make her a present of his scalp.

These marauders also took her stock of cattle. Mrs. Simpson begged them to leave one milk cow for her little children, but her request was refused. The property was restored, however, in an unexpected manner. After going two miles further on the way, the robbers put the cattle in a pen until morning. Two large steers broke out during the night and opened the way for the whole flock to return home.

Rev. Simpson remained with the army until victory from oppression was assured. He is believed to have been engaged in most of the battles fought.

After the war he continued in charge of Fishing Creek and Bethesda churches, occasionally supplying Catholic. Between 1790 and 1800, he moved to the district of Pendleton where he spent the remainder of his days.

Rev. Simpson bestowed on his children superior education and moral training. One son married a daughter of General Andrew Pickens, another a daughter of Col. Moffatt; another, Dr. James Simpson, a daughter of Col. John Bratton; two others into the family of the Sadlers.

Jane was married first to James Neely of Fishing Creek by whom she had a son named for her father, and later to James Boyd, by whom she had two daughters.

Jane White

Jane Brown White was born in the county of Antrim, Ireland in 1758. William White who became Jane's husband was born in the same county in 1753. Both families emigrated to South Carolina at the same time and settled on adjoining farms in the "centre of Chester District, three miles south of Chesterville, one mile from Purity Church on the Rocky Mount Road, branching from the main Columbia Road which forms ... the backbone of the district, passing through its entire length, and separating the waters that flow into the Broad River from the tributaries of the Catawba."

Jane and William were married and had one child when hostilities commenced in the South. Two of William's sisters were married, and three others lived upon his premises. When it became necessary to take sides in the contest, White and his brothers-in-law had no difficulty in making up their minds. William joined McClure in the attack at Mobley's Meeting House on the banks of Little River in Fairfield District.

The British commander at Rocky Mount issued a summons to the people in the vicinity to assemble, take protection, and enlist in the royal army. This official soon wearied in the performance of his duties (as no one showed up) and indulged himself with a nap. A fellow officer waked him and asked, "What if McClure should come upon us?" He replied, "I wish to heavens he would, for I am full of fight."

Mrs. Ellett says this same redoubtable champion was found after the battle ensconced in the chimney corner.

When Cornwallis was marching from Charlotte to Winnsboro, he encamped for some days on the plantation of John Service, two miles east of White's residence. During his stay, his soldiers robbed Jane White of all her clothing, provisions and cattle, taking also some lambs on which she set a high value.

She went to the encampment, and through John Service presented her petition for redress to his lordship. But the great man drove Service from his presence with angry oaths. Mrs. White was thus compelled to return home empty handed. But her tongue being "a free and fearless member, she did not fail to give her spoilers some of its lessoning ... that a day of retribution was not far distant."

At the close of the war, White returned home and resumed his agricultural pursuits. It was always his particular delight to describe to the young people among his kin and friends the Revolutionary experiences through which he had passed.

Jane and William White had eight sons and one daughter. Two sons served with Jackson in his war with the Creek Indians; five others were at Charleston as volunteers in 1812. It was this principle "that impelled them to count no sacrifice too great in the acquisition of that liberty which cannot be prized too highly by those who inherit its blessings."

Early cotton press built in 1798, powered by oxen or mules rotating the beam to tighten the press, it was rendered obsolete by modern machinery.

COTTON PRESS   L. ADAMS

VII COTTON KINGDOM

"KING COTTON" DOMINATED SOUTH

Cotton was the main force behind the Cotton Kingdom's (S. C., Ga., Ala., Miss. and La.) culture and economy. It enriched the planter, impoverished the soil, made big farmers out of little ones, and planters out of farmers. It paid the taxes, bought the supplies, paid off the mortgages and built the railroads. Finally, it sustained the institution of slavery, making it a central element of the regional society and economy.

Like the major theme in a symphony, it wore its way through the entire area, on occasion light and subtle, but more often strong and distinct — and dominant.

In 1860, South Carolina was literally covered in cotton fields. Only the tip of Oconee County and a few beach sections were sparsely cultivated in cotton.

Chester County was one big cotton patch. It was interspersed with fields of grain and pastures needed to sustain the hordes of people and animals that cleared the land, planted and harvested the crops.

THE PLANTER

W. J. Cash in his inimitable way describes the development of the planter class by the strong, the pushing, the ambitious among the old coon-hunting population of the backcountry. The frontier was their predestined inheritance. They possessed precisely the qualities necessary to the taming of the land and the building of the cotton kingdom.

The plantation family was self-contained because it had to be. It grew, slew and preserved its own food, bred and grew its own

66

transportation, dug its own water supply and sewerage disposal holes, organized its own social life with neighbors and kinfolk, treated most of its own ailments. It even provided its own vices, from its tobacco and cornfields.

W. J. Cash's epic description of the development of the planter class:

A stout young Irishman brought his bride into the Carolina upcountry about 1800. He cleared a bit of land, built a log cabin of two rooms, and settled down to the pioneer life. One winter, with several of his neighbors, he loaded a boat with whisky and the coarse woolen cloth woven by the women, and drifted down to Charleston to trade. There, remembering the fondness of his woman for a bit of beauty, he brought a handful of cotton seed, which she planted about the cabin with the wild rose and the honeysuckle — as a flower. Afterward she learned, under the tutelage of a new neighbor, to pick the seed from the fiber with her fingers and to spin it into yarn. Another winter the man drifted down the river, this time to find the half-way station of Columbia in a strange ferment. There was a new wonder in the world — the cotton gin — and the forest which had lined the banks of the stream for a thousand centuries was beginning to go down. Fires flared red and portentious in the night, to set off an answering fire in the breast of the Irishman.

Land in his neighborhood was to be had for fifty cents an acre. With twenty dollars, the savings of his lifetime, be bought forty acres and set himself to clear it. Rising long before day, he toiled deep into the night, with his wife holding a pine torch for him to see by. Aided by his neighbors, he piled the trunks of the trees into great heaps and burned them, grubbed up the stumps, hacked away the tangle of underbrush and vine, stamped out the poison ivy and the snakes. A wandering trader sold him a horse, bony and half-starved, for a knife, a dollar, and a gallon of whisky. Every day now — Sundays not excepted — when the heavens allowed, and every night that the moon shone, he drove the plow into the earth, with uptorn roots bruising his shanks at every step. Behind him came his wife with a hoe. In a few years the land was beginning to yield cotton — richly, for the soil was fecund with the accumulated mold of centuries. Another trip down the river, and he brought home a mangy black slave — an old and lazy fellow reckoned of no account in the rice-lands, but with plenty of life in him still if you knew how to get it out. Next year the Irishman bought fifty acres more, and the year after another black. Five years more and he had two hundred acres and ten Negroes. Cotton prices swung up and down sharply, but always, whatever the return, it was almost pure velvet. For the fertility of the soil seemed inexhaustible.

When he was forty-five, he quit work, abandoned the log house, which had grown to six rooms, and built himself a wide-spreading frame cottage. When he was fifty, he became a magistrate, acquired a carriage, and built a cotton gin and a third house — a "big house" this time. It was not, to be truthful, a very grand house really. Built of lumber sawn on the place, it was a little crude and had not cost above a thousand dollars, even when the marble mantel was counted in. Essentially, it was just a box, with four rooms, bisected by a hallway, set on four more rooms bisected by another hallway, and a detached kitchen at the back. Wind-swept in winter, it was difficult to keep clean of vermin in summer. But it was huge, it had great columns in front, and it was eventually painted white, and so, in this land of wide fields and pinewoods it seemed very imposing.

Meantime the country around had been growing up. Other "big houses" had been built. There was a county seat now, a cluster of frame houses, stores, and "doggeries" about a red brick courthouse. A Presbyterian parson had drifted in and started an academy, as Presbyterian parsons had a habit of doing everywhere in the South — and Pompeys and Ceasars and Ciceros and Platos were multiplying both among the pickaninnies in the slave quarters and among the white children of the "big houses." The Irishman had a piano in his house, on which his daughters, taught by a vagabond German, played as well as young ladies could be expected to. One of the Irishman's sons went to the College of South Carolina, came back to grow into the chief lawyer in the county, got to be a judge, and would have been Governor if he had not died at the head of his regiment at Chancellorsville.

As a crown on his career, the old man went to the Legislature, where he was accepted by the Charleston gentlemen tolerantly and with genuine liking. He grew extremely mellow in age and liked to pass his time in company, arguing about predestination and infant damnation, proving conclusively that cotton was king and that the damyankee didn't dare do anything about it, and developing notable taste in the local liquors. Tall and well-made, he grew whiskers after the Galway fashion, the well-kept whiteness of which contrasted very agreeably with the brick red of his complexion — donned the long-tailed coat, stove-pipe hat, and string tie of the statesmen of his period, waxed innocently pompous, and, in short, became a really striking figure of a man.

Once, going down to Columbia for the inauguration of a new Governor, he took his youngest daughter along. There she met a Charleston gentleman who was pestering her father for a loan. Her manner, formed by the Presbyterian parson, was plain but not bad, and she was very pretty. Moreover, the Charleston gentleman was decidedly in hard lines. So he married her.

When the old man finally died in 1854, he left two thousand acres, a hundred and fourteen slaves, and four cotton gins. The little newspaper which had recently set up in the county seat spoke of him as "a gentleman of the old school" and "a noble specimen of the chivalry at its best"; the Charleston papers each gave him a column; and a lordly Legaré introduced resolutions of respect into the Legislature. His wife outlived him by ten years — by her portrait a beautifully fragile old woman, with lovely hands, knotted and twisted just enough to give them character, and finely transparent skin through which the blue veins showed most aristocratically.

PLANTERS AND PLANTATIONS

DAVIE HOUSE
1828

LUCY ADAMS

Chester County was not plantation country until after the invention of the cotton gin in 1793 and the spread of short staple cotton to the Piedmont, writes native son Chalmers Gaston Davidson. According to the Census of 1790, James Knox was one of the country's earliest planters who owned twenty-nine slaves. William McDonald and William McDaniel owned twenty-six each.

Dr. Davidson writes that the first great planter in Chester was William Richardson Davie who was raised in the Waxhaw section and became Governor of North Carolina and Envoy to France. After his distinguished public career, he returned to his native river plantation as a planter and established Tivoli on the Catawba, near Lands Ford, in 1805. General Davie owned several hundred slaves and his plantation is the only one mentioned by name for Chester District on the Mill's Atlas map of 1825.

Major Allen Jones Green established Rose Hill plantation, above Land's Ford, around 1815. The Census of 1830 for Chester District lists General Davie's son, Hyder, as the largest slave owner in the District with 160 blacks. Next came Major Green with 155, T. G. Blewett with 145, and General Davie's second son, William with 135. Edward Mobley, the first of a notable planting family in Chester and Fairfield had 105 slaves.

Wealthy planters from the low-country of South Carolina came into Chester District. The Izards of Charleston, who intermarried with the Greens, had plantations on the Catawba. Wilmot S. Gibbes built a summer home, later his principal residence, about 1825, which is still standing. The residence known as Oakley Hall (in Rodman community) was originally a typical double-galleried mansion with gardens, a show place to this day. It is owned by Miss Margaret Saye.

On the 1825 Mills map appears "W. Gibbs" on the Lands' Ford Road and "major Green's" above Tivoli on the Catawba. Also appearing are "Dr. Cloud's" near the "Beckhamville Post Office" in East Chester and Degraffenreids on Fishdam Road in West Chester. Dr. William Cloud owned ninety-eight slaves in 1840. By 1860 he owned 128 slaves and 2,800 acres of land. He also had six beautiful daughters, the youngest of whom married William Calhoun, youngest son of the Statesman John C. Calhoun. The Beckhamville Mansion, three stories with fourteen rooms, burned in 1895.

The DeGraffenried family were descendants of Christopher, Baron de Graffenried, one of the early Landgraves of Carolina, according to Dr. Davidson. They intermarried with the Thomas and Blewett families of Chester, both of whom owned over a hundred slaves in 1830. The Degraffenried property in West Chester was referred to as The Baron's Estate.

The last of the great planters of the DeGraffenried name was Tscharner Hobson DeGraffenried who owned 108 slaves in 1860. He lived on original DeGraffenried property on Sandy River. His residence was known as Oakland. The house site and family burial ground, with elaborate marble memorials, is now only a pile of rubble on Fish Dam Road.

Other large plantation owners in Chester District in 1850 Census were: Col. Davie's estate, Thomas De Graffenried, Charner Scaife, Thomas McLure, R. E. Kennedy, C. J. Jones, John G. Smith, Nancy Mobley, Samuel McAliley and Dr. Isaiah Mobley.

Thomas De Graffenried lived in a very large home in Chesterville which later became Brainard School for Negroes and was torn down in 1960.

Old Wyoming was owned by the Pride family. The plantation house still standing in northeastern Chester County is one of the finest ante-bellum houses in the up-country.

Worthy's Bottoms with address Carmel Hill P. O. was the home of Henry Worthy who owned 107 slaves and 3,200 acres on Broad River in the 1860 Census. The property was sold to Sumter National Forest by the last heir, Hood C. Worthy. Woodside was owned by the Cassels family. The house was built in 1856 and owned by Thomas Tresvant Cassels who had nineteen slaves and six slave houses in 1860 Census.

Rose Hill was property of Mrs. Allen Jones Green. Her brother, Halcott Pride Jones, reversed his last name to inherit the Pride property in Chester District and left a fortune when he died in 1817.

Redcliffe, home of the Randells and McLures was built about 1843 by Col. Theodore Randell.

A third wealthy planter, James Stringfellow McLure, was brother of John Joseph McLure and Col. Edward C. McLure. He purchased the Randell estate built in 1843 in West Chester and lived in lavish style of the storied plantations.

Both E. C. McLure and John Jr. McClure were listed at Smith's Turnout P. O. in 1860 Census. E. C. McLure owned 2,600 acres, 110 slaves and 33 slave houses. James McLure owned 152 slaves, 32 slave houses and 2,300 acres (1,800 improved and 600 unimproved).

Red Hill's large ante-bellum mansion was built on the plantation of Adam T. Walker in western Chester District. The house was restored by Mrs. T. L. Eberhardt. It burned in 1929 and the land was sold to David A. Gaston who owns it today.

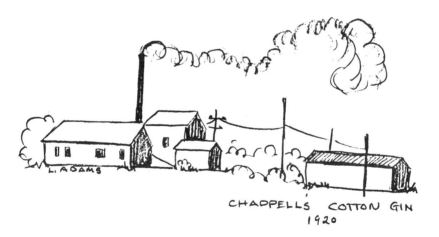

CHADPELLS COTTON GIN
1920

Among the most imposing Chester County mansions were the twin Mobley mansions, one on Lancaster Road and one on Peden Bridge Road. Perhaps the handsomest of all survivals into the Twentieth Century was the house built for Jack Rice about the year 1830 in present Wilksburg community. Rice sold it to his son-in-law, T. C. Scaife who sold it to Mr. Tucker who gave it to his daughter, Mrs. John W. Wilks. It was a handsome Classical Revival house known as Tin-tops. It burned in 1910.

Thomas McCullough Boulware, the largest slave owner in the County in the Census of 1860 (157 Negroes) had a very handsome house near Blackstocks that was burned by Sherman's men near the end of the War.

On Highway 72, six miles north of Chester, Robert Stringfellow operated a 1,130 acre cotton plantation known as Hillbright. He built his house in 1852, and from it five sons went into the Confederate Army. As troop trains passed through the area, wounded soldiers too ill to travel further were taken to the Stringfellow plantation for care. Among the wounded treated there were Dr. Gill Wylie who later became a prominent New York gynecologist. The plantation and house are now owned and occupied by the William Brawley Stringfellows.

The Oaks or Nine Mile House belonged to Dr. Isaiah Mobley. Mary Mobley (perhaps a kinsman) in the 1860 Census owned 2,700 acres and 78 slaves. The house burned in the 1940's when Col. "Tuck" Cunningham lived there.

Millwood, the plantation home built shortly before the War by Edwin R. Mills was later owned by the Frank Hicklin family. In the 1860 Census E. R. Mills owned 30 slaves.

Hazelwood was the home of the Caldwells. It sat on what is now Highway 97 or Great Falls Road and was an original land grant from King George III of England. The house was demolished in the 1950's.

Samuel McAlily's address in the 1860 Census is listed as Smith's Turnout P. O. At that time he owned 2,786 acres, 76 slaves and 17 slave houses. His plantation homestead was as unpretentious as he was. It is now the property of his great-granddaughter, Miss Margaret Colvin, and is located on the Highway 72 By Pass near Chester. Samuel was famous in his day for his outstanding opposition to secession.

Other plantation owners in the 1860 Census were Valentine Atkinson of West Chester with 2,000 acres and 69 slaves; John Sanders with 6,300 acres and 77 slaves; R. N. Hemphill with 3,000 acres and 39 slaves; Jane Hemphill with 98 slaves, James Atkinson (Smith's Turnout P. O.) 3,400 acres, Churchill Carter 2,300 acres and 47 slaves and Richard Woods (Carmel Hill P. O.) 2,300 acres and 84 slaves. Thomas Boulware reported 182 slaves, Bigger Mobley 83 and L. C. Hinton, administrator for six children, 122 slaves.

The 1860 Agriculture Census was taken by R. E. Alexander who went from house to house, often staying for several days, and recorded information by hand. A typical accounting, that of Richard Woods, whose plantation was on Broad River, stated he had 1,200 improved acres, 1,100 unimproved, valued at $27,600. He had 14 horses, 24 asses and mules, 20 cows, 4 oxen, 20 other animals, 35 sheep, 155 swine. He produced 260 bushel wheat, 300 rye, 3,500 Indian corn, 600 oats, 116 bales of cotton, 100 lbs. wool,

800 bushel beans and peas, 50 bushel Irish potatoes, 300 bushel sweet potatoes, 800 lbs. butter, 15 tons hay, 10 lbs. beeswax and 200 lbs. honey.

A large land grant was made by the King of England to seven Osborne Brothers in the northwest corner of Chester County near the York County line. Some of the land is still in possession of the Osborne family.

According to the 1860 Census there were 124 slave owners in Chester County with a total of 10,936 slaves.

DESCRIPTION OF CHESTER COUNTY PLANTATION IN 1860

Description of a Chester County plantation was found in an old diary, author unknown. It describes the trees and flowers indigenous to the area, and the concerns of the planter.

In selecting his plantation, Thomas showed his usual sound judgment in practical matters. It comprised twenty-five hundred acres in a compact body, not all bought at one time, but as he saw opportunity to secure the property of small farmers whose land adjoined his. Sandy River crossed it. The lowland bordering the creek, call "The Bottom," was always fertile, and insured heavy crops in the dryest season.

Stringfellow House, built prior to the Civil War.

From the creek bottoms the land rises and runs back in a series of gently rolling hills. Those not already cleared for cultivation were covered with a magnificent growth of timber, — oaks of many species, yellow pine, hickory, elm, sweet and blackgum, besides a variety of other shrubs and trees. Walnut trees of magnificent size, magnolia, beech and laurel grew on the banks of the creek.

Crops raised on the hills flourished best in wet weather, so with the rich and diversified soil on the plantation, there was never a failure of a whole crop in the most unfavorable season.

The land was well watered throughout by Sandy River, with its tributary branches. In the hills springs bubbled out, giving rise to spring "branches" which did not go dry in the most prolonged drought. There was always pasturage for cattle along these water-courses, and in the bitterest cold of winter they found abundant green food in the canebrakes of the creek.

Many wild flowers adorn the fields and woods till late in the fall. Tiny blue innocents and dandelions dot the grass as early as January. Later come wild violets, roses, the wild honeysuckle, clematis, woodbine and a host of flowering trees, shrubs and vines. Among these we find the red-bud, honeysuckle, maple, dogwood, crabapple, hawthorn, wisteria and wild peach; but supreme in beauty and fragrance we have the yellow jasmine. It is the crown and glory of Southern woods, throwing its drapery of golden bells over trees and shrubs for whole acres.

An indigo patch for each family was an indispensable requisite. Sulphate of iron, indigo, maple and red oak bark, walnut hulls, holly leaves, sumach, the long moss that grows on trees and madder constituted their dye stuffs. With such consummate taste and skill did they combine these colors in the manufacture of male and female attire that they are impressive to this day.

VIII CIVIL WAR

CHESTER IN PRE-CIVIL WAR ERA

Chester in 1855 was a typical Southern community. The government was headed by an intendant, similar to the present day mayor, four wardens, a magistrate and a marshal. They were selected annually, and generally the same men managed to retain their posts.

Laws and ordinances were enforced by a marshal who was appointed by the town council and approved by the people. Chester had more than its share of marshals during the 1850-1860's with some leaving because of poor pay, and others being asked to leave for various reasons. Average pay was $100 a year.

The marshal was over a group of men called the Night Watch. The men were required to patrol one night every two weeks on the watch. One might exempt himself from this compulsory duty by paying a fee of $3.00 per year. Since most men did not have extra money on hand to afford this convenience they were compelled to serve. Those who defaulted were summoned before town council and fined $2.00 or sent to jail.

Some of the duties of the Night Watch were set forth in an ordinance passed by town council on March 4, 1854:

1. Ring Howerton bell (curfew) regularly at 10 p.m. from March 20-September 20, and 9 p.m. from September 20-March 20 for curfew.

2. Enter any kitchen or yard where unlawful gatherings of Negroes, either slave or free, were suspected.

3. Patrol streets within corporate limits from minutes after the bell rings until daylight.

4. Report and stop any acts contrary to any active ordinances.

5. Test fastenings of doors and windows of all business buildings and report any peculiarities to the manager or owner.

6. Report fires and alarm the town.

These duties were rigidly enforced and records show that crime and violence in Chester during this period were kept at a minimum.

Ordinances that the marshal and his deputies had to enforce were the prevention of hogs running loose in the corporate limits, the discharge of firearms or other combustible materials, disorderly conduct and speeding through town with a horse and buggy. They also pressed property owners to build sidewalks and maintain their homes and businesses.

Disorderly conduct was Chester's main problem during this period. Open bars were licensed in the city and patronized by many. After a few shots of Southern bourbon, intoxication and brawling often followed.

History records that bars were numerous and very successful. One was owned and operated by a woman, Mrs. E. McAfee. Licenses, renewed annually, were $1,000 and the licensee was required to sign an oath that he would not sell or deliver "any spiritous liquors" to any slaves, to close by 10 p.m., not to open on Sundays, and to keep the quality of their establishments at the highest.

Amusements

For entertainment, other than bars and "Tin Pan Alleys," local people enjoyed the annual fish fries at the falls near Great Falls, the best of which were held when the shad were running. Also, there were numerous religious revivals that were going on almost continuously from 1845-1870 at Bonnet Rock near Armenia. It was a Methodist campground near a large rock which was said to point in different directions and thereby prophesy the weather.

Visiting was probably the greatest enjoyment during antebellum days where one visited in terms of months instead of days. Barbecues, picnics, parties and balls were favorites among the distinguished planter class of the area, while simple get-togethers provided entertainment for the poorer class.

As for the slaves, they reportedly received good treatment and were permitted time for their own social lives "until conditions up north worsened and required a clampdown."

Town Well

Chester's newspaper, The Chester Standard, at this time was owned and edited by George Pither.

A town well was proposed and accepted in Chester on April 20, 1860. Its estimated cost was $175.00 and it was given the name of Agurs Well in honor of a prominent Chester family. The well became a bone of contention as its cost increased and its workmanship was questioned. The war prevented its completion. Toward the end of the war, a pump previously bought for the well had to be sold to finance the city's debts.

About this time, the first Board of Health was established in Chester County. Due to an epidemic of smallpox in Columbia, the Chester Town Council appointed Dr. J. A. Reedy as chairman of a committee to formulate measures to preserve the health of local citizens. On November 28, 1860, the Board met and passed two resolutions: (1) to use all methods necessary to prevent persons from the infected districts from coming to town, and (2) that any such persons who have not been subjected to vaccination be liable to such immediately.

It was agreed to enforce an ordinance forbidding persons within the corporate limits from letting water stand for long periods of time on their premises. These measures were effective, for during the period of this epidemic, Chester lost only one citizen, Thomas Hellam.

NULLIFICATION

Chester County, along with all of South Carolina, suffered through the pangs of nullification. A local incident points to the problem.

In 1828, a subscription was begun for the purpose of erecting a new church building for Purity Presbyterian Church in Chester. It is recorded that "the great political tornado Nullification" sprang up and swept over the state. Both church and state were affected by it.

At the time, James Hamilton, ancestor of Herman P. Hamilton of Chester, was Governor of South Carolina.

After the War of 1812, the national government needed money. The debts of the war had to be paid, and money was needed for highways and other internal improvement. For this reason a tax was placed on all imported goods. Markets were flooded with cheap goods made in England and manufacturers demanded that a tariff be placed on the imports to protect them from competition they considered unfair.

South Carolinians generally opposed the tax. They felt that it protected Northern manufacturers at their expense. The people of South Carolina had to sell cotton and buy manufactured products. If they did not buy abroad, they would have trouble selling abroad. The tax meant also that they would have to pay higher prices for the manufactured products they bought. South Carolinians felt that the tax helped the North and hurt the South. The passing of the tariff law of 1816 marked the beginning of trouble between the two sections.

The tariff, designed to be temporary, became permanent and more burdensome. Each Congress after 1816 was faced with demands for new and heavier duties on imports.

A mass meeting condemning the tariff was held in Charleston. The Up Country, including Chester County, sent a petition to Congress stating that the people of the state did not object to a tariff to provide money for national defense. They were opposed, however, to a tariff that would take money from the farmer and merchant in order to give it to the manufacturers.

Another tariff law was proposed in 1824. The average duty on imports was increased to 37 percent, nearly twice that of 1816. The South voted solidly against the new tariff law, but it was passed.

In South Carolina there was great indignation. The General Assembly adopted resolutions of protest, and citizens met to express indignation. There were rumblings about leaving the Union.

A new tariff imposed in 1828 was so high it became known as the "tariff of abominations." Statesman John C. Calhoun was called upon to draft a protest. He drafted The Exposition stating it was the right of the states to refuse to obey any act of Congress they considered to be in violation of the Constitution. This refusal to obey came to be known as nullification. Those who favored it were called Nullifiers, while those who opposed it were called Unionists.

In July, 1828, a meeting was called at Edgefield. The people at this meeting, the largest ever held in the state, pledged themselves to buy neither manufactured goods from the North nor livestock from the West. Similar meetings were held in Chester and around the state. Everywhere there was threatening talk about leaving the Union.

Bitterness over the tariff was aggravated by related problems. The price of cotton had dropped to new lows, and so had the volume of exports from Charleston. At the same time prices of manufactured goods bought by South Carolinians had gone up.

The state's economic troubles were aggravated by two other developments. Cotton had worn out the land and slavery was no longer profitable. Another source of trouble was the state's failure to develop manufacturing and other industries as well as farming and planting. Because the South's resources were tied up in land and slaves, it did not have the great outlay of capital needed to diversify.

As the land wore out, many Chester Countians and other South Carolinians moved westward, festering with resentment toward the national government. They felt that the policies were dictated by the North in order to make the rich richer and the poor poorer.

After the famous debate between Robert Y. Hayne of South Carolina and Daniel Webster of Massachusetts on states rights, matters grew worse in South Carolina. The state was about evenly divided between the Nullifiers and the Unionists. Every county courthouse and every crossroads became a place of bitter argument. Families were divided and men went armed at all times.

Daniel Greene Stinson in his autobiography says that, in 1830, Chester District became politically divided and "many of my best friends were in the ranks of the Nullifiers. Yet differing from them, my motto was 'Principles, not men'. "

He says "the press of the state espoused the cause of the Nullifiers, and established a paper called *The Hive* in Columbia, an organ of the Union party, that was edited by Dr. Landrum." Stinson frequently contributed short articles to this paper.

In a story entitled Nullification Grows Bitter in Chester District, Stinson wrote:

In the canvas of 1830, all the lawyers were with the Nullifiers. They first proposed to nullify the tariff through the legislature, but this did not take well with the people. They then went for a convention, called a mass meeting of the citizens of the District to assemble on the first Monday of September, and argued before the people to leave it to a convention which might nullify the tariff or not, just as might be thought best.

A young man opposed the call of the convention. He was denounced as a submissionist and an order given to throw him out of the door. This was promptly met by the crowd, "Do if you dare; your blood shall sprinkle this floor."

Several old men tried to say something, Stinson wrote, but they could not be heard, so great was the confusion. The legislature in 1830 failed to call a convention. The Nullifiers took the name of "Jackson and States Rights," and the other party took the name of "Union and States Rights," and the two parties became very bitter toward each other. The Nullifiers denounced the Union men as submissionists and soaptails, and tariff men. The Nullifiers, having formed associations all over the state by the name of "Free Trade Associations," issued monthly tracts to circulate among the people. The Union party then retaliated by calling them "Jacobin Clubs" and "Bombsuckers."

Arthur Cornwall wrote of a later meeting in Chester District.

A CITIZENS' MEETING IN 1831

A general meeting of the citizens of Chester district was held at the Court House on Friday, November 11, 1831, pursuant to previous public notice. John Roseborough, Esq., was called to the chair and George W. Colemen, Esq., appointed secretary.

On motion of James Chestney, Jr., Esq., it was:

Resolved, that a committee be appointed to draft resolutions, expressing the sentiments of the people of Chester district on the present state of public affairs.

Whereupon, John McKee, Thomas McLure, George Gill, James Chestney, Junior, John McCreary, Burr H. Head, and Samuel Lewis were appointed said committee.

The letters of the Honorable William Smith, and the Honorable James Blair, of Yorkville in answer to the committee of invitation, were then read.

William Ellison, Esq., of Fairfield, who attended the meeting by invitation was then called on, and entered into an elaborate and finished argument, exposing the fallacy and danger of the doctrine of nullification, and its incompatibility with the best interests of South Carolina and of the Union.

John McKee, Esq., chairman of the committee, then reported a detailed preamble and resolution. After the reading of the resolutions a spirited debate ensued as to the form they should assume, in which several gentlemen participated. On the reading of the second resolution R. G. Mills, Esq., desired to be heard in support of nullification which was promptly refused by the meeting, when Major Mills and a few other gentlemen withdrew. The resolutions were unanimously adopted.

A general committee of thirty citizens was appointed to promote the objects of this meeting.

The following letter was written:

"His Excellency Andrew Jackson — President of the United States of America. Dear Sir: — In conformity with a resolution of the citizens of Chester district, we have the honor to forward to Your Excellency, a copy of the proceedings of a meeting held by them on the 11th, instant. In discharging this duty permit us to express the high regard we individually entertain for your eminent public services and elevated character; the desire we feel for the prolongation of your valuable and useful life, and the sanguine hope we confidently cherish for the complete success of your administration.

Very respectfully, we have the honor to be Your Excellency's most humble servants,

John Roseborough
Chairman of the meeting.
G. W. Coleman,
Secretary.

Chester Court House, 12th, November, 1831.

President Jackson answered this letter as follows:

Washington, Dec. 28th, 1831.

Gentlemen: — I received, in due time, your letter of the 12th of November, last, transmitting to me a copy of the proceedings of a meeting of the citizens of Chester, held on the day before, and expressing the favorable opinion which you entertain individually of my character and services.

I hope you will excuse the delay which has occurred in tendering my thanks for so flattering a proof of the friendship and support of a respectable body of my fellow-citizens. The multiplicity of public business with which I have been surrounded for the last two months, not allowing me at the moment of its receipt an opportunity to acknowledge it, prevented also a recurrence to it earlier than this.

The approbation of my fellow citizens, at all times cheering to me was peculiarly grateful, when received under the circumstances which elicited that expressed by the meeting, of which you are the organ. In reply to it now I can only say that it shall be my endeavor as long as I am in the executive chair, by a faithful discharge of the duties confided to it by the constitution, to draw closer the bonds of our Union and promise the welfare and happiness of our beloved country.

Andrew Jackson

Messrs. J. Roseborough and G. W. Coleman, Chester Court House, South Carolina.

President Andrew Jackson issued a proclamation claiming South Carolina as his birth place and addressing the "fellow citizens of my native state." Stating that nullification was lawless, he said he spoke in order to "use the influence that a father would use with his children whom he saw rushing to certain ruin."

As he admonished them, Jackson was using his influence to persuade Congress to reduce the tariff. The Ordinance of Nullification was dropped and the slow healing of differences began.

In 1831, the Nullifiers carried the State, and the District of Chester by a majority of over three hundred. In the meantime, another quarrel between the North and South had arisen over the spread of slavery to new territory. This controversy led to the War Between the States.

SECESSION

Historian Louis B. Wright says, "Like Biblical Eden, South Carolina from early in its history was betrayed by a serpent — the serpent of Pride, chief of the Seven Deadly Sins. Pride led to many collateral faults, all flowering freely in the Scotch-Irish stock: overweening individualism, an unwillingness to submit to authority, every man's conviction of the rightness of his opinions, and a thousand contentions that flowed from these characteristics. South Carolina has been one of the most contentious states of the union."

Every one in Chester County was not supportive of the Southern cause. Many families, especially those from Rocky Creek area, went out from the county to Ohio, Indiana, Arkansas or Tennesse to avoid, as some of them declared, "the judgments which would some day befall on the South because of her sins."

Another example of pro-Northern sentiments was the prominent George Pither, a native of New York and editor of the Chester Standard. With the outbreak of hostilities, he sold his newspaper to C. Davis and Samuel W. Melton and moved back North. But the majority of citizens supported the Southern cause.

No matter what people were doing between 1850 and 1860, a feeling of stress and strain was pervasive. There was dissatisfaction with the national government, open resentment toward the bitter campaigns of the abolitionists from the North, and angry threats to secede from the Union.

For years abolitionists had worked to abolish slavery and free the Negro slaves in the South. Hundreds of abolition societies were organized and Northern lecturers spoke out violently against the South. They sent agents into the South to stir up the Negroes and urge them to rise against their masters. Some of the agents were seized in the state and were tarred and feathered.

In 1851, a book called Uncle Tom's Cabin, written by Harriett Beecher Stowe, began to appear in Northern newspapers in serial form. It was an exaggerated and inflamatory picture of slavery that enraged both North and South — but for different reasons. Southerners hotly resented being pictured as cruel monsters. Northerners found fuel to feed their fight against holding slaves.

In the 1850s another source of friction was the question of admission of Kansas to the Union. The Kansas-Nebraska Act of 1854 had declared that a territory might vote itself slave or free. When Kansas was opened to settlement, people poured in from both North and South. Among them were families from Chester County and surrounding areas. There were clashes that resulted in bloodshed. Kansas was eventually admitted as a free state.

Chester Countians joined neighboring counties in a meeting three thousand strong on Magazine Hill in Abbeville to urge South Carolina to withdraw immediately from the Union. There were some, however, who urged that the state wait until other states joined them before seceding.

When the election for governor was held in the fall, Robert Barnwell Rhett, the "father of secession" was defeated. The new governor was Francis Wilkinson Pickens of Edgefield, who favored delay.

The new Republican party which had been formed to oppose the spread of slavery to the territories met in Chicago and nominated Abraham Lincoln for President. South Carolina declared it would secede from the Union if Lincoln were elected.

Lincoln was elected President in November, 1860. A convention was called immediatley in South Carolina. It met in the first Baptist Church in Columbia, with General David F. Jamison as president. The convention had to be moved to Charleston because of an outbreak of smallpox in the capital city.

On December 20, 1860 the Ordinance of Secession was passed without an opposing vote. It declared South Carolina to be an independent state, as she had been at the end of the Revolution. A committee prepared a statement giving the reasons for secession. The convention sent delegates to other Southern states, inviting them to join South Carolina in a Southern confederacy of states.

South Carolinians were united. The state went wild with joy. Bells rang, drums beat, cannons roared — and the imminence of war loomed over the land. They knew the North would not allow the Southern states to withdraw in peace. But they had no doubt that the South could and would win a war. They did not for a moment realize that the odds were overwhelmingly against them.

CHESTER COUNTY'S DELEGATES
TO SECESSION CONVENTION

Chester District had four delegates who attended the Secession Convention and signed the Ordinance of Secession.

Alexander Quay Dunovant was born in Chester on August 18, 1815, the son of Dr. John Dunovant and Margaret Sloan Quay Dunovant. He was descendant of pioneer families to the area. William Dunovant, his paternal grandfather, moved to Chester from Amelia County, Virginia, with his bride whose maiden name was Nancy Williams. He was a planter. His maternal grandparents, Alexander Quay and Catherine Leslie were also among the pioneers of Chester. His father, Dr. John Dunovant, was born in Chester, graduated at Philadelphia Medical College, married Margaret Quay of Chester, and served as State Senator for several terms.

Alexander Dunovant began his business life in his father's store in Chester. He married Mary McLure Lowry October 11, 1838. In 1841, he moved to Columbia, and in 1844 bought a large plantation on Broad River. He was intendant (mayor) of Chesterville in 1855, and a member of S. C. Legislature 1850-52. Family papers show that he was a member of Palmetto Lodge, Independent Order of Oddfellows in 1842.

Alexander Dunovant had two brothers, General Robert Mills Dunovant, who was also a signer of the Ordinance of Secession from Edgefield County, and General John Dunovant who was killed in battle during the Civil War. He had nine children; one of his sons, William D. entered the Confederate Army at the age of 16 at Sullivan's Island. He later became a captain in the 17th Regiment and lost an arm at the Battle of the Crater.

During the war, Alexander Dunovant was on Governor McGrath's staff, with the rank of Colonel. After the surrender, while he was at his home one afternoon, he was arrested for resisting the intrusion of United States soldiers upon his premises, and taken to Charlotte, North Carolina for trial. After a hearing, he was released.

The winter following the surrender, he decided to move with his family to Texas where he had bought a large plantation. In the undeveloped country of hardship, struggle and disrespect for law, Dunovant and his son, William, brought endurance, courage and stamina. But the scourge of malaria felled him at a fairly early age. He died in Texas in 1869.

John McKee

John McKee, oldest signer of the Ordinance of Secession, was born in Rathfriland, County Down, Ireland, November 4, 1787, the son of Andrew McKee and Jane McKee McKee, first cousins. He came to America by way of Charleston and settled on Rocky Creek in 1799. While there he learned the watchmaker's trade.

Later he moved to "Chester Hill," as the site of Chesterville was then called. Establishing himself as a merchant (on the hill on corner across from present City Hall), McKee earned an enviable reputation. In addition to the general stock of goods, his store carried a selection of books ranging from popular novels to the classics. He made many grandfather clocks, some of which are still in homes of Chester County.

On February 5, 1818, John McKee married Mary Alexander Hayden, who rode from Hanover County, Virginia, to Chester on horseback. They had ten children, all of whom died in infancy except John McKee, Jr., and Mary Ellen McKee.

John McKee was elected to the House of Representatives for one term, 1824-26. In 1842, he went to Europe and took his two children with him. In his diary of the trip he included enthralling descriptions of the grandeurs of the British Isles, all written with a pleasant charm and wonderful skill in word painting.

In 1860, he was elected to the Secession Convention from Chester District, and signed the Ordinance. His son, John McKee, Jr. served in the first company raised in Chester for service in the Confederate Army.

John McKee died in Chester early in 1871. The year before his death, his home with his store annex was burned. In the early 1890s, John McKee's grandson, J. Langdon McKee, presented to the Chester Public Library the signer's portrait and his framed copy of the Ordinance of Secession.

Thomas Wade Moore

Thomas Wade Moore, physician of Chester District, was born near Blackstock, Chester District, in 1809, the son of John Michael Moore of Fairfield, who came from Ireland, and Rebecca (Wade) Lunsford Moore, widow of Capt. Swanson Lunsford, the Revolutionary soldier buried on the State House grounds in Columbia. He entered the South Carolina College at the age of 16, leaving after his junior year. He was graduated from the Medical College of South Carolina in 1829, at the age of 21, and settled in the Fishing Creek section of Chester District.

Moore gave up the practice of medicine and turned to planting. He married first Sarah Dabney Chisolm of Charleston, and second, Marian McDonald of Albany, New York. He was a member of the House of Representatives from Chester for several terms, 1838-40, 1848-52, and 1855-56. He was defeated in the race for the State Senate on the secession issue, but was elected to the Secession Convention and signed the Ordinance.

During the war, he was Confederate district fund treasurer. A son, Thomas Wade Moore, Jr. was killed in battle in the war. Dr. Moore died in Chester in 1871, in his 62nd year.

Richard Woods

Richard Woods, another signer of the Ordinance of Secession from Chester District, was born August 10, 1813, in the western part of the district near Broad River. He was the eighth of ten children of Matthew Woods and Margaret Faucett Woods, married in 1804 in Orange County, North Carolina, moved to South Carolina soon after their marriage.

Richard Woods attended an old field school where he received a sound basic education. He also attended Mt. Zion Academy at Winnsborough, and he taught school at Lowrys, Chester District, for at least one term. He was a successful planter and owner of a large plantation.

Woods was known as a kind and indulgent master to his slaves. The quarters provided for them were models of neatness and comfort, the frame houses built along a regular street, each with its little garden in the rear.

Richard Woods was married three times. His first wife, Elizabeth Pinchbeck, died while very young, leaving two children. His second wife was Mrs. Susan (Kelley) Hopkins, who likewise lived only a short time. He married Mrs. Lou (Hawthorne) Wilks.

Woods' only public service was that of delegate to the Secession Convention in 1860-62, and signer of the Ordinance of Secession. During the war, he contributed largely of supplies to the Confederate Army. His only surviving son, Thomas Matthew Woods, went out with the boys aged 15 and 16 toward the end of the war.

After the war, Woods was able to retrieve his fortunes on the Broad River plantation. He died at his home December 16, 1884, and was buried in the family graveyard on his plantation.

CHESTER COUNTY ENTERS WAR

Chester County, as did the rest of the South of the 1850s, existed in a relative state of tranquility and the people, as a whole, did not contemplate war.

The tranquility was due in part to the enormous agricultural growth of the South at this time. With the combined help of Eli Whitney's cotton gin and the South's rapidly developing railroad system, the antebellum economy flourished. King Cotton was by far the most dominant agricultural crop. Southern soil, climate and slave labor provided advantages over other countries, and gave this region the cotton monopoly.

Southern planters were so busy making money and enjoying the fruits of their labors that they paid no attention to the rumblings in the North.

Cotton, according to W. J. Cash, beat back the wilderness, mowed the forest, poured black men and plows and mules along the streams of the South, spun out the railroads, freighted the waters with panting sternwheelers and barges — in brief created the great and fabled South.

It was 1820 before the plantation was fully on the march, striding over the hills of Carolina. The whole period from the invention of the cotton gin to the outbreak of the Civil War is less than seventy years — the lifetime of a single man. But this is the period that the growth and development of the great South, and of Chester County, took place. Men who, as children, had heard the war whoop of the Cherokees and Catawbas in the Carolina back-woods lived to hear the guns at Vicksburg and smell the smoke as Sherman burned Atlanta.

The South completely dominated all phases of the government at this time. It possessed complete control of both the House of Representatives and the Senate, and almost all important government positions were filled by Southerners. It was not until the South lost this majority that it was ready to secede, and when the inevitable happened, it did.

On April 11, 1861, several companies left Chester to answer the call to arms, reporting to Charleston, and from there to be mustered into the Sixth Regiment of South Carolina.

Before the first gun was fired on Fort Sumter, before there was any civil war, and before President Lincoln had called out 75,000 militia or one million volunteers, Chester County responded to the call of the Palmetto State. She responded with five companies:

Company "A" under Captain Alexander Walker
Chester Guards under Captain Obadiah Hardin
Chester Blues under Captain Ed McLure
Catawba Guards under Captain Lafayette Strait
Pickens Guards under Captain Michael Moore

The Pickens Guards went out from the Hopewell neighborhood.

During the war Chester furnished eight companies of infantry, two companies of calvary, and in the last year of the war, three companies of reserves.

Chester County furnished 2,428 men to the Confederate Army; 367 never came back: 164 lost their lives on battlefields and 203 died of wounds and diseases at home and in hospitals. Out of this number, the highest ranking officers were Generals R. G. M. and John Dunovant, Lt. Col. Culp, Capt. Obadiah Hardin, and Lt. Col. William Alexander Walker. Capt. J. Lucious Gaston of the infantry was killed at the Battle of Seven Pines May 31, 1862.

The war years in Chester were ones of great hardship for blacks and whites alike. Money was scarce since the Confederate bills were practically worthless. Food, clothing, salt, medicines and other necessities were hard to come by.

Although Chester did not become a battlefield, it saw much of the perils of war, because it was situated along the Charlotte-Columbia Railroad, one of the lifelines of the Confederacy. Soldiers by the hundreds passed through Chester daily, either going to or from battle. Many who were sick or wounded were taken off the train for treatment.

With conditions so desperate, Chester was fortunate to have had a loyal group of slaves and freedmen who were not interested in revenge at a time when it could so easily have been obtained. They took care of aged parents, defenseless wives and children, largely dependent on them.

Both blacks and whites shared misfortune, loss, injustice, confusion and poverty. The land, once greening and productive, was desolate, picked clean of crops, livestock and young men. War resulted in the loss of the South's finest manpower on the battlefields, loss in land values and the millions invested in slaves, and loss of property of every description by Sherman's deliberate destruction.

BURREL HEMPHILL STORY

A poignant account of how a Chester County slave, Burrel Hemphill, was cruelly put to death by Sherman's soldiers rather than to betray the trust of his master has been handed down through the generations in Blackstock.

History records that the Federal Army left Columbia and marched north to the vicinity of Blackstock. There they made a right turn and moved toward Cheraw. Raiding parties called "bummers" fanned out in every direction from the line of march to pillage and plunder for food and booty.

Such a group came one day to the home of Robert Hemphill, three miles northeast of Blackstock. Hemphill was a planter of considerable wealth and prestige, owning scores of slaves who worked the 2,200 acres of the estate. A bachelor, he was widely known for his kindly attitude toward his slaves.

Upon the approach of the soldiers, Hemphill fled to North Carolina, leaving Burrel to talk to the raiders. According to "Uncle" Charles Hemphill, a grandson of Burrel who was a 12-year-old witness to the happening, the soldiers were convinced that Burrel knew the hiding place of the family silverware and other valuables, and also the hiding place where a considerable amount of money had been buried by Robert Hemphill before he fled.

Sources say that Burrel knew only where the silverware was, for the master had carried away what money there was on the premises. Though cruelly tortured, tied to a horse and dragged half a mile from the Hemphill home to Hopewell Church, Burrel would give no information. Soldiers then carried him into the woods near the Hemphill house where he was hanged on a limb from a blackgum tree and his body riddled with bullets. As a final gesture of violence, the frustrated soldiers burned the nearby cotton house to the ground and, with it, 300 bales of cotton.

In later years, members of the Hopewell community chipped in and erected a granite marker with this inscription: "In Memory of Burrel Hemphill Killed by Union Soldiers February, 1865. Although a Slave He Gave His Life Rather Than Betray a Trust, He Was a Member of Hopewell."

SHERMAN'S MARCH THROUGH THIS AREA

Dr. Barrett paints a graphic picture of General William Tecumseh Sherman's army as it moved across Fairfield County toward the Catawba crossing. Men trudged "along in company with pets acquired along the line of march. It was not an unusual sight to see a squirrel perched on a knapsack, a coon on a string, or a fighting cock in hand. Many of the men mounted on mules or horses, generally of the plug variety, had little to occupy their attention, while others on foot were busy tending to the large number of sheep, cattle and hogs that were necessary to this fighting force."

Probably one man in a dozen had a full suit of clothes, but this suit was patched or full of holes — many had on hats they found in the houses along the line of march, an old worn out affair in every instance — tall crushed silk hats, some revolutionary styles, many without tops, caps so full of holes that the hair was sticking out.

General Beauregard who was expected to order Hardee or some portion of the Army of Tennessee to defend Columbia against Sherman, enraged Governor Magrath by ordering Hardee on February 11 to evacuate Charleston immediately and march northwest to Chester, near the North Carolina line. Beauregard first chose Chester as an assembly point and then successively Charlotte, Greensboro and Salisbury in North Carolina. But the fall of Wilmington on February 22, brought him back to his original destination, Chester.

Kilpatrick on his feint toward Chester destroyed the railroad tracks as well as telegraph lines as he went. This put the town of Chester "truly in a dark corner," thought Charles Holst, a resident of Chester, but he was thankful to have a shelter over his head.

The most vindictive of Sherman's officers was his calvary commander, Brigadier General Judson Kilpatrick. He is described as "a viscious, mean-spirited little man." Kilpatrick expressed pleasure at the opportunity for wreaking vengeance on what he called "the hellhole of secession."

After burning Columbia, most of Sherman's troops crossed the border into North Carolina during the second week of March and concentrated at Fayetteville. After destroying everything of value there, they moved on to Goldsboro on March 14. South Carolina had been left in ruins.

By February 23, Sherman's entire army had reached the Wateree and some divisions had crossed. Heavy rains set in on this date and lasted three days, causing the river to flood. At Rocky Mount, the left wing encountered great difficulty in effecting a crossing. The bridge, heaving like a ship in a storm, held up under the crossing of the Twentieth Corps and the cavalry. Before Davis' Fourteenth Corps could cross, it gave way to the logs and driftwood swept downstream by the swift current. The Fourteenth Corps, stranded on the west bank of the Wateree, could only wait the recession of the waters.

SHERMAN'S ARMY IN THE ROCKY MOUNT SECTION

The writer who tells of Sherman's march through South Carolina has a prolific as well as a sorrowful theme.

Several days before the arrival of the army at Rocky Mount February 22, 1865, the southern skies were covered with the smoke of burning buildings. Each day the smoke appeared nearer and nearer, and the hearts of the people beat faster. Next came a throng of fugitives, fleeing from their homes endeavoring to save their stock and a few valuables. Then came straggling soldiers with many tales of woe and horror.

Next was heard the skirmish near Gladdens, then the smoke of the neighbor's buildings was seen in black columns ascending heavenward, then came the sound of the taps of the drums. The Yankee soldiers dashed up to the doors and demanded gold and silver watches and silver plate. Whether given or not, the homes were thoroughly searched and everything they wanted taken. Often when the soldiers did not wish the articles themselves, they took them and gave them to Negroes.

Yards were cleared of dogs. In one instance a soldier presented his gun to shoot a dog which had fled to its mistress' feet for protection. Had not an officer ordered him to desist, death might have been the result to the lady (Mrs. Robert Ford). Firearms were taken away and destroyed, a great many thrown into the Catawba River.

The poultry was all taken. Bacon, flour, corn, meal, and provisions of all kinds were removed. Every locked door was forced open, ginhouses and cotton burnt in every instance. This much was done by the first group of Sherman's advancing army.

Late in the evening they put pontoon bridges across the river and a part of the army went over in the afternoon of the 22nd. It rained and the water rose and broke the pontoons. By the morning of the 22nd the encampment reached from Caldwell's Cross Roads on both roads to Rocky Mount Ferry. The six days and nights that the army spent there was a time of much sorrow and fear to the ladies and the few old men who were at home.

General Jeff C. Davis of the U. S. Army had his headquarters at the house of Robert Ford for twenty-four hours. He drove Mrs. Ford, her aged mother-in-law, and the children of the family from their rooms to an open portico to spend the night, an unpleasantly cold and wet one. He occupied the grandmother's room, much to her discomfort. Gen. Davis traveled in a fine silver mounted carriage drawn by two fine white steeds stolen on the march. His meals were served on silver waiters.

General Sherman traveled through this vicinity on horse back, and save the wanton destruction of property, did nothing to render himself obnoxious. He had burnt ten buildings belonging to Mrs. Robert Ford, among them a large barn and stable. Several secret efforts were made to burn the dwelling house, but it was saved through the efforts of an Indiana private soldier, whose name is now unknown.

The family of Mrs. Ford had a steadfast friend in the chief of artillery. He found some Masonic articles about the house and asked Mrs. Ford if her husband was a Mason. On being answered in the affirmative, he had the house and yard cleared of pillagers, gathered a few provisions and sent them in and placed a guard over the premises. When he moved he left a paper which he hoped would be some protection, but there was but little to protect.

The Yankee soldiers shot down all kinds of stock, destroyed all farm implements and burnt the fencing. During the six days at Rocky Mount, they foraged the country for miles, going in squads of from four to ten, sometimes without arms. General Sherman's headquarters were near the Barkley mansion. He treated the ladies in this section politely.

The neighborhood was so pillaged that the people for several days had to subsist on the gleanings from the camps. Mr. J. H. Stroud of Chester County was very kind to the people in their dire distress. He sent an ox cart regularly with meal and flour. His name will ever be green in the memory of the unfortunate people of the Rocky Mount section. The good people of Bascomville, Chester County, and others also aided them. All aid received was from private persons. For two years the rations were mainly cowpeas boiled in water and a bit of cornbread. Without money, clothing or credit, there was real fear of starvation.

After the army passed, persons in the track of the march came and claimed all unknown stock and broken down and abandoned vehicles of all kinds. A few had some cattle left. They had to keep them under guard, or they would have been claimed and driven away.

Mr. Stephen Ferguson of Chester County, an aged man, asked for a detachment of Wheeler's cavalry, and came down and skirmished with the Yankees in the yard of Mr. Robert Ford and Dr. Scott's, which greatly frightened the ladies. Ferguson rode boldly up to the window and told them to stand between the chimneys. He captured a few stragglers and left.

The army began to move across the river about ten in the night, seemingly in great excitement. Ferguson came with a large detachment, but was too late. The army had crossed and the bridges were raised.

Sherman's army bypassed Chester; the Federal occupation of Lancaster was accompanied by some disorder, but in comparison to Winnsboro the town suffered very little.

His army was constantly foraging and looting. It was reported of Kilpatrick's men that their "most lucrative prize was ten fully loaded wagons belonging to an unfortunate party of refugees from Chester, South Carolina, who arrived in Monroe almost simultaneously with the Federals." (Charlotte Democrat March 7, 1865.)

CHESTER DURING WAR

Chester in 1863, in the midst of the War Between the States, is described in these vignettes printed in *The Chester Standard*. The eight-page newssheet was "devoted to general and local intelligence and to the political, agricultural and educational interests of the state."

Advertisements

A. N. McNinch's ad for Hides "tanned on the old Plan — one half for the other" states that "Persons forwarding hides to me this spring will receive half in leather next Fall."

Wanted:

An overseer to attend to about 20 negroes. None need apply unless over conscript age and well qualified for such business.

C. J. McKee.

Notice To Farmers, Etc.

Our army, now in Virginia, is in want of all the corn that can, under any circumstances be spared by the good people of South Carolina, — also hay and fodder baled in good order. — Let every man put his shoulder to the wheel and continue to push until our independence is gained — the army is entirely dependent on the people, and the people are more than dependent on our suffering army.

John M. White
Gov. Forage Agent

Mr. Lonnegan, the Government Agent, notified the people of the District that he "is now ready to receive all the Bacon which they can spare for which he is prepared to pay $1.00 per pound when delivered to Dr. Cornwell's store."

He also appealed for dried fruit, peas, etc., all for use by the Confederate soldiers.

Jordan Bennett, Dentist —

Would inform his friends and the public generally that he is now fully prepared to insert teeth, on the Vulcanite base, or on metal; also, with pivot on the old stump.

In consequence of the advance in the price of Gold, now costing five times as much as formerly, I am compelled to advance my prices:

Gold Plug — $4.00
Tin Plug — $2.00

Bathing Tub
Large Tin Bath (never been used) for sale. Apply at this office.

$200 Reward
Some black hearted scoundrel set fire to my fence destroying about 15 or 20 pannels. It was discovered in time or it might have been very serious. In hopes of detecting the villian I offer the above reward for proof to conviction.

O. P. Farrar

For Sale
Three houses and lots in the town of Chester.
The store and Dwelling House opposite the Bank of Chester.
Two houses on Pinckney Street, occupied by Col. Secrest and Mrs. Neal. All of which contain good out buildings and excellent wells.

D. Carrol

Directory for Chester District
A complete list of all public officials appeared in every issue of The Chester Standard, also a calendar for the year 1863, and a list of members of the First Permanent Confederate Congress with Jefferson Davis of Mississippi as president.

Chester officers serving were: Sheriff — Wm. M. M'Donald; Ordinary — Wm. H. Anderson; Clerk of the Court — Geo. W. Curtis; Com'r in Equity — Giles J. Patterson; Tax Collector — Israel McD. Hood; Coroner — W. H. Anderson; Escheator — S. Alexander.

Commissioners of Public Buildings were Saml. McAliley, Chairman; John McKee, Jr., W. A. Walker, W. H. Gill, S. Alexander, John J. Mclure, W. T. Gilmore.

Commissioners of the Poor were Alex W. Smith, Minor Montgomery, F. A. Hardin, Henry Hardin, one Vacancy.

Commissioners of Free Schools were Giles J. Patterson, Chairman; Rev. W. Banks, W. H. Gill, Nicholas Colvin, John Atkinson, C. Rives, Jas. F. Wherry, Rev. Wm. Banks, Sec. and Tr., T. A. Kendrick, Agt. for Treasurer.

George S. Cameron was president of the Bank of Chester. Business hours from 9 a.m. until 2 p.m. Discount Day every Wednesday.

John J. McLure was Intendant of Town Council. Wardens were S. Alexander, S. W. Mobley, John W. Walker, W. M. Nicholson. G. W. Curtis was Clerk and Treas.

Candidates announcing for election to the office of Tax Collector were Matthew White, E. C. Wilks, J. H. Smith, Robert Wallace,

Maj. E. M. Mills, B. H. Corder, John B. Cornwell, James A. Thomas, Wm. P. Cassells and Thos. Mayfield.

Candidates for Sheriff were Dr. S. C. Morrison and Maj. W. P. Gill.

What Was Funny 100 Years Ago

Under the title "Rebelana" is the notation "Our witty contemporary at Chattanooga continues his daily fusilade of puns. We copy a few specimens from a recent issue.

President Lincoln, at the close of his late Washington Fourth of July speech remarked "having said this much, I will now take the music." We are at a loss to divine what kind of instrument he "took" it in, but presume it was "in a horn."

The dignified President of the United States did himself injustice when he declared that "all men were created equal." There isn't as large a fool in Christendom as himself, He is unequaled in history.

The Yankees claim that their artillery at Vicksburg threw against the city 25,000 tons of iron. To judge from the swine who threw it, it must have been pig-iron.

It is hard to tell which are most plentiful in Yankeedom since the war broke out, blue bellies or green backs.

Morgan's invasion of Kentucky is said to have thrown General Boyle into a perfect stew.

CONFEDERATE WAR HEROES

Captain Obadiah Hardin

Captain Obadiah Hardin was a son of William Hardin and Elizabeth Cornwell Hardin and was taught bravery, industry and self-discipline in their home. Obadiah Hardin was one of the brave Chester County men who gave their lives for the Southern Cause.

At early life he was called to the command of the 26th Regiment, South Carolina Militia, and the duties of his position he discharged with credit to himself and with satisfaction to the Regiment. He offered his services to his country in her hour of need and was elected Captain of the Chester Guard.

An advocate of strict discipine he shunned no duty and dealt out even-handed justice to all. He was conscientiously just and impartial to all. No captain of the Sixth Regiment was more deserving of the confidence of his command and none had it in a higher degree than Captain Obadiah Hardin.

At the Battle of Drainesville, December 20, 1861, Lieut.-Colonel Secrest was in command of the Regiment, Thomas W. Woodward was Major and Captain William McAliley was Color-bearer.

Major Woodward said to Captain McAliley (of course, not a captain then), "Colonel Winder will not ask who is killed or who is wounded, but how the colors have been borne." Captain McAliley replied, "I will take care of the colors as long as I am able."

A little later he was shot through the hand, so that he could not hold the flag staff. When he showed his hand to Major Woodward, the latter said to Captain Obadiah Hardin, whose company was in the center, "Name a brave man to take the colors!"

Captain Hardin, instead of assigning one of his men to this dangerous duty, took up the flag himself and went forward holding it aloft. He was shot through the body December 20, and died December 28, 1861 in the hospital in Richmond.

Major Woodward remarked afterward that he had never seen a more game looking soldier than Captain Hardin that day as he moved forward with the colors. Major Woodward was also wounded that day.

Several others from Chester county fell that day: Joseph Caldwell, William McDill, John Barber, and perhaps others.

The company known as the Chester Guards, under Captain Obadiah Hardin, came from the western section of Chester County. This company consisted of Carters, Cornwells, Hardins, Estes, Hudsons, Brakefields, Sanders and divers others.

They went out in 1861 with thirty-eight men. Of that number, twenty-four lost their lives in the Confederate War. Captain Hardin, himself, was one of the twenty-four. Of the fourteen who survived, one went through life with an empty sleeve and another hobbled through on one leg. This company was organized near New Hope Methodist church at what was known as "Carters Field."

Captain Hardin's brother, George Hardin and George Brakefield were killed on the battlefield. After the gallant captain's death, Lieutenant W. H. Sanders was promoted to Captain and John Wesly Wilks was First Lieutenant.

William Randolph Sims

Chester had a distinguished Confederate veteran, William Randolph Sims who lived to be more than 94 years old. He heard the first shot of the Confederate War fired on the "Star of the West" by the Citadel cadets stationed on Morris Island, and was at Appomatox Court House when General Robert E. Lee surrendered to General Ulysses S. Grant. Few Confederate soldiers earned this distinction, having witnessed the curtain's rise on the terrible drama of the war, served in its ranks for four strenuous years, and then saw the curtain descend on the war's end.

Abraham Gibson

Abraham Gibson was of distinguished ancestry. His grand-father, Captain William Watson, was a renouned veteran of the Revolutionary War who was at Yorktown when Cornwallis surrendered.

In the Confederate Army, Mr. Gibson was a member of General Wade Hampton's famous cavalry. He was commended for outstanding deeds of daring and heroism during the War Between the States.

He was a merchant, magistrate and farmer. He was a Mason, a champion checker player as well as a champion wrestler. He established a championship record in checkers which he held for 30 years in both North and South Carolina. In wrestling he held a record in the Southern states as having never been thrown. He was a fine athlete. At age 86, before his death on April 3, 1932, he could leap from the ground and click his heels twice before descending. He was father of 24 children.

HISTORY OF CONFEDERATE MONUMENT

The idea of a monument to honor Confederate soldiers from Chester District began the very year the War Between the States ended.

In the latter part of 1865, the pupils of Miss Ellen Elmore's School undertook to raise funds by putting on theatricals. They raised a small amount of money which was used to enclose the graves of Confederate soldiers in Evergreen Cemetery, and to mark the graves.

In 1870, a movement was begun by Miss Mary Ellen McKee for the erection of a monument. Owing to the impoverished condition that prevailed in the South after the war, it failed.

Twenty years later, in 1890, Mrs. Maude McLure took up the task, and by a theatrical performance raised $200.00. She, too, became discouraged, and turned the money over to the City for the Park.

Determined that Chester should not lag behind, Mrs. Julia Killian Campbell, president of Chester Chapter, United Daughters of the Confederacy, took up the work about 1900.

She staged and directed a theatrical performance, "Under the Southern Cross," and raised one hundred and twenty-five dollars. Local talent was used in the play.

It was slow work to increase the fund and many discouragements were met. But the United Daughters of the Confederacy were dedicated and untiring in their efforts, and finally succeeded.

By February, 1904, they had $300.00 on interest, and decided to ask the cooperation of Walker-Gaston Camp, Confederate Veterans.

Walker-Gaston Camp raised $372.00. The U.D.C.'s gave many entertainments to raise funds and had in the Treasury January 1, 1905, $416.52.

The contract for the monument was given on January 31, 1905, to the McNeel Marble Company of Gainesville, Georgia, for $2,000.00. It was to be erected on top of the City's hill where the Calhoun Guards and the Chester Blues swore allegiance to the Confederate States forty-four years earlier.

According to the contract signed by the above Committee, the McNeel Marble Company agreed "to build and erect in the city of Chester, South Carolina, one Confederate Monument, the material to be of Oglesby, Georgia granite" and to be 41 feet high. The Monument was to be placed on a good foundation of sufficient depth "to go below the freezing line." The Committee was to "do all draying of the monument from railway car to place of erection, and to get permit from city for erection, and on completion of the contract to pay to McNeel Marble Co. the sum of $2,000.00." The cornerstone by contract was to be laid on April 11, 1905 and the monument was to be erected by May 10, 1905, if possible or as soon thereafter as the work could be done.

Records show there were some objections to placing the monument on the town square.

The Committee in a letter to City Council dated June 6, 1904, pointed out the many reasons why it should be placed on the square.

They wrote: "They (the reasons) are patent to every one who has given the subject a moment's reflection. We wish to direct your attention to two. The proposed monument has been talked of and devoutly hoped for by many of our devoted men and women for many years, and only one location has been considered suitable — the public square — the most prominent spot in our County."

"The Monument," they wrote, "is to be a witness unto this and succeeding generations of our love and admiration for every man and every woman of Chester County who endured the sufferings and sacrifices of the Confederacy."

DEDICATION OF MONUMENT

The cornerstone was laid on May 10, 1905 with appropriate Masonic ceremonies.

On June 27, 1905, the Monument was unveiled at 6:30 in the afternoon.

It was noted that "the timely and eloquent address of S. C. McFadden was a complete vindication of the South."

The Monument was unveiled by four little girls, all granddaughters of Veterans: Eliza Walker, granddaughter of General Alexander Walker and William McAliley; Nancy Brice, a granddaughter of William H. Hardin and Thomas Brice; Savilla Barber Shannon, granddaughter of Edward Shannon and Hemphill Mc-Daniel; and Mary Grace Douglas, granddaughter of Alexander Wise and Alexander Douglas.

Inscriptions engraved on the Monument were written by Judge William A. Brawley.

East side: "This monument guards the memory of the men of Chester District, who, obeying the call of their State, died for the Confederate Cause 1861-1865."

"Time may crumble this marble into dust, but time can not dim their glory, their patriotism, their valor, their faithfulness, and their fame remains forever the heritage of their countrymen."

NON LIBI PATRIAE.

West side: "Their fame increases like the branches of a tree, through the hidden course of time."

North side: Crossed Sabres.

South side: Crossed Guns.

CARPETBAGGER

IX RECONSTRUCTION

PLIGHT OF BOTH BLACKS AND WHITES

The victory of the industrial North over the agrarian South not only brought the end of slavery and the agricultural economy based on it; it also shattered the myth of Southern superiority. The war was a psychological as well as a military and economic defeat for the South.

Attempts to rebuild South Carolina and Chester after the Civil War had to take into account several significant results of the war. A great amount of property had been destroyed; the Negro had been made free; and the Negro and the Northern white man for the first time were able to compete with the native white man for the control of many aspects of local life.

The Negroes' ability to adapt to Reconstruction was far less adequate than that of the white man. It is true that the war had been won for his benefit but he had few assets with which to exercise his freedom.

In the first place, he was very poor. He had no property, no home, no possessions. The utter poverty in which most Negroes emerged into freedom is described thus: "a band of refugees partly covered with every conceivable thing that could be put on. Some of the women had an old, cast-off soldiers' coats and 'crocus bags, fastened together with their own ravellings. . . . Many of the men had strips of gay carpeting, or old bags, or pieces of blankets in which they cut arm-holes and wore as jackets. . . . Their pants were tied around the waist with pieces of rope."

The Negroes were completely bewildered. Their first heady response to "freedom" left them in utter confusion as to what to do with it. That the race was able to survive the ordeal of freedom was due more to its large numbers and to the blind instinct of self-preservation than to acquired social habits.

The Negro was not, however, devoid of qualities helpful in his new situation. He was capable of hard manual labor and had a knowledge of farming and certain industrial crafts. He knew how to live on little; he had been moved about as a slave and knew how to make the most of that hardship. He was instinctively too wise or too timid to attempt actions beyond his powers. He was seldom vindictive. He was capable of touching loyalty to old associations, and was contented under conditions which would have made a more sensitive race miserable.

Moreover, he knew how to dance and sing in the midst of physical distress. He could almost turn a funeral into an occasion of joy, and he could give rags the semblance of a fancy dress.

About five percent knew how to read and write. The Negro was adept at imitating the whites in dress, in manners and in speech.

In September 1865, Governor James L. Orr called a special session of the legislature to enact the so called "black code," designed to regulate the status of the freedmen. The code declared the regulations of slavery no longer in force, ratified the Thirteenth Amendment, and allowed Negroes to acquire property, sue and be sued, receive the protection of law in person and property, testify in court and enter into marriage contracts. Their children were given the status of legitimacy. Provision was made for the care of indigent blacks.

On the other hand, a series of restrictions assigned colored persons to the position of an inferior caste. Use of the terms "master" and "servant" in the code was interpreted to the victorious North that South Carolina, a few months after its defeat, was attempting to reestablish slavery. The legislature was highly impolitic in not making itself aware that it was flaunting a red flag in the face of the conqueror, according to Simkins and Woody in *South Carolina During Reconstruction.*

Butler McCallum's Early History, (unpublished):

I share some of my impressions and some of the things I heard years ago about the difficult years that followed the Civil War. When we read the records of the events of those days, the hardships and violence of the times are usually played down.

When the war ended, much of the wealth of the South had been used up. The people had financed the Confederacy with their savings as far as possible, additionally with credit for the supplies required for a war.

There were very few large towns. The county seats were usually villages, and most of the people lived on farms. The value of the land and slaves represented a major part of the wealth of the people. When the slaves were freed it was a long time before land had much market value. It was several years before farmers could make a fair living by raising crops for cash income.

It was a time of confusion. Many of the negroes, after being freed, were unable to make their personal decisions about what they should do and where to start. Many of them just rambled off to another place.

At first only part of them were willing to work for wages or farm as sharecroppers. Naturally the freed slaves felt unshackled. It was a new freedom and they wanted to live it up. Many had not developed the restraints and self controls required among civilized people.

Veterans of the Confederate forces, and all others that aided the Confederate States, were disenfranchised by laws newly enacted. These people were prohibited from holding public office. The result was that these privileges were largely restricted to the negroes and to new people from the north. The latter were called "carpetbaggers." For about ten years in South Carolina there was a time of misrule, of waste and graft, a time of high taxes and unrealistic bad laws. The courts were often unjust.

I will recite here two incidents that occurred then. South Carolina had a law that assessed a road tax on adult males. Instead of paying the tax, a man had the option of working three days annually on county roads. Mr. William Stroud was a neighbor of the Atkinsons and lived on an adjacent farm. Mr. Stroud received a notice to report for work with a road crew on a certain date. The Stroud's first child, an infant, died the day before the work date. Mr. Stroud asked the road official at the court house to give him a later work stint so that he could bury his child. This request was refused and he had to work that day.

The other incident shows how incompetent one public official was. Miss Emma Star Woods lived near Broad River in Chester County and she expected to teach at a rural school near her home. She went to the court house in Chester to get a teacher's certificate and to sign the contract. The official was not able to write in the required data on the forms so Miss Woods had to make out the forms herself.

Every county seat in South Carolina was occupied by unfriendly soldiers. Usually the office of sheriff was filled by an incompetent man.

Men did not like to risk leaving their families at home without protection so the original Ku Klux Klan was started.

NEGROES' ROLE

The United States Congress, feeling that the State of South Carolina, along with the other Confederate states, was not making an honest effort to recognize the results of the Civil War in reforming its government, decided to place the state under military control and force another plan of reconstruction. The plan, known as the

Congressional Plan, embraced the Civil Rights Bill, giving the freedmen all the civil rights of citizens. It also embraced the Fourteenth Amendment, which each ex-Confederate state was required to accept and approve before it could be readmitted into the Union. During 1867, the great Commonwealth of South Carolina was called Military District No. 2. Soldiers had been put in entire control of the people.

Thus the Negroes were given the power to vote and help destroy the "Black Codes" and other legislation prejudicial to their interests which the white people of the southern states had passed to revitalize slavery.

Just as the white people of the North had found themselves unable to complete the task of freeing the Negroes physically without the aid of the latter in the armies of the Republic, so now they found it impossible to preserve the Negro's freedom and assure his progress without his own assistance.

W. E. B. DuBois in his book, *The Gift of Black Folk,* says, thus Negro suffrage was forced to the front, not as a theoretical and dangerous gift to the freedmen, not according to any preconcerted plan but simply because the fruits of war made it necessary to keep a freedman's bureau for a generation and to use the Negro vote to reconstruct the southern states and to insure such legislation as would at least begin the economic emancipation of the slave. Negroes at this time comprised the majority of the population of the State.

In other words, the North being unable to free the slave, let him try to free himself. And he did, and this was his greatest gift to this nation.

South Carolina was received back into the Union under her "Black-and-tan" Constitution of 1868, as that truly democratic document was derisively called.

In South Carolina in 1868 a Negro government was formed. Every Negro man had the right to vote and hold office. White men who had helped the Confederacy could not vote. This meant that almost all of the white people of the state were cut off from taking part in the government.

The period from 1868 to 1874 was known as the time when South Carolina was under the "Rule of Robbers." All power was in the hands of the Negroes and a few white men from the North and West.

Under the desperate and chaotic conditions in the South at this time, it is not surprising that in the selection and election of men to carry out the work of reconstruction serious blunders were made; that some thieves and plunderers forged to the front and filled some of the offices.

Circumstances were propitious for this. The South had gone far beyond her financial ability in the persecution of a disastrous and wasteful war. She had no public monies, and her private fortunes were wrecked. A billion dollars in slave property had evaporated.

Money was needed to operate state and local government. Taxes were assessed. Bonds were issued. From 25 to 75 percent of the par value of these bonds remained in the safes and lockers of bondholders in the North. In fact, the northern bondholders got a larger proportion of money which should have been used to run these state governments than it was possible for "carpetbaggers" to steal.

Under the so-called carpet-bag government, South Carolina and Florida were so controlled for eight years, longer than any other states. North Carolina was controlled for about six years; Louisiana, Mississippi, Virginia, Alabama and Arkansas for three or four years; Georgia, Tennessee and Texas for less.

Kelly Miller, a native South Carolinian, who lived in the state during this period described the situation:

Negroes filled all stations in the government, with the exception of governor, which was always accorded the white race. The Lieutenant Governor, Secretary of State, Treasurer, Legislators and Congressmen were plentiful. . . . I used to hear of the fabulous happenings going on in Columbia. I had relatives who went from Fairfield and Chester Counties as representatives and senators. They would tell me that Negroes often lit their cigars with five-dollar bills. Nowhere on earth did Negroes ever exercise so much political power as in Columbia. Nor did they ever revel so extravagantly in the excrescenses of power.

With reference to Negro suffrage, the giving of the ballot to the Negro became the necessary means for the rehabilitation of the southern states. It achieved the following results, according to Sinclair in *The Aftermath of Slavery:*

— It established the sovereignty of the nation.

— It destroyed all that was viscious, mischievous and menacing in the doctrine of states rights.

— It made effective the Thirteenth Amendment, and enacted the Fourteenth and Fifteenth Amendments to the Constitution of the United States — giving rise to the strange paradox, unique in the history of the world, that the ballot of the ex-slave had become necessary to save the face of a conquering nation, preserve the fruits of victory, and assist in the enactment of laws which made his own freedom secure; and it wrote his own citizenship ineffaceably into the constitution, the law of the land.

— It was effective in causing the adoption of free constitutions for the southern states, the establishment of orderly government in them . . . and restoring them to practical and proper relations with the Union.

— It gave the South its first system of free public schools, a benefaction of incalculable value.

These good accomplisments partly recompensed the state of South Carolina for the money which was lost or stolen, and the uncouth manners in the legislative halls which replaced the polished, and often worthless, activities of the aristocrats who had formerly ruled at Columbia and led the state into rebellion, war, and economic ruin, according to writer Asa H. Gordon.

This reconstruction legislation was good enough to last the state of South Carolina up to the 1930s and beyond.

X BETWEEN RECONSTRUCTION AND FARMERS MOVEMENT 1868-1877

AFTERMATH OF WAR

It was an era of Victorian houses, courtly leaders who were as poor as they were polite, small wooden schoolhouses with Friday afternoon spelling bees or declamation contests, dusty streets with opera house, livery stable and Confederate monument, railroad excursions loaded with exuberant passengers, rocking chairs on front piazzas, and mournful pilgrimages to the local cemetery on Confederate Memorial Day.

What was true of Chester was true of the entire South after the war. From 1865 to 1876, radical domination prevailed everywhere. The heel of the despot was on the neck of "the prostrate state." Carpetbaggers, scalawags, and negroes "had our commonwealth by the throat, well nigh choking all decency to the death. Greedy seekers after gain and position flocked to our southland, taking advantage of the franchise hastily thrust upon the ex-slaves who were totally unprepared for it, and who were manipulated by selfish adventurers who for 10 to 11 years, ruled in politics."

According to Dr. R. W. Sanders, the State was brought under military control in 1865, and continued so for years. True patriotism was banished or shackled by foreign control. As Col. Rutledge, of Charleston, expressed it, the Legislature, surcharged with incompetency and covetousness on the part of negro representatives and their imported leaders, was composed of "a black spot here and a white spot there — a thing by folly out of tyranny."

Chester, with all the rest of the state was writhing under the unparalleled ills of the situation. But the pride and smothered patriotism of the good people of the State at last said in 1876, "we will suffer it no longer. At the peril of life and every other interest we will shake off the oppressor and bring our country back to its former condition of just home-rule and civil glory."

The people met, here and there, resolved to unite and proceed with the unshakable determination to cast off forever the unrighteous yoke of radicalism. The brave and wise Wade Hampton, while spending the summer at his mountain resort in the Blue Ridge, was asked to return home and take up the leading of the well-remembered campaign of 1876.

He complied, and the result was such a movement as was seldom, if ever, known in the annals of history. The ex-Confederate soldiers of the State, numbering thousands then, together with the younger and older men of the country, rallied to the Hampton standard and stirred the people to active resistance from the mountians to the sea. The whole State was traversed by General Hampton and his band of able public speakers who went everywhere arousing the people to join the solid phalanx and march on to victory. Men, women and youths everywhere determined to dare, do, or die for the right.

In the late summer or early autumn of 1876, a great political meeting took place one day in the oak grove of Mrs. Margaret Woods, near the heart of Chester. Hundreds, perhaps, thousands, of Red Shirts mounted on horses and mules, together with other excited citizens, assembled around the roughly built platform to hear the speeches of the peerless Hampton and his colleagues who were his fellow-travelers.

Ringing appeals, designed to stir indignation and impel to united action, were made by Hampton, Connor, Hagood, Rion, Youmans, and possibly others. The large, dense crowd was literally swayed by the oratory of intrepid leaders. Col. Youmans, one of the State's most brilliant speakers, seemed to eclipse all the others with his fervid eloquence. A Red Shirt, near the stand, mounted and about "three sheets in the wind," exclaimed vociferously: "Hurrah for Leroy Youmans! He ought to be president of the United States!"

In similar manner "the political pot boiled" from center to circumference throughout ill-starred Carolina. And when the election came off in November, the popular resentment of determined people smashed the bonds of political slavery, hurling the tyrants down to political despair. After much dispute and contention in the State in Washington, Hampton became Governor and better citizens at last resumed control of the Government.

There was much excitement and turmoil in Chester on the day of the election. The box for ballots was in the Court House, and the court yard teemed with voters. A few negroes voted with the Democrats. A riot was reported to be raging around the ballot box, and a "runner" rushed to a company of U.S. troops in camp, near the C.C.&A. depot, and asked their immediate haste to the Court House to quell the impending row. They came, found no real trouble, however, "stacked arms" in front of the Court House and remained on the grounds until convinced that there was really no trouble.

During the early part of the night, eager crowds gathered on the hill at the center of the town to "hear the news" as the telegraph operator caught the rapidly passing messages and reported them to the waiting squads. It was announced that North Carolina had elected General Vance, Governor; that Hampton had defeated Chamberlain, and that these former Confederate generals, respectively, would be installed as governors early in 1877.

Under all of the agitations that followed for the next few months, Hampton went to confer with the authorities in Washington. On his return, it having been settled that he would be Governor, when his train halted at the Chester depot, a crowd had assembled and he was called out for a speech. He came to the platform of the coach in which he was riding and made a brief talk. He announced the death of Radical oppression in South Carolina. Among other words spoken he said, "I shall be the Governor of South Carolina, and I will be the Governor of the whole people."

Following Reconstruction, Chester County was faced with many of the problems that other counties in the state experienced that were primarily dependent on agriculture. As a result of the lien law, Chester County farmers were committed to the one crop system which added to the depletion of the land. Geographically small in comparison to some counties, farmers were compelled to cultivate marginal land to increase production.

When Governor Benjamin Tillman offered organization for agricultural reform, the farmers of Chester County responded. The period in which Tillman's influence was most evident was also the period in which Chester County experienced growth unparalled in the history of the county.

Tillman was a colorful and forceful member of the "Red Shirt" campaign to overthrow northern carpetbaggers and install Wade Hampton as governor. After this successful campaign, Tillman was soon in the forefront of the farmers' revolt that swept the state.

During the 1870s and 1880s, cotton prices fell and the farmers experienced hard times. Many lost their land. Their farm supplies had to be bought on credit, and many others became deeply in debt to local merchants.

FARMER'S ALLIANCE

Farmer's Alliance originating in Texas in 1874, gained a foothold in South Carolina in 1887 and in Chester County in 1888. Improving farming methods was foremost among the goals of the leaders of the Alliance. Other goals were a rigid economy, diversification of crops, prevention of erosion, and more intelligent use of fertilizers.

In 1882, forty-three percent of the tilled land in the county was in the production of cotton. Farm land rented for $2.00 per acre. Most of the land was tilled by blacks which comprised 64 percent of the population at that time. The majority worked on shares, a system whereby the landlord furnished the land, implements, seed and stock and took one-half the crop.

When the Farmer's Convention met in Columbia on April 29, 1886, there were 300 delegates in attendance. Delegates from Chester County were F. P. Moore, Julius Mills, J. H. Hardin, F. M. Shannon, R. T. Mockbee, W. H. Hardrix, T. J. Cunningham and J. B. McFadden.

Following the Columbia convention, farmer's clubs began to be organized throughout Chester County. In May, 1886, the Baton Rouge Township farmers met at Armenia, organized a club, and elected Jesse H. Hardin as president. In May the Sandy River Township met at Capers Chapel and chose Dr. A. F. Anderson, president. The farmers of Lewisville Township met at Capers Chapel and selected S. T. Lewis to be president.

Black farmers of Chester County were active members of the Colored Alliance which was "always content to play a supplementary role to the white Alliance."

The Chester County legislative delegation supported the aims and ideals of the Farmer's Alliance. Elections of 1890 through 1898 show that Alliance men were elected and reelected to the legislature. Peter T. Hollis, of Pleasant Grove Alliance was elected to the House of Representatives in both 1894 and 1896. Jesse H. Hardin of Baton Rouge Alliance was elected to the House in 1890. P. L. Hardin of Bascomville Alliance was elected to the House in 1890 and again in 1892.

The Alliance during the years of its heyday was considered to be politically formidable according to Joseph Church of The Farmer's Alliance.

In 1897-98, farmers began to take interest in organizing county auxiliary experiment clubs to cooperate with Clemson College in disseminating information relative to farms and gardens. There was now considerably more emphasis on methods to improve farming and less on political involvement and political candidates.

By 1904, the almost twenty year long Farmer's movement in Chester County had ended to be replaced by an organization which was primarily interested in upgrading agricultural practices, Clemson University Extension Service.

KU KLUX KLANS

Reconstruction days following the War between the States are described by E. Alston Wilkes:

"It was a time of darky domination, and negro bucks of the old plantations, backed by the United States government, held sweet sway over the realm. . . . The Ku Klux Klans arose about this time, organized in the dark cavern of secrecy. They would go forth at night in companies of a dozen or more in fantastic shapes and grotesque garb and spread terror in negro quarters, inflicting punishment by whipping and otherwise on evil doers. They did some good and were an arm of protection in some communities, and much harm to the cause of reconstruction."

Negro militias were organized and were furnished guns by a corrupt government.

About 110 negroes or more congregated in martial order near New Hope church in West Chester and fortified themselves behind high rocks near the roadside three hundred yards from the church building. About thirty white men gathered in the rear of the church and behind trees. A round or two was fired, and the negroes retreated precipitously, leaving a few dead on the field. One white man was wounded.

Then the Yankees came around again and people were greatly troubled for a while on account of martial law. Negroes would report citizens as Ku Klux, or for complicity in their work, and they would be tried and frequently convicted on the oath of ex-slaves. Some were released after a time, the sufferings of others were extended. Some Chester County men who had been active in the Klan were arrested, tried and found guilty and were sent to Charleston to federal prisons.

The Ku Klux Klan made its first appearance in South Carolina in 1868 as a minor factor in the attempt of the whites to intimidate the newly enfranchised black majority.

The general purpose of the organization was made clear by the constitution which was used in neighboring York County. The members were obligated by oath to take "the side of justice, humanity, and constitutional liberty as bequeathed to us in its purity by our forefathers," to aid fellow members in sickness, distress, and pecuniary embarrassment, and to be of special protection to female friends, widows and their households, and to oppose the principles of the Radical party. These high aims conflicted with the later activities of the Klan.

The penalty of death was provided for any member who revealed the secrets of the order. Members were required to become acquainted with designated signs and passwords and to provide themselves with arms and disguises.

After the Radicals defeated the white Reform party in the election of 1870, Ku Klux activities became evident in Spartanburg, York, Union, Chester, Newberry, Fairfield and Chesterfield Counties. They reached their height in March and ceased by midsummer 1871.

The evidence of the Klan in South Carolina leads to the conclusion that it was made up of haphazard groups which acted independently of a state or regional organization.

Members did their work at night, attired in hoods, masks and other regalia sufficient to disguise the wearer and calculated to impress the black man or Radical white that the wearer was a spirit from another world.

The Klan for the most part was made up of low-type men, and did not enjoy among respectable contemporaries the esteem with which later generations have invested it.

Although of less importance than political motives, social and economic factors were causes of Klan visits. Adultery between the races especially led to terrorizing of blacks. Negroes were whipped for refusing to work for whites; some were maltreated because they deserted the farms to become railroad workers. Klan activities were more violent in upper rural counties, in which the mass of the white population had to work with their hands for a living, thereby coming into economic competition with the Negro.

A delegation of the South Carolina legislature went to Washington to complain of the conduct of the Klan. An investigation followed and President Grant on October 12, 1871, issued a proclamation that since "a condition of lawlessness and terror existed" in the nine counties of York, Newberry, Fairfield, Lancaster, Chester, Chesterfield, Spartanburg, Laurens and Union, he suspended the writ of habeas corpus in these counties.

Federal authorities began rounding up alleged Klansmen and several hundred were arrested and charged with conspiracy to prevent the exercise of the rights of citizenship guaranteed by the Fourteenth and Fifteenth amendments.

In the early 1900s, the vitriolic pen of Shelby (N.C.) native Thomas Dixon produced "The Clansman." Set in Chester's neighboring town, York, "The Clansman" glorified the Ku Klux Klan, villified carpetbaggers and caricatured blacks. Dixon's central villain bore a close resemblance to arch-Republican, Thaddeus Stevens. Abraham Lincoln came across as a well-meaning but bumbling dupe.

"The Clansman" was made into a movie by Director D. W. Griffith. Dixon suggested that the title be changed to the more epic "The Birth of a Nation," and this was done.

The panoramic and controversial silent movie spread across the nation like a forest fire. It aroused intense opposition and calls for suppression. Tradition has it that a Chesterite was so incensed at a local showing that he threatened to fire shots into the screen to save white womanhood from black radicals. Theater owner Fred Powell never let it happen.

Dixon appealed to President Woodrow Wilson, a former Johns Hopkins classmate. He and his cabinet viewed "The Birth of a Nation" in the East Room of the White House, February 18, 1915. "Like writing history with lightning . . . so terribly true," Wilson said afterward. North Carolinian Josephus Daniels, the Secretary of the Navy, arranged a second showing for the Supreme Court and Congress the next night.

Opposition still raged all across the land. Demonstrators battled police for 24 hours on Boston Common. But the presidential approval had given "The Birth of a Nation" a crucial infusion.

Nine months later it opened in Charlotte, N.C. and sometime later in local theaters. "No Southern Man can See It Without a Lump in His Throat," the advertisements claimed. Thousands flocked to see it. As an artistic offering it was stupendous. But more important, "The Birth of a Nation" rallied the long dormant Ku Klux Klan, and opened a Pandora's Box for the embittered South to contend with.

Members of United Daughters of the Confederacy and Veteran's organizations were vocal and vociferous in their opposition to the film and, of course, the Klan.

The Klan in Chester County

Allen W. Trelease in *White Terror* writes: Chester County, north of Columbia, was one of those in which Ku Klux activity became most common after the 1870 election. Night riding and the attendant outrages occurred all over the county but were most common in the western part, where plantations were largest and the Negro population greatest. Many blacks regularly slept out in the woods at night, but others determined to fight back. The obvious means of resistance lay in the militia companies which had been organized and armed for just this purpose.

In February 1871, one of these companies, under a Negro captain, Jim Woods, began to picket the roads at night, sometimes turning back white men whose business they were unsure of. On the night of March 4 they repulsed a Ku Klux attack on Captain Wood's house, wounding one of the attackers and capturing some disguises. The next night they drove off a larger Klan assault. Fearing still worse to come, they mustered in the following morning, about eighty strong, and began marching toward the town of Chester, the county seat, to get reinforcements and more ammunition. Apparently they expected a massive white turnout against them, for they

hoped to get help from another militia company in town and sent
out runners as far as Union and Newberry counties to summon
additional men. On reaching Chester they stacked their arms, stationed pickets, and obtained more ammunition from John C.
Riester, a white Republican leader and the major in command of the
county militia. The sheriff ordered them to disperse and return
home, but they refused to do so, arguing that their purpose was
wholly defensive.

The white men in town believed otherwise and proceeded to
organize for their own defense. They sent messages as far as North
Carolina calling for reinforcements to put down an impending
Negro rising. During the night there was an exchange of gunfire
between a small group of whites and a squad of militia. Around
dawn the whites advanced in a body toward the railway depot,
where they found the militia drawn up in line of battle to meet them.
Stopping to parlay, they persuaded the blacks to agree to leave town
and return home. But instead the Negroes went to a church five
miles away, stationed themselves in a strong defensive position, and
again sent out runners for rations and reinforcements. Their fear
was that if they dispersed as the whites demanded, they would
render themselves helpless in case of any white attack.

By this time hundreds of white men were converging on the
county from all directions, responding to appeals and reports that
grew more exaggerated the farther they spread. Many of those who
responded — perhaps all of them — were Klansmen out of disguise.
Some came down by train from Rock Hill, Charlotte, and Cleveland
County, North Carolina; others came up from Winnsboro and
points south. One contingent of fifty or sixty, coming toward
Chester from the west, had to pass by the militia camp and found
that they had blockaded the road. The blacks themselves opened
fire, using trees and rocks for cover. The whites, led by Colonel
Joseph F. Gist of Union, returned the fire and drove the militiamen
back with a flank attack. The Negroes lacked the training, leadership, and morale to contest the field for very long against seasoned
Confederate veterans. They retreated for three-quarters of a mile in
fairly good order, occasionally turning and firing, but then broke
and ran in all directions. The largest group, about twenty in number,
headed northward toward York County, where a small federal
garrison was posted. News of their coming preceded them and
coincided with a local panic among whites there arising from similar
causes. The York County sheriff went out with a posse, intercepted
the militiamen, and took them into protective custody for a short
time. They were then released and returned to their homes.

The "Chester riot" scared almost everyone. Major Riester went
down to Columbia and returned with a company of federal infantry
which was soon augmented by additional troops. A few days later

Governor Scott sent up an officer to disarm the local militia companies. Riester wound up his affairs in Chester and left the county permanently, to the cheers of his Conservative neighbors. With the militia rendered powerless, the Ku Klux continued raiding in the countryside without any real hindrance either from it or from the federal garrison in town.

XI OTHER WARS

MEXICAN WAR

Citizens of Chester responded with patriotic ardor to the call for volunteers for the Mexican War. This was in 1846, following the great drought of 1845.

People forgot all about the drought and its sufferings, and burned with fire of patriotic enthusiasm and local pride in the praiseworthy effort to organize the first company. She almost achieved that honor.

The town was aroused. Public meetings were held in the courthouse week after week, attended by both men and women. Patriotic songs were composed and sung. In a short time a company of volunteers was organized to match the famous Palmetto regiment. Captain R. G. Dunovant was major of the regiment.

Those meetings in Chester to raise this company, and the glory it won on the fields of carnage in Mexico, had a lasting effect upon the boys of Chester, which made it easier in 1861 to raise volunteers for the terrible war between the states. Their valor was unsurpassed by any communities in the State in marshaling her sons for war.

Chester's division of the Palmetto troops left Chester in 1846 for the Mexican War and came home in 1848. Company B, Palmetto regiment, was composed of R. G. M. Dunovant, captain, John T. Walker, 1st Lt., W. B. Lilley, 2nd Lt., Benjamin Culp, 3rd Lt., G. W. Curtis, 1st Sgt., R. A. Pagan, 2nd Sgt., William W. Triplett, 3rd Sgt., Jackson Hood, 1st Cpl., E. T. Gibbes, 2nd Cpl., William Wilks, 3rd Cpl., and 85 privates.

During the Mexican War, Major John Kennedy organized a company of men in case they should be needed. He was elected major and was ever after given that title.

SPANISH AMERICAN WAR

In February, 1898, a great explosion shook the harbor at Havana, Cuba. The blast destroyed the United States battleship, Maine, which burst into flames and sank in the harbor. Two hundred and sixty American seamen were killed. The sinking of the Maine set the stage for the war between the United States and Spain.

The Spanish-American War began in April, 1898, and ended four months later. It grew out of American sympathy for the oppressed people of Cuba. But some Americans favored the war for other reasons. They saw an opportunity for the United States to become a great world power.

The war ended in an American victory and the United States won possession of Puerto Rico, Guam and the Philippines, and independence for Cuba.

Company D., First South Carolina Volunteer Infantry, 76 strong, was organized at Chester May 4, 1898, and left for Columbia where they were mustered into service May 12, 1898. They went by rail from Columbia to Camp George H. Thomas, Chickamauga Park, Georgia, on June 6, 1898. They remained in camp until July 29, 1898. From there they went to Camp Cuba Libre, Florida, where they were assigned to Second Brigade, Third Division, Seventh Army Corps.

On April 24, 1899 they returned to Columbia and were furloughed for thirty days. At the expiration of the furlough the company was mustered out of service by Capt. Ezra B. Fuller, Seventh United States Calvary.

WORLD WAR I

America declared war on Germany April 6, 1917. South Carolina's contribution in money, including bond purchases and donations, approached $100 M, which ranks the State by capacity, among the highest in the Union. The official roster of her soldiers, sailors and marines contains almost 65,000 names, of whom 2,085 died in service, 460 in battle or of battle injuries.

South Carolina soldiers won a remarkable proportion of distinctions for bravery. The Congressional Medal of Honor, highest American award, was made to 78, 6 of them to South Carolinians of 118th Infantry, Thirtieth Division. The Distinguished Service Cross was won by 88 South Carolina soldiers, five of them officers from South Carolina.

The State's mild winter climate caused the establishment here of Camp Jackson at Columbia, Camp Sevier of Greenville, Camp Wadsworth of Spartanburg, the Marines' recruiting depot at Parris

Soldiers camped in Chester County, World War I.

Island and the Marine Corps Supply Service at Charleston.

During World War I, Mary Adair Chapter of D.A.R. in Chester was organized into a "National League for Woman's Service." They did Red Cross work, knitted garments, supported a French orphan, contributed to rebuilding a French village, Tilloloy, bought war bonds and War Saving Stamps, practiced economy and in every way gave loyal service.

During World War I soldiers were cared for in Chester. They were taken off troop trains, and isolation rooms were set up for their care as their diseases were contagious. Mrs. George T. Gregory was one of the faithful nurses.

Life in every village and town changed from leisure to a feverish pace to win the war. All men between the ages of 21 and 30 were required to register for the draft. "Four Minute" men promoted the sale of Liberty Bonds and support for the draft. Draft Boards were hastily set up in each county.

Billboards shouted slogans such as "Food Will Win the War." A stern-looking Uncle Sam appeared on army recruiting posters to announce "I Want *You.*" Everybody was singing "Over There" to let the world know that the Yanks were coming.

Chester families read the papers fearfully for news from places that heretofore had been only names on a map: Belleau Wood, Chateau-Thierry, the Hindenburg line, Meuse-Argonne, and Flanders Field.

The war was costly both in lives and money. About 63 of every 100 servicemen who died came from the allied armed forces. During the first three years of war, the fighting nations spent more than

$85,000 every minute. The United States borrowed money from its citizens through Liberty Loans.

Chester furnished 930 soldiers in the World War. Of this number 346 were white and 584 black. The total number of registrants physically examined was 1700.

Local registration board members were Col. Arthur L. Gaston, Dr. John E. Cornwell, Dr. W. B. Cox, Z. Vance Davidson, clerk, and Miss Marie Cornwell, assistant.

When the Armistice was signed on November 11, 1918, there were no radios or television services to broadcast the good news. But every whistle and bell in working order tooted and rang for hours in a frenzy of thanksgiving that the war was over.

CHESTER COUNTY WAR MEMORIAL BUILDING

Erected in honor of the men and women of Chester County who served their country in World Wars One and Two and dedicated to the memory of the following men who made the supreme sacrifice.

World War One

Robert L. Atkinson, Walter Campbell, King Castle, William F. Cauthen, Leander T. Dixon, David W. Drennan, William M. Edmonds, Edward B. Foutz, James Hemphill, James A. Love, Charles Lefevre, William E. McGarity, Fred T. Miller, Obed Loughbride Nichols, James Nunnery, Thomas M. Robinson, William D. Roof, John A. Simpson, William H. Stewart, Robert M. Wilson, William D. Woodward, Austin H. Young, Manuel Able, Israel Boyd, Edmund Brown, William Chapple, John P. Cockrell, Ernest Coleman, Claud Craig, Elmore Gray, Lawrence Crockett, Robert De-Graffenreid, Robert Burrough, Ned Earl, Sam Ervin, Ed Hemphill, William Hodge, Jr., McCaniel Lee, Leo Manley Lewis, William McLurkin, Alexander Stinson, Jr., John Woodward, Golden Wright.

World War Two

South Carolina and Chester County bore their full share of the terrible losses of life and treasure in that frightful conflict for the very preservation of freedom, World War II. From November 1, 1940 to June 30, 1945, accessions of South Carolinians to U. S. Army totaled 119,000 men and 1,886 women. Navy enlistments from December 1, 1941 through June 30, 1947 totaled 52,000 men and 732 women. Again the State stood true to her motto, "Ready with Minds and Fortunes."

World War II killed more persons, cost more money, damaged more property, affected more families and probably caused more changes than any war in history. It opened the Atomic Age and changed the methods of warfare. Bombers and ballistic missiles rained destruction on land and sea. Airplanes, warships and ground forces worked together in split-second timing. Paratroops dropped from airplanes.

More than fifty countries took part in the war, and the whole world felt its effects. Causes of the war were: (1) the rise of dictatorships; (2) the desire of Germany, Italy, and Japan for more territory; and (3) the problems of international peace left unsolved by World War I.

Japan's attack on Pearl Harbor in 1941 brought the United States into the war on the Allied side. It was truly a war for survival.

Chester's men fought and lost their lives in the Coral Sea, Midway, Guadalcanal, Kwajalein, Iwo Jima, many thousands of miles from home.

On August 6, 1945, a B-29 called "Enola Gay" dropped the first atomic bomb used in warfare on the city of Hiroshima. More than 92,000 persons were killed or missing. Three days later a bomb was dropped on Nagasaki killing at least 40,000. The Japanese realized they were helpless if one atomic bomb could cause so much damage. On September 2, aboard the battleship Missouri, the Allies and Japan signed the surrender agreement.

The men and women behind the man behind the gun helped win World War II. People on the home front built weapons, produced food and clothing, paid taxes, bought war bonds, and practiced stringent self-sacrifice. War production by the Allies was the real key to Allied victory. As men went into armed forces, women took their places in war plants.

Urgent requirements for war materials caused many shortages in consumer goods. Chester Countians remember rationing of meats, butter, sugar, fats, oils, coffee, canned goods, shoes and gasoline. Each family carefully handled its ration books.

Motto on the home front was:

> Eat it up
> Wear it out
> Make it do
> Or do without

People were repeatedly warned not to give away information that might be of value to the enemy. Mail was carefully censored. Slogans on billboards included "Loose talk costs lives" and "A slip of the lip may sink a ship." Civilian Defense offices were set up to protect the country from attack.

Selective Service Act called up all males 18 to 45 elegible for military service. A local 3-man selective service ("draft") board was established in each county. A lottery system determined the number assigned to each male registered.

Teenagers, women and elderly men became welders, riveters, machinists, metal workers, carpenters, electricians and mechanics of all types.

Rationing boards doled out 1½ gallons of gas per week for pleasure driving, set a national speed limit of 40 miles per hour, held drives to collect scrap metal and paper.

Volunteers served as air raid wardens and aircraft spotters, others rolled bandages for Red Cross or studied first aid to help the injured in case of an enemy air attack.

CHESTER COUNTY IN WORLD WAR II

Herman P. Hamilton was appointed chairman of Chester Civil Defense. He and Angus Macaulay were co-chairmen of the War Savings Bond Program. John M. "Buck" White, Jake S. Colvin and J. Boyce Bankhead were heads of the Draft Board.

William Moore, son of Mrs. Lillian P. Moore was one of Chester's first heroes. When he came home on leave, a large citywide banquet at Bethel Methodist Church was given in his honor.

There were 99 Gold Star Mothers in Chester County who lost a son in World Wars I and II.

Leeds area in western Chester County was the center of army maneuvers between the Reds and the Blues in 1941. The farm of Lucille and John Bramlett was a mock battle site where hundreds of half-tracks and trucks were "captured" and concealed under their pecan trees. Over 1,000 calvary horses were moved along the dusty, unpaved road in front of their house and tied to trees in the nearby forest until they were loaded and shipped away on the train.

The Bramletts remember the site along the road where General George Patton had his headquarters — soldiers coming to their kitchen for breakfast when the army kitchen had been captured — troops riding their small children on tanks and showing them movies at the bivouac — soldiers borrowing the Bramlett truck to drive into Chester and buy liquor and beer.

John Bramlett said the soldiers were paid twice while they were in the area. They spread blankets on his sawdust pile and gambled all night long.

Eva W. Bramlett was postmistress at Leeds Post Office during maneuvers.

Chester Theater, operated by Fred J. Powell, Sr., was used by the Army during maneuvers here. Powell allowed the Army officers to use the theater for planning sessions when movies were not being shown.

Powell often recalled the sight of the famed General George Patton standing on the stage at the theater talking loudly in a booming voice and slapping the tops of his boots with his ever-present riding crop.

Nearby, Winthrop College in Rock Hill was asked by the federal government to house, feed and teach 300 young men involved in Civilian Pilot Training Program. A contract was signed with the U. S. War Department, and the first contingent of trainees arrived in Rock Hill by train on March 7, 1943.

The presence of hundreds of young men on the all-girl campus proved to be mutually enjoyable, as well as of great benefit to the war effort. The training continued until July, 1944, when it was phased out.

Palmetto Literary Club of Chester stressed defense work and adopted a defense creed for club women. Mrs. H. S. Adams and Mrs. R. A. Oliphant were recognized for their success as chairmen of garment cutting and production for Red Cross. Club members all volunteered to finish garments for Red Cross.

Members supported the war effort in these ways:

— Furnished a day room at Fort Jackson; "the soldiers seemed pleased with it."

— Filled soldier's kits.

— Discussed ways and means of doing their part in the sale of war bonds.

— Mrs. Will Craig reviewed the novel, *Signed With Their Honor* by James Aldridge. Members were "thrilled by this beautiful and moving love story of an English pilot and a Grecian lady, the first novel to deal with air power in action in the Second World War."

— Mrs. Bernadine Patterson was conducting bi-weekly classes on United Nations and peace at the high school.

— Subject for the Club 1943, "Leaders of the World at War."

— Voted against Sabbath Day dancing and card playing, and for stricter chaperoning at local Soldier's Center.

— Office of Price Administration asked members for cooperation in price control of foods.

— On account of tire and gas rationing, district meeting was called off.

During World War II, Chester County was one of eight counties in South Carolina chosen as a site for military maneuvers. Khaki tents sprang up like toadstools in the fields and woods around Lowrys. Mock battles from October 6 to November 30, 1941 were staged between the "Red Army" and the "Blue Army." Long convoys of jeeps and trucks moved through the county. The troops in army drab who came from many different places in the country found friendliness and warm hospitality in the county.

Chester had a practice evacuation of a textile factory. The workers were then taken to a ball park where the army had a picnic dinner for them.

The South Carolina counties directly involved in the war games, or maneuvers, were Chester, Lancaster, York, Fairfield, Chesterfield, Kershaw, Marlboro and Richland. They were chosen because of the rolling wooded terrain and numerous streams in the area. There were adequate roads, yet the population was not so dense as to interfere with the soldiers' training or civilian routines.

Nearly one third of the entire U. S. continental army participated — more than a half million troops. One line of over 2,500 military vehicles stretched from Fort Benning, Georgia to Rock Hill, a distance of over 400 miles.

The first big battle between the Reds and the Blues occurred on October 4th on a 30-mile front which stretched along the Chester-Fairfield county line. That weekend Chester had a huge street dance for the soldiers and invited them to church on Sunday. The soldiers responded to both invitations with enthusiasm. Several romances budded between the soldiers and Chester's pretty girls.

On Monday the soldiers were back learning the lessons of war. When the Blue Army "blew up" a bridge near Blackstock, it meant a seven mile detour and a 21-mile hike for the Red invaders.

Maneuvers in the area ended in late November. Four days later the Japanese bombed Pearl Harbor.

SOLDIERS WHO LOST THEIR LIVES IN WORLD WAR TWO

Stewart S. Abell, Jr., Robert E. Abell, Jr., William J. Aiken, Lonnie L. Albert, Robert M. Anderson, William R. Baumil, Charles Bolin, Roy C. Bruce, Johnny W. Brassell, Joel F. Bacon, Francis Campbell, Walter Green Cathcart, Fred Christopher, Jake S. Colvin, Jr., James Craig, James Mitchell Dickerson, David Edwards, Robert Lee Edwards, Jr., Lee Morris Ellington, Henry R. Ferris, John V. Faulkner, John Dixon Ferguson, John T. Fowler, James E. Gabbert, Milton S. Gable, Jr., John E. Gardner, Chalmers M. Gaston, Claud E. Gatlin, Max E. Good, William A. Gregory, Henry F. Gurley, Robert A. Guy, William C. Hefner, Lyles Glenn Hardin, Arthur H. Hammonds, Wilton Harbin, James E. Harvey, Roy B. Hayhurst, Rufus A. Helms, John M. Hemphill, Jr., Robert P. Hinson, Wade Hazel Hough, Joe Herbert Kobret, James L. Land, William T. Undenzweig, John Marion Love, Marvin F. Matkins, Ben E. Morrow, Hugh Mobley, Robert W. Mendenhall, John T. Moore, Ralph W. Morris, Paul L. McCants, Benjamin R. McElduff, Charles E. McGowan, Arthur L. McKeown, Dewey M. McKeown, Jr., R. A. Oliphant, Jr., Thomas W. Patrick, Jr., Cecil Everett Pierce,

Harry Milburn Plyler, Fred William Ramsey, James Franklin Roberts, Dwight Roddey, Walter Avery Roof, Joseph G. Saye, Warren Simpson, Arthur W. Smith, Jack Stewart, Jessie M. Stroud, Richard Viars, Lawrence W. Wade, James Daniel Wessinger, James B. Wheeler, Guy M. Wilkes, Jr., Wilbur H. Willis, Crawford Henry Wise, Therman H. Woodle, Joseph J. Woodward, James Niel Yongue, Charles C. Young, Jr., Joseph D. Young, Lawrence Barnes, Coleman Bagwell, William A. Cornwell, Tommie Mobley, Avis Davis, Ross Graham, Frazier Mayfield, Robert Sea Poag, Nathaniel Walker, Augustus C. Smith, J. D. Small.

GAYLE MILL

XII DEVELOPMENT OF COTTON MILLS

CHESTER TURNS TO TEXTILES

After Reconstruction pangs began to ease, the South's most pressing internal need was for money. To get money it had returned with absorbing passion to the only practice which, in its experience, had yielded it: the cultivation of cotton. But cotton, always fickle and dangerous was actually bearing the South into deeper and deeper trouble.

They called into use old, poor lands which, in the antebellum South, had been adjudged of no worth for growing the fiber. Cotton is a voracious plant and to grow it required fertilizer in growing quantities. Cotton had also long ago begun to exhaust those plantation lands which in the golden 60s seemed eternally fecund.

Farmers ceased to be self-sufficient in food: they no longer produced provender enough at home to take care of themselves and their animals from crop to crop and must, therefore, somehow manage to secure it from outside. They were in no position to finance these needs and had to have credit.

The whole credit machinery of the Old South, as much else, had gone with the wind. There were few solvent banks left and no capital to set up a proper banking system.

The supply merchants stepped into the breach. Practically every man who could lay his hands on a few hundred dollars and persuade the wholesale houses in the North to extend him some credit set up shop to supply guano and bread to his neighbors. By the 1880s, almost every crossroad had at least one banker-merchant and the necessary credit was achieved.

The evil thing was the price that had to be paid. These new masters of Southern economics quickly saw that they could exact whatever rate of payment they pleased. The farmer had to mortgage his crop, mortgage the land on which the crop was to be grown —

123

often on all his land and chattels, and to pay charges or "time prices" that averaged from 40 to 80 percent.

He might have made it if cotton prices had held up but cotton became a glut on the world market. As early as 1878 the price had dropped to ten cents and the trend was constantly downward. In 1898, it plunged to below five cents — the lowest in history.

In mounting numbers, the farmers crashed into disaster. Every year saw thousands fail. Land in these years of plummeting cotton prices and forced sales got to be almost as cheap as it had been on the original frontier; in most places it could be had as low as two or three dollars an acre.

About this time, there began to grow up in the minds of many (the old Confederate captains in large part), that another line must be found to pull them out of their economic difficulties — build cotton mills in the midst of the cotton fields.

Dr. Broadus Mitchell in his *Rise of the Cotton Mills in the South* says "an enthusiasm — so naive, so headlong, so uncalculating and uncautious as to be almost beyond belief" swept the beleaguered populace. He was "dumfounded by the blithe disregard to rudimentary business principles displayed by the early entrepreneurs. Aspiring hamlets built cotton mills without any sort of investigation into the advantages of the locality for textile manufacturing. Only in rare instances was the enterprise headed by a man of any experience in business. . . . The usual plan was to select the man in the community who possessed the people's confidence to the highest degree and draft him into service regardless of his previous training. Thus the new mills were headed by doctors, lawyers, teachers, bankers, planters, even clergymen."

By 1882, South Carolina had 26 cotton mills according to S. C. Department of Agriculture, A. P. Butler, Commissioner. Two were listed in Chester County.

Cedar Shoals Factory on Fishing Creek, 40 H. P., 612 spindles, $21,000 capital, 16 hands, $2,400 annual wages, 130,000 pounds of cotton consumed; value of products $21,500, 125,000 pounds of yarn; market value of stock $110 per share.

Fishing Creek Factory on Fishing Creek, 50 H. P., 3,000 spindles; $100,000 capital, 35 hands; $5,000 wages; 468,000 pounds of cotton used; $75,348 value of products and $100 per share value of stock.

By 1900, the number of S. C. mills had increased to 115, with 30,201 workers; and by 1930, the mills numbered 239 with 94,756 workers. The great development took place in Greenville, Spartanburg and Anderson counties while smaller towns in the upcountry, including Chester, longingly watched their progress and sought to get on the textile bandwagon.

And so the cotton mills came. From Greensboro in North

Carolina to Greenville in South Carolina, on to Atlanta, Georgia, there was an almost uninterrupted succession of mills and mill villages and mill people. They sprang up along the Southern Railroad and along the towered procession of James Buchanan Duke's power lines which he delivered before he died to the new shrewd "mortmain of benefaction," according to Jonathan Daniels.

Textile mills first brought a modicum of prosperity to the region. An immense reservoir of cheap labor was available, and the cotton mills lured men and women from the hills and from hardscrabble farms. Farmers with their families, usually large ones, deserted their rented shacks on the land and flocked to the mill villages where all of them could find work and better houses than they had ever known.

For all the mills, there were villages of clapboard or asphalt shingle cottages, all within walking distance of the workers' jobs. They were company owned and controlled. Before the days of automobiles and modern transportation, employees had to be within walking distance of the mill and in the hearing distance of the shrill, sonorous mill whistle that regulated their days. If the mill owners had not constructed villages they would have had no employees.

The village in time revolutionized the social condition of the workers. Management was forced to provide schools for their children after the S. C. Child Labor Law was passed in 1907. The law prohibited children under 12 from working in the cotton mills. It became necessary to find a place for them to be while their parents worked. This was how the law requiring compulsory attendance in the schools came into being.

A law requiring marriage licenses was also introduced and passed to prevent marriages of children below the age of 14. Child marriages were common in mill villages at the time. In order to enforce the child labor laws, the state needed to keep vital statistics on births and deaths. South Carolina recorded none of these until 1911.

Management built churches and supplied preachers, and set aside land for gardens and recreation as well as cow pastures, hog pens and chicken yards. The company store provided charge accounts for all items of necessity.

Many of the mill villages organized baseball teams that challenged neighboring mills. The schools and churches became centers of social activities previously unknown in the country. Although later generations, especially in the north, condemned the mill villages as paternalistic, they were essential at the time they were created, and they served a useful social purpose in educating a generation of poor whites, many of them illiterate, to a better way of life: W. J. Cash says — "by far the greater number of him were literally in the intellectual status of Lula Vollmer's old mountain woman of our time who knew of France only that it was, 'somers yon side of Ashville."

During this period of industrialization, first "Pitchfork Ben" Tillman and then Cole Blease came upon the South Carolina scene as paladins of the burning issue of white supremacy politics. Blease got to be governor in 1910 by championing the sort of millhands who were carried on the books at the company store. "Cotton Ed" Smith and Olin D. Johnson carried on the tradition.

Colonel Elliott White Springs, one of the nation's most successful and colorful entrepreneurs tells the story of the development of textile plants, in which he played a dominant role, in Chester County. His narrative, written in 1949, delineates the progress from 1888 to 1948.

In 1888 the town of Chester was stirred by the coming of another railroad, the Georgia, Carolina & Northern which was being built from Monroe, N. C. to Atlanta, Ga. It already had the Lancaster and Chester, the Charlotte, Columbia & Augusta, and the Chesterville and Lenoir.

The town at the time contained 2,800 people. It had a score or more of business firms, five white churches, three Negro churches, and a good academy. It had no industrial enterprises and had not made any appreciable progress in thirty years.

In that era, the coming of a new railroad — it mattered not how large or how small the line — served to set off a spark of enthusiasm in every city, town, and hamlet through which it was to pass, and would lead every one to expect some sort of a "boom" to follow. Chester was no exception to the rule. The coming of the Georgia, Carolina & Northern (now the Seaboard Air Line) made it begin to dream dreams.

Along about this time the cotton textile industry was beginning to dig its roots in the South. Textile plants had sprung up in other communities near Chester, and in every instance had been followed by an increase in the population and a business stimulation due to the payrolls. Every community got the idea that the quickest and surest way to promote growth was to build a mill. Machinery agents were ready with plans and acted as engineers and promoters for the new enterprises. That is why so many early mill buildings appear to be duplicates.

And so it was decided by the people of Chester that they needed a cotton mill. Some of the leading merchants and business men talked the matter over and an open meeting was called. At this meeting the promoters secured sufficient promises of subscriptions to the capital stock to justify an organization.

Chester Manufacturing Company

On July 10, 1888, the Secretary of State issued a charter to the Chester Manufacturing Company. The incorporators were listed as J. L. Agurs, J. H. Smith, S. M. Jones, G. D. Heath, J. J. Hemphill, G. W. Gage, and W. H. Hendrix.

The capital stock of the proposed company was fixed at $100,000.00 in shares of $100.00 each. W. H. Hardin was elected president.

About two-thirds of the capital stock was subscribed. The Woods property was secured as a site, the most eligible in town with abundance of free stone water for dyeing and steam purposes. A two-story brick building was erected, and fourteen homes were built for operatives. Masonry and plastering were done by J. R. Simrill and the wood work by George Alexander Allbright, both skilled artisans of Chester.

Work progressed slowly, however, for the plant did not begin operations until 1890.

In the Chester Reporter of January 23, 1890, it was recorded:

"Stream was raised in the engine of the cotton factory for the first time last Friday. The machinery was set to running and this will go on for several days for the purpose of testing adjustments of the whole outfit of machinery. The big wheel is the object of much wonder and remark. It is about the biggest of the kind ever seen by most of the people about here. Some of the factory hands have moved in and others are expected soon."

And so Chester's first cotton mill began operations with its own dye works to color the yarns. It almost immediately became known to the public as "the gingham mill."

The new venture did not have very smooth sailing, for in the Chester Reporter of April 17, 1890, it was recorded:

"A meeting of the stockholders of the Chester factory was held here last Monday to consider the question of adding to the subscriptions to the capital stock. Most of those present agreed to add 50 per cent to their subscriptions. It has been decided to abandon the plan of putting in spinning machinery.

Mr. Hardin, the first president, resigned and was succeeded by Dr. W. S. Gregg. While Dr. Gregg was president a disastrous fire swept the plant and, according to an old Chester paper, $90,000 worth of beautiful cloth was burned, and there was but little, if any, insurance to cover the large quantity of goods already packed and ready for shipment.

The mill was rebuilt and John Gilligen of Providence, R. I., became superintendent and general manager. J. W. Dunovant was made president, and S. B. Lathan, secretary.

The management decided that one of the causes of the woes besetting the plant was that it had to buy yarns from a distance, and that it would be to its advantage if it could spin them in Chester. Thus it was decided to attempt the building of a yarn mill in Chester.

A separate corporation, the Catawba Manufacturing Company, was formed, but the stockholders were practically the same as those of the Chester Manufacturing Company. The first brick on the new plant was laid on June 1, 1892. D. A. Tompkins designed the mill and provided the machinery. It began operation with 5,000 spindles.

And then came the panic of 1893 when business all over the United States tottered, and orders were cancelled by shaky customers. The two mills at Chester were caught in the whirlpool and lacked enough working capital to weather the storm. A receiver was appointed by the court in behalf of the creditors and the company liquidated.

On July 1, 1894, the Chester Manufacturing Company was sold at public auction to D. A. Tompkins of Charlotte, N. C. for $100,000. Mr. Tompkins also bought the Catawba Manufacturing Company to protect his interest in the machinery, and proceeded to operate the two mills as a unit. 212 people were employed.

The gingham mill's troubles were recurring, however, and it was taken over again by the Court for its creditors in 1898. This time considerable trouble seems to have been experienced in finding a buyer, but it was finally sold in 1899 to O. P. Heath of Monroe, N. C. and Eli Springs of Charlotte, N. C.

Springsteen Mill

Colonel Leroy Springs, of Lancaster, was made president of the new company and took over the operation of the plant, and its name was changed to Springsteen, which was the name of the Springs family in Holland before they came to New Amsterdam.

Colonel Springs set out immediately to enlarge the plant. A mortgage of $65,000 was placed on the plant to borrow money from W. E. Holt. From thirty to fifty additional houses were built, and the company bought an adjoining lot from Mr. M. A. Carpenter."

The addition to the plant seemed to have brought joy to everybody in Chester but the boys who played baseball, for the new houses were being built on the lot where they played.

In "Curbstone Chat" in the Chester Reporter of October 19th, 1899, appeared the following:

"There is a howl of lamentation among baseball players. They are all 'broke up' by the building of houses on the playground, the front part of The Springsteen Mills property. These sportsmen say they 'always knowed that wasn't no fittin' place for no factory nohow.' "

But a new diamond was found and the enthusiasm for baseball continued. Not too many players used gloves then and one player recalls that "Our pitcher caught a linedrive ball and it turned his hand blue to his elbow." A padding of leaves stuffed in the side of pants was concocted to prevent too many skinned thighs. "This wasn't much trouble as the spectators were sitting in a clump of trees nearby, anyway." laughed one of the fellows.

In the Columbia State of October 31, 1899, there was a writeup of the exhibits at the State Fair, from which we quote:

"The Springsteen Mill of Chester has a superb exhibit of samples from its spun, woven, and finished products made from cotton grown in the state of South Carolina, which they claim is the finest colored cotton goods made in the South."

But even under the smart management of Colonel Springs, the Springsteen Mill continued to have its troubles for a while. The story is told in Chester that on the night the Carolina and Northwestern Shops, located on property adjacent to Springsteen burned, Colonel Springs on hearing of the fire, exclaimed: "Why in the hell didn't the Springsteen plant burn, too?"

In 1902, W. H. Fries, of Salem, N. C., attempted to form a merger of a dozen small mills in the Carolinas, and took an option on the Springsteen Plant. However, a depression destroyed his plans and the option was never exercised.

The Springsteen Mill incurred a heavy debt and, after O. P. Heath sold his stock to Colonel Springs, the two Springs brothers

Springstein Mills, Chester, S. C.

endorsed the notes of the company to keep it out of bankruptcy a third time. They carried them until the war in 1915 raised prices to a profitable level, and the notes were paid. Meanwhile, the plant had been increased to 16,000 spindles and 375 looms.

In July, 1898, the Catawba Spinning Company was sold for its debts by the Clerk of Court, and its buildings and machinery were purchased for $49,000 by D. A. Tompkins, who later resold them to Colonel Leroy Springs, C. J. Webb, a yarn broker of Philadelphia, C. B. Skipper, formerly superintendent of Eureka but then superintendent of The Lancaster Cotton Mills, and Waddy C. Thomson.

The name was changed to the Eureka Cotton Mills, and it was operated as a yarn mill, but in 1909 the new owners decided to build a weave shed and install 600 Draper Model E looms to weave sheeting.

It was merged with the Springsteen Plant in 1931, and the name Eureka used for both. Colonel Springs had studied the classics at the University of North Carolina, and Eureka was the only Greek word he could remember.

Just after the Chester and Catawba Plants had been sold at auction, Chester decided to build another mill, and in the Chester Reporter of January 25, 1900, appeared this story:

"The new cotton mill, which it was stated last week was assured, may be called doubly assured now. The commission was received from the Secretary of State Tuesday night. The corporators are J. L. Agurs, and T. H. White. The capital stock is $100,000, a majority of which is already assured. This site of the new mill is on the Withers place, 367 acres and work will begin by April 1st. The new mill will be called the Wylie Mill in honor Mr. Joseph Wylie."

The mill managed to keep its head above water until the depression in 1912 when it ran out of capital, and on May 24, 1912, the stockholders voted to go into liquidation and to sell the mill at public auction.

The mill was sold at public auction on June 28, 1912, and was bid in by H. J. Haynsworth. Mr. Haynsworth was representing the Parker Mills and the Wylie Mill was assigned to Hampton Mills division of the Parker Mills Company, and F. S. Dupre became its superintendent.

The Parker Mills was caught in the cotton break at the beginning of the War in 1914, and in 1916 the Chester Plant was sold to Lockwood Greene & Company, that immediately sold it to Carroll Baldwin. The name of the plant was changed to the Baldwin Mills.

In 1920 J. P. Stevens & Company bought the controlling interest of stock in the mill, and in 1924 the Baldwin Mills went into liquidation as such, wound up its affairs, and dissolved. The property and assets were exchanged for shares of the common capital stock of the Aragon Baldwin Cotton Mills, which was then being organized. The plant then became known as the Baldwin Plant of the Aragon Baldwin Cotton Mills, which company also owned the Aragon Plant at Rock Hill and the Glenn Lowry Mills at Whitmire.

The Baldwin Plant finally contained 31,480 spindles and 876 looms.

In 1919 A. H. Robbins, who had been superintendent of the Lancaster Plant, went to Chester to become Manager of Springsteen and Eureka. In 1934 he assumed responsibility for Baldwin, and served in this capacity until his death. His son, Eugene, was superintendent of Eureka from 1933 until 1945.

Harry S. Adams was Secretary of Springsteen and Eureka from 1910 until they were merged with Lancaster. He later was in charge of the Social Security Department for the whole Springs Cotton Mills.

In 1931, after the death of Colonel Leroy Springs, the Springsteen Plant was abandoned and the machinery moved to the Eureka Plant, where the building was enlarged, giving a total of 45,000 spindles and 1,100 looms. For two years the Springsteen buildings were used as a cotton warehouse, and the people living in the Springsteen houses were employed at the Eureka Plant, running their old machinery, which had been moved two miles.

In 1933 the Eureka Cotton Mills was merged with The Lancaster Cotton Mills and the Fort Mill Manufacturing Company, and enough capital became available to rebuild the Springsteen Plant and fill it with modern machinery. It was one of the first plants in the South to be entirely equipped with Model X looms, long draft spinning, long draft roving, one process picking, automatic spooling and warping, and continuous card strippers. It was enlarged in 1938 to 29,744 spindles and 624 looms. It ran continuously since 1934.

During all these vicissitudes the workers in the mill were steadfast in their loyalty to the management, and only that encouragement preserved the management's determination to operate. The citizens of Chester as a whole, though they had long before lost their financial interest in the mill, still gave the management and the workers their heartiest cooperation, and this has made Chester a profitable and pleasant place to live.

Gayle Mill

In December, 1933, The Lancaster Cotton Mills purchased the Chester Plant from the Aragon-Baldwin Cotton Mills, and changed its name to the Gayle Plant in honor of Walter Gayle, who had inherited D. A. Tompkins' mantle as the leading machinery salesman and textile engineer of the South.

Immediately after its purchase, the mill was rebuilt, enlarged and new machinery installed. It was enlarged again in 1937 to

40,648 spindles and 1,184 looms. Gayle Mill was closed down permanently in 1975.

The Springsteen Plant made carded poplins. It was closed in 1983. The Eureka Plant made rayon gabardine, buffing cloth, and meads cloth. The Gayle Plant made pillow tubing, Birdseyes, and sheeting yarn poplins. At Gayle also was a sewing plant where 100 machines were operated on two shifts, sewing sheets, pillowcases, Birdseye, and table covers. When Gayle plant closed the sewing room was moved to Grace Plant at Fort Lawn.

Springs Mills Formed

By the time he died in 1959, Col. Elliott White Springs had transformed the obsolete, financially troubled empire of the 30s into a modern muscular textile giant. The value of plant property had risen from $7 million to $109 million. Sales had risen from $8.1 million to $184.3 million. By 1980 it was one of the ten largest textile companies in the nation.

The progressive spirit spawned by Col. Springs continued under his successor, son-in-law Hugh William Close. Close began to build, modernize and renovate.

The modern Springs Cotton Division warehouse at Fort Lawn was completed in 1962. Elliott Plant was completed nearby in 1963, Frances Plant in 1964. In the same general area, Leroy Plant was completed in 1966 to turn out the polyester-cotton blends that were playing an increasingly large role in the industry.

A $9 million expansion at Fort Mill Plant and an $11 million expansion at Grace Finishing were completed. Many workers from Chester commuted to these plants.

In 1966, the selling company in New York was merged with the manufacturing company in the Carolinas and the corporate name was changed to Springs Mills, Inc. In 1959, Springs Mills, Inc. sold enough springmaid cloth to circle twelve times around the earth.

In 1968, the company made still another departure from the past. It undertook indirectly, its first long-term debt financing. This happened when Chester County issued industrial revenue bonds to finance construction of Katherine Plant on Highway 9 near Chester. It is the world's largest shuttleless loom plant. Springs leases the building from the county.

COLONEL ELLIOTT WHITE SPRINGS

The history of Springs Mills is synonomous with that of its founder, Elliott White Springs.

Springs, World War I ace, pilot, author and textile manufacturer left an indelible and significant imprint in this area. A native of a small South Carolina town, he first rose to national prominence as the fifth-ranking American ace of World War I.

Capitalizing on his war experiences, he launced a literary career that earned him the title of "the foremost chronicler of World War II aviation."

In 1931, turning from his successful writing career to the family textile business, he assumed the presidency of five small mills, and advanced the business to the position of the largest producer of exclusively cotton textiles in the world.

During the post-war period of the 1940's, Elliott Springs began a national advertising campaign based on satirical imitation of other advertising. The campaign attracted national attention through its ribald copy and went on to become a textbook case history of advertising success. What was more significant, it sold the Springmaid brand name in a remarkably short time.

With the success of Springs' products came the increasing growth and prosperity of communities such as Chester, where Springs plants were situated. It was a success due in large measure to the productive genius and the unpredictable, highly imaginative brilliance of Elliott Springs.

The only son of Colonel Leroy Springs and Grace Allison White Springs, Elliott White Springs was born in Lancaster in 1896 where he spent his early childhood. During his youth he spent summers in the Carolinas and winters at preparatory schools, first at Asheville School and later at Culver Military Academy. After graduation from Culver in 1913, he entered Princeton University from which he graduated in 1917.

In the spring of 1917, Springs enrolled in Princeton's new aeronautical school in preparation for service as an Army fighter pilot in World War I action. After two months of training, Sergeant Springs reported for active duty at Mineola, N. Y. for an overseas assignment in the United States Air Service.

Sent first to Oxford, England, for flight training and later to Turnbery, Scotland, for gunnery schooling and combat flying, he completed training in March of 1918 and received his commission as a first lieutenant.

Lt. Springs was appointed to the 85th Aero Squadron, Royal Air Force, under the command of the famed Canadian Ace, Major Billy Bishop, who led his new squadron across the English Channel to France to join the fighting Allied forces.

Arriving late in May of 1918, the 85th Squadron spent two weeks in a rigorous training program. On June 5, 1918, Major Bishop led a small flight on patrol to the front, and during the encounter with six German planes, Springs shot down a German Pfalz scout. It was the first of eleven official downed planes. Many other unconfirmed victories that were not recorded under the rigid

British system were unofficially credited to Springs. He had begun his outstanding record as an American ace.

Transferred to the 148th Aero Squadron, U. S. Air Service, in July, Springs was appointed a flight commander. At the close of the war, he was the squadron's leading ace, recipient of the Purple Heart, and Distinguished Flying Cross of Great Britain and the American Distinguished Service Cross.

Returning to the United States, the young Air Corps officer and ace was heralded as a national hero. He received the commendation of the United States government and was decorated by the Prince of Wales.

Springs, promoted to the rank of Captain, continued his interest and activities in aviation. He was an officer in the Air Force Reserves and a test pilot for L. W. F. Airplane Company. In August of 1919 he entered the first cross-country air race between New York and Toronto, Canada.

After his return to South Carolina, Springs embarked on several new careers. He was much in demand as a speaker and as a stunt pilot. He became an officer in Fort Mill Manufacturing Company, and a popular writer of books, magazine articles and short stories. In 1922, he married Frances Hubbard Ley of Springfield, Massachusetts, and brought her to the ancestral White home in Fort Mill.

Captain Springs upon the death of his father in 1931 became president of the mills. He divided his time between his textile and writing careers. He consolidated two Fort Mill plants and three other textile plant operations under the name of The Springs Cotton Mills.

Captain Springs spent considerable time visiting offices of publishers and magazines in New York to sell his stories. In 1926, a serialized version of his book, *War Birds: Diary of an Unknown Aviator* appeared in Liberty Magazine.

Almost overnight he was a success. During the next few years he wrote and published scores of short stories and several books including *Contact, Nocturne Militaire, Leave Me with a Smile,* and *Clothes Make the Man.*

During his twenty-eight years as president, Springs Mills experienced unprecedented growth. Its property value increased from about $7½ million to $114 million and annual sales from $8 million to $184 million in 1959.

While a majority of textile plants in the country either curtailed or halted production during the depression of the 1930s, the Springs Cotton Mills began an extensive expansion while the mills ran full time. Warehouses were often filled with unsold goods, but when the nation began to recover, Springs Mills had cloth to sell the plants that were in good running order. Business continued to thrive and grow.

In 1941, Captain Springs left his business to return to active duty with the Air Force. He was promoted to lieutenant colonel and served briefly as executive officer of the Charlotte (N. C.) Army Air Base until he was retired in 1942 on a disability incurred during the war.

Returning to the textile plants, Colonel Springs turned over the entire production to the Army and Navy. In 1943, 1944 and 1945, all the plants were awarded the coveted Army-Navy "E" Award for excellence of production achievement.

Springs Mills continued an expansion program that is evident to this day. A mammoth bleaching, dyeing and finishing plant was built near Lancaster.

In the wake of national economic recovery, Colonel Springs initiated his innovative, tongue-in-cheek advertising campaign which caught the public eye and focused it on the new Springmaid brand name of sheets and pillowcases. It spoofed the contemporary type of advertising and sent the Springmaid line to the top of the national market.

The most widely known and memorable ad featured a sprightly Indian maid standing over a weary Indian chief who is reclining in a Springmaid sheet hammock. The ad is captioned with the line, "A buck well spent on a Springmaid sheet." It has become a classic in advertising history.

Elliott Springs was an innovative leader in employee and community benefit programs. He installed cafeterias to provide hot meals for employees on all shifts. He set up the Leroy Springs Foundation to finance recreation facilities such as softball fields, tennis courts, community centers, golf courses and swimming pools. He developed Springs Park near Great Falls Springmaid Beach on the coast near Myrtle Beach, and a camp in the North Carolina mountains.

Springs instituted a profit sharing program and medical programs including clinics and full time doctors and nurses. Many of the things he pioneered to help his employees and their communities were carried out quietly and without fanfare behind the scenes.

Springs corporate office building in Fort Mill is a monument to Springs' progressive ideas. It received nationwide attention for its unusual architecture and unique features. The two-story building contains furniture created from textile machinery. In the president's office a control panel on the executive desk, similar to an airplane cockpit, has push button controls to open sliding panels, remote controlled curtains and a conference table that rises from the floor. The windows, set at a forty-five degree angle, permit indirect lighting without glare.

Elliott White Springs, a legend in his own time, died in 1959 at age 63. He left a remarkable record of accomplishment in war, business, writing, advertising, employee and community concern and involvement — and hundreds of delightful stories of the unpredictable things he said and did, many of them true.

CLOSE BECAME PRESIDENT

Hugh William "Bill" Close held the reins of the massive Springs Industries for nearly a quarter of a century after the death of his father-in-law Elliott White Springs in 1959.

In 1946, Close, then a Springs trainee in New York married the only daughter of Col. Springs, founder and head of the textile empire.

That year Close was fresh back from World War II where he had been assigned to the aircraft USS Franklin, one of the most battle-scarred ships of the war.

In 1947, Close and his bride, Anne, moved to Fort Mill where he began his rise to the top by doing a variety of jobs from carding, spinning, spooling, weaving, repairing machinery and being a self-described "lousy left-handed doffer."

Close became Springs president in October 1959. Under his leadership, Springs underwent the most intensive growth in its 96-year history. During the 1960's, the company grew from eight plants and 12,000 employees to 22 plants and 19,500 employees.

In 1966, the company went public, selling its stock for the first time on the New York Exchange. In 1969, Peter Scotese was named president, the first non-family member to hold the spot. Close became chairman of the board. He and his family own 58 percent of the company's stock, according to a recent proxy statement.

Springs had annual sales of nearly $1 billion with 29 plants in eight states, Mexico and France. Non-manufacturing interests such as Kanawha Insurance Company and the Lancaster and Chester Railroad are operated under the Springs Company in Lancaster. The company has a professional management team since Bill Close's death on Wednesday, August 17, 1983.

TEXTILE TRENDS IN 1985

Springs Industries, a giant of the Carolinas textile empire, which was built on cheap labor, ruled the industry for much of this century. The empire is crumbling.

In the past 12 years 52,100 textile jobs in South Carolina have been lost — nearly one out of three, according to a report by Charlotte Observer of September 15, 1985.

For J. P. Stevens, which has closed 13 of its Carolinas plants including three in Great Falls since 1982, the competition from cheaper labor overseas has its irony. It was Stevens move to the South in the 1950's, lured by low wages, that contributed to the demise of textiles as a major employer in New England.

The decline of the Carolinas textile empire takes with it more than the state's largest industry. Textiles have shaped life in South Carolina and Chester County for generations and dotted the landscape with red brick mill towers and villages of wooden mill houses. Scattered across the countryside a network of thriving industrial villages nurtured a small-town way of life throughout a thickly populated region. Many of the old mills are abandoned to kudzu or converted to other uses.

The Carolinas are the heart of the U. S. textile industry, with nearly half the nation's textile workers. Some 106,000 in South Carolina work in textiles, far more than in any other industry.

In 1948, textile mills employed 65% of all manufacturing workers in South Carolina. By 1984, these proportions had fallen to 30% in the state.

Between 1973-1984, Chester County lost 1463 textile jobs. Neighboring Great Falls suffered a lethal blow in 1984 when all three of its J. P. Stevens plants closed with a loss of 630 jobs.

Springs Industries, reeling from competiton with foreign imports, for the first half of 1985 earned $5.1 million, down 73% from $18.8 million a year ago. Springs plants in Chester County in 1984 lost 508 jobs.

Textile companies profitable and still in business are becoming more flexible, more automated and more market oriented. Along with marketing there is a lot more product development and innovation, newer technology and a swing away from classical paternalistic managments that prevailed most of this century.

Textile executives still dominate South Carolina politics. As one astute observer says, "You have to dance around those boys." Their economic power and the gratitude they earned enabled them to dominate local politics, and influence education and religion. Their paternalism still touches every facet of life in Chester County from recreation to retirement.

Brushy Fork Baptist Church
Chester County

XIII CHURCHES AND MINISTERS

RELIGION WAS DOMINANT FORCE TO EARLY SETTLERS

With the Bible of the pioneer came the preachers, some of them itinerant, some settled. The minister was the faithful shepherd of the flock, one with great influence. He exhibited learning, courage and steadfastness. He was willing to carry a ploughshare and a rifle along with his Bible. Because of his education and calling, he was of exalted rank.

The first dissenters in the Chester area were anti-Anglican, those who opposed the Church of England. They were Independents, Congregationalists, Hugenots or Presbyterians. Sometimes they were known as Separatists, Commonwealthians, or Dissenters. They joined themselves together because of a mutual history of resistance to ecclesiastical and royal tyranny.

Several branches of Presbyterianism were transplanted to this new settlement. The first Churches in Chester County were Presbyterian because the majority of the first settlers carried this belief, and for geographical rather than Calvinistic beliefs.

According to Robert Lathan in his *History of the Reformed (Associate) Synod of the South* facts warrant the conclusion that the Presbyterian Church had an origin in a blending of Irish Presbyterianism and English Congregationalists together with a slight mixture of Scotch Presbyterians.

Chesterville District had an organized church as early as 1752. In 1758 the Rev. William Richardson came into the settlement described as one "where the Catawbas pillaged, the Cherokees stalked and burned, and taverns dispensed whiskey, wine, home brew and English beer."

138

Mr. Richardson began his mission work in the Waxhaw and Fishing Creek churches and extended his message along "Rocking Creek" which was lined with Covenanters, Associate Presbyterians as well as Scot Presbyterians. Eventually those groups would unite and call themselves "Catholic."

After some years the five or six presbyterian groups combined to build a union Church, which they called "Catholic" as all groups were to worship there. It was located "on the Rocky Mount Road, 15 miles southeast of Chester." Rev. Richardson was for a time the preacher. In 1770, the Covenanters began to hold society meetings, and soon wrote to Ireland for a minister.

It was partly in response to this call that Rev. William Martin came to South Carolina, the first Covenanter minister settled in the south. While the party he brought could not get their lands together, many were able to settle in the Rocky Creek area, where their leader located. He not only took up land by grant in 1773 but later bought a square mile (640 acres) and built a stone house on it.

At first he preached at Catholic regularly. In 1774 the Covenanter congregation withdrew from Catholic and built a log church on the same road as the Catholic church and two miles east of it," on the dividing ridge between Great and Little Rocky Creeks." This was described as being near the house of Mrs. James Barbour Ferguson. There he preached to his own congregation.

In early years the Revolutionary War did not particularly affect the settlers in the area, but by 1780 the situation changed. In that year the British and Tories were ranging the country. Mr. Martin then preached a sermon described vividly by Dr. Lathan. There are several accounts of this sermon, but all agreed on the sense of what he said. He reminded the congregation of the hardships their fathers had suffered, in religious persecutions and economic poverty, that they had been forced out of both Scotland and Ireland, had come to America and cleared their lands and built their homes and their church and were free men. Now, he told them, the British were coming in, and the soldiers would again be depriving them of the fruits of their labors and be driving them out. They should not stand meekly and idly by while all they had wrought was taken from them; there was a time to pray and a time to fight, and the time to fight had come!

As a result of his sermon, two companies were immediately formed under Ben Land and Captain Barbour, provided with arms and horses and joined to the American forces fighting the British.

The British retaliated by burning the church and taking Martin prisoner. He was confined for six months in Rocky Mount and Camden. He and Col. Winn were taken before Lord Cornwallis where Col. Phillip a member of the staff recognized Martin as a fellow countryman he had "known and respected in Ireland."

He was released, it appears, on condition that he would not return to Chester County or else, because of extreme Tory activity in Chester County, it was felt that it was unwise for him to return there. He went to Mecklenburg County, North Carolina.

After the surrender at Yorktown, Reverend Martin returned to Chester County. His log church had burned down, so he took charge of the congregation at Catholic.

When, in 1782, the Convenanter ministers Cuthberton, Debbin and Linn of Pennsylvania pulled away to form the Associate Reformed Presbyterian Church, he refused to go into it with them. That left him the only Covenanter minister in America "who professed to teach the whole doctrine of the Reformation, and who kept alive the Covenanter Church in America."

Whether this difference of opinion on doctrine had anything to do with it is not known, but in 1765 he was dismissed by Catholic congregation for intemperance. As one writer phrased it, "He was somewhat less temperate than became him in the use of strong drink." Others insisted that during cold weather everyone was offered whiskey on arrival at a house, and he took no more than anyone else. The argument raged for many years after his death.

Rev. Martin did not cease preaching and apparently his services were in great demand. During the next few years he preached at school houses, from Edward McDaniel's down to Jackson Creek, at Richard Gladney's in Fairfield, across the Catawba at William Hicklen's "who had moved from Rocky Creek to Lancaster County." He also supplied the Society at Long Cane in Abbeville County. His preaching during that dreary period did much to keep alive the Covenanting cause.

Later his congregation in the Rocky Creek area built him another church, east of the one burnt down, on the Rocky Mount Road on a beautiful hill in a grove of trees. There he preached until his death.

Rev. Martin continued to have problems. Since he was of the "Gentry" class and had been a leader in his area and his church, he did not accept advice from younger men representing the Reformed Presbyterian Church of Scotland. They were preparing charges against him that he had been intoxicated three times, had sold a negro, and had not properly administered a matter of church discipline. He and his congregation ignored the charges and all attacks on him and he continued to preach to his own congregation and to administer baptism until his death.

About 1804 the stone house he had built in 1774 burned down. He then built a log cabin nearby in which he lived the rest of his life.

In 1806 he was injured by a fall from his horse, resulting in a fever, from which he died 25 October 1806. He was buried in a small graveyard near his cabin. He is described as "a large, fine looking man, a proficient scholar, an eloquent speaker, and an able divine."

A deed dated October 10, 1840 of Bethany Church in Chester County indicates another segment of Presbyterians were worshipping together. The deed states that the property is for use of all denominations "with the exception of the denomination of Christians called the Independent Presbyterians to have EXCLUSIVE use of said church the first Sabbath in each and every month."

Settlers from Maryland and settlers moving from Union, South Carolina district, soon came into Chesterville District bringing the Baptist faith. A church was organized in 1789 under William Woodward, and the church meeting house was built on the Eli Cornwell property.

The Methodists, organized under the evangelistic fervor of John Wesley, were particularly suited to society in the back country. They were outstandingly successful in the woods, the swamps, the pine barrens and in small and dispersed settlements. Their itinerant preachers ministered to those who could ill-afford to support an assigned clergyman. They were effective in civilizing and evangelizing remote and destitute settlements.

Indian threats had the effect of bringing all nationalities and creeds together for mutual support and protection.

Chester district gradually began to lose its primitive look and to acquire resemblance to an organized court center. The settlers' extreme individualism and the essential need for preservation of national class, ideals, dialects and religion were their trademarks. The necessity of sharing and helping each other melded them into a cohesive community.

The Scotch-Irish settlers are characterized as "undisciplined, aggressive, pugnacious, fiercely intolerant, highly emotional, hard-driving and hard-drinking." As such, they were in contrast to the few Germans and Swiss who settled in Chester County, put down deep roots and set about to cultivate, harvest and build to help each other.

Not all the settlers were restless, unrefined, atheistic or hard-drinking. Men of education and culture advanced to Chester County and spread their knowledge and gentility over the district. They participated in politics, attended to their lands, supported their churches and actively influenced the community.

OLDER CHURCHES IN CHESTER COUNTY

Early settlers in Chester District were assidious in building "meeting houses" for religious worship and set this priority ahead of building homes for themselves. Earliest churches along Fishing Creek and Rocky Creek date back to 1752.

These plain temples of God, often started in crude brush arbors, were the gathering places to share the "old time religion." Services were held nearly all the Sabbath day, or week days whenever a minister was able to come to them. Cemeteries were adjacent to the churches as were the little primitive one-room school houses.

Among early churches were:

1. Armenia United Methodist Church on S. C. Hwy. 29 was organized in 1832, and its first building erected in 1843. The present structure was built in 1930. The church got its name from the Armenia section, one of the earliest settlements in the county.

2. Associate Reformed Presbyterian Church, Main Street, Chester was built in 1897 on land purchased by Joe Wylie for $2,000 and given to the church.

3. Bethel United Methodist Church at Saluda and York Streets in Chester was built in 1898 on a granite base. Its stained glass windows are unusually beautiful.

4. Bethlehem Baptist Church on S. C. Hwy. 42 in Baton Rouge grew out of Calvary Church. It is quite old; the date of construction is not known. As was the case with many older churches, members first assembled in a brush arbor for worship.

5. Bethlehem Methodist Church, Blackstock, owes its beginnings to a family named Stockdale who came to America in 1795. They had belonged to a Methodist Society in Ireland and formed one in their new home. Services were held once a month in their home and were conducted by circuit riders. In those early days when travel and roads were uncertain, circuit riders served in pairs. Records show that the first pair served in 1808. In 1824, a camp meeting was held on the site.

6. Black Rock Baptist Church on S. C. Hwy. 56. Some of the blacks who had been baptized at a white church, Smyrna Baptist, started a movement about 1853 for a church of their own. They were led by a slave, Leroy Featherstone, who became their minister, served for 67 years, and baptized more than 4,000 people.

7. Brushy Fork Baptist Church and Cemetery, State Hwy. 49. Dates from 1822. The graveyard contains the graves of early families and Confedereate soldiers, Obadiah Hardin, R. C. Montgomery and E. T. Wade.

8. Calvary Baptist Church, S. C. Hwy. 25, Baton Rouge Community. First church was a tent about a mile from the present church on Brushy Fork Creek. Second church was a wooden building called Sanders Meeting House. It was a crude structure used for both a meeting house and a school. Present church was built in 1859.

9. Capers Chapel, on U.S. Hwy. 321, north of Chester. Originally Smith Chapel, moved to present site in 1855. Wooden building was replaced by brick structure in 1881. Bricks were made by hand from clay dug from the valley behind the church.

10. Carmel United Presbyterian Church on Walnut St. in

Chester. Organized in 1869 by New York Presbyterian Home Mission Board as a part of Brainerd Institute for blacks.

11. Catholic Presbyterian Church (the name Catholic being used to signify broad and liberal). 1 mile off Hwy. 97 between Chester and Great Falls. Has held congregational meetings since 1758, said to be second church organized in county. (First was Richardson Church.) Revolutionary soldiers are buried in an adjacent rock walled cemetery.

12. Ebenezer United Methodist Church, off Hwy. 97 west of Great Falls. The first church was a log building erected in 1845 and used until the present one was built in 1892.

13. First Baptist Church, College Street, Chester. Major John Kennedy, in 1836, gave the Baptists a lot which he stipulated to be "used forever as a place of worship." The wooden church had a weathervane with the Christian symbol of a fish. It had a gallery for slaves and a baptismal on the "beautiful clear stream" of Tanyard Branch.

FISHING CREEK CHURCH
1752

14. Fishing Creek Presbyterian Church. This church pre-dates the Revolutionary War. Organized in 1752 it was built on land donated by George Kelso who held a land grant dated May 7, 1774. People who lived around this church suffered much during the conflicts between the British and the Tories.

15. Gethsemane Baptist Church. This church on Old York Road is on the site of the brush arbor where Chester County's first black congregation worshipped. It was founded in 1852 on a lot donated by Mrs. Annie Tims. Present church was built in 1908.

16. Harmony Baptist Church in Northeastern Chester County was organized in 1839 in an old building known as Republican Church. Present church was built in 1911.

17. Hopewell Associate Reformed Presbyterian Church on S. C. Hwy. 44, organized in 1787, was originally a log house and is one of the oldest A.R.P. churches in the South. At least two Revolu-

tionary War soldiers, Robert Kilpatrick and Edward McDaniel are buried in the church cemetery.

18. Mount Prospect Methodist Church on S. C. Hwy. 901 was built in 1851 after the original log building burned. For more than fifty years, Mount Prospect was best known for its camp meeting grounds.

19. New Hope Methodist Church on S. C. Hwy. 9 West of Chester records one of the earliest groups of Methodism in the area: "Bishop Francis Asbury preached at New Hope in 1794." Services were held here only occasionally by circuit riders. A brush arbor was followed by a log house, then a wooden building in 1861.

20. Pleasant Grove Methodist Church on S. C. Hwy. 46 was organized in 1848 and met for several years in school houses. In 1855, Mrs. Jane Hemphill deeded three acres and the church was built with slave galleries on each side.

21. Pleasant Grove Presbyterian Church dates back to 1831 when a part of Catholic Presbyterian Church pulled away and began worshipping at the "Brick Church" which became known as "Upper Catholic." This was on the present tract of land owned by Pleasant Grove. In 1847, Upper Catholic became a church and the name became Pleasant Grove.

PURITY PRESBYTERIAN CHURCH

22. Purity Presbyterian Church on Wylie Street in Chester was established in 1787 on the present site of Old Purity cemetery. In 1839, members built a Lecture Room on West End and used it until 1854 when it was sold to St. Joseph Catholic Church. The present building on Wylie Street was dedicated in 1855.

23. St. Joseph's Catholic Church, built in 1839 as Presbyterian Lecture Room, and purchased from Purity Presbyterian Church in 1854, is the oldest church in Chester.

ST. MARKS EPISCOPAL CHURCH
1878

24. St. Mark's Episcopal Church on Center Street was built in 1879 by ARPs. Of Gothic design, it was designed by celebrated Philadelphia architect, Samuel Sloan.

25. Union ARP Church was founded at Richburg in 1795 by Presbyterian Covenanters who had been worshipping at Rocky Creek Meeting House since 1775. The first church was built of logs. In 1848, members erected a new building behind the cemetery, and in 1913 it was moved to its present location.

26. Woodward Baptist Church on S. C. Hwy. 16 south of Chester was built in 1830. This church gave unexpected sanctuary in April, 1865 to Mrs. Jefferson Davis, her children and attendants on their flight from Richmond. Heavy rains made stagecoach travel difficult and the party chose to spend the night in the church. Organized in 1789, the first church building was a log cabin on Fish Dam Road (West End).

27. Zion Presbyterian Church at Lowrys had its beginnings when land was donated by Major James G. Lowry in 1850. In 1890, the congregation decided to move the church from its original location on S. C. Hwy. 78 to the present location in Lowrys.

Other old churches of record are Pisgah, Hebron (below Catholic), Uriel, Beaver Creek Baptist (on Ashford Ferry Road), Cool Branch Baptist (Hwy. 215), Liberty Baptist, Ebenezer Methodist, New Bethel, Heath Chapel Methodist near Great Falls, Cedar Shoals Presbyterian (near Bascomville), and E. Bethel Methodist (Hwy. 21 near Fort Lawn).

CAMP MEETINGS

Camp meetings played a big part in the South in the early 1800's when the so-called Great Revival or Second Great Awakening swept across the Southern frontier. Some were held in and around Chester

County; one of them was at Bonnett Rock in Armenia Community. Baptists, Presbyterians and Methodists reportedly participated. From 1810-1870 Bonnett Rock was a camp meeting ground.

Meetings were held in late summer after crops were laid by. The weather was warm and dry enough for "camping" out.

Some wags described camp meetings as:

All day meeting
With dinner on the ground
Devil in the bushes
And whiskey all around.

These lines were probably penned by hecklers and carousers who, attracted by the crowds, came to scoff and disrupt, and perhaps get a free meal. Some set up whiskey kegs in the nearby woods and retailed whiskey by cupsful.

Besides the ministers, who preached from Friday to Tuesday all day and much of the night, there were numerous trial ministers who visited the tents and counseled and prayed with individuals.

There was shouting, speaking in tongues, jerking, and falling into trances during the highly emotional services.

Other camp meeting sites were in the county. For more than fifty years, Mount Prospect Methodist Church on S. C. Highway 901 was best known as a campground. In July and August, people gathered in a large arbor to preach, pray and sing. Both the arbor and the church were also used as a school.

In 1824, a camp meeting was held on the site of the present Bethlehem Methodist Church at Blackstock.

The Bonnett Rock Campground arbor is vividly recalled in a history of the Grant family written by Mrs. A. N. ("Miss Marie") Grant in 1935.

The lives of these people were so closely associated with the church that history cannot be recorded one without the other. The first record of a church or a preacher in Armenia community was in 1832 when the Chester circuit extended from near Columbia to four miles northwest of Chester. The preacher was the Rev. J. H. Robinson, a circuit rider and a Methodist. Preaching was held whenever the circuit rider came, regardless of the day of the week. In 1859, the circuit was divided and east Chester included New Hope, Armenia and Capers Chapel Churches.

The preacher at Armenia was the the Rev. John Watts. Sometime during the existence of this church, the Bonnett Rock Camp Ground arbor was built. According to Mrs. Grant, there were thirty acres in the grounds. The arbor was good size. There were two aisles crossing in the center, and the seats were made of slabs. Behind the pulpit there were seats for the colored people. Fresh wheat straw was spread across the altar. The arbor was lighted by candles. One large chandelier holding about fifteen candles was suspended from the center of the roof.

The grounds around the arbor were lighted by pine knots. Four stobs were driven in the ground, a plank laid on them and then shovels of dirt. On this the lighted knots were placed.

Each family had a rude cabin or tent. The whole family would "pack up" and come in wagons and stay a week while the meeting was going on. Some member of the family would go home each day to tend to the livestock.

Not only the families from the immediate neighborhood, but people from miles away attended the meeting.

Mrs. Grant described the religious fervor of these "all-day and half the night" meetings: "Oh! What glorious services were held there in 'lay-by' time. At night the children were put to bed and the others went to services. The grand old hymns and fervent prayers of those devout worshippers have never been forgotten."

The arbor was torn down sometime between 1875-80, shortly after Armenia's second church was built.

Camp meetings had long been a powerful agency in the evangelization of Methodists. They were held in conveniently located groves where rude benches and a shelter of rough boards were erected. A group of "tents," really wooden shacks, where provided for the overnight shelter of those who attended the week or ten days session.

These "feasts of the Tabernacle" were adaptations to local demands of what supposedly had been the custom of ancient Jews. They provided convenient opportunity for extended fellowship to a people who normally lived in rural isolation. Organized religion had a greater influence on the outlook and daily lives of our ancestors 100 and 200 years ago.

CAMP WELFARE

Camp Welfare near Great Falls is owned by the African Methodist Episcopal church. The organization, an outgrowth from "brush arbor" camp meetings in the time of Bishop Francis Asbury's fervid preaching (1785-1815), was set up shortly after 1865 when Negroes withdrew from white churches. They had previously attended white camp meetings, of which Indian Fields near St. George is the only South Carolina survival.

Camp meeting is still the highlight of the year for folks who grew up in the Mitford Community between Great Falls and Winnsboro. All during the week before the fourth Sunday in August each year they come from all parts of the United States to the Camp grounds.

Beginning with the first arrivals about 7:00 a.m. Monday, the crowds grow and grow until about 2,000 persons are on the grounds by Saturday night. They come and bring all the family from grandma to the baby, plus enough water and food to last during the week.

About 200 rustic one-room wooden cabins or "tents" make up the camp, and most of them are in use. They are scattered over the eleven and one-half acres of wooded, hilly land that was deeded to the Camp's trustees more than 100 years ago. The cabins belong to families who pass ownership along from one generation to the other. Each family repairs, furnishes and maintains its cabin. New cabins are built each year. Others are patched up and used.

Camp meeting can be described as one of the oldest and hardiest traditions of the South and is, at the same time, a series of religious services, family reunions, community picnics and homecomings.

Camp Welfare, according to the best resources available, was started during the Civil War, when Negroes in the area met in the woods to pray. Brush arbors provided a place to worship and a place to sleep, as well as a place to hide from the dreaded Northern soldiers.

One of the founders of Camp Welfare was Mary Mitchell whose husband, Jerry Mitchell, was fighting with General Robert E. Lee's Army at the time of his surrender at Appomattox. Mary's granddaughter, Mrs. R. M. Graham of Salisbury, North Carolina, recalls her grandmother's stories of the war, the camp, and the Negroes' "prayers for freedom and peace."

The camp grounds are part of a large tract of land known as the McMaster place in Fairfield County. It is located on a secondary, hardtopped road about twenty miles from Winnsboro. In the early days of the camp only a crude, unpaved road led to the camp, and campers came in farm wagons. Because of the lack of refrigeration or ice, live chickens were brought in coops strapped to the wagon bed. The chickens and sometimes a pig or a beef cow, were butchered, dressed and cooked after arrival on the grounds. The cooking fires were built in the open, and the pots rested on rocks around the brush fire. Light was provided at night by a flambeau tied to a tree. Water was "toted" from the spring in a wooden bucket.

The best foods the family had were saved for camp meeting. All during the summer youngsters were instructed to "catch that fryer and let's fatten him up for camp meeting." Country hams and other delicacies were saved for the big week.

The practice continues, but food preparation is much easier now. Many cabins have refrigerators and all have stoves. The foods prepared and consumed during the week are an Epicurean delight, and the feasting goes on and on.

Preaching services are held in the open "arbor" three times a day at 12 noon, 3:30 p.m. and 8:00 p.m. The interdenominational services are led alternately by eight to ten visiting preachers. Singing and shouting with religious fervor reverberates over the hills. The collection plate is passed to pay the preachers. The sawdust trail is there for penitent sinners to traverse, if the spirit moves them.

Visiting goes on day and night. Children run, play, climb and eat ice cream cones from the small store that operates for one week only. Teenagers gather in a cabin where transistor radios bridge the gap between the old order and the new. A jet plane streaking overhead emphasizes the great difference between the two.

A lonely cemetery, gradually being engulfed by the surrounding forest, lies behind the camp ground. Grave stones date back to the early 1800s.

A church sat in the compound and was used for services until it burned about twenty-five years ago, and was replaced by the open shelter or "arbor."

Older people recall a time when a few disorders were caused by visitors who imbibed too freely from the bottles they brought along. The offenders were handcuffed and chained to a tree until a car load was ready to be transported to the Winnsboro jail.

Bethel United Methodist Church in Background,
at End of Main Street, Chester

XIV *BROAD RIVER AREA*

WOODS FERRY

Wood's Ferry that provided crossing of Broad River from Chester County to Union County in antebellum days got its name from Colonel Richard Woods, a member of the Secession Convention from Chester County. His handsome brick home, whose crumbling walls were still standing when the Woods Ferry Recreation Area was started in 1965, was one of many elegant antebellum plantation homes built up and down the river.

Col. Wood's father, Matthew Woods, came to the Broad River area and settled on a large land grant about 1800. A map of Chester District contained in Mill's Atlas of 1825 does not list Wood's Ferry. This substantiates the belief that his son, Col. Richard Woods, later gave the ferry its name. The survey was made in 1818 by Charles Boyd, D.S.

The area along the river, originally Indian territory, was settled after the Revolutionary War. Among earliest families who migrated and settled down, most of them on land grants, were the McCool, Moore, Johnson, Wm. Hill, Stevens, Mitchell, Triplett, Shaw, Hughes, Cranford, Morris, Worthy, Love, Chalk, Wilkes and Pendergrass families. Their descendants still live in Chester County. Thompson Worthy was the first white settler.

Many places of unique interest lay along the river in Chester County. From north to south, as listed in Mill's Atlas, they are: Lockhart's Canal built around a 47 foot fall in the river over 1¾ miles; Love's Ford and one of the largest known Indian mounds; McCool's Ferry, later called Worthy's Ferry; Major Hill's Distillery near the present park site; Lyles Ferry that was in use as late as 1845, and located near Neal's Shoals and Bennett's Bottoms; the home of the Rev. William Hughes; the point where Terrible Creek runs into the river; Moman's Ferry later known as Fishdam Ferry; and Fishdam Ford, site of the major battle led by Gen. Thomas Sumter in the Revolutionary War.

Family cemeteries dot the area along the river. Among them are those of the Woods, Shaw, Chalk, Triplett, Cahill, Cranford, and Moore families. Hopkins family cemetery that once contained many marble markers now has only one. Three Indian cemeteries are known to be in the area. Two family burial grounds near Bennett's Bottoms have no markers and those interred there are unknown to the present generation.

Dr. Sam McConnell years ago dug into the Indian mound by the river, and reportedly found a wealth of Indian artifacts. John Bramlett, who knows the area well, believes there are others in the area.

"Sally Johnson Hill" in the area was named for a woman who lived there for 40 years after the death of her husband.

Chalkville in west Chester and named for the Chalk family once had a thriving school and post office.

Early settlers on the Broad River gained their wealth by cotton farming with slave labor.

Cotton was loaded on flat boats and poled down the river to Columbia where it was sold. Boats on the return trip brought sugar, coffee, whiskey and other supplies for the family and slaves on the plantation.

William Worthy, his son Martin, and grandson, Henry were listed as among the eight largest slave owners in the county. When Henry Worthy died he left a safe full of gold to his heirs. Worthy's plantation site consisting of more than 2000 acres is now a part of Sumter National Forest in Chester County.

Woods Ferry Recreation Area

Wood's Ferry Recreational Area, 14 miles west of Chester, beside the Broad River in Chester County was dedicated Sunday afternoon, May 16, 1965. This area, once the center of the county's wealth, culture and cotton farming, lay dormant after the Civil War spelled doom to the cotton kingdom, and river transportation was replaced by railroads.

Grant of a quarter of a million dollars under the federal Area Development Administration was made in 1963 to pump new life into the depressed area. Work was started in October 1963 to develop 35 acres along the river. Forest Service of U. S. Department of Agriculture supervised construction and maintains the area.

A winding road was built leading to the park. The rugged, hilly, wooded terrain made the park and road construction a major engineering project. Park facilities include 28 camping spurs, two group camping areas, 87 picnic tables with shelters, 58 barbecue pits, a manmade harbor, boat dock and boat launching facilities. Water fountains, rest rooms with showers, paved walkways and parking areas are completed. Park benches along the river and in the deep shade of giant trees are plentiful and inviting.

WEST CHESTER GOLD STRIKE

The Broad River area of Chester County made national headlines in 1937 in an incident that read like an Arabian Nights tale.

Tradition, based on some known facts, was that a large land owner and blacksmith, Littleton Land, amassed a fortune and converted it into gold coins. When Sherman and his Union army headed toward Chester, it was rumored he brought three buckets of gold coins and buried them on his Broad River plantation. A servant, Zed Land, who cared for his master for many years reportedly told of helping to bury the money under the anvil block of the blacksmith shop.

Littleton Land, whose son was killed in the Civil War and whose daughter died young and unmarried, himself died of cancer around 1885, leaving no heirs. He deeded a portion of land to his faithful servant, Zed. The three buckets of gold over a period of years became no more than a tradition and a good topic of conversation and speculation.

On Easter Sunday, 1937, Tobin Crank, a young Negro truck driver and descendant of Zed Land, was chopping wood in the front yard of his home on the former Land farm. His axe went into the ground and struck a pile of gold coins in a rotting bucket.

Tobin Crank, 24, had struck it rich. A count of the money made by Mrs. Hattie Y. Harden, Probate Judge of Chester County, revealed there was $6,900 worth of gold coins, most of them in $20 gold pieces. Crank's wild excitement spread to his family and over the entire surrounding area, and the curious beat a path to his door. Rumor goes there was considerable digging in those parts, also. The remaining two buckets of gold have not yet been found.

XV *LANDSFORD CANAL*

WATER TRANSPORTATION ROUTE

Landsford is a quiet and remote corner of Chester County that bears a lingering aura of great historical events. The muted roar and ripple of the rushing Catawba River brings to mind the Indian crossing nearby, and the Red Men who hunted and fished along its banks in the long ago.

Nothing visible is left to remind one of the Revolutionary War skirmishes in the area led by the Fighting Gamecock, General Thomas Sumter, or William R. Davie, or of the retreat of General Cornwallis across the Catawba.

Fragments of stone masonry remain to attract tourists to the Landsford Canal site of one of the State's most ambitious engineering projects, started in 1817 by the great architect and engineer, Robert Mills.

History was made at Landsford. The Chester County Historical Society, South Carolina Parks, Recreation and Tourism Department, and interested individuals have made sure that present day citizens and their posterity are aware of it.

Visitors in increasing numbers are coming to Landsford. Fishermen have always beat paths to the water's edge where they found an abundance of fish. Wildlife is luxuriant and natural. Legendary tales affirm that the area once had more snakes "than you could shake a stick at."

Small cemeteries, most of them family graveyards, are slowly being engulfed by the forest. A black topped road winds through the isolated area and to the recently developed picnic area.

LANDSFORD CANAL
1823

Building of Canal

Landsford Canal was built on a large tract of land granted in 1754 by the King of England to Thomas Land, who gave the site its name. The area is owned by Duke Power Company, but is leased to the South Carolina Parks, Recreation and Tourism Department.

The site was at first a crossing for the Indians. There was a big stone near the crossing, and if it was not covered with water, the Indians knew it was safe to cross. This stone was called the "Sign Stone."

During the Revolutionary War, General Sumter and his Patriot Army camped nearby. A great deal of fighting and skirmishing took place around the crossing, at that time called Land's Ford. It was the mustering ground for the forces of Sumter and Davie when they were getting ready for the attack on Hanging Rock.

General Cornwallis crossed the river at Land's Ford on his retreat from Charlotte to Winnsboro after the defeat of the British under the command of Patrick Ferguson at the Battle of King's Mountain.

In 1795, Thomas Sumter realizing the value of water transportation to the landowners and farmers, applied for a charter to build a canal at Land's Ford. He did not pursue the project because he became interested in South Carolina politics.

In 1817, the South Carolina Legislature passed an Act to establish the office of Civil and Military Engineer for the State. Robert Mills, a famous architect and engineer, was appointed to this office. In 1818, one million dollars was appropriated for internal improvement in the State. This money was to be spent at the rate of $250,000 a year for four years. The official appropriation for Landsford Canal construction in 1822 was more than the entire appropriation for the free schools that year in South Carolina.

The Landsford Canal was a part of this general plan for internal improvement planned for South Carolina. Great men in the state and nation who took part in designing and building the canal were: Joel Poinsett, William R. Davie, Abram Blanding, State Senator Billy Hill from York County, and others.

Mills, at this time, was just beginning to develop his genius for architectural design that made him famous. He later designed the Washington Monument, Treasury Building and Post Office Building in Washington, D. C. William R. Davie, former Governor of North Carolina and Father of the University of North Carolina, had retired to his plantation at Land's Ford where he occupied himself with farming and serving his native state in an advisory capacity.

It was the dream of Robert Mills to build canals and inland waterways to facilitate transportation in the area. In doing this the upcountry planters would be able to trade with the low country and seaport merchants.

In 1819, Joel Poinsett, president of a newly created Board of Public Works, asked and received from the Secretary of War, John C. Calhoun, permission to put one of the four canals through lands belonging to the United States government at Rocky Mount. This canal became one of four built to circumvent the sharp water fall between Land's Ford and Great Falls.

Poinsett wrote to Boston and Philadelphia for 100 workmen in stone, contracted for 20 tumbling carts, 12 scrapers, and four ploughs, and the canals were begun. John Shillinglaw was brought all the way from Scotland to supervise the construction.

There were four principal falls around which canals were to be dug and locks to be built. They were at Wateree Creek, Rocky Mount, Catawba Canal and Land's Ford. This inland waterway was planned to extend from Charleston to the North Carolina mountains. After a fifty mile trip by land to the Wautega, the system could connect with the Tennessee River and on to the Mississippi River.

The Land's Ford Canal, designed by Mills, combined the beautiful with the practical, showing his liking for stone masonry and the use of the arch. Construction was begun October 20, 1820, by Robert Leckie, contractor, working under Mills' direction. It was completed in 1823.

Typhoid fever took a heavy toll of the Scotch workmen brought over to do the skilled work.

Some of the Negroes employed also became sick and died of the fever. Several graves of workmen are in the Sturgis Cemetery not far away. The workers camped on the work site and had no netting for protection from mosquitoes. Typhoid and malaria fevers spread.

Thomas Leckie and his family had it. His wife, Mary, and son, John Bomford, died. Their graves are enclosed by a high granite wall in the Waxhaw Cemetery, and can be reached only by stones projecting from the walls.

Landsford Canal was completed and in use from 1823-1827. From official records, John Carter, the lock keeper, was paid $114.50 for his first half year, and $250.00 each of the following years for his services. The foundation of his house is still visible near the canal entrance.

William Richardson Davie gave the land on which the canal was built. It was from the channel of water of Davie's grist mill and sawmills that the river entered the canal. On August 12, 1823, Davie was paid $500.00 for damage done him in stopping his mills for nearly eight months while work on the canal was being done.

The canal was built of smooth granite blocks, many five feet long and two feet wide, cemented together. The walls are straight and smooth. The stones are laid with such exactness, that although it was completed over one hundred and fifty years ago, from the appearance of the splendid engineering and masonry, it could have been completed just a few years ago.

The Landsford Canal was 12 feet wide and 10 feet deep. It ran along a two mile stretch of the Catawba River, overcoming a fall of over thirty-two feet. There were five locks built in steps to raise and lower the shallow bottom boats or barges. Six storm culverts carried streams under the canal to the river.

There were two wooden bridges and one stone bridge over the canal. Still standing today are three of the lock chambers, each about fifty feet long, and the arched stone bridge.

Canal Traffic

Only large trees growing in the canal bed suggest the years that have passed since barges of cotton and other goods floated down the river to market.

Some smaller boats traveled down the canal with other products, but it was never used as much as was planned. There is only one known record of a cotton barge having used this canal and it was piloted by James Cloud Hicklin, a farmer and man of means who resided in the Fishing Creek District of Chester County. He had experience and knowledge as a boatsman, having been connected with the Fishing Creek and Rocky Creek canals.

The canal around the falls at Landsford has been preserved. Its giant granite blocks have weathered the passing of years and idleness. It is a joy to gaze at some of man's most beautiful works and know they will always live as a memorial to him and to early settlers.

Old records show that on March 23, 1832, a barge with 46 bales of cotton paid a toll of $2.76 to travel through the canal. The same barge returned upstream on April 2, 1832 carrying millstones on which $2.25 toll was collected.

A letter preserved by Mrs. Eli Springs, Yorkville, S. C. March 1832, tells the story:

Dear Leroy:

This will introduce to your acquaintance Mr. Benjamin Chambers, Jr. of this place who goes on a visit to your city (New York) for the purpose of purchasing goods ——

Twelve days ago Austin and myself took water at the old Nation's Ford with 46 bales of cotton and in five days landed it safe in Camden and sold it for 10 cents.

And the boat on its return is bringing two pair millstones for a mill William E. White and myself are now engaged in erecting at the Ford.

Affectionately, your father,

John Springs

Note: Nation's Ford is on the Catawba River near its crossing by U. S. Hwy. 21 (Rock Hill to Charlotte).

LANDSFORD CANAL GATEHOUSE

Landsford Park Development

In the summer of 1965, both State and National attention became focused on Landsford Canal. Dr. E. T. Crowson, professor of history at Winthrop College, researched and wrote a history of the canal he described as "a great landmark in South Carolina, and one of the most valuable historic properties in the nation."

Development of the canal into a recreational area was begun. A shot in the arm came in the form of financial aid from the 1965 Federal Land and Water Conservation Fund. The South Carolina

Wildlife Department was chosen by Governor Donald S. Russell to serve as liaison agency between the Federal Bureau of Outdoor Recreation and the state and local groups promoting the project.

Fred H. Hambright, representative of Chester County Historical Society and an enthusiastic proponent of the park development, said the Canal project was listed in 1965 by Charles Lee of the South Carolina Archives Department as sharing top priority in state projects along with the restoration of the British Star Fort at Ninety Six in Greenwood County.

In 1965, South Carolina's share of funds was $142,000.00. In 1966, over one million dollars became available on a matching fund basis. Funds were used to restore the two-mile canal area and its locks and bridges. The canal keeper's house was moved to the park and restored to be used as a museum. A hardsurfaced road leads to the site from U. S. Hwy. 21. Parking areas, restrooms, picnic tables and water fountains were constructed. The 100 acre site, with two miles on the river front, was leased from Duke Power Company.

It was placed on the National Register of Historic Places.

A two-room log cabin that dates back possibly to the 18th century was donated to Chester County Historical Society by Blair and Margaret Wise Knox before selling land the cabin was on to Boise Cascade Corporation. The Society gave the cabin to the Park.

Department workers of South Carolina Parks, Recreation and Tourism Department, led by historian Mike Foley, marked the cabins' pine logs in February 1978 and Chester County Stockade inmates took the logs apart. The cabin was rebuilt in a wooded area 150 feet from the river in August 1979. Two new chimneys, windows, a roof, floor and porch were added. The cabin was opened to the public in April 1982. It can be rented for family, church or company picnics.

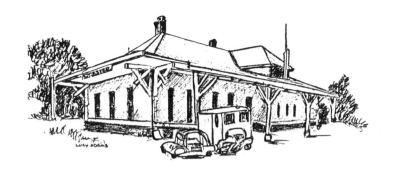

XVI *RAILROADS*

TRANSPORTATION BY RAIL

A correspondent signing himself "H", on November 22, 1821, in a letter to the Charleston City Gazette was in all probability the first to suggest a steam railroad in South Carolina. He stated:

"Having during an excursion Eastward, seen a speciman of the patent railway, I was led to believe that the plan would be useful in this State. . . . The season for discussing the great subject of Internal Improvement has arrived and this may add to the materials." H. "H" is believed to have been Robert Y. Hayne.

Under this communication was published the plan headed "The Patent Railway" which included a description of the combination iron and wood railway. This plan is so novel many persons think they see insurmountable difficulties, without understanding all the details, the writer said.

As Fulton was ridiculed for his attempt to apply steam to boats, he continued, those that pronounce that horses cannot walk on a plank must allow that steam can and has been used and considered as cheap as horses.

He gave an example. In South Carolina suppose a pair of railways were laid from Charleston to Augusta, and a fork run to Columbia — in all, 150 miles, cost $400,000; a load of cotton could be carried in five days, instead of thirty, by water. Two dollars per bale would be readily paid for carrying same, and proportionately for rice and tobacco, and $25 per ton for carrying goods up. There is sufficient transportation to make the work valuable, he concluded.

The suggestion of the Charleston-Columbia-Augusta steam railway was made five years before the three-mile road to Quincy, Massachusetts, operated by horse power was even commenced and within a dozen years Charleston mechanics were to design and build the first locomotive which ever turned a wheel in America.

On January 30, 1828, the S. C. Legislature granted a charter to begin a survey of the proposed railway and means of raising money for building it. The advantages of Charleston as a future emporium of trade and commerce for the southern and western United States were pointed out. By increasing its transportation system through a railroad the vast hinterland and the seacoast would be brought within a few hours of each other, a brilliant prospect that should be hastened.

The South Carolina Canal and Railroad Company was organized in May, 1828. On the 28th of December, 1829, contracts were let for the construction of the railroad, and on the 9th of January, 1830, the enterprise was actually put under way by the driving of piles for the roadbed at Lines Street near Charleston. In October, 1833, the entire line from Charleston to Hamburg, 136 miles, was completed and opened to the public.

E. L. Miller, one of the directors of the company, undertook, at his private risk, to provide a locomotive that should draw three times her own weight at a speed of ten miles an hour, and the contract was accepted by the Board of Directors on the 1st of March, 1830. The locomotive was built in New York under Mr. Miller's direction, and was the first constructed in the United States for actual service on a railroad. It weighed four tons, had four wheels made with spokes, was called the "Best Friend," and arrived in Charleston on the 23rd of October, 1830.

In December, trial trips were made. Upon these occasions the "Best Friend" accomplished from sixteen to twenty-five miles an hour, drawing four or five cars with forty or fifty passengers. Without the cars, the locomotive made thirty-five miles an hour, to the amazement of all spectators.

In 1831, the entire line from Charleston to Hamburg was placed under contract. In November, 1832, the road was opened to Branchville, 62 miles; in February, 1833, to Midway, 92 miles, and in the following October, the entire 136 miles to Hamburg. In February, 1832, the first United States mail ever carried on a railroad was transported over the 12 miles then in operation.

EARLY CHESTER RAILROADS

The first train on the Charlotte and Columbia railroad arrived in Chester in August 1851. Construction was started in 1840 and extended to Augusta, Georgia in 1852. The station of this, Chester's first railroad, was at the intersection of Lancaster and Walnut Streets where Southern Railroad Station is now.

Great preparations were made for the coming of this first train. In the woods near the depot a grand barbecue was prepared for the crowd that began assembling the night before. It was estimated that about eight thousand people flocked in to see the wonder and enjoy the feast and fellowship. Most of the people had never seen a moving railroad engine and train of cars.

About 11 a.m. the shrill whistle of the engine announced the approach of the train, and it soon came in sight, bearing banners and evergreens and a number of people from Columbia and Winnsboro. It is reported that "the enthusiasm of the people and the consequent confusion beggars description." It was with difficulty the steam

powered engine plowed its way through the human mass to the depot.

The president of the railroad company, the Hon. Edward G. Palmer, then addressed the crowd from the platform of the car amidst vociferous applause. All then repaired to the grove and feasted on barbecue. The table was erected on three sides of a square, and in measurement was of great length.

Such an assemblage of people at a feast had never been seen in Chester, and probably never in the state. Thousands inspected the engine and cars with great curiosity and admiration, but none seemed more amazed than Obadiah Farrow. He prided himself upon his skill as a blacksmith and believed that no man could excel him as a worker in iron and brass. After a close inspection of the engine he proclaimed it the greatest wonder of the world, and now that he had seen it, announced his readiness to die.

The trains left Columbia in the morning and stopped at Cornwell for dinner. This had also been the stopping place for stagecoaches. The house was owned by Elijah Cornwell whose father, Eli Cornwell, came to South Carolina from Dinwiddie County, Virginia.

The train stopped ten minutes at small stations and twenty minutes at the large ones. The first conductor was Mr. Fowler and the engineer was Mr. Davis. No tickets were sold, the conductor collected cash payments at the rate of five cents a mile. This subsequently became the Southern Railway Company.

By way of this Railroad, Mrs. Jefferson Davis and her children arrived in Chester at daylight on August 15, 1865. After a brief pause in the city, they were forced to flee by wagon to escape capture by the Yankees.

Southern refugees, including Mrs. Mary Boykin Chestnut, author of *A Diary From Dixie,* and many high ranking Confederate officers found the Chester depot the last rail stop. Consequently, in the spring of 1865, the town became the hub for Southern soldiers and partisans.

In April, 1865, the Constitution of the Confederacy was rescued at the Chester Depot by a visiting newspaper reporter, Felix Gregory De Fontaine. Hearing that important papers of the Confederacy were at the railway station in Chester and that Union soldiers were marching toward the town, DeFontaine found and rescued from an uncontrollable mob such records as the Constitution, Patent Office records, and papers from the Attorney General's office.

The Confederate Constitution has remained in a vault at the University of Georgia since the 1930s.

Chester's other railroad of the fifties was the Kings Mountain Railroad, now Carolina and North Western. W. T. Vandiver of Indiana was the first engineer to run this road. The first agent was John T. Walker.

Along with the trains came the telegraph. The first telegraph line to Chester was erected in 1850. C. H. Brennecke was the first operator. The office was in the freight depot of the Charlotte and Columbia railroad.

Trains did not run on telegraphic orders but by certain rules. If a train did not come on time, the one at the station waited twenty minutes and then allowed five minutes for difference in time. It then had the right of way until the other train was met. Freight trains had to observe the same rules.

The trains were woodburners and speed was slow. Freight trains had no conductors. The engineers had all the responsibility. The business of the road was heavy in Chester because all the freight from Union and York had to be shipped from Chester.

In the later years of the Civil War, Sherman demolished the railroads of South Carolina as thoroughly as those of Georgia. When he quitted the state its steam communications had been utterly disrupted. He had nearly erased the South Carolina road from the map. The old main line was gone between the Edisto and Windsor; its Columbia branch was little more than a smoking scar through the woods.

Terminal facilities in Columbia had suffered the same fate as those in Atlanta. Above the capital the tracks were gone from the Spartanburg & Union, from Alston to its crossing of the Broad River. Northern wrecking parties had obliterated the Charlotte & South Carolina as far as Blackstock's depot. The Cheraw & Darlington was broken up in a score of places.

All told, the state lost, at the hands of Sherman, nearly two hundred line miles of railroad.

LANCASTER AND CHESTER RAILROAD

In 1873, a Special Act of the South Carolina General Assembly granted a charter to the Cheraw and Chester Railroad Company, and provided:

"That the said company is hereby authorized to construct a railroad from Cheraw in Chesterfield County to Chesterville, in Chester County, by such route as shall be found most suitable and advantageous."

The corporators named in the act were F. A. Kehew, W. A. Greenleaf, C. B. Stuart, Henry McIver, H. Craig, S. Jackson, J. S. Miller, W. A. Evans, John Erwin, W. A. Moore, Williams Stevens, C. A. Plyler, J. R. Welsh, George W. Melton, A. H. Davega, T. H. Moffatt, William B. McMillin, and John Lilley.

The railroad was a development of the early efforts of the great coastal cities of the Atlantic to reach the Ohio and Mississippi valleys, and bring to their docks the produce of the Middle West, which was being floated down the Mississippi to New Orleans, and thence to the world.

Philadelphia, Baltimore, Norfolk, Wilmington, Charleston and Savannah all lavished their capital upon efforts to cross the mountains by rail and tap the wealth of the Mid West. In this effort, Charleston was the earliest and most successful pioneer.

Robert Mills who designed the Washington Monument, the Lancaster Court House and the Lancaster County Jail, was an engineer of the Charleston Canal and Railroad Company. He had previously advocated the use of canals, and had designed and erected locks extending the inland waterway from Charleston via the Cooper to the Santee, and made navigation possible up the

Congaree, Wateree and Catawba to York County by building five masonry locks at Landsford near Fort Lawn.

From here he proposed to continue up the Catawba to the mountains and with a canal and a tunnel reach the Swannanoa, the French Broad, and eventually the Tennessee and Mississippi. This plan was abandoned in favor of a railroad to connect Charleston with the Savannah River which was completed in 1832 and was then the longest railroad in the world.

By 1848, the Charleston capitalists had built railroads to Augusta, Columbia and Camden. The Charleston, Cincinnati and Chicago was chartered in 1853 to run from Camden to Lancaster, to York to Marion and north westward. However, it was not built until 1887, and then only by use of public funds. Lancaster County, as late as 1948, was still paying interest on some of these bonds. Other railroads were built in the South. Sherman's March to the Sea ended the service of these for years.

However, after the original lines were rebuilt, a fever of construction began in the Piedmont to tie in with the flow of traffic and direct modern transportation by their doors.

The Cheraw and Chester was designed to take the produce of the mountain valleys and Middle Western plains to Cheraw where it would be floated down the Pee Dee River to Georgetown Harbor. It connected at Chester with the Kings Mountain Railroad to Yorkville, then with the projected Chesterville and Lenoir Narrow Gauge Railway through Dallas, Lincolnton, Newton, and Hickory to Lenoir, and thence on across the Blue Ridge to Cincinnati and Chicago.

The Yorkville Inquirer of August 10, 1873, printed a half page account of a mass meeting held in York Court House in behalf of the Chesterville and Lenoir Railroad. Judge T. J. Mackey was the principal speaker, and the Inquirer said of his talk: "Judge Mackey pictured a plethora of staple products in the mountains that were virtually without value because there was no way of getting them to market, and said that the building of the railroad would reduce the cost of flour, corn, potatoes, and the like down at this end of the line."

The railroads were built in sections under different contractors, and very often a contractor or a company gave out of money before the entire line was tied together. In the case of the Cheraw and Chester, rail was laid in 1879 from Chester to the Catawba River, but money was lacking for a bridge, and from Cheraw to Pageland, before the capital was exhausted.

For three years it was operated in three sections and then it was split. The Chester section was leased to the Charlotte, Columbia and Augusta in 1882, and it built a wooden bridge and completed the line one mile beyond Lancaster in 1883. The Charlotte, Columbia and Augusta was released to the Richmond and Danville, which in turn went into receivership in 1893, and emerged as the Southern Railway in 1897.

The road from Cheraw to Pageland became the Chesterfield and Lancaster, but was never extended further.

Meanwhile a flood on the Pee Dee filled the channel with sandbars, and it was no longer navigable by steamboats.

The receivers for the Richmond and Danville operated the road from Lancaster to Lenoir as one line, but failed to pay expenses, and turned the Cheraw and Chester back to the stockholders in 1894. In 1896, the Cheraw and Chester was sold by Court Order at an advertised sale to satisfy its debts.

Colonel Leroy Springs of Lancaster purchased the road at auction for $25,000.00, renamed it the Lancaster and Chester Railway Company, and organized a company to operate it. The incorporators of the new company were Leroy Springs, William Ganson, R. C. McManus, W. T. Gregory, L. C. Payseur and James M. Heath, all of Lancaster, and W. H. Hardin of Chester. The capital stock of the company was $50,000.00.

At a meeting of the Board on June 22, 1896, W. H. Hardin was elected manager and auditor of the road. He was also manager of the Chesterville and Lenoir. It is recorded in the minutes that "The salary of the conductor was fixed at $60.00 per month, the assistant conductor at $25.00 per month, the express allowance of $12.50 per month, to go to the two conductors to be divided between them as they may agree. John M. Moore is designated Conductor and E. H. Hardin, Assistant Conductor."

While the railroad business as a whole was not prosperous at the time, the new owners did not sit and wait for traffic to come to their platforms, but sent out and brought the traffic in.

Colonel Springs held interest in three cotton mills in Chester and built one in Lancaster. He operated a large mercantile business in Lancaster and a large cotton business in Chester. All of the directors were merchants who supplied traffic to the L. and C.

However, the road had the great disadvantage of all narrow gauge lines, being unable to interchange carload traffic with the main lines. All cargo had to be unloaded from the big box cars at Chester and Lancaster, and reloaded into the L. and C. small editions. Among other things, the L. and C. engines had to burn wood because the coal mines were on broad gauge railroads, and it was uneconomical to reload it. The wooden bridge across the river burned in 1899 and was replaced with one of steel.

Mr. Hardin, in his report to the directors on June 1, 1897, states that in its first year's operation the road used 1,289 cords of wood for which it paid $1.34 a cord. He also reported that the road was paying 11⅛ cents each for crossties.

In 1902, Colonel Springs and his associates succeeded in borrowing $125,000.00 from the Southern Railway by bonding the railroad, and changed it to standard gauge. New engines and cars were purchased, and coal became their regular diet.

Also in 1902, a big addition was built to The Lancaster Cotton Mills, and in 1914 it was again enlarged and became the largest textile mill in the world under one roof. Colonel Springs and Captain John Stevens built an oil mill and later a fertilizer plant in Lancaster. This accordingly increased the traffic of the L. and C., and its earnings became impressive.

In 1913, the town of Chester engaged in a baseball series with the town of Dillon and since most of the Lancaster citizens were baseball fans, the L. and C. was persuaded to run a special train for the occasion. The train left Lancaster with three coaches of fans, the greatest number of passengers ever hauled by the L. and C. In fact, there were as many passengers on this one train as were ordinarily hauled in a year.

When the train reached the Hooper's Creek Trestle, a freight car jumped the track and plunged the three coaches into the creek. Every passenger was bruised, shaken and injured, and five did not survive.

Two Chesterites, now deceased, were members of the L. and C. train crew and riding the train at the time of the accident. They were W. W. Pegram, Sr., father of W. Ward Pegram, former editor of The Chester news, and J. S. Stanback, of 149 Center Street.

With this misfortune went not only the L. and C.'s only rolling stock, but the entire capital of the company. It was two years before Colonel Springs emerged from the Court House with his rails intact, but without means to purchase new rolling stock. The L. and C. never purchased another passenger car.

Colonel Springs succeeded in borrowing enough capital to get the road back in operation, and for a short time traffic improved, and it was making its way back to solvency when disaster struck again. The flood of 1916 carried away the three-span bridge across the Catawba River. For weeks the L. and C. detoured over the Southern and Seaboard by Catawba Junction and Fort Lawn. Then a ferry was built to take the place of the bridge, but operation in this manner was slow and costly.

A new bridge would have cost $90,000.00 which was much more than the railroad was worth even before the old bridge washed away. For a year it was a question of whether or not to abandon operations and take up the rail for scrap.

Colonel Springs then heard of a bridge on a main line railroad which was being abandoned in favor of a double track bridge. He negotiated for the bridge which happened to fit the stone piers of the L. and C.'s old bridge, which were not washed away by the flood.

The L. and C. resumed operations in time to be taken over for two years by the National Government during World War I.

Fate, not content with impeding the L. and C. by both fire and flood, brought up its reserves in the form of a tornado. This tornado struck a train traveling from Chester to Lancaster, lifted the first box car behind the engine, which was loaded with 50 bales of cotton and deposited it gently, bottom side up, clear of the tracks.

The engineer took little notice of this, however, as the rear cars coasted forward and coupled themselves to the engine which then proceeded on to Lancaster as if no accident had occurred. A picture of the overturned freight car was carried by the nation's newspapers, bringing the L. and C. more fame than its many court battles.

Since then the railroad has had a quiet and prosperous existence. A. P. McLure came with the L. and C. as superintendent in 1898 to succeed Mr. Hardin. He could and did fill every position on the railroad at one time or another. He was a qualified engineer, an expert railroad mechanic, and until he retired as president in 1945, had a personal acquaintance with every crosstie and rail owned by the L. and C., past and present.

He was succeeded by three men — Elliott Springs as president, W. H. Gladden as comptroller, and W. S. Barfield as superintendent.

The railroad now uses Diesel engines which burn about the same amount of oil that the old steamers used for lubrication. The old steam engines have long been retired.

But so the children, who for half a century have waved at the old steamers as they puffed by, may not be completely deprived of this pleasure, the railway acquired and put into operation the only miniature steam driven railway in the world, which has delighted passengers since the Charleston Exposition in 1902. Any weekend the engineers, firemen, switchmen and brakemen can be seen at the Springs Recreation Park operating their Lilliputian Branch on schedule.

A unique feature of the L. and C. railroad is its distinguished list of honorary vice-presidents. Among the most famous on the list were Admiral W. F. "Bull" Halsey, R. J. Reynolds, Samuel Hopkins Adams, James Mongomery Flagg, Lowell Thomas and Gypsy Rose Lee.

CHESTER COUNTY COURT HOUSE

XVII *CHESTER COUNTY ESTABLISHED*

BOUNDARIES SET

Chester County was originally a part of Craven district laid out in 1682 and named for one of the Lord's Proprietors. It covered most of the upcountry of South Carolina. In 1785 when South Carolina was divided into 37 minor judicial subdivisions, Chester as a county is mentioned for the first time. Lines were surveyed and marked and its present boundaries established as Chester District for the purpose of holding court. Chester County records begin that year. Its name came from Chester, Pennsylvania and Chester, England from which the first settlers emigrated.

For about ten years court was held at the Gill house at a place called Walkers, near what is now known as Lewis Turn Out, and later designated as a stage coach stop. Mr. Gill was the judge and there were three magistrates. Alexander Walker moved that he be made clerk and it was done.

In 1798, the state was again divided into 23 districts, Chester still holding to the original survey of 1785. Chester received its town charter in 1849 and its city charter in 1893.

(Chester District in 1792 had 1,446 white males of 16 years and upwards, 1,604 free white males under 16 years, 2,831 free white females including heads of families, 47 "all other persons," and 938 slaves, for a total population of 6,866.)

About 1791 commissioners were appointed by Charles Pinckney to locate and build a courthouse. Their first selection was the present site of Old Purity (now Trinity) Presbyterian Church. The final selection was on top of Chester's hill, now occupied by the Balsar building in front of the Confederate monument.

Judge A. L. Gaston in his *Remarks and Reminiscences* published in July, 1948 wrote that Chester city's major growth took place in the second half of the Nineteenth Century. It began with the construction of the Court House in 1852. On the 6th of January,

William A. Rosborough conveyed to the State of South Carolina a lot "for to build a Court House upon" situated on Saluda Road, joining lands of James Graham, Esq., Samuel McAliley and John Rosborough, for the sum of $3,400 paid by the commissioners of public buildings for Chester district.

The building was probably built shortly after the date of deed and before the Civil War. The building was of the style of one of the Princeton University buildings and was proposed by John J. McLure, then a young lawyer and graduate of Princeton. The old court house was eventually torn down and the bricks sold. The present building was erected in 1850 in a style reminiscent of Robert Mills and considered to be one of the handsomest in the state.

CHESTER COUNTY COURT HOUSE

Chester County's T-shaped Court House, 140 Main Street in Chester was built in 1852-1855 on land purchased from William A. Rosborough for $3,400. The architect is not known, but conjecture is that it could have been designed by Robert Mills, but this is not substantiated. It has Mills' grace, style and magnificent simplicity. The fact that Mills was the national architect and living in Washington when this court house was built does not exclude the probability of its having been constructed from one of his designs.

The court house was added to in 1896 and again in 1928 when the improvements were made according to plans drawn by A. D. Gilchrist, architect.

A transverse structure of three stories, wings have been added on both sides of the original building. A rotunda to give light and beauty was added near the back, all in harmony with the original. Still later Mr. Gilchrist designed the wing on the rear that reaches to McAliley Street.

The Court House, a gray stuccoed brick building is entered through a six-columned pedimented portico that rests on an arcaded basement. Windows have corniced headings supported on consoles.

An earlier Court House was built near the site in 1795. It was torn down.

Citizens of Chester County regard the Court House as the town's most distinguished building.

A memorial stone on the grounds in front of the Court House was erected by Chester gentiles in honor of Jack Simmons, a childless Jew who loved children.

MILLS' STATISTICS OF CHESTER COUNTY, 1826

Chester is one of the upper districts of the state, and lies within what is geologically termed the granite region. It is bounded west by the Broad river, (which runs a course a little to the west of north, and in a straight line nearly 18½ miles,) which divides it from Union; on the north by a straight line, beginning at a point on Broad river, one mile below Pinckney's ferry, and running nearly due east about 32 miles, until it intersects the Catawba river, in Major Green's plantation, 8 or 10 chains above the mouth of a branch called Frenel branch, which divides it from York district; on the east by the Catawba river, (running a south course nearly 18¼ miles in a straight line), which divides it from Lancaster; on the south by Fairfield, from which it is divided by a straight line, beginning at the mouth of Rocky creek, and running nearly due west 30 miles, or until it intersects Broad river, a few yards below the mouth of Sandy river. The average length of the district is 31 miles, and breadth 18¼ miles. It contains 361,600 acres.

The soil of this district embraces every variety, from sand to rock, but the largest proportion is what may be called clay, at least a substratum of clay, with a covering of vegetable matter, more or less mixed with primitive substances. The ridges between the water-courses are generally sandy, with a thin soil. The low grounds present a rich loam, some parts very stony. There is not much small gravel.

The whole of this district fit for cultivation is well adapted to the growth of corn, wheat, rye, oats, and in short, all grains; but owing to the wretched state of its agriculture, the small grains are not a profitable crop. Cotton grows well on all lands suited to its growth; also flax, hemp, tobacco, &c. Pease, beans, and all the esculent tribe thrive well.

Corn and cotton are the only crops run upon, (as it is termed), or are staples: wheat, rye, &c. are considered as incidental, no calculations being made upon them.

No rotation of crops is established further than answers the immediate view of the planter.

Corn may be said to average, on first, second, and third quality lands, 15, 25, and 35 bushel per acre. The average price for the last ten years, may be rated at between 75 and 90 cents per bushel; the last year it was as low as 35 cents. Some good land will yield 75 bushels per acre.

Cotton will average on the same quality of land, 4, 6, and 800 pounds per acre, although some lands will produce 1,500 to 2,000 pounds per acre. In 1824, Wm. H. Gibbs, Esq. gathered upwards of 1,400 pounds from one acre, though the land was not rich, but well cultivated.

The average price of cotton for the last five years, may be rated as netting to the planter, about 11 cents per pound, prepared for market. The proportion of clean cotton to that in seed is as three of the latter to one of the former.

Columbia now takes a large share of the business of this district; Charleston being very seldom resorted to as a market for the sale of its produce.

Lands in this district are valued, according to quality, from $2 to $20 per acre. Property is generally very equally divided, as much so as could be expected from the nature of things; none very rich, and none very poor.

The lands through a great portion of the district are mostly a red, sometimes a bluish, clay; apparently of primitive formation. The whole country is a continued succession of hill and dale. The soil from the sides of these hills, when cultivated, soon washes down into the valleys, and leaves them barren.

It would be well if our farmers were to adopt the Dutch custom in Pennsylvania and Maryland, to leave the tops of the hills in wood, and clear the bottoms.

Chesterville is the seat of justice of the district, and is situated upon the dividing ridge, between the waters of Broad and Catawba rivers, at the head of the east branch of Sandy river. The town has a very romantic appearance as you approach it. A learned traveller has likened it to one of those strong places used in the feudal times of Ireland, when tenants built around the tower of their lord to claim his protection; with this difference, that here was no moated tower, no tyranny, and no oppression. It is a little St. Marino, and on it dwell fit citizens for such a place, good and intelligent republicans. The town is erected upon the top of a small hill — the houses crowded together, very neat, and some of them elegant.

The grounds about Chesterville slope, in the manner of a glacis, on all sides; and the woods are cleared around it about the range of cannon shot. The village contains twenty-five dwelling-houses, a handsome court-house and jail, and a male and female academy of respectable standing.

The Broad river is now navigable the whole extent of the district. The Catawba is also, except at the point now under improvement by the state, at or near Rocky Mount; which, when finished, will make the navigation of this noble river complete, from near the foot of the Alleghany mountains to the ocean.

None of the creeks are navigable; the great rapidity of their current prevents this. The names of the principal interior water courses are Rocky, Fishing, Turkey, and Sandy rivers; all which have numerous branches; the two first are waters of Catawba, the latter of Broad river.

The falls of Catawba are a great natural curiosity. They lie in this district just opposite Mount Dearborn, where the United States government began to form a military post, but afterwards abandoned it.

Good laboring hands are hired at $880 a year, or by the day at fifty cents. The price of labor is fluctuating, being regulated by the price of cotton. The expenses of living are very moderate in families, never exceeding $880 a year; the rates of boarding at taverns about $100 per annum. The price of beef is four cents a pound, pork five cents, bacon ten cents.

The climate here is very variable in winter. The thermometer in summer ranges generally between 83 and 88 degrees. Along the water-courses fevers prevail in summer, but generally through the district it may be considered healthy. Several instances occur of persons living over eighty years, some exceeding one hundred.

The census, taken five years ago, gives to this district 14,189 inhabitants; namely 9,611 whites, 4,542 slaves, and 36 free blacks. The increase in the interval must be considerable, not only from natural causes, but by emigration from other states, and the lower parts of this state. Emigrants from the district have been rare lately, though some few occasionally occur to the states of Alabama, Georgia, and Mississippi.

The taxes paid by this district into the treasury, the last year, amounted to $5,132.66.

Taxes in South Carolina in 1826:

On land, city and town lots 37½ cents ad valorem on every $100.

On slaves, 75 cents per head. On free negroes $2 per head.

On professions, 75 cents in every $100. On stock in trade, 75 cents per 100 dollars.

Lands belonging to the first class are valued at $26 per acre, and the last class at 20 cents per acre.

Chester sends three representatives and one senator to the state legislature.

Schools are very common through the district. The subject of education commands much attention. An academy for teaching male and female youth in the higher branches is established at the village, and has able teachers.

By the munificence of the state, the poor have the means provided for the education of their children. Not less than between three and four hundred dollars are annually expended in this way here. The two last years 259 children received the rudiments of education, and this excellent system is still pursued.

Colonel Lacy, who so highly distinguished himself in the battles of Hanging Rock, King's Mountain, and Blackstock, belongs to this district. He was a cool and intrepid officer, and rendered important services to the state.

The Presbyterians are the most numerous religious sect in this district, and next to these are the Methodists, then the Baptists. The habits and education of the people make this one of the most religious and orderly districts in the state.

The number of poor, supported by the charity of the district, amounts annually to twenty-five; their expenses to $1,400. The number of blind 15; deaf and dumb 7; lunatics 3.

There are no manufactures carried on in the district, except in the domestic way.

The few pines found in this district are what are called the short leaf pine; but the most common native trees are the various kinds of oak, walnut, beech, poplar, &c. The apple, peach, pear, and plum, thrive well, though no attention is paid to forming orchards of them. Cotton so completely absorbs the attention of the people, that every thing else is neglected. The materials now used for building houses are chiefly pine and oak; though abundance of fine stone is found in various parts of the district, and excellent clay for making brick. Both of these however are gradually getting into use. Mr. Rice (on the road leading from the court-house to Symnes' ferry on Broad river) has set a good example, by having the basement wall of his house built of cut stone, executed in the handsomest manner.

If our planters would adopt the practice of erecting their houses of stone, or brick, it would secure the permanent settlement of their farms, induce their further improvement, and check the spirit of emigration.

This district abounds with the finest granite and soapstone. The canal locks, both on Broad and Catawba rivers, are executed in granite of the most beautiful and substantial kind.

No minerals or metals have yet been discovered in the district.

The fish in the waters of this district are the shad (in season), redhorse, trout, cat-fish, eel, perch, round-fish, or sucker, with several others. The game are the deer and fox, besides the rabbit, squirrel, raccoon, and opossum, which are plenty. The shad leave the rivers in the fall, and return in the spring.

The birds are those common to this state.

NAMES IN CHESTER COUNTY

Baldwin Station — named for Baldwin (Gayle) Mill.

Baton Rouge — named by French colonists for a red boundary mark (red stick) which separated their land from the area of the Indians.

Blackstock — named for Edward Blackstock, first postmaster.

Broad River — so named because of its width. The Indian name was Eswan Happedaw, meaning Little River, dividing the lands of the Catawba and Cherokee Indians.

Carlisle — First called Fish Dam; renamed in 1890 for the Rev. Coleman Carlisle, a Methodist Minister.

Catawba — so named because of the nearness of the Catawba Indian Reservation and the Catawba River.

Chester — created in 1785, named by early settlers from Chester, Pennsylvania, which in turn had been named from Chester, England. It comes from the Latin word, castra, or camp.

Dinber — Composite name of Mr. Hardin and his wife who was Miss Barber.

Edgemoor — originally named Ashlund, was changed to Edgemoor about 1907 at suggestion of General R. F. Hoke, president of Seaboard Airline Railway.

Fishing Creek — so named by the colonists before the Revolution because of its abundance of fish.

Fort Lawn — named for Mr. Fort who had an unusually beautiful lawn around his home.

Great Falls — named for an awesome waterfall in Catawba River.

Lando — named by Calvinists who settled there in 1787, from Bavaria, Germany, in memory of Landau, from which came the carriages called landaus.

Lewisville — named for the Lewis family, prominent there for more than 100 years.

Lowrys — formerly Lowryville, named for the Lowry Family who came with Scotch-Irish settlers from Pennsylvania in the 1750's.

Mount Dearborn — named in 1803 for Henry Dearborn when, as Secretary of War in President Jefferson's cabinet, he went there to lay the cornerstone of an arsenal for what was then planned as a southern military academy, similar to West Point. Congress failed to act and the project was abandoned in 1825.

Nitrolee — formed in 1917, named for William States Lee who came to this place in 1917 with a machine he hoped would take nitrogen from the air. The experiment failed, but a power plant was erected and the village grew around it. Combining the word, nitrogen, with that of Mr. Lee, the inhabitants called the place Nitrolee.

Richburg — named it is said for the fertile soil in the vicinity.

Rocky Creek — named for the rocky foundation of its course.

Rossville — named for an early Associate Reformed Presbyterian minister who established a church there.

Suzy Bole Creek — named for a prominent land owner in the area.

Turkey Creek — named for the abundance of turkeys in the area.

Wilksburg — named for Major John Wilks, an early settler and a noted Baptist minister.

Woodward — formerly Yongueville, renamed for Captain W. B. Woodward who gave land for station and post office when the Charlotte-Columbia-Augusta Railroad, now Southern, came through.

CHESTER COUNTY'S SENATORS

Lewis P. Jones gives this profile of South Carolina legislators: they were more predominately native-born than those of any state in the lower South (92 percent in 1850), and their median age higher (1850: House 39; Senate 45) than elsewhere. More than half of them owned over $25,000 in personal property in 1860, and 26 over $100,000.

For real property, the statistics were equally impressive — about triple that of legislators in other deep South states. Of this group in 1850, 80 percent were slaveholders, and 53 percent owned enough slaves to be classed as planters.

As Ralph Wooster summarized it, South Carolina "was still the stronghold of the landed aristocracy and the least democratic state in the lower South."

Rosser Taylor lists the traits of the gentry: individualism (partially due to isolated living), exaggerated concept of personal honor, benevolence, military-mindedness, hospitality and charm of manner, deference for women. Not all their traits were admirable, as Mary Chestnut in her *Diary of Dixie* described one, "Yes, he is easy to find. Wherever there is a looking glass, a bottle, or a woman, there he will be also."

In 1692, when the first Commons House of Assembly in South Carolina was called, the State had only four counties — Albermarle, Berkeley, Colleton and Craven.

Legislative Council, forerunner of the Senate had 13 members. The Constitution of 1778 provided for a Senate, members having terms of two years; the Constitution of 1790 gave Senators a four year term.

Two sessions were missed, both as the result of national conflict: that of 1781 when the State was almost entirely in the hands of the British, and that of 1867, when the State was placed under military rule as the beginning of Reconstruction.

Chester County's Senators, in alphabetical order:

Ashbel Greene Brice, 1915-1918, died in office 30 January 1918

Joseph Brown served in Eighth General Assembly representing the District between Broad and Catawba Rivers, Fairfield, Chester, Richland

Green Berry Colvin, 1828-1830

John Douglass, 1840-1844

John Dunovant, 1820-1824 and 1832-1840

Nathaniel Ridley Eaves, 1844-1852

John Lyles Glenn, 1898-1902

Wilbur Gill Grant, 1942-1964, died 15 June 1964

David Hamilton, 1922-1926

Peter Lawrence Hardin, 1902-1914

James Hemphill, 1865-1867

Ferdinand Hopkins, 1819-1820 filled vacancy of John McCreary

Daniel Huger, Sixth General Assembly, represented District between Broad and Catawba Rivers

P. L. Hardin, 1902-1914, died 17 December 1914

John Lee, 1872-1874

John Hardin Marion, 1918-1922. Elected Associate Justice of Supreme Court; resigned 19 January 1922

Samuel McAliley, 1852-1865

John McCreary, 1810-1818, resigned 18 December 1818, elected to Congress to represent new election district created by Constitutional Amendment of 1808. He was born near Fishing Creek, son of James McCreary and Margaret Gaston. He served in the Revolutionary War.

J. Hemphill McDaniel, 1890-1898, served in Confederate Army, was wounded at Battle of Seven Pines, was member of Hopewell ARP Church

Giles Jared Patterson, 1882-1890

John Pearson, 1806-1810, represented Fairfield, Chester, Richland

Robert Robinson, 1824-1828

Thomas Taylor, Fourth General Assembly, represented District between Broad and Catawba Rivers, Fairfield, Chester, Richland, 1790-1794, and 1802-1806

John Turner, Fairfield, Chester, Richland, 1798-1802

Dublin J. Walker, 1874-1877, resigned 25 April 1877

William Alexander Walker, attorney, 1877-1882, served in Confederate Army, wounded at Gettysburg, died in office 21 April 1882

Lucius Wimbush, 1868-1872, Negro, member of colored band in Columbia before Confederate War, died in office 17 October 1872

John Winn, District between Broad and Catawba Rivers, 1778-1780 and 1782-1784, was member of both Third and Fifth General Assembly

John Mahan Wise, 1926-42, was President Pro-Tempore 3 March to 21 April 1942. He was mayor of Chester 1911-1913.

Chester County is now in District 7, under reapportionment, comprising Chester, Fairfield and Richland counties. District Senators are: Heyward Elliott McDonald, Isadore Lourie, Hyman Rubin and John Alfred Martin (1984).

CHESTER COUNTY'S REPRESENTATIVES

Craven district, between Broad River and Catawba River, had representation at the First Provincial Congress held in Charleston in 1775.

Delegates were Henry Middleton, John Chestnut, Robert Goodwyn, John Winn, Henry Hunter, Thomas Woodward, Thomas Taylor, John Hopkins, William Howell, Dr. Benjamin Farrar and Joseph Kirkland.

Delegates to Second Provincial Congress were John Winn, John Nixon, William Lang, William Barrow, William Howell, William Lee, Thomas Taylor, John Turner, William Strother and Henry Hunter.

First General Assembly 1776
District Between Broad and Catawba Rivers

William Barrow	John Nixon
William Howell	William Strother
Henry Hunter	Thomas Taylor
William Lang	John Turner
William Lee	John Winn

There are no extant Journals for Second General Assembly 1776-1778.

Simon Hirons	Thomas Taylor
John Nixon	John Winn

Information taken from Hemphill, Wates and Olsberg: Journals of the General Assembly and House of Representatives 1776-1780.

Third 1779-1780

Robert Ellison	John Knox
Robert Patton	John Pearson
Richard Winn	Robert Goodwyn
John Milling	George Hancock
John Nixon	William Reaves
James Taylor	

Fourth General Assembly (not held in 1781 because of War)

John Adair	Robert Lyell
Henry Hunter	Charles Miles
Joseph Kirkland	John Pearson
William Kirkland	William Reeves
Edward Lacey	Richard Winn

Fifth 1783

William Reeves	James Knox
Col. Edward Lacey	Col. Richard Winn
Robert Lyell	Capt. Charles Miles
Col. David Hopkins	John Adair

Sixth 1785-1786

Capt. Field Farrar	James Taylor
Minor Winn	Capt. Kemp Taliaferro Strother
Capt. John Milling	Col. David Hopkins
Richard Winn	John Turner
Col. Edward Lacey	Capt. Thomas Baker
Dr. James Knox	Henry Hampton

Seventh 1787-1788

Minor Winn	James Craig
Capt. Thomas Baker	Henry Hunter
John Cooke	John Turner
John Gray	James Pedian
Aromanus Lyles	Field Farrar
James Knox	Edward Lacey (resigned to become sheriff of Chester District, later of Pinckney District)

Eighth 1789-1790

John Cook	Arthur Brown Ross
Jacob Brown	James Pedian
John Turner	Aromanus Lyles
William Meyer	George Gill
John Gray	James Knox
Edward Lacey	

Apportionment Under the Constitution of 1790 — Chester became an election district.

1791	Col. Joseph Brown, Col. Edward Lacey, John Mills
1792-1793	Joseph Brown, James Knox (died 10 August 1794)
1794-1795	John Pratt, John McCreary
1796-1797	John Pratt, John McCreary
1798-1799	Joseph Brown, John McCreary (elected Ordinary of Chester District 21 December 1799)
1800-1801	George Gill, Clayton Rogers
1802-1803	Thomas Baker Franklin, John McCreary (elected sheriff of Chester District 10 Dec. 1802), George Gill
1804-1805	Charles Boyd, George Gill
1806-1807	George Gill, Dr. Charles Boyd
1808-1809	George Gill, Hezekiah Donald
1810-1811	John Walker, Hezekiah Donald, Ferdinand Hopkins

1812-1813	Hezekiah Donald, Robert G. Mills, Ferdinand Hopkins
1814-1815	Ferdinand Hopkins, Hezekiah Donald, Henry Bradley
1816-1817	Robert Gill Mills, Henry Bradley, Charles S. Sims
1818-1819	John Dunovant, Charles Boyd, John E. Gunning
1820-1821	John Cherry, William Anderson, William Woodward
1822-1823	Robert Robinson, John Mills, William Woodward, William Anderson (Woodward moved from the State in 1823)
1824-1825	Green Berry Colvin, John McKee, Nathaniel Ridley Eaves
1826-1827	Green Berry Colvin, Nathaniel Ridley Eaves, Frederick William Davie
1828-1829	William Lowry, Nathaniel Ridley Eaves, James Faucett Woods
1830-1831	Nathaniel Ridley Eaves, James Faucett Woods, Joseph Gaston, George Gill, Jr.
1832-1833	James Faucett Woods, Robert Robinson, Green Berry Colvin, Frederick William Davie
1834-1835	Green Berry Colvin, Robert Robinson, Theodore Randall, Frederick William Davie
1836-1837	Frederick William Davie, John Douglass, Robert Gill Mills, William Woods (Mills elected Supt. Public Works, SC, 18 Dec. 1837)
1838-1839	John Douglass, Thomas Wade Moore, John A. Bradley, William Woods
1840-1841	Frederick William Davie, Lemuel Jackson, John W. Rice
1842-1843	Frederick William Davie, Nathaniel Ridley Eaves, Thomas McLure
1844-1845	James Y. Mills, James B. McCully, Lewis A. Beckham
1846-1847	Frederick William Davie, James B. McCully, Thomas McLure
1848-1849	James B. McCully, Samuel McAliley, Thomas Wade Moore (McCully elected Comptroller General of S. C. on 6 Dec. 1849)
1850-1851	Samuel McAliley, Alexander Quay Dunovant, Thomas Wade Moore
1852-1853	Cyrus Davis Melton, William Alexander Rosborough, Tillman Ingram
1854-1855	Cyrus Davis Melton, William Perry Gill, Thomas Wade Moore
1856-1857	William Perry Gill, John Simonton Wilson, Cyrus Davis Melton, James Hemphill (Melton denied a seat 4 Nov. 1856 by House because he did not own requisite amount of property at time of his election)

1858-1859 John Simonton Wilson, Swanson Wade Douglas, W. Taylor Gilmore

1860-1861 John Simonton Wilson, Churchill Benjamin Jones, W. Taylor Gilmore

1862-1863 Nathaniel Ridley Eaves, James Hemphill, James McDaniel, A. F. Anderson (McDaniel died 19 May 1863. Tombstone inscription copied from grave in Hopewell ARP Church Cemetery.)

1864 James Hemphill, Edward Conrad McLure, Jared Giles Patterson

Apportionment under the Constitution of 1865

1865-1866 William Alexander Walker, T. A. Lipsey, Thomas C. Howze

1868-1869 Under Reconstruction
Barney Humphries, Sancho Sanders, Barney Burton

1870-1871 Barney Humphries, Sancho Sanders, B. G. Yocum

1872-1873 John Lilly, Prince Young, Charles Simms

1874-1875 S. J. Crouch, J. Jordan, John McCullough, Samuel Coleman (McCullough died about 15 May 1875)

1876-1877 John Lee, Purvis Alexander, Samuel Coleman, John James Hemphill (House ruled Lee not eligible to serve because at the time of his election he held the disqualifying office of Postmaster of Chester)

Note: Some members were expelled from House for "committing the crime of bigamy," "because of his gross contempt and defiant attitude assumed against the law and dignity of the house;" for accepting a bribe to vote for a U. S. Senator; for attempting to bribe certain publishing houses concerning the supply of school textbooks," etc.

1878-1880 A. F. Anderson, Osmond Barber, John James Hemphill

1880-1882 Osmond Barber, John Bennett Cornwell, John James Hemphill

1882-1883 James F. Barber, William Stuart Mills, R. T. Mockbee

1884-1885 William R. Davie, R. T. Mockbee, John Wesley Wilkes

1886-1887 S. P. Hamilton, James Hemphill McDaniel, Osmond Alexander Wylie

1888-1889 F. L. Whitlock, Jesse H. Hardin, James Hemphill McDaniel

1890-1891 Jesse H. Hardin, Peter Lawrence Hardin, Cantor Walker McFadden

1892-1893 Ashbell Green Brice, Peter Lawrence Hardin, Samuel Moffatt Wylie

1894-1896 Joseph Nunnery, Samuel Thompson McKeown, Peter Turner Hollis

Apportionment under the Constitution of 1895

1897-1898   George Williams Gage, Peter Turner Hollis, Samuel Thompson McKeown (Gage elected Judge of Sixth Judicial District 18 Feb. 1898)

1899-1900   James Wilbur Means, Peter Turner Hollis, John Hardin Marion

1901-1902   Arthur Lee Gaston, Peter Lawrence Hardin, Peter Turner Hollis

1903-1904   Arthur Lee Gaston, Thomas C. Strong, John Mahon Wise

1905-1906   Paul Hemphill, Thomas C. Strong, Arthur Lee Gaston

1907-1908   Paul Hemphill, Ashbell Green Brice, Samuel Thompson McKeown

1909-1910   Ashbell Green Brice, Samuel Thompson McKeown, John Edgar Nunnery

1911-1912   Ashbell Green Brice, Samuel Thompson McKeown, John Edgar Nunnery

1913-1914   Ashbell Green Brice, Richard O'Neale Atkinson

1915-1916   Richard O'Neale Atkinson, Samuel Thompson McKeown

1917-1918   Elliott Holmes Hall, John McLure Hemphill

1919-1920   Richard O'Neale Atkinson, David Hamilton

1921-1922   John Lyles Glenn, Jr., Richard O'Neale Atkinson

1923-1924   John Lyles Glenn, Jr., Richard O'Neale Atkinson, Arthur Grier Westbrook (Glenn was appointed Solicitor of the Six Judicial District by Gov. Thomas G. McLeod 27 March 1923)

1925-1926   Charles Boyd Abell, Arthur Grier Westbrook

1927-1928   Charles Boyd Abell, Arthur Grier Westbrook

1929-1930   Thomas Hardin Brice, Arthur Grier Westbrook

1931-1932   George Wesley Chitty, Arthur Lee Gaston

1933-1934   Josiah Griffith Jordan, Arthur Lee Gaston

1935-1936   Wilbur Gill Grant, Josiah Griffith Jordan

1937-1938   Wilbur Gill Grant, David Hamilton, Jr.

1939-1940   Josiah Griffith Jordan, Charles Williams McTeer

1941-1942   David Aiken Gaston, Wilbur Gill Grant

1943-1944   David Aiken Gaston, Ben Nunnery

1945-1946   James Hicklin Craig, James Carl Gibson

1947-1948   Robert Witherspoon Hemphill, James Carl Gibson

1949-1950   Thomas Booker Hamilton, Samuel Edward McFadden

1951-1952   George Tillman Gregory, Jr., Fred Heyward Strickland

1953-1954   William Thomas Jeffers, Josiah Griffith Jordan

1955-1956   Harry Rankin Gardner, George Tillman Gregory, Jr. (Gregory elected Judge of Sixth Judicial District 8 Feb. 1956)

1957-1958   Harry Rankin Gardner, Luther Clark Wright, Jr.
1959-1960   Harry Rankin Gardner, Luther Clark Wright, Jr.
1961-1962   Harry Rankin Gardner, Luther Clark Wright, Jr.
1963-1964   Harry Rankin Gardner, Luther Clark Wright, Jr.
1965-1966   Jimmie Ernest Nunnery, Luther Clark Wright, Jr.
1967-1968   Jimmie Ernest Nunnery, Luther Clark Wright, Jr.
1969-1970   William Ross Hare, Luther Clark Wright, Jr., Richard
            O'Neale Atkinson, III (Wright died of heart attack 31
            August 1969)
1971-1972   John Porter Gaston, John Reid Justice
1973-1974   John Porter Gaston
1975-1981   Melvin Ernest Nunnery
1982-   Paul E. Short, Jr.

CHESTER OBSERVES BICENTENNIAL

Against a background of red, orange, blue balloons and hundreds of onlookers, the Chester County Bicentennial committee kicked off the county's 200th birthday celebration Saturday, April 17, 1985.

Part of the celebration was the dedication of Chiefs' Park, built on top of the hill in downtown Chester to resemble a park constructed for the CBS television miniseries "Chiefs," which was filmed in and around Chester in 1983.

Following the dedication ceremony, a white dogwood was planted in the park by Bicentennial committee chairman Barry Wilson, Downtown Business Association president Sharon Wilson, Main Street director Susan Evans, Chester County Chamber of Commerce president John Sherer and Chester City Councilman Terry Ehrlich.

Officially, the Bicentennial was observed April 19, which in 1785 was the day that South Carolina's Upcountry was divided into seven counties. Events were planned through December, 1985:

— a tour of six historic Chester Homes, sponsored by the Diversity Study Club, on Sunday, April 28.

— an arts extravaganza, sponsored by Chester Arts Council, Saturday, May 4, Chester Mall.

— Chester County Historical Society spring banquet, 7 p.m. Monday, May 6, Purity Presbyterian Church Social Hall. Speaker, Dr. William Bruce Ezell Jr., president of Erskine College.

— home furnishings show, Thursday and Friday, May 9 and 10, sponsored by Clemson Extension Service.

— Chester Little Theatre production of "Hello Dolly," Thursday through Saturday, May 9 to 11.

— Flopeye Fish Festival, Great Falls, Saturday, May 25.

— archery tournament, 2 p.m. Sunday, June 2, Chester State Park.

— Bicentennial Ball, Saturday, June 15, Chester Mall.

— concert on the Chester County Courthouse lawn, sponsored by Chester Arts Council, September.

— dedication of new Chester County Library, corner of Center and West End street, October 6.

— tour of eastern Chester County historical churches and cemeteries, October 12.

— Extension Services's holiday showcase and "Taste and See," November 22.

CHESTER COUNTY HISTORICAL MUSEUM

Louise Gill Knox provided the dream. J. B. McDowell, Chester County manager, provided the nuts and bolts. Their aim was the establishment of a Chester County Historical Museum.

Miss Knox began by organizing a sponsor, the Chester County Historical Association. It became a reality in December, 1959, and promptly went to work.

Goals of the Society were (1) to establish the museum (2) to restore the Landsford Canal and its surrounding landmarks, (3), to organize a tour of antebellum homes, churches and public buildings in order to foster appreciation and preservation of Chester County's rich historical heritage.

Through the efforts of McDowell and County Council, a safe and ample space in the basement of the County Court House was provided for the growing collection of museum pieces. This official Chester County Historical Museum was opened with ceremonies on May 2, 1960.

Headlines in local papers chronicled the Museum's progress: Exhibit of China, Glass and Silver (October 1960), Confederate Centennial Exhibit (May 1961), Old Portraits Before 1875 (November 1961), The T. Price Gibson Civil War Collection (May 1962), Reminders of Kitchens Past (May 1963), Cultures of Other Countries (May 1964), the Claude E. Gatlin Indian Collection (May 1966).

The museum was headquarters for first tour of homes in May 1966 when more than 250 visitors registered from the two Carolinas.

In 1970, when South Carolina celebrated its 300th birthday, the State's spotlight was on Chester September 29-October 3. The museum displayed flags from around the world as well as its treasured collections.

Chester County councilmen in February 1980 allowed the

Museum to move into the old Chester County jail behind the Courthouse on McAliley Street. The fortress-like masonry building, erected in 1914, has been spruced up to provide space for the Museum to continue growing.

GUERNSEY FESTIVAL

Some of the most aristocratic blood lines that flowed in Chester County are gone and almost forgotten.

The haughty males bore such high-sounding names as King George of Sunnyside, Imported Governor of the Vanquidor, Golden Noble II of the Briquet, Lord Bonny of Sitka, and Longwater Hollister of Rockingham.

Euphonious epithets borne by the females were Amelia's Rose Gold of Ophir, Rilma Hawthorne Hilda, Imported Flower of the Jenemies, and Violet of Orchard Springs.

All were purebred Guernsey cattle.

In addition to lending Chester County its name, Chester County, Pennsylvania, fostered the breeding and selling of Guernseys in the South Carolina "grass belt" encompassing Chester, York, Lancaster and Fairfield Counties.

Early in 1884, David R. Flenniken of Winnsboro exhibited three purebred Guernsey heifers and a Guernsey bull at Chester County Fair. Judge J. Lyles Glenn, Sr. and his father-in-law, J. C. Hardin were so taken with the showing they bought the lot and kept them in Chester County. Later in the barnyard of Judge Glenn's home in Chester, South Carolina Snowdrop was born.

The influence of this purebred Guernsey calf may well have been the spark which kindled the growth of the Guernsey industry in Chester County, for her son, Scot of Delta, and his daughters were responsible for the first notable sale of Guernseys outside the county, proving that the breeding of these cattle was a profitable business.

This sale and the combination of circumstances leading to it was accepted as a milestone of importance in the development of this Guernsey County. Soon after the sale, J. T. McDill, a young farmer, and W. A. Barber, attorney, formed a partnership and established Chester County's first Guernsey breeding farm. It was known as Delta Farms and was located in Peden Bridge community.

After McDill died in 1902 as a comparatively young man, and Barber joined a New York law firm, the Guernseys were sold at auction. Among local buyers were W. A. Darby and brothers, H. T. Boyd, T. C. Faley, J. J. McDaniel, Alex McDonald, A. Mayo McKeown and others who continued to breed and enlarge their stock.

In the February, 1919, issue of the *Guernsey Breeder's Journal,* one of Alex McDonald's finest bulls, Billy's Raymond of the Manor, had his picture featured on the cover, and his Imported Flower of the Jenemies, grand champion female at the Chester County Fair in 1918, also was pictured. In the same issue appeared an article: "The Guernsey Army of Occupation in the Piedmont," with Chester County prominently recognized as a Guernsey center.

W. B. Stringfellow of Hillbright Farm owned Bessie of Cornwell and Famous Princess Pat both of whom set records in pounds of milk and pounds of butterfat produced. Stringfellow's Dairy Maid for several years was a leader in South Carolina, as was Imported Governor II of Les Grants.

Other famous cattle and their owners were Governor's Dairy Maid, L. E. Stroud; Raider's Pride of the Sandhills, H. T. Boyd; Victor of the Prairie, A. Mayo McKeown; Gerrar Royal, James S. McKeown.

J. Watt Weir of Hopewell community owned Flora of High Point, a heifer who had the misfortune of having her tongue bitten off by a stallion as they shared a bale of hay.

In 1917, at the Wysacky farm of Robert M. Cooper, Jr. the State Guernsey Association was organized; on March 20, 1917, the State Guernsey Cattle Club was organized with Alex McDonald of Chester County as president. Tri-County Association encompassing Chester, York and Fairfield counties was organized with officers: W. M. Patrick of Woodward, president; Dr. W. W. Fennell of Rock Hill and R. B. Caldwell of Chester, vice-presidents; E. M. Kennedy of Blackstock, secretary-treasurer; J. J. McDaniel of Cornwell, T. L. Johnson of Winnsboro and Alex McDonald of Chester, executive committeemen.

This association held an annual picnic at Hopewell A.R.P. Church. Members brought their Guernseys and staged a show, heard an address by a prominent cattleman, and enjoyed a family outing.

R. B. Caldwell, attorney, and later president of the Commercial Bank, was a leader in the development of Guernsey breeding and cattle sales. Two of his famous animals were Imported Governor II of Les Grantes and Rilma Hawthorne Hilda.

By 1936, Chester County was established as the outstanding Guernsey County in the South and was known as "Wonderful Guernsey Center of Dixie", the call letters still used by Radio Station WGCD.

The Guernsey Festival, an annual event, began in the fall of 1946 and reached its apogee September 3-6, 1949. W. T. "Goat" Betts was chairman of the four-day festival that featured a mammoth stage spectacle "Pirates to Purebreds." Miss Augusta Buck of Edgemoor reigned as Queen of the Guernsey Festival, and was escorted by Senators Olin D. Johnston and Strom Thurmond.

Winners in the parade were floats by the Republic Cotton Mills and Rossville Community. "Hillbright Dainty" was Grand Champion Cow and "Sunshine's Lucky Max King" was Champion Bull.

A significant event in the march of Guernsey breeding progress was the opening of the Borden evaporated milk plant in Chester in 1940, with its many milk routes extending to all parts of the area. Through this system of marketing, 1,200 farmers had a daily market for milk.

S. C. COOPERATIVE EXTENSION SERVICE

Chester County will forever bear the beneficent imprint of the South Carolina Cooperative Extension Service. Work done by the many thousands of agents who fanned out across the state laid the foundation for much of the social and economic growth in South Carolina's rural and mill communities in the 20th century.

The Smith-Lever Act passed by Congress in 1914 provided for cooperation between the U.S. Department of Agriculture and the land grant colleges in conducting extension work. An earlier bill, the Morrill Act in 1862, provided for at least one land grant college for each state. In 1889 a law was passed establishing an experimental station at each of these colleges. Clemson was named South Carolina land grant college.

To a state and county that were 80 per cent rural at the time, research findings in agriculture and home economics benefitted practically everybody. Clemson Agricultural and Mechanical College spearheaded the farm program and Winthrop College the homemaking program.

Well trained graduates with the designation of Farm Agent and Home Demonstration Agent went out with missionary zeal to help improve the quality of life in the rural areas. They showed South Carolinians how to properly use and conserve the land, how to improve health conditions through proper sanitation and a balanced diet, how to use improved methods and tools for farming, how to grow and preserve food, and how to beautify the home and its furnishings.

Each little rural area soon had its own Home Demonstration Club that met monthly. Club members received free instruction, demonstrations, and publications.

By the summer of 1911, Clemson and Winthrop were cooperating fully in the highly successful programs. That year they sent a train for a 10-week summer tour that covered every county in South Carolina. They demonstrated steam canners and cookers, washers with wringers, steam irons, food preparation and all the labor-saving devices to relieve the drudgery of work on the farm. Talks were devoted to sanitation and health, preventable diseases, and physical care of family members and farm animals. Many "how to" bulletins and other publications were generously distributed.

In 1921, at one of Winthrop's short courses, the farm women organized the South Carolina Council of Farm Women, the first of its kind in the nation. The Council, which eventually had 6,000 members, made a concentrated effort to develop leadership and initiative among the farm women. The success of this effort has been extraordinarily effective.

Clemson University's Extension Service and widespread research projects are recognized and respected worldwide. Representatives from many countries come to study the Service.

The South Carolina Cooperative Extension Service remains vigorous and active. Although the purpose remains the same, it has adjusted to meet changing conditions and needs as well as changing technological innovations.

CHESTER AIRPORT AND BERMUDA SOARING

Chester's Airport on Hy. 321 North is as pretty a piece of property as the county affords. Cleared and leveled from row-crop fields, near the end of World War II, the site was to be used as a training field for Air Corps pilots but was never fully put into operation. It was built by the U. S. Corps of Engineers, with Henry Mitchell, supervisor.

Three 5,000 foot runways were built, one of which is automatically lighted at night. It is designed to take any piston aircraft and some small jets. Unicom, the standard ground to air communication for small airports, is used.

After the war, the airport took on the look of many other abandoned military sites. Its major uses became drag racing and coon-hound trials. Disenfranchised quail and doves moved back and built nests around the runway.

A transplanted Yankee who came to Chester during maneuvers, stayed after the war and saw possibilities for developing the airport. Joe Giltner and his wife, Lucille, made a plan and made it work.

Chester, they knew, was one of the best soaring areas in the eastern United States because of the bumpy air, level open areas, and good thermals created by wide plowed fields. Another soaring enthusiast was Stanley Hoke, a native of Chester who lived in Charlotte. Hoke brought his sail plane and started soaring over Chester.

The airport, owned by the city and county of Chester became

base to Bermuda High Soaring School. The runways are leased by the county to the South Carolina State Aeronautics Board who, in turn, leases it to Bermuda High Soaring. The first local airport commission members were Fred Powell, chairman, W. T. Betts, R. A. Oliphant, H. R. Woods and W. C. Stone.

Hoke rented the airport and Giltner became the manager in the early 1960s. A 90′ x 65′ foot hangar with 5,400 square feet and 400 square foot office building were built. 100 octane unleaded fuel and tie downs were provided.

Bermuda High Soaring offered gliding and power aircraft training. It has been busy and successful largely due to the Giltners' enthusiastic efforts.

Since 1969, the Regional soaring meet has been held annually the third week in April. National Sanctions Meet was held here in 1973 and National Open Class Meet in 1976. The meets bring an average of 200 visitors to the area, including 65 to 70 contestants with three crew members each. A survey in 1980 determined that about $150,000 revenue came into local coffers during the week.

Bermuda High was sold to Giltner and Gayle Coffman, then in 1972 to Fred McFawn, Jeff Dishongh and Kent Hughes who are the present owners. McFawn is manager and instructor.

(Left to Right) Matchline House; Cotton Boll; Landsford Canal; Thistle; Catholic Pres byterian Church; Magnolia Blossom; Log Cabin; Pine Cone. (Center) Chester County Court House.

Confederate Monument on top of Chester's hill is a memorial to soldiers who fought in the Confederate Army during Civil War.

Chester's Confederate Monument centered in "Chief's Park," built in 1985 to commemorate the making of miniseries, "Chiefs."

Chester County War Memorial Building on Main Street was built to honor Chester County men who fought in World War I and World War II.

St. Marks Episcopal Church built in 1879 on Center Street.

Purity Presbyterian Church, Chester, S. C., was established in 1787. Present church was dedicated in 1855.

Old Catholic Presbyterian Church on Rocky Creek has held meetings since 1758. It was the second church organized in Chester County.

Fishing Creek Church

Fishing Creek Presbyterian Church pre-dates Revolutionary War. Organized in 1752, it was built on land donated by George Kelso who had a land grant dated May 7, 1774.

LANDSFORD

Lock Kesper's house at Landsford Canal near Great Falls. Structure was moved there in 1973 from Mt. Dearborn.

RAILROADS

Old Seaboard Railroad depot on Wylie Street is no longer in use.

Seaboard Depot

Chester County's handsome Court House was designed in a style made popular by Robert Mills. It was built in 1852-1855.

Chester's Federal Building on Main Street was formerly the Post Office.

MISCELLANEOUS

Chester County was known as "Wonderful Guernsey Center of Dixie" in the 1950's. An annual Guernsey festival was held with shows and sales at County Fairgrounds.

National and Regional Soaring meets are held at Chester Airport. Bermuda High Soaring School operates here 12 months a year.

Tracy Barnes launched balloon at Chester Fairgrounds in 1960.

Foote Street Elementary School

First Floor:
Left front — First Grade; Bea Heron, teacher. Right front — Second Grade; Mrs. Mary Johnson, teacher. Back — Third Grade; Mary Lindsay, teacher and principal.

Second Floor:
Left front — Fifth Grade; Dorothy Smith, teacher. Right front — Sixth Grade; Mrs. Blanche Hafner, teacher. Back — Fourth Grade; Jennie McKinnell, teacher.

Foote Street School was opened in 1898.

College Street School built in 1891. Second graded school in state.

Brockman High School on Columbia Street in Chester was opened in 1924.

Rossville Graded School near Great Falls. Building is now Rossville Community Center.

Roddey Colored School.

Edgemoor School.

Finley Grammar School in Chester.

Eureka Elementary School in Eureka Mill Village in Chester.

BRAINERD INSTITUTE

Campus of Brainerd Institute, on Loomis Street in Chester, one of the South's first black schools established in 1866 to educate children of freed slaves.

Classroom building of Brainerd Institute in Chester. Brainerd was one of the first black schools established in the South.

Lowrys Library in Lowrys is no longer in use.

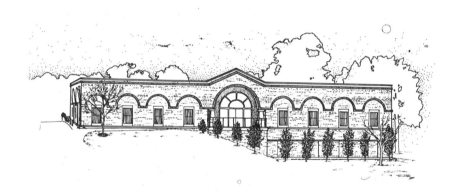

Chester's new 15,000 sq. ft. library on Center Street opened in early 1985.

Main Street on the hill. A club house was located on third floor of Agurs Building.

A gala day on Chester's hill during the "horse and buggy days."

Farmers attending a mule auction in Chester in early 1900's. In background is Stahn's Jewelers and Masonic Temple.

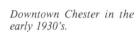

Downtown Chester in the early 1930's.

Chester's leading department store on the hill in 1930's with its all male staff posing for pictures.

Chester's York Street in early days. Bethel Methodist Church in background. In foreground is Madeline Pryor Steinbeck, daughter of Dr. S. W. Pryor, in yard of Pryor home and hospital.

Main Street in Chester. Note Esso station on left and movie theater on right. (Circa 1940's)

Chester's Volunteer Fire Department with Belvin B. Roddey at the wheel.

Chester's City Hall on the hill was formerly the Opera House.

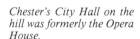

Old Chester County Jail built in 1914 on McAliley Street now houses Chester County Historical Museum.

Early Chester County Jail on Center Street. Jailor lived on first floor; prisoners were housed upstairs.

Magdalene Hospital, established by Dr. S. W. Pryor, stood on corner of Saluda and Hudson streets. It was destroyed by fire.

Chester Sanitorium was established by Dr. Robert E. Abell on York Street. It is now the property of Maranatha Church.

Chester's first hospital was established in the mid 1880's by Dr. Torbit Henry and Dr. Marion of Richburg. The house, on Pinckney Street, is now the home of Dr. R. J. Gosh.

Chester's second hospital was upstairs in the home of Dr. S. M. DeVaga on Wylie Street. It is now Barron's Funeral Home.

Pryor Hospital was built in 1917 on York Street. It was torn down and an A&P grocery store was built on the site.

Chester County Hospital was built in 1952. Nursing Center was added in 1969. Both are on Great Falls Road.

Will Durham's country store at Blackstock was operated for 84 years until it was auctioned in 1982.

Will Durham operated his large country store at Blackstock for 84 years.

Metal Signs Attracted Buyers

David Baker Auctions Off Bridle Rings

Old Set Of Scales

Assorted Merchandise

Items at the store include some old style corsets, above, which were removed from their original packages. The grocery side of the store, left, contained a variety of old and new produce

Photo By DAVID HARRIS

"Nitrolee"
General Electric Chemical
Co. First plant in the United
States built to extract nitro-
gen from the air for use in
manufacturing fertilizer.

Company store of Republic
Cotton Mills built around
1910. School was held up-
stairs until first school was
built. Belk Department
Store is in building now.

Great Falls in early 1900's. First Republic Cotton Mill was built in 1909.

First Republic Cotton Mill
in Great Falls.

Little "Dinky" train used in building first Duke Power Co. dam on Catawba River in 1907.

First dam on Catawba River at Great Falls was built in 1907.

Hundreds of these massive rocks lie along the Catawba River and all around Great Falls.

Flop Eye near Great Falls.

Chester's first cotton mill, named The Gingham Mill, Baldwin Mill, and Gayle Mill at various periods of its use. It was closed in late 1960's.

Pg 162 - the engineer was
Mr. Davis

Pg 168 - Population stats

Pg 172 - Pop stats - 1826

Pg 212 - Ann P. Collins
215

174 - Chester settlement facts 1785

176 - John Winn served in govt,
and   1778 - 1780 + 1782 - 1784
177

177 - Richard Winn - in govt.

178 - Col. Richard Winn - in govt,
Minor Winn - served in govt.

189 - "Old Field Schools" + Free
School Act of 1811,

==================

"HISTORY IS
AN OMNIBUS
ON WHICH
OUR ANCESTORS
RIDE."

Anne Pickens Collins
March 28, 2001

Designed by Robert Emory Anderson

XVIII *CHESTER COUNTY SCHOOLS*

EARLY ACADEMICS AND COUNTRY SCHOOLS

E conomic conditions in the Upcountry improved steadily and consistently during the first half of the nineteenth century. Living standards rose perceptibly while educational facilities for the youth of the area remained woefully inadequate. During the early years of the century, children had to be taught at home by their parents or, if affluence permitted, by a tutor. Some families in Chester County joined together to provide schoolrooms and teachers.

In the Chester area, as in most of the state, early education was frequently connected with the churches and, in many cases, the minister was also the teacher. Sometimes classes were taught in the church and sometimes in a one-room cabin nearby, or in the teacher's home.

Finally, the General Assembly made a feeble attempt to rectify the situation that existed not only in Chester County but throughout the state. On December 21, 1811, the Free School Act was passed, with an appropriation of $300 for each of the 124 schools authorized for the state. This was considered to be the first real effort to establish a system of public education.

This Act mandated that "free schools be established in each of the forty-four election districts equal to the number of members in the House of Representatives to which the district was entitled."

As a result of this Act, the first Commissioners for Free Schools for Chester County were appointed. They were John Roseborough, Christopher Thompson, Ferdinand Hopkins, Samuel McNeal, the Rev. J. B. Davies, Dr. J. Curry and John McCreary.

This meager but well-meant effort resulted in the establishment by the government of "old field" schools. These were usually conducted in crude one to two room huts or log cabins, often located at the edge of a field abandoned because of decreased fertility — hence

189

the name often given to these schools. Students lived in walking distance or came by horse and buggy to the school. Parents of the pupils paid a fee to the teacher for his services and, more often than not, provided him living quarters in their homes. Sometimes the teacher was paid in money and sometimes in farm commodities. This haphazard method of payment was not conducive to attracting a high caliber of instructors.

School terms lasted only a few months, the session being determined by the ability of the parents to pay the teacher. School usually opened late in the fall after the crops were harvested and the children were no longer needed to help with farm chores. Only the fundamentals of reading, writing and arithmetic could be taught under these circumstances and to such a mixed age group. But the schools produced a surprising number of proficient students who found learning exciting and playground associations fun.

Support for schools continued to be sparse and sporadic. In 1840, the state appropriated $1,200 annually to all of Chester County for instruction. Twenty years later, by 1860, there were twenty-three teachers in Chester County, conducting classes for 241 pupils. Teachers were paid according to the number of students taught. At that time $1,800 was appropriated for the entire county.

Some children attended school as "poor scholars." Parents paid as much as they could and the rest was taken care of by "the greatly inadequate free school fund." Unfortunately, these schools became known as "pauper schools," causing some poor families to refuse to accept what they deemed governmental charity. Although they kept their children at home, others prized education above pride and sent their children at the State's expense.

For a number of years there continued to be private schools where students paid tuition. They co-existed with the so-called Free Schools. The increasingly prosperous planters in the area became less and less complacent with limited opportunities for their children and were instrumental in founding a number of academies. These were financed by tuition paid by each student, with fees sufficiently high to support an adequate, well-equipped building and to employ capable teachers. Students from distant homes found room and board either at the school or with families in the neighborhood.

Lewisville Female Seminary

According to existing records, one of the earliest and best of the boarding schools in Chester County was Lewisville Female Seminary, 10 miles east of Chesterville, S. C. The exact date of its beginning is not determined, but it was in the early 1840s. It closed in 1854 at the death of Mrs. A. S. Wylie, principal. The only remaining school building is the home of Mrs. W. W. Gaston, Jr.

Rev. L. McDonald, pastor of nearby Union A.R.P. Church, is listed as superintendent and visitor, with Mrs. Wylie as principal, "assisted by Mrs. Lewis of the Columbia Institute, Tennessee, and Miss Kellog of Castleton Female Seminary, Vermont, etc. & etc." Trustees were Col. L. A. Beckham, James B. McGill, James Drennan, John Cherry, Wilmont S. Gibbes, Wm. A. Rosborough, Wm. Knox, Dr. A. P. Wylie and James A. Lewis.

The scholastic year was divided into two sessions of five months each "commencing the 5th day of January and the 21st of July." Terms per session were:

Pestalozzian Department (educational reform as proposed by Johann Heinrich Pestolozzi, a Swiss educator), $4.00; Junior Department, $6.00; Senior, $9.00; Music, Piano or Guitar, $18.00; Wax Work, $8.00; Oil Painting, $18.00; Fancy Needle Work, $8.00; Use of Drawing Patterns and Books, 50¢; Use of Instruments, $2.00; Languages, each, $8.00; Boarding, $27.00; Washing per month, $1.00; Stationary, $1.00.

Printed sheets announced that "the Rev. L. McDonald, influenced only by his anxious desire to further the interest and increase the advantages of the Institute, will lecture on Mental and Moral Philosophy, Evidences of Christianity, etc. & etc. Lectures will be delivered on the circle of the Physical Sciences by Drs. William and A. P. Wylie and Dr. W. W. Mobley."

Parents and guardians were assured that "this school will be very desirable, and recommends itself to Parents and Guardians, as well by the moderates of tuition as by the healthiness of its location. — They (pupils) will be required to write home every fortnight, and such attention and criticism will be devoted to the composition and penmanship of their letters as to make the exercise improving to their scholarship. The P.S. is never to be read by the teacher."

Minimum age for admission was thirteen. Classes were offered in four levels, Preparatory, Primary, Junior and Senior. Among subjects taught, in addition to the three Rs, were Grammar, Ancient Geography, History Universal, Natural Philosophy, Astronomy, Algebra, Rhetoric, Geometry, Physiology and Botany. Emphasis was placed on constantly reviewing orthography, penmanship, calisthenics and Scripture History.

Lewisville Female Seminary's circular listed as references His Excellency, Gov. John H. Means, Fairfield; Ex-Gov. John P. Richardson, and Hon. F. J. Moses, Sumter; Gen'l James W. Cantey and Samuel Spence, Camden; James H. Witherspoon, Dr. R. E. Wylie and Rt. Rev. Thos. F. Davis, D.D., Lancaster; A. Q. Dunovant and R. E. Kennedy, Chester; and Rev. William Martin, also of Camden.

A final note in the circular stated: Parents and Guardians Are Ernestly Requested Not To Furnish Their Daughters With Jewelry, or Needless Articles of Clothing. And, "A carriage will meet any pupils coming as far as Lewis Turn Out, on the Charlotte & S. C. Rail Road, when timely notice is given."

Building that housed Lewisville Female Academy dormitory is now Mrs. W. W. Gaston's home. She is the fifth generation of the Wylie family to live there. Dr. Wylie, husband of Mrs. Wylie who ran the school was a great uncle of Mrs. Gaston. When the Gastons observed their Golden Wedding anniversary there on August 30, 1943, the building was then over 150 years old.

In 1853, there were fifty girls at the Academy. Antonia Wylie, niece of headmistress Amanda Wylie, wrote her name on the dormitory wall and it is still there, according to the present owners.

Chesterville Academies

The first school house in the town of Chester was the Chesterville Academy, established by an Act of the General Assembly in December, 1818. Seven trustees were appointed: John McCreary, George Kennedy, William Bradford, John Walker, Henry Bradley, John Roseborough and John E. Gunning.

The school was a two-story frame building which stood on the site known as McLure Hill. It was near the property now owned by Fred A. Triplett, Jr. whose home faces West End Street. The school, supported by tuition fees and private funds was attended by both boys and girls. The original building burned and was later replaced by a brick structure which was used for boys only. A girls' school was opened in 1841 by the Rev. D. McNeal Turner.

Just before the outbreak of the Civil War, the lot on West End on which the Academy stood was sold and a new brick building was erected across town. The new school, known as Brick Academy, was opened with 125 pupils. It stood on the present site of the brick house formerly owned by the Jospeh Walker family on the street appropriately named Academy Street.

After the first academy was burned, Ann Foster, a northern lady, operated a school in a building that later became the residence of Dr. A. P. Wylie, and still later of Thomas White. After Miss Foster married and left Chester, Wylie P. Jones opened a school in the building on Pinckney Street near the blacksmith shop which later became the carriage factory of C. Holtz. (According to older Chester residents, this was located on what is now called Center Street between St. Mark's Episcopal Church and the corner which turns to Pinckney.)

Joshua Hillary Hudson in his autobiography says, "Mr. Jones taught here a year or possibly longer and was succeeded by Mr. Sealy who taught a year. Up to this time the school had been mixed, male and female. By this time the Academy on McLure Hill had been rebuilt of brick and was for males only. Mr. Sealy was succeeded by teachers Davie, Sherrell, Shelton, Bansemer a German, and Giles J. Patterson, the last named for 1848-1851."

It has been an erroneous belief of many that the quaint brick house on Academy Street, which was owned for many years by the Joseph Walker family is the original Academy. According to Miss Elizabeth Lindsay whose father attended school there "the Walker house on Academy Street was never used as a school but was closely associated with one. It is on the same lot and built of the same brick."

"According to Mrs. Rebecca Walker Miller, the Academy was nearer the street and had a solid wall front and a gable end on the street side. Her father, Joe Walker, had the building razed and a home constructed of the brick but farther back from the street than the former building."

Mrs. John G. White in *Old Homes of Chester* (1946) states that in a house "lordly in appearance," on the corner of York and Smith Streets a school was once operated. The house with fourteen rooms and a basement was built in 1819 for Dr. John Dunovant, and was moved from York Street to Smith Street in 1913. In 1841, Dr. Dunovant sold his house to the Rev. McNeal Turner. There Mr. Turner conducted the Chesterville Female Seminary, having as trustees Wm. D. Henry, Thos. McClure, John McKee and David Wilson.

Other academies operated in Chester County in the 1800s included Mills Academy in the Hazelwood section near the Fairfield County line. It was taught by Miss Lizzie Mills in a one-room building in her back yard. Families in the area were Dixon, Douglas, Mobley, Thorne, Bigham.

Hicklin School was built in 1853 by J. B. Hicklin on his property at Knox Station on the old McDaniel Road.

Blackstock Academy at Blackstock was started by Miss E. J. McCulley. She was succeeded by W. Banks Thompson. This academy grew and became Blackstock High School.

Fishing Creek Church School was organized in 1893 in the Church Session House, Miss Lizzie Reid, teacher. A new school was built in 1926.

Purity High School organized by Purity Presbyterian Church was operated prior to 1880 under the direction of J. K. Henry, a graduate of Erskine College.

Bascomville School was started in the 1800s. Teachers were Miss Anna Webster and the Rev. Joseph Wilson.

Hopewell School near Hopewell A.R.P. Church. Families there were Tennants, Sterlings, McDaniels, Weirs, Boyds, Nichols.

Leeds School in Leeds District.

Baton Rouge School: McCallum, McDaniel, Worthy, Cunningham, Stevenson, Wilkes families.

Sealeys Creek School: Pressley, Gregory, Benson, Roddey, Allen, Wade, Lucas, Turner, Fennell families were served by this school.

West Chester School.

Douglas School — on site where Woodward Baptist Church parsonage is now. Community families were: Yongue, Douglas, Tennant, McKeown and Hare.

Sandy River Academy, later Capers Chapel School, on S. C. Hwy. 321. The second floor housed the Sandy River Academy Band directed by Brooks Hardin. The school was the focal point of the community's educational and social life. Many graduates went on to Clemson, Erskine, Wofford and Columbia Colleges.

Rossville School was housed in a one-room building, then in Ebenezer Methodist Church and later in a Stevenson home.

In a local newspaper April 11, 1889, it is recorded that Wilksburg Academy "is a useful building to the community," and a reminder to "get well fixed before summer comes."

Matthew Elder, Jr. in his autobiography tells of a pre-Revolutionary school held at Hopewell Associate Reformed Presbyterian Church. Texts used were American Spelling Book, New Testament, The Bible, Gough's Arithmetic, The English Reader and Murray's Grammar. One teacher was John Hemphill, afterward Chief Justice of the Republic of Texas and United States Senator from the Lone Star State.

Daniel Green Stinson says that when he was eight years old, in 1802, he attended a school "three miles from home on the other side of Big Rocky Creek, teacher Robert Boyd." Stinson wrote: "In 1807 the fortification of Mt. Dearborn near Beckhamville, was completed and garrisoned by regular soldiers. Military schools were established all over the country, preparing for the war that took place in 1812. In 1810 I attended one of these schools and received considerable military training."

Other one-teacher schools in Chester County:

Landsford School on Hwy. 21.

Rowells School near S. J. Cornwell's store on Hwy. 21.

Jordan School in El Bethel community.

El Bethel School near El Bethel Methodist Church.

Fort Lawn School.

Harmony School near Harmony Baptist Church.

Starmac School named for families it served: Sloans, Thrailkills, Allisons, Roddeys, McWatters.

Wylie's Mill School, Catawba, Piney Grove, Mount Pleasant, Knox Station, Carters, High Point, Old Aurora, Tip Top were country schools.

Halselville School was near Beaver Creek Church. Families

served were: Durham, Wright, McLurkin, Coleman, Cunningham.

Ford School was near Orr's Station. Families nearby were Ford, Minter, Chambers, Wrenn, Lewis, McDaniel, Bennett.

Cornwell School built on land given by Dr. W. J. W. Cornwell, near Cornwell Turnout on Southern Railway.

Lewisville School was near the E. B. Burns and Mrs. Virgie Martin homes at Richburg Junction.

Wellridge School was in existence over 100 years ago.

Pleasant Grove School sat near Pleasant Grove Presbyterian Church.

Sunshine School on Highway 72 was established on land donated after the Confederate War by Alexander Walker Wise.

There was a log school house named Armenia at Bonnett Rock in the early days. Each family paid so much toward a teacher's salary. The school term varied in length, but the children stayed from early morning until late afternoon.

The school was just one room with a big fireplace and no windows. The door stood open to give light. The benches were made of slabs and there was one big desk where the children did their writing. Text books were the old Blueback speller and McGuffy's reader.

Armenia's next school was held in the preacher's tent on the old camp ground. Here Mr. Buchanan, first editor of the Chester Reporter, and "Humpy-Back" Jim Sanders taught.

The first Armenia school was built between 1876 and 1880. John Grant gave the land, Taylor Grant supervised the building and Neely Grant and Zack Roof built the chimney. Later teachers who boarded with the Neely Grants were Molly Lackey, Catty Lucas, Mary Traywick, Mattie Mills, Eli Alston Wilkes and Lizzie Lowry.

CHESTER COUNTY SCHOOL WAS LIKE THIS

One water bucket, usually filled from a spring nearby, and one long-handled dipper were used by all.

A wood-burning stove provided heat. Wood for the stove was hauled to the school by parents.

The teacher, with what help she got from pupils, had to start the fire in the mornings, keep it stoked during the day and provide janitor service in the building.

A bench in front of the teacher's desk was used for the group reciting their lessons. The others studied until their turn came.

Roll call was answered every morning with a Bible verse. Friday afternoons were set aside for "speeches," songs or other performances by the pupils. Often parents and visitors were invited for this.

Teacher supervised simple playground activites and often

joined them. Favorite games were jump rope, hopsctoch, hide-and-seek, drop the handkerchief, ring-around-the-rosey, and baseball.

School "took in" at 8 a.m. and "let out" at 4 p.m. Noon recess was one hour long while pupils ate lunch from a tin pail brought from home. Ham biscuits and baked sweet potatoes were two favorites.

There were no toilet facilities. Permission was granted to "be excused" which meant "going to the woods."

Pupils walked to school, often several miles.

FOOTE ST. SCHOOL   LUCY ADAMS

BEGINNING OF GRADED SCHOOLS

In 1879, the Legislature passed the Act granting the town of Chester the right to establish a graded school. Dr. W. H. Witherow who had come to Chester to take charge of the Chesterville Academy, organized in 1880 the second graded school in the state. Winnsboro had the first. This was indeed a milestone.

The new school was known first as the Chester Graded School. The name College Street School was adopted when the building was completed and opened for classes in February 1892.

Prior to opening day, school classes were held in the Cotton Hotel located where Peoples Furniture Company is today.

Progress in providing schools moved rapidly during the next few years. In 1895 a High School charter was granted to College Street. Student fees were $2.50 a month. This school was in the Court House District, and its opening was the beginning of a new day for education in Chester County. It was the flagship for standards of organization, housing, instruction and support for the rest of the county.

First Rural High Schools

According to Historian Louise Gill Knox, about the year 1906, the South Carolina Legislature passed a law providing for rural high schools. In Chester County, one was organized at Richburg and one at Edgemoor but they were not highly successful and soon reverted to rural graded schools.

In the year 1911, Lowryville District voted bonds and built a modern brick school building, the first of its kind in the county, and set a precedent. In 1915, Fort Lawn and Cornwell Districts issued bonds and built large school buildings.

The first consolidated high school district was created in 1922 by the consolidation of Knox, Pleasant Grove, Pryor and Rodman Districts. Bonds of $15,000.00 were issued to build and equip Oakley Hall, a two story red brick high school building. Harry E. Hicklin was its principal and a pioneer educator of distinction.

Handsome Oakley Hall remained a high school and community center until the consolidation and integration of county schools in 1970. A large cannery was built behind the school during World War II to help the community preserve foods in season and to feed themselves in a time of rationing. (Note: Oakley Hall in a deplorably vandalized state, and its grounds were sold at auction to Sidney Blaney, Jr. The property was transferred on July 29, 1985.)

In quick succession rural high schools were built in Blackstock, Edgemoor, Richburg, Leeds and Wellridge Districts. Some of the buildings are still standing in 1985 although long converted to other uses or left to the ravages of time.

Records show that six school houses were built between 1924-26. They were Chester High School, Edgemoor High School, Leeds Grammar School, Rossville Grammar School, Richburg High School and Wellridge Grammar School.

BROCKMAN HIGH SCHOOL

Seven white high schools were accredited in 1925-26; Chester, Great Falls, Edgemoor, Blackstock, Fort Lawn, Richburg and Oakley Hall.

Thirty years later in 1924 a new high school was built on Columbia Street, relieving the pupil load that had grown apace at College Street School. Brockman High School, named for Supt. Myron E. Brockman was a handsome, commodious building for its day.

The Class of 1923-24 was the first class to graduate from Brockman. This was also the first class to issue the school yearbook, the Cestrian. Three issues yearly were of literary content and the fourth was an annual. Elizabeth Anderson was editor and Ambrose Wylie was business manager.

Brockman served white high school students until 1954 when a new modern high school was built across from Brockman on Columbia Street. Chester County schools were integrated in 1964.

In 1973, a new Senior High School was built on the Highway 72 ByPass adjacent to Area Vocational School that had been constructed in 1965. Brockman was abandoned for school use but its auditorium continued to be used until vandalized and burned.

The new Chester High School was dedicated on Sunday, March 31, 1974. T. J. Bratton, superintendent, D. C. Reid, Jr., chairman of trustees, John Porter Gaston, member of House of Representatives, T. Quincy Smith, principal, Mrs. Jean Cann, director of music, and David Green, band director, participated. Hon. Tom S. Gettys, U. S. Congressman, made the address.

Dora Jones Elementary School was built in 1910 on a parcel of land on Reedy Street given by S. M. Jones. It was named in honor of Mrs. Jones.

Foote Street Elementary School was opened in 1904, operated for sixty-four years, and closed in 1968. In March, 1948, a cafeteria was opened in an old army barracks next to the school with Mrs. Blanche Hafner as director. The cafeteria burned December 17, 1954; and a new one was built onto the school building.

HISTORY OF BRAINERD INSTITUTE

Brainerd Institute had its beginnings in 1866 in Chester as one of the South's countless efforts to aid the hapless ex-slaves. Once a thriving and productive Negro school, today it consists of several fast decaying, lonely and ghostly buildings surrounded by weeds and piles of rubbish. The biggest and most imposing building has had no human inhabitants for years, save the weird vague echos of the dead past.

Brainerd's beginnings stretch back to Freedmen's Bureau created by law March 3, 1865, following the War Between the States.

BRAINERD INSTITUTE
1869-1959

The Bureau, functioning within the War Department, was designated a "Bureau of Refugees, Freedmen and Abandoned Lands" and was given the main task of promoting the well-being of the freedmen and of white refugees. It was commissioned to provide fuel, clothing and medical care for the destitute of both groups, to make provision for their education, and to make available, either for rent or sale, abandoned lands in the South that were held by the Federal government.

Miss E. E. Richmond, a white woman, came all the way from New York to help carry out this mission. She established her headquarters in a log cabin five miles north of Chester, on the Brawley plantation. She was soon joined by another white woman, Miss Carolyn I. Kent, from New Jersey. The school was moved to a large storage building in Chester.

For two years these two "angels of light" conducted a day school, a night school and a Sunday School and did untold good through their work among all the Negroes, old and young. Here preaching was held at frequent intervals by invited Negro ministers. School was taught by the two women in this storage building until 1869. Their work is described as "another of those unwritten pages of history where indispensable good was done for bewildered people." Just a few months earlier, these freedmen who had known white people only as masters came to know two of the finest of that race as their tireless devoted servants.

In the Fall of 1869, the Board of Missions of the New York Presbyterian Church sent the Reverend Samuel Loomis, a white minister, on a mission to upper South Carolina with instructions to establish churches and schools among the freedmen, at such points as seemed advisable, to begin religious and education work.

After pioneering through the section, Reverend Loomis chose Chester as the most favorable location from which a far-reaching work could be inaugurated. He began with the work which the two women were operating and spread out to the adjoining counties of York and Fairfield.

Rev. Loomis was designated by his church as a Home Missionary. Born In Twinsburg, Ohio on February 3, 1829, he earned an A.B. degree in 1849 (college unknown) and was graduated from Union Theological Seminary, New York, in 1853. The same year he was licensed by the Fourth Presbytery of New York. In 1856, he was ordained by the Presbytery of Pataskala, New York and began preaching. He and Mrs. Loomis, in December 1868, started the parochial school which soon developed into Brainerd Mission. The name Brainerd was chosen in honor of David Brainerd, a man Rev. Loomis knew and admired as a pioneer in mission work among the Indians. Historians recorded that "light began to dawn." The work of Brainerd Mission began to grow more noticeably and soon Brainerd Institute was established and recognized.

A church was organized by Rev. Loomis in the Fall of 1869 and the school work continued with Mrs. Loomis and Miss Kent as teachers. Both the school and church were moved to a new location then known locally as the "Old Commissary."

Rev. Loomis is remembered as a dedicated and dignified person. He always wore a black broadcloth Prince Albert with trousers to match the coat and vest, and a tall silk hat.

Among the clergymen Rev. Loomis trained and sent out to preach were the Rev. Baker Russell, the Rev. I. A. James, and the Rev. Reuben Nance.

To meet the growing needs of the school, in 1882, Professor H. A. Green came from New Jersey to work with the Loomises. The Freedmen's Board purchased the "DeGraffenreid Place," ten acres of land and a house east of the railroad and on a hill. In 1888, Centennial Hall was begun. The main part of the building was thirty-five feet by seventy-six feet, the ell on the west was twenty-five feet by fifty-five feet, all two and one-half stories high.

The lower floor was used for chapel and recitation rooms, the second floor as young men's dormitories and the printing room.

A workshop on the grounds was made possible by donations of Chester friends of the school. Records show that "the location of this school is a wise one, as it is situated in the midst of a dense colored population and is the only school of its class in all this section of the country."

Purpose of Brainerd is stated as "not only to fit young men and women for college and seminary, but to give those who wish a good academic education a chance to receive one. Our aim is to give our pupils such a religious, moral and mental training as will fit them to go out and found homes in which God is worshipped, purity and morality honored, and industry, thrift and self-respect constantly upheld."

Rev. and Mrs. Loomis continued their work in Chester for a quarter of a century. He resigned his position as principal in 1892. They were succeeded by another white couple, Professor and Mrs. J. S. Marquis of Washington, Pennsylvania, who continued at this work for thirty-six years. In 1928, the leadership of Brainerd was turned over to a Negro professor, J. D. Martin of Johnson C. Smith University. After conducting the school for six or seven years, he was succeeded by Professor L. S. Brown who continued as its head until the closing of the school at Commencement time in 1939.

Leverett Loomis, son of Rev. Loomis and an ornithologist who taught in Brainerd Institute, one day showed eleven varieties of wild ducks, mounted, that he said he killed in Chester County.

He was also a taxidermist and had a beautiful collection of Chester birds mounted. He afterwards became a professor at the University of California.

In the Historical Files of the Educational and Medical Unit of the Presbyterian Church, U.S.A., 1874, is found these items on Brainerd Institute:

Brainerd, Chester, South Carolina, Rev. Samuel Loomis, superintendent; well located on the edge of Chester upon a lot containing one acre and a quarter, has a neat two-story frame building combining school rooms and rooms for a missionary home, also two cottages for additional purposes.

There were 145 pupils receiving the highest educational advantages to children of Presbyterian families of the Chester Mission. A plain but neat house of worship had been erected on campus by Mrs. A. C. Brown of New York City.

Thirty-nine years later (1913) Thomas Jesse Jones described Brainerd as "a well-managed school of ten grades providing some industrial training" to 175 pupils, elementary 132, secondary 43. There were nine teachers, seven white and two Negro; seven females and two males.

Jones reported that the classroom work was well done, instruction in sewing was provided for all girls and woodworking for the boys. Boarding students also had cooking lessons and "fairly good home training."

The Presbyterian Board provided $5,628.00 that year, with $742.00 coming from tuition and fees. Salaries for the nine teachers was $4,540.00, supplies and equipment $3,380.00; power, light and heat $800.00 and repairs $150.00.

The campus had grown to twenty-one acres inside the town of Chester and its value was estimated at $2,100.00. The buildings were estimated at $41,000.00 and were reportedly "clean and well kept."

Twenty years later on January 13, 1933, Church records show Brainerd was a co-educational accredited high school. The boys and girls at Brainerd "invariably carry off all first prizes at the County Fair."

Among projects attempted by the new administration under Dr. J. D. Martin which followed a white faculty was the building of a school library, staffed by a trained librarian.

It is significant for Brainerd that it enjoyed the leadership of and fellowship with white leaders over so long a time. It was inevitable that these true missionaries should breathe into their Negro pupils an indispensable something, an experience of racial equality, an experience of self-worth, a cultivation which mere books could never give. This influence affected to a great extent the life of the Negro in the town of Chester and in the area.

Brainerd became a four-year high school in the early 1920s. In the mid 1930s it became Brainerd Junior College with its purpose that of teacher training. Its predicament was that of a vanishing high school enrollment and thus the necessity of expanding into college work or simply going out of existence. Its doom was sealed and Brainerd ceased to exist with the Spring commencement of 1939.

Some Distinguished Graduates of Brainerd

The Rev. Thomas Henry Ayers, A.B., A.M., D.D., pastor of Carmel Presbyterian Church in Chester.

Professor Robert James Boulware, former president of Clinton College of Rock Hill.

The Rev. James Henry Colerman, A.B., D.D., organized and built Second Wilson Baptist Church in Chester and James Chapel in Carlisle. He baptized between three and four thousand in the six churches he served as pastor.

The Rev. David Cordoza Crosby built the Clinton Chapel in York, S. C. and served as a Presiding Elder.

The Rev. Jerry Calvin Gilmore, L.I., A.B., long time pastor of Calvary Baptist Church in Chester.

The Rev. Mansel Phillip Hale, A.M., D.D., first president of Friendship Normal and Industrial College, minister and educator. His grandfather was a native African.

The Rev. Hugh L. Harry, A.B., A.M., had charge of the Presbyterian work in Manning, S. C.

The Rev. George Waldo Long, A.B., S.T.B., had charge of the Presbyterian work at Cheraw, and was head of the parochial school that later was named Long High School in his honor.

Dr. Isaiah Alvin Macon, practiced medicine in Chester and Rock Hill where he established a hospital and taught at Friendship College. His wife, Fannie Easler, also attended Brainerd.

The Rev. David Brainerd McLure spent all of his life serving Baptist churches in Chester County, was Moderator of Sandy River

Association and a trustee of Morris College.

The Rev. John Martin Miller, minister and principal of Emerson Industrial Institute.

The Rev. George A. Pratt, B.Th., member and teacher at Calvary Baptist Church in Chester. His mother, Amanda Williams Pratt was brought from Mobile, Alabama to South Carolina before Emancipation.

The Rev. David Eugene Rice, B.D., was private secretary to Bishop B. F. Lee of South Carolina Conference and pastor of a number of churches from 1909.

The Rev. Benjamin F. Russell, D.D., spent the first fifteen years of his life in slavery. He completed his study of theology at Biddle University and preached at Blackstock for forty years.

The Rev. Joseph Cyrus White, A.B., D.D., was pastor of Zion Baptist Church, the largest black church in South Carolina, where, under his leadership, membership grew from two hundred to twenty-seven hundred. He was a member of the Executive Board of State Convention, editor of People's Advocate, and trustee of Morris College.

Captain Phillip Thomas White taught at Friendship College and was Grand Orator of the Masons of South Carolina and editor of Rock Hill Messenger.

Mrs. Mamie Featherstone Woods was successful as a business woman in hair culture with an establishment in Chester and agents operating all over the state. She made generous contributions to Friendship College.

County Schools 1985-86

Chester Department of Education 121 Columbia Street, in 1985-86 school year had administrative personnel: Edward L. Laughinghouse, superintendent, C. T. Gaskins, Clyde L. Nelson and James A. Wilson, assistant superintendents. Annual budget is $14,500,955.

Board of Trustees are Willis Crain, chairman, D. C. Reid, Jr., Brenda Fort, J. Charles Killian, W. Earl Cameron, Bill Stringfellow, Jr. and Linda Short.

Schools, enrollment and teachers: York Road Elementary (Kindergarten) 275 students, 14 teachers, College Street Elementary on Hinton Street (1st and 2nd grades) 585 students, 42 teachers, Southside Elementary on J. A. Cochran By-Pass (3rd and 4th grades) 650 students, 45 teachers; Dora Jones-Gayle Elementary on Columbia Street (5th and 6th grades) 685 students, 45 teachers.

Chester Junior High on Caldwell Street (7th and 8th grades) 725 students, 44 teachers; Chester Senior High on By-Pass (Grades 9-12) 1400 students, 65 teachers; Chester Career Center on By-Pass 600 students, 27 teachers.

Fort Lawn Elementary has 180 students, 16 teachers; Lewisville Elementary (formerly Lando) 300 students, 23 teachers; Lewisville Middle School 315 students, 25 teachers; Lewisville High School 365 students, 30 teachers.

Great Falls Elementary 562 students, 37 teachers, Great Falls Middle 277 students, 22 teachers, Great Falls High 435 students, 26 teachers.

XIX *CHESTER COUNTY LIBRARIES*

FIRST LIBRARY IN COUNTY, 1771

W hen Scotch-Irish settlers in the 1750's arrived in what is now Chester County they brought with them their Bibles. For a good many years Bibles were their only library. As writer Bruce Barton wrote: "The Bible is not one book, it is a library." It contains history, drama, poetry, love stories, biography and autobiography, geography, genealogy, philosophy, astrology, religion, and mathematics. It touches on every facet of both human and divine knowledge. The Bible was used as a textbook in homes and early schools.

In 1771, the Reverend William Richardson, eminent Presbyterian divine and founder of Old Catholic Church in Chester County and Waxhaw Church in Lancaster County left a sum of money in his will "for purchasing Bibles and other religious books to be distributed among the poor in America." This legacy was implemented in 1800 and books were put into circulation among the church congregation.

During the Revolutionary War, the Rev. John Simpson, pastor of Fishing Creek Presbyterian Church was owner of a fine private library that was saved by his wife when the British set fire to his house. She rushed into the fire, piled the books into her apron and almost lost her life.

Records show that in 1815 an act was passed by the State of South Carolina to incorporate the Fishing Creek Circulating Library Society in Chester County. Books in the library were valued at $1,000.00. Since ministers were usually schoolmasters, too, the books were highly prized and widely used.

PEOPLE'S FREE LIBRARY OF SOUTH CAROLINA AT LOWRYS

Chester County is believed to be the first county in the United States to have had a circulating library.

The story of its beginning and of its unique services to rural citizens and to scattered little one-room schools across Chester County is an intriguing one.

In the early 1900s, Dr. Delano Fitzgerald, a physician of Baltimore Maryland, attracted by the good hunting and the friendly folks, came for many years to spend his winters at the Joe Wilson home in Lowryville.

Wishing to contribute something of value to the town where he had passed so many pleasant months, he donated a library in 1904, the first free library in Chester County. It was named the "People's Free Library of South Carolina."

He built a small pretty building on the edge of Zion Presbyterian Church property in Lowrys and furnished it completely with book shelves, tables and chairs, a Bible, an unabridged dictionary, a set of encyclopedias, and filled the shelves with classics and other books. The hand-written list of books reached a total of 1,381. Records of users were kept in a ledger.

Dr. Fitzgerald employed a librarian, Mrs. Florence Guy Anderson (Mrs. Ernest T. Anderson, Sr.), afterwards Mrs. Jake Jenkins. All expenses of establishment and operation were borne by Dr. Fitzgerald. The community accepted his gift with enthusiasm, and the facility was eagerly used. A love of good books and reading was generated in the Lowrys community that is still strong to this day.

In order to make the books more widely available, Dr. Fitzgerald had 22 strong cabinets made that would hold several dozen books. These boxes were distributed to the homes and schools of the county. The boxes were exchanged every month. Each box had a number and a record book listing the contents.

Dr. Fitzgerald hired Walter Bankhead to circulate the books once a month by horse and buggy. Among regular stops of this early "bookmobile" were Armenia, Sealy's Creek, Guthriesville, McConnellsville, Mt. Pleasant, Delphos, Wilksburg, Baton Rouge, New Hope, Chalkville, Brattonville, Olive, Dinber, Capers Chapel, Carters, Lewis Turnout and Airlee. Regular stops were also made at the Lathan's, M. M. Grant's, Gwin's, Mrs. C. H. Smith's and Mrs. J. N. Brice's homes.

In addition to a choice selection of books, Dr. Fitzgerald subscribed to top magazines of the day and had them come to the People's Free Library of South Carolina. Old record books dating back to 1908 reveal how popular these magazines were. Among the most widely circulated were the Delineator, Harper's, Little Folks,

Short Stories, Etude, American Boy, Pictorial Review, Ladies' Home Journal, McClure's Modern Priscilla, American Poultry Journal, World's Work, Munsey, Review of Reviews, Suburban Life, Success, Everybody's Southern Cultivator, and Cosmopolitan.

Records show $17.00 was spent in March, 1908 to renew magazine subscriptions. In the same month, money to maintain the library was spent as follows: gummed numbers 50¢, a load of wood 75¢, postage 10¢, delivery of books 5¢, glue 25¢, fixing chairs 50¢, ink 10¢, cleaning yard 15¢, and a postal card 1¢.

After Mrs. Anderson ceased to serve as librarian, volunteers kept the library open for a while. It was finally closed and remained closed for several years. It was reopened and operated as a branch of Chester Public Library from 1948-1954. L. C. Berry, a member of the library board, was instrumental in having it re-opened. Mrs. Helen B. Bradford was employed as librarian.

The library again fell into disuse in 1955 when the Book Club and the Bookmobile made an abundance of literature available. The books were sent to Chester County Library and the building turned over to Zion Presbyterian Church as stipulated in the deed.

Many books from the Fitzgerald collection are still in the Public Library. Among them are the large leather-bound Bible, a rare picture book on American Presidents, two volumes of Life of General Stonewall Jackson, and many volumes of fiction. Several of the book boxes are there on exhibit.

HISTORY OF CHESTER COUNTY LIBRARY

The Palmetto Literary Club might be called the mother of the Chester County Public Library because this club was instrumental in getting the library started.

The Palmetto Club was organized in 1898. It, along with the Up-to-Date Club, was a charter member of the South Carolina Federation of Women's Clubs (SCFWC). The president of this infant club was Mrs. G. B. White, mother of the late M. Henry White who served for a long time as president of the People's National Bank.

Mrs. White, keenly interested in educational and cultural life of her community, had a vision, and that was the establishment of a community library. When a group of club women attended the organizational meeting of the SCFWC the delegates from the Palmetto Club returned from this meeting inspired to organize a public library.

Early minutes of the Palmetto Club reveal that, at Mrs. White's instigation, an organizational meeting was called in August, 1898. The Club members received the idea enthusiastically. The interest of the Up-to-Date Club and that of prominent citizens was enlisted and a Library Association was formed.

In 1900, the long talked of library became a reality. It had a home ready and waiting in a large second-floor room of City Hall that overlooked the square.

When the Chester City Hall was erected on top of the hill in 1892, Giles J. Patterson, an attorney-at-law and a far-sighted citizen had incorporated in the charter a provision that certain space be designated for use as a Public Library. The Library was named the Patterson Free Library in his honor.

In 1900, the formal opening of this first library took place in the City Hall with dignified and appropriate ceremonies. A son of Chester, Judge Joshua Hilary Hudson was speaker for the occasion. His speech is recorded in his book *Sketches and Reminiscences* which is a rare and treasured volume to those fortunate enough to own one.

The first board of governors for the library were Mrs. A. G. Brice, Mrs. Julia Campbell, the Reverend D. N. McLaughlin, and Mrs. G. B. White. Financial support of the library came from paid memberships, small fees, plus many musicals, teas, plays and ice cream suppers.

The first librarian was Mrs. Julian (Julia Gott) Sloan, one of three Gott sisters who, when the history of education in Chester is written, should have a chapter dedicated to them.

Mrs. Sloan was a lady of culture and mistress of a private school. She instilled into many boys and girls of that day a love for good reading and a taste for good literature.

She was succeeded by Miss Julia Spratt. Miss Poston succeeded Miss Spratt and during her administration the library became a free library. The Chester Free Library continued to serve the community well under the guidance of Mrs. Ada C. Stone, and enjoyed a marked degree of success.

About 1921, interest in the library lagged and it was closed for a time. The Chamber of Commerce finally came to the rescue and kept it open for a year. Then, when it seemed in danger of being closed again, the club women under the leadership of Mrs. T. S. Leitner, took it over.

The twelve Women's Clubs of Chester banded together and each club pledged $50.00 a year toward the support of the library. A Board of Governors in 1925, composed of the presidents of each of the 12 clubs, elected the following officers from their number: Mrs. T. S. Leitner, chairman; Mrs. John G. White, vice-chairman; Mrs. R. R. Moffatt, treasurer; and Mrs. R. E. Abell, secretary.

The Board elected Mrs. S. E. (Ethel Means) McFadden librarian. With Mrs. McFadden's literary knowledge and organizational ability, the circulation and stock of books began to grow, magazines and newspapers were subscribed to, and the Chester Free Library gained a firm place in the life of the community.

During Book Week each fall, the club women canvassed the business houses for funds to help buy new books, and directed the destiny of the library for six years.

In 1929, City Hall was destroyed by fire. Many valuable books and documents were burned. Fortunately, the portraits of the four signers of the Ordinance of Secession itself were saved and are now the property of the Chester County Historical Society and are housed in its Museum. Only 600-700 volumes in circulation at the time of the fire were saved.

The morning after the fire, Chester citizens hastened to call a meeting in the Sunday School rooms of the Associate Reformed Presbyterian Church to make plans to continue the library. On July 26, 1929, the Board of Governors accepted the responsibility of securing a new home for the surviving books.

With the cooperation of Superintendent of Education John E. Nunnery, a room in the Chester County Court House was secured as a temporary home, and on the first afternoon when the library service was resumed, 78 volumes were donated by friends of the library.

The Chester Free Library continued to serve the people from the Court House until 1930 when the original quarters in the rebuilt City Hall were ready for occupancy. A room for the children's books and a storage space on the top floor were added to the original space alloted to the library. To avoid further loss by fire, a fireproof safe was purchased for the storage of irreplaceable records and documents.

The six-year period for which the club women had pledged their support to the library was drawing to a close. They kept plugging away for a tax-supported library. In 1931, the citizens of Chester School District, in the midst of the depression, voted to tax themselves and additional 1.2 mills, rather than to dispense with the services of their libraries.

A part of the tax was pro-rated for a Negro branch library to be housed at Finley High School. The wife of Professor S. L. Finley served as first librarian without remuneration. Later the library was taken over by the school librarian.

The new Board of Governors appointed by the Chester County Board of Education consisted of Mrs. H. S. Adams, Mrs. T. S. Leitner, Mrs. C. W. McTeer, Mrs. W. C. Miller and Mrs. John G. White.

When the Women's Clubs of Chester turned the responsibility for the running of the library over to the new board, they donated the sum of $125.00 toward the purchase of new books for the Caroliniana Collection.

Mrs. McFadden continued to serve as librarian. She was a woman of wisdom and dedication. She possessed in a very special way the two necessary qualifications for a good librarian. She knew and loved people; she knew and appreciated books. She received a very meager salary but she was selfless in service. She spent countless hours overtime tidying up the library, dusting the books and shelves, and gathering material for club and term papers.

Mrs. McFadden retired in 1956 after 30 years of service to the library. She made her home in Columbia with her son, Attorney Means McFadden, until her death in April, 1966.

As citizens grew more library conscious, the interest became county-wide. Through proper legislation, a tax-supported county library came into being. This was made possible by a 1¾ mill property tax imposed.

In 1946, plans for a tax supported Chester County Library were completed and the board of the Chester Free Library turned its assets over to the county. The library was henceforth known as Chester County Public Library with branches at Great Falls, Lowrys and Finley High School.

Trustees appointed by the County Board of Education were L. C. Berry of Lowrys, Thomas B. Hamilton, Mrs. William C. Miller and Mrs. John G. White all of Chester, J. W. Keistler and L. W. Pittman of Great Falls, and J. G. Hollis of Richburg.

In 1950, the ground floor of the handsome new War Memorial Building adjacent to the Court House was dedicated to the use of Chester County Library. It remained in use for thirty-five years, until 1985.

Librarians who succeeded Mrs. Ethel Means McFadden were Mr. Maude Q. Kelsey, Mrs. Elizabeth C. Williams, Miss Jame Porter, Flint A. Norwood, Mrs. Elizabeth Dixon, William Kay and Ms. Patricia Ryckman.

During Norwood's tenure in 1958, the Library Services Act was passed. It authorized the State Library Board to make available to one library in each Congressional District, a special local history depository for Caroliniana. The Chester library was designated for Fifth Congressional District including Chester, Cherokee, Chesterfield, Lancaster, York, Fairfield and Kershaw counties.

Among Caroliniana's approximately 1,500 volumes are many that are out of print and irreplaceable, including early South Carolina histories by McCrady, Snowden, Wallace and Rivers. Other rare volumes are Mrs. Ellet's *Women of the Revolution* in three volumes, Gen. Robert E. Lee's *Letters and Recollections,* and *Colonial Records of the South Carolina House of Commons* from 1749.

Of unusual interest are three volumes of *Men of Mark in South Carolina* and several volumes of *Kinfolks*. On microfilm are *Southern Intelligencer* of Charleston, S. C. dating back to 1822, the

Chester Standard from 1854-1857, and the *Chester Reporter* from 1874-1906.

Rare volumes of biographies, South Carolina churches and gardens, genealogies, schools and colleges are on file. A new vertical file set up in 1983 by Mrs. Gladys Dixon Douglas contains a wealth of collected materials and pictures pertaining to Chester County and South Carolina.

A new branch library in Great Falls was dedicated in February 1976.

During Ms. Ryckman's administration since 1979, library staff has been expanded to include a professional children's librarian and an adult services librarian. Dial-a-story has been added along with regular services to nursing center, children's story hour, and summer reading program. More local newspapers have been microfilmed, and local history and genealogical records expanded.

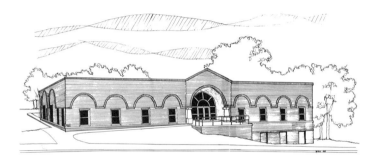

A DREAM COMES TRUE

After more than five years of planning, Chester County councilmen voted in September 1983 to build a new Chester County headquarters library at the corner of West End and Center streets if voters approved an October 25th bond referendum to pay for it. The 600-square-foot space in the Memorial Building had become inadequate and there were no parking spaces.

Councilmen and library trustees considered about a dozen possible sites before settling on the Center Street site. Architect Frank Williams of Matthews, N. C. recommended this sloping site that would allow for a 7500 square foot basement under the 15,000-square-foot proposed library. The site, made of five lots, included ones owned by the Chester County School District and J. Edward Davis. The lots total about 3.2 acres.

County voters approved the bond referendum by 1,760 to 947 vote margin on October 25, 1983. Voters authorized County Council to issue up to $1 million in general obligation bonds to purchase the library site and construct a new facility.

Friends of the Library, a support group organized in 1983, concentrated efforts to promote passing of the referendum, and in raising funds through a public subscription campaign. A $100,000.00 grant from federal jobs bill was made through State Library. It was made to create jobs in the County where unemployment was 14%, one of the highest in the state, at the time. Library officials set a goal to raise $500,000.00. Private citizens donated $44,928.00 toward the project to lower the tax burden. Funding sources such as the Elliott White Springs Foundation and the Chester Foundation, businesses and industries, federal and state agencies made donations to further lower the cost.

The library, designed to blend with Chester's existing City Hall and other on-the-hill buildings, was built by Leitner Construction Company under the supervision of J. D. (Jimmy) Leitner, Jr. Jimmy's grandmother, Mrs. T. S. Leitner was one of the library's founders in 1922.

The library, completed in July 1985, has a spacious meeting room, kitchen and toilets that groups can use without entering the main part of the building. It has a well-stocked local history room, a conference room and children's special area. There are 82 parking spaces at the corner site, with entrances from both Center Street and West End Street.

Ground Breaking

On a blistering hot Sunday afternoon, August 5, 1984, ground was broken with a golden beribboned shovel for the new library. Speaker for the occasion was the Hon. Heyward McDonald, South Carolina Senator, who grew up in Chester. In the wilting heat, he made a few gracious remarks then handed his well-prepared speech to news reporters — and invited the approximately 100 guests to join him at City Hall for a brief reception and a cooling libation.

The Hon. Paul Short of South Carolina House of Representatives, wielded the shovel and managed a meager crack in the dry and hard-packed soil on the site. The Rev. Gene Forrest Couch, pastor of Bethel United Methodist Church gave the invocation. Mrs. Anne P. Collins, chairman of Library Trustees, presided over the meeting and introduced guests.

Bookmobile

Chester County has a long tradition of bookmobile service. Soon after the People's Free Library was begun in Lowrys in 1903, the first attempt to circulate books to the rural population was made by means of horse and buggy. Twenty-two sturdy oak boxes were constructed and passed around to schools, stores and homes.

The Library put its first motorized bookmobile on Chester County roads in 1938. John Edgar Nunnery, Superintendent of Education, was instrumental in its planning and purchase. This vehicle was used for ten years, but its design — with books shelved behind windows on the outside of the truck — exposed both patrons and staff to the weather.

Three later bookmobiles, including a converted bread truck, served Chester County over the years. The new bookmobile, manufactured by the Gerstenslager Company of Wooster, Ohio, was put into service January 17, 1983. It has shelving for 1500 books and cost $35,500.00

Bookmobile staff 1938-1983: Nelle Wilkes, Lorene Roof, LaVerne McLane, Daisy Browning, Helen Bradford, Marie Hatchell, Ethel Hollis, Frances Lee O'Neal, Anne Cassells, Cathy W. Bryant, Elizabeth Lawson.

The new bookmobile was dedicated on Sunday, March 6, 1983 with Betty E. Callaham, South Carolina State Librarian; Carlisle Roddey, Chester County Supervisor; the Rev. Charles Elliot, pastor of Purity Presbyterian Church; Anne P. Collins, Chairman and Henry L. Sneed, Jr., trustee, Board of Library Trustees participating.

Friends of the Library

Friends of Library was organized on June 6, 1983 as a supporting arm of Chester County Public Library. Organizational procedures were set up by Mrs. Anne P. Collins, Chairman of Library Trustees, and Miss Susan Grant Hasty who drafted the by-laws and called the first meeting.

Charter officers were president, Miss Hasty; vice-president, William White; secretary, Mrs. Mary Beth Anderson; treasurer, Mrs. Doris Schumacher; board members, Mrs. Harriet Stringfellow, Mrs. Lou Cecil and Mrs. Betty Caughman.

Friends, with upwards of 300 members, has to its credit successful lecture and classic film series, book sales, the campaign supporting the successful bond referendum for a new library, and printing and selling note paper designed by Chester County artists.

Masons Lay Cornerstone for New Library

Performing a ceremony that dates back to the earliest days of masonry in Italy, S. C. Grand Master of Masons Harry T. White of Spartanburg formally laid the cornerstone at the building site of the new Chester County Library on Center Street Saturday, December 15, 1984.

The members of Chester Masonic Lodge No. 18 A.F.M., along with Grand Lodge masonic officers from all over the state, the latter of whom wore formal attire, gathered on a bright, warm day to add a bit of history to Chester's new construction. It was the first time since 1891 that a cornerstone ceremony had been conducted in Chester by masons.

The cornerstone itself contains some history sealed in a time capsule. Two copper boxes hold artifacts of the masons, including lists of local and Great Falls Lodge officers. Also in the boxes is information on the library architect and builder, and current issues of newspapers.

In Saturday's ceremony, White pronounced "the stone to be sound and true, through the test of level and plumb." As has been done by masons for centuries, the stone was then sprinkled with the corn of nourishment, the wine of refreshment, and oil of joy from small silver pitchers.

Finally, the stone was edged by a trowel, which is the South Carolina Masonic order's most prized possession. White said the trowel was made of Mexican silver coins by the Marquis de Lafayette in 1825. Lafayette used it to lay the cornerstone at the monument to Gen. Barron DeKalb, whom he had fought with in the Revolution.

The trowel is so prized by masons, White said, because it is one of the few ceremonial pieces that was not taken or destroyed by Sherman's troops in the Civil War.

Also speaking briefly at the cornerstone ceremony were County Supervisor Carlisle Roddey, Mayor Willie Cranford, Library Board Chairman Anne P. Collins, Head Librarian Pat Ryckman and Worshipful Master Calvin Price of Chester Masonic Lodge No. 18. Chester City Manager Penn Colvin, a mason, presided.

The ceremony was followed by a reception in City Hall in honor of the visiting Grand Lodge officers, who came from as far away as Charleston to participate in the ceremony.

CHESTER COUNTY LIBRARY DEDICATION

Chester County Library was formally dedicated on Sunday, October 6, 1985 at 3 p.m. On Center Street at convergence of Main, the 15,000-square-foot brick building was completed in August and the move from War Memorial Building was made on September 10.

The Hon. John M. Spratt, Congressman from Fifth Congressional District made the dedicatory address. He was introduced by South Carolina State Librarian Betty E. Callaham.

Two special rooms in the library were presented. The S. Lewis Bell local history room given in memory of the late civic leader and library patron was presented by Henry L. Sneed, Jr. member of Library Board of Trustees. The Anne Pickens Collins conference room honoring current trustee and Board chairman Anne P. Collins was given by her three sons and three daughters. Presentation was made by Joel Wyman Collins, Jr. Both rooms were accepted by Jeff D. Brown member of Board of Trustees.

The Bell room was donated by a local foundation. The Collins room was donated by Joe Ann Collins Dickson of Jamestown, North Carolina, Nancy Collins Anderson of Rock Hill, Dr. Andrew Pickens Collins of Durham, North Carolina, Margaret Collins Boshamer of Charlotte, North Carolina, Joel Wyman Collins, Jr. of Columbia and Richard Wilkinson Collins of Newberry and their families.

Other program participants were the Rev. Rhett Y. Winters, Jr., pastor of St. Marks Episcopal Church and the Rev. Dr. James L. Jackson, pastor of First Baptist Church. Chairman Collins presided.

Friends of the Library, Margaret Hamilton, president, and library trustees and staff served as hosts following the dedication. They conducted guests on tour of the building and served refreshments.

XX *A LOOK BACK*

CHESTER IN 1869

When John A. Bradley, Jr., Chester attorney-newspaperman, founder of Chester Reporter, looked at Chester in January, 1869, here is what he saw:

About 1,000 residents in the town.

No automobiles but lots of horse-drawn wagons, buggies, people on horseback or on foot.

Streets were muddy quagmires, and there were no sidewalks.

Public school system was limited to a two-story, six-room brick building on Academy Street, plus two small wooden buildings at the rear of the house for first, second and third grades.

Three drug stores: A. H. DeVega in a room on top of the hill where Duke Power Co. later had an office.

Dr. S. E. Babcock and J. J. Stringfellow in a building across the street from City Hall.

Leard and Jordan in the McAliley building on the square.

(Later Stringfellow did business in the Cotton Hotel Building.) Leard opened his own business where the Lynn brothers later operated Lynn's Drug Store in the valley.

Doctors: Dr. S. E. Babcock, Dr. A. P. Wylie, Dr. Robert Jordan, Dr. W. Melton. Dr. Wylie was the father of Dr. Gill Wylie, famous New York physician and founder of Bellevue School of Nursing.

Dr. Babcock had two sons, Dr. James Babcock who headed S. C. State Hospital for years, and W. F. Babcock, secretary-treasurer of Chester Mill.

Attorneys: Samuel McAliley, William H. Brawley, James Hemphill, Giles J. Patterson, W. A. Walker, C. S. Brice, Major S. P. Hamilton, J. J. McLure, E. C. McLure, J. J. Hemphill, T. C. Gaston, John A. Bradley, Jr.

William H. Brawley later moved his practice to Charleston where he was appointed to a federal judgeship by President Grover Cleveland.

Major Hamilton who had lost an arm in an accident was one of the more colorful lawyers and a playwright. Many of his plays were hit attractions at the Chester Opera House when they were presented by local amateur groups. Major Hamilton was a son of James Hamilton, Governor of South Carolina during the turbulent Nullification Period. He also served as president of South Carolina Bar Association. Herman P. Hamilton of Chester is a descendant.

OLD NICHOLSON HOTEL

CHESTER 1876

Hotels in Chester in 1876:

The Nicholson House near the Southern Railway depot conducted by Mrs. Catherine ("Mrs. Tatt") Nicholson and her daughter Sally and her son, William.

The Chester Hotel in the center of town.

The Cotton Hotel. "Another good boarding place of good capacity not far across from the Court House."

J. Hillary Hudson lists the following tradesmen in Chester:

Lawyers: Samuel McAliley, Nathaniel Eaves, James Hemphill, M. Barron, Alexander Walker, C. D. Melton, Dudley Culp, John J. McLure.

Clerk of the Court of Common Pleas and General Sessions was John Rosborough.

"Whipping post was in use as an instrument of punishment — white men were led from the prison cell, stripped to the waist, fastened to the post and given thirty and nine lashes on the bare back, well laid on with rawhide." It was a shocking sight — but had a most salutary effect in deterring men from committing crime.

Merchants: Thomas McLure, Amzi Neely, John McKee, Brawley and Alexander, Dickson Henry, James Graham; all these — accomplished business men, noted for strict integrity and purity of character.

Boarding House on the decline of the street leading to McLure Hill, John McAfee and his maiden sister, Ellen, proprietors.

The George Kennedy house, kept by Mr. Colvin, M. Howerton,

Mr. Mid McDonald.

"Miss Ellen McAfee was the most famous caterer, in this line in advance of her day."

Dram Shops: Joshua Gore "Eccentric, humorous and loud-swearing," and John McAfee.

Carpenters: George Albright who came from North Carolina with a family of sons, and George McCormick.

Tailors: Dabney Hudson, Rush Hudson, Jefferson Clark, Angus Nicholson.

Jefferson Clark is described as "a good tailor and a noted ventriloquist which faculty was a source of much amusement both to himself and friends. The negro blacksmith often dropped the foot of the horse he was shoeing and fled the premises upon hearing the horse curse him. Others destroyed the dozen eggs one by one which they were offering for sale on hearing chickens chirping in them."

Leading Farmers in early 1900s: W. Holmes Hardin, John W. Grant, John Darby, Major John W. Wilks, Robert Love, John B. Cornwell, William Cornwell, Joseph Smyer, Andrew White, Matthew White, Joshua Abell, Amaziah Triplett, D. B. Rothrock, Alex Rosborough, Obadiah Farrar, Biggers Mobley, Hamilton McCandless.

Merchants: F. M. Nail owned Valley Racket Store in the valley on Gadsden Street. S. B. Nail owned hotel in 1887, later Chester Hotel. Wylie and Agurs, General Merchandise.

J. L. Gunhouse & Co., General Merchandise.

Pinkston M. Nail, Groceries and Confectioneries; owned Red Racket store 101-105 Main Street where Peoples Furniture Company is now. Racket stores were fore-runners of Five and Ten Cent stores.

H. C. Rothrock, Soft Drinks & Confectioneries.

Henry Samuels, Dry Goods.

Myer Wachtel, Dry Goods.

Jake Kaufmann, Men's Cothing.

John Gibson, Groceries.

J. J. Stringfellow, Drugs.

A. H. Davega, Drugs.

James Parish, Furniture and Coffins.

W. Holmes Hardin, Groceries and Farm Supplies.

E. C. Stahn and R. Brandt, Jewelry.

Miles Hunter, Confectioneries.

Bob Alexander, W. T. D. Cousar, Culp & Irwin, Saling Heyman, and Nix Grocery Co., Groceries.

John McIver, Baker.

Parker and Woods, Saddles.

James Pagan, General Merchandise and Farm Supplies.

Buck Massey, General Farm Supplies.

Bennett and Moffatt, Farm Implements.
Bob McNinch, Monuments.
John Yongue, Depot Agent.
Tom Brennecke, Express Agent & Telegraph Operator.
George Albright, Contractor.
John Albright, Cotton Buyer.
George Melton and Harvey Smith, Cotton Buyers & Capitalists.

CHESTER COUNTY IN 1883

Chester County has 16 towns and trading settlements; with 125 stores, as follows: Chesterville, 87 stores; Blackstock, 9 stores; Richburg, 7 stores; Fort Lawn, 4 stores; Bascomville, Chestnut Grove, Hazlewood, Lowryville, and Crosbyville, 2 stores each; Carmel, Cornwell, Landsford, Rossville and Wylie's, one store each.

Of this number five sell liquor, two hardware, twelve drygoods, 47 miscellaneous articles and 59 general merchandise. The stock of the storekeepers is estimated at $904,000. Chesterville is the county seat.

It has three hotels, and a large hall for public exhibitions, is let for $5 to $10 a night. Nine churches with accommodations to seat 3,000 persons were built at a cost of $35,000. There are two graded schools; the buildings cost $9,000 with a capacity for 500 pupils, a female academy, and an Institute exclusively for colored pupils.

Taxes are two and one-half mills, with a street tax of $2.50 on all able-bodied males. There is an indebtedness of $3,000, the balance due on the cost of constructing five water tanks for fire protection, with a capacity of 100,000 gallons.

Three railroads unite here, the Charlotte and Columbia, and two narrow gauge roads, the Chester and Lenoir linking the Atlanta and Air Line railroad, and the Chester and Cheraw completed to Lancaster.

The National Bank has capital of $150,000, surplus $80,000.

Besides fruits, hides, etc. about 30,000 bales of cotton are shipped annually to Charleston, New York, Baltimore and Philadelphia. Yearly sales are given as follows: provisions $300,000; dry goods $150,000; hardware $50,000; miscellaneous $20,000.

Among industries of the town is a large wagon and carriage manufactory, the Chester agricultural works and machine shops, a saddlery, and a cotton seed oil mill. Recent attention has been given to grape culture.

Two newspapers are published in the town, and the County Agricultural Society has extensive fairgrounds.

In 1840, the population of Chester was 250; in 1880 it was 1,899.

XXI *TOWN OF CHESTER*

ESTABLISHED ON HILL

The name Chester was derived from that of the county in Pennsylvania from which the first settlers migrated. They brought it from Chester, England when they came to America. The word Chester comes from the Latin words, castra, which means camp. That first little settlement was called Chesterville.

The people from Pennsylvania were accustomed to bringing their cattle into the fertile plains of the south to graze. The site of the town of Chester is believed to have originally been a cowpen, or camp.

Two classes of people generally advanced in front of the regular settlers or cultivators of the soil. These were the owners of cowpens, and traders with the Indians. An uncultivated country covered with canes and natural grasses possessed many advantages for raising stock. These were greatest where the settlements were least. Central spots in which cattle might be occasionally rallied, and so far domesticated as to prevent their running wild, were sought for and improved. They were often located in front of the settlements. Some of them suffered greatly at the hands of the Indians.

Traders advanced without ceremony into the heart of Indian settlements. Individuals sometimes turned their backs on civilized society and chose a residence among the Indians. Anthony Park, one of the first settlers of the back country, traveled in 1758 a few hundred miles among the Indians. He found several white men, chiefly Scotch-Irish who said they had lived as traders among the Indians, some from twenty to fifty years. One of these said that he had upwards of seventy children and grandchildren in the nation.

In *Kinfolks,* several traders with names common to Chester District are recorded. They lived among the Cherokees.

220

A General View of the Upper Country, (According to Anthony Park and Dr. Davis)

In the year 1750, when the settlement of the upper country began, there were so many buffaloes, which have long since disappeared, that three or four men with their dogs could kill from ten to twenty in a day. Wild turkeys were also in the greatest plenty. Deer were so numerous that a rifleman with a little powder and shot could easily kill four or five in a day. A common hunter could kill in the autumnal season as many bears as would make from two or three thousand weight of bear bacon. The waters abounded with beavers, otters and muskrats. Twenty beavers have been caught by one man in one season on Fairforest. The country was also overrun with wolves, panthers and wild cats. There was a great facility of raising stock from the profusion of native grasses and canes. When the whole country was within the grasp of a few settlers, the preference of one spot over another was generally decided by the comparative plenty of canes. Though provisions were easily raised, the labor of raising them for sale was but indifferently rewarded, for there was no regular market for any crop nearer than 100 miles. The skins of wild beasts were the most profitable crop taken to Charlestown: next to them was butter and tallow, afterwards flour and hemp.

The town of Chester grew around the farm of the Stewart family where the Great Wagon Road from Pennsylvania and the road from Columbia intersected. By 1835, there were at least twelve buildings including a Baptist Church and a court house. By the 1850s the village had grown to include many more houses, stores and offices. The great change, however, came with the advent of the railroad in August, 1851.

Hub of the little town of Chester was established on top of the area's highest hill. Tradition holds that the streets were laid out by rivulets from a keg of rum bursted in a boisterous launching of the township.

CITY HALL

Chester's City Hall was built in 1890-91 under the supervision of Captain A. D. Holler who was also the builder of College Street School the same year. The four-story brick building with basement constructed in Romanesque Revival style on the crest of Chester's hill cost $15,902.

It is 115 feet wide on the west side, 56 feet on south side, 124 feet on east side, and 67 feet on north side. It contained a high clock tower with a bell in it. The bell sounded the alarm for fires and alerted volunteer firemen.

City Hall was one of the most impressive structures built in early Chester. On the first floor were city offices and city jail. Upstairs was the Opera House, which served as the civic center of the community. Graduation exercises, minstrel shows, chatauquas and home talent plays were held there. The first moving picture in Chester, "The Birth of a Nation" was shown there; it was a silent picture.

The Opera House, handsomely fitted and furnished, consisted of a "pit" containing the choice seats, a gallery with two box seats, and two closed box seats in the pit area.

James Hamilton was city engineer and treasurer, and was also manager of the Opera House.

The first company to play in the new auditorium was Barlow's Minstrels in September, 1891. The scenery for the stage was painted by E. Cramer of Columbia. Coburn's Minstrels also performed in Chester as did Redpath Chatauqua.

Mrs. W. R. Wallace (Lucille Melton) was one of Chester's most outstanding and capable directors and actresses in amateur theatricals. The plays she produced at the Opera House were excellent and memorable. Costumes used were elegant as they were ordered from New York.

Lucille Melton's talent was widely recognized. She was offered the role of Jo March in a pretigious touring company production of *Little Women,* but turned it down when her mother, Mrs. Lizzie Melton expressed her strong opinion that acting was not a proper pursuit for a young lady of quality.

A fire on July 25, 1929, badly damaged City Hall. Many treasures of the library, valuable pictures such as that of Edward Strobel, the statesman, and others were destroyed. It was rebuilt, this time omitting the auditorium or opera house but including a community room and library. The bell and clock were not replaced.

City Hall in 1981 stood with its age showing and little left of its former stateliness and style. The library was moved to War Memorial Building. The fire department in 1980 was moved to a new station on Columbia Street. City jail was moved to City-County Law Enforcement Center on Dawson Drive. City offices and council chambers and a police substation are in the building now.

City Hall underwent a restoration in 1983. The exterior was sandblasted and repaired, the trim painted. The interior was painted and redecorated. Funds were provided by matching grants from the City of Chester and the South Carolina Department of Archives and History. Only nationally registered historic and endangered properties were eligible for this grant under the Special Emergency Jobs Act. The City of Chester received the largest grant amount in the state for the year.

Chester's downtown area, or Hill District, was designated as an

Historic District in the National Register of Historic Places in 1972. The Chester City Hall was also placed as an historic building in the National Register in 1973.

On May 14, 1984, the Chester City Hall Reopening Ceremony was held in observation of National Historic Preservation Week. Participants were Mayor William A. Cranford, City Manager Penn Colvin, the Rev. James Jackson, Charles E. Lee, director of S. C. Department of Archives and History, Calvin Price, Master of Chester Masonic Lodge #18, and Chester High School Concert Band directed by Tom Fort.

MAYORS OF CHESTER

Like most small southern towns, Chester's city hall in the 1970s was old, sparsely furnished, and had few creature comforts to make administering city government a plush job. Council chamber was a monotone of brown walls, heavy tables, dark benches and chairs.

The cushionless benches arranged under the tall windows had been polished through the years as councilmen sat, pondered, squirmed and wrestled with civic matters.

A big old-fashioned, four-bladed oscillating fan hung from the high ceiling. From its inanimate vantage point it doubtless witnessed Chester's growing pains for many years. It had ruffled the papers bearing official seals and signatures. It fanned not only a procession of councilmen but reams of rhetoric through the years.

HAMILTON COMPANY

The fascinating feature of City Hall is the collection of framed photographs of Chester's 29 mayors who have served the city since the 1850s. They look down from their mounted frames with varying degrees of dignity, high starched collars, bearded styles and bow ties. All their visages are austere and unsmiling except His Honor R. D. "Reg" Wilson whose smile is, to those who know him, built in and permanent. He served as mayor from 1959-1967 for a eight-year term.

There is a hint of an Irish twinkle in the eyes of His Honor Robert Frazer, mayor from 1930-1943. He brought it with him when he emigrated from Ireland to Chester while still a young man. He holds the distinction of serving as Chester's mayor longer than any other — 13 consecutive years.

His Honor E. Booker Bagby who was mayor from 1945-1955 and again from 1957-1959 ran him a close second with twelve years of service to the city. He looks down from the wall with the warmth and friendliness that were so much a part of him. He looks as if he were about to begin one of the funny stories he enjoyed telling.

Next in length of service, His Honor W. H. Hardin, 1884-1885 and 1899-1907, served as mayor for nine years, His Honor S. C. Carter for seven years, and His Honor S. M. Jones for six years.

Mr. Jordan Bennett had the honor of serving as Chester's First Intendent, a title later supplanted by that of mayor. He served prior to 1860 for an unspecified term.

Intendents and their terms of service were: John J. McLure, 1860-61 and 1863-64, John A. Bradley, 1862-63.

There is a gap during Civil War period 1863-68.

Dr. Eli Cornwall, 1868-1870, A. H. Davega, 1870-1872, G. W. Melton, 1872-1876, John L. Agurs, 1877-1881, John L. Chambers, 1881-1884, W. H. Hardin, 1884-1885, John McIver, 1885-1886, J. Lyles Glenn, 1886-1887, S. M. Jones, 1887-1893, J. C. James, 1893-1895.

Beginning with Mayor Barnett M. Spratt who served 1895-1899, the title of mayor was given the city's head of government. Succeeding mayors were: W. H. Hardin, 1899-1907, R. B. Caldwell, 1907-1909, Henry Samuels, 1909, E. H. Hardin, 1909-1911, John M. Wise, 1911-1913, W. J. Simpson, 1913-1915, Z. Vance Davidson, 1915-1919, J. B. Westbrook, 1919-1921, George Washington Byars, 1921-1923, Samuel Church Carter, 1923-1930, Theodore N. Tinsley, Mayor Pro-Tem 1930, Robert Frazer, 1930-1943, Fred J. Powell, 1943-1945, E. Booker Bagby, 1945-1955 and 1957-1959, Herman P. Hamilton, 1955-1957, Reginald D. "Reg" Wilson, 1959-1967, Edward Hood Dawson, 1967-1975, James T. Funderburk, 1975-1983, William A. Cranford, 1983-.

A portrait of John Colvin Cornwall shows that he served continuously as City Councilman for twenty-four years, 1943-1967.

Other pictures bearing information on Chester's history are those of James Hamilton, engineer and treasurer from 1890-1918, J. H. McLure, clerk and treasurer 1918-1945, Hood C. Worthy, city manager from 1945-1966, and Sam T. Weir, chief of police from 1933-1947. City policemen were photographed in 1941, 1948, 1956, 1958 and 1960 and bear the likeness of many stalwart men who have served as law enforcement officers in the city.

This all-male picture gallery reflects about 120 years of Chester history, the ancestry of many present day citizens, and the imprint of great and good men who served the city well.

CITY POST OFFICE

Chester Post Office was established either in 1794 or early 1795. Records reveal that the first receipts were taken on April 1, 1795. The first postmaster was Samuel Lacey and the first post office was operated out of the county court house where old Chester Hotel building stood on top of the hill. On November 27, 1886 its official name became Chester Post Office.

The first post office building was built at the corner of Main and Wylie Streets on land purchased by the federal government in 1907 from Congressman John J. Hemphill and Dr. G. B. White. On this corner stood a wooden building which housed a grocery store operated by J. A. Owens, father of the late Mrs. J. H. James.

When the property was sold to the government the store was demolished and the house moved to West End, just beyond Tan Yard Branch. It was later demolished.

FEDERAL BUILDING

The post office became the Federal Building in 1964 when a new post office was built on Saluda Street. The property was bought from Miss Ocey Corkill and Mrs. Faye McDonald.

The 9,111 square-foot modern building was started in early Spring in 1964 and completed November 15, 1964. The first day of operation was November 30 for the staff of 30 men.

The old Post Office (now Federal Building on corner of Main and Wylie Streets) was built in 1908 by Blue Ridge Construction Company of Asheville, N. C. It was first occupied on July 13, 1909. Prior to 1909, the Post Office was housed in a part of the Eberhardt building (later Carolina Inn) on Main Street. Rent was $65.00 per month.

Old records show that in November, 1902, there were six rural routes emanating from the Chester Office. Routes were 20-27 miles in length and carriers' pay averaged $846 per year.

Records point out that Stoneboro, Sampit, Tindal and Old Point post offices were in operation in 1911 but fail to state where they were located and their relation to Chester.

Railway mail clerks operating at that time on the Edgemont and Lancaster railroad received $4.44 per day wages. One to three wagon loads of mail were transferred daily between Southern and Seaboard Railroads.

City delivery service was inaugurated in Chester on December 1, 1907. By April 8, 1910, the Chester postmaster had under his jurisdiction four railway mail service clerks, three city carriers, four regular mail clerks and six R.F.D. carriers.

One duty of the post office in early days was reporting on the "foreign" population of Chester. On April 12, 1911, the "foreigners" consisted of five Greeks, six Italians, two Germans, and four Irish.

On April 23, 1911, the Chester Ministerial Association circulated a petition to all patrons of the Chester Post Office recommending that the city carrier window be closed on Sunday. All patrons signed, and the window was closed on Sundays after April 30, 1911.

Other 1911 records show that the salary of the postmaster was $2,400, and the assistant $1,000. City carriers made four trips daily, and the Postal Savings System began in Chester. The citizens of Hemphill Avenue, Gaston and Hampton Streets asked for city delivery of mail but service was denied at that time because the streets had no lights, and only foot paths for sidewalks.

The Chester Post Office has been first class since 1941 when receipts passed the $40,000 mark.

Chester's present Post Office on Saluda Street was dedicated Sunday afternoon, February 14, 1965, at 2:00 p.m. C. Banks Gladden, Chester County native and Regional Post Office director of Atlanta, Georgia, was guest speaker. Dedication services, attended by about 200 persons, were held indoors due to rain and cold weather.

Appearing on the program were Fifth District Congressman Tom S. Gettys, Mayor R. D. Wilson and Joe Penner of Los Angeles, California, owner of the building. Telegrams were read from Judge Robert W. Hemphill and Senator Olin D. Johnson.

Assistant Postmaster Walker Huggins accepted the name plaque and flag from Gladden. The flag was one that had flown from the Post Office and from the Capitol in Washington, D. C.

Postmasters who have served Chester are: Samuel Lacey, April 1, 1795; George Kennedy, November 28, 1798; William McClure, September 5, 1827; William Roseborough, November 2, 1832; Thomas McClure, December 31, 1836; Hiram C. Brawley, October 28, 1842; William Walker, November 11, 1851; William H. Anderson, October 14, 1853; John R. Allen, May 29, 1854; John McCaughin, May 28, 1866; J. Edward Wylie, July 11, 1870; Alexander S. Richardson, September 22, 1873; John Lee, April 27, 1875; Thomas M. Graham, November 27, 1876; Samuel B. Lumpkin, May 16, 1882; Thomas N. Youngblood, April 28, 1886; Carolina A. Youngblood, November 26, 1886; John W. Dunovant, July 12, 1898; T. J. Cunningham, September 10, 1916; Thomas M. Douglas, October 24, 1918; Samuel L. Myers, May 1, 1923 (acting); Samuel L. Myers, January 9, 1924; Thomas W. Barrett, September 30, 1929 (acting); Seabrook C. Carter, June 24, 1930; John Crawford, September 1949; P. Haynes Wilkes, Sr., September 1949; Carl C. Wilkes, September 1949; Joe H. Giltner, July 1, 1955 (acting); P. Haynes Wilkes, Jr., April 1960; Walker K. Huggins, 1969 (acting); Sam L. Grant, Jr., 1969 (acting); Alex Boyd, January, 1976; Alvin Terry, February, 1980; Leroy Rabon, 1980-.

JAILS

According to Mrs. Eliza Walker Welborn, Chester in the early days had stockades for lawbreakers. One was close to where First Union Bank (formerly Commercial Bank) is now. These stockades were torn down in the early 1870s. The first stockade was located across from where Pundt's Restaurant is now. A long porch faced the muddy unpaved street. A debtors' room was a large room which held those who had been convicted of not paying their debts. They could look out the windows and see those whom they knew ought to be in there, too, but had managed to evade the hands of the law.

Later a large brick jail was built on Center Street. It had a "hanging" room upstairs, and some clever marks where a prisoner managed to cut a hole with a teaspoon and make his escape. This jail was later converted to an apartment house.

The first jail built in Chester was located just off Church Street on the site of present Cestrian Square. It served the area in the early 1790s until another jail was built on the hill in 1798.

The third jail was a log structure and stood on a lot between Gadsden, Hudson and Wylie Streets. It was used from 1819 until 1842. The next jail was built in 1842 on Center Street. Land was bought from the estate of General Henry Bradley for $300.

Another jail was built in 1914 on McAliley Street. Following construction of new city-county Law Enforcement complex on Dawson Drive in the 1970s it was turned over to Chester County Historical Society for use as a museum.

OLD WATER WORKS PLANT

The old West End Water Works plant was located where the American Legion Pool later stood on West End.

On June 28th, 1895, the citizens of Chester held a mass meeting to discuss whether or not Chester should have water works. At this meeting citizens asked that city council secure the services of a hydraulic engineer to investigate the matter of boring a well and to furnish tentative figures as to the cost of a water works plant of sufficient capacity to supply the needs of Chester. The late B. M. Spratt was Mayor of the city at that time.

In order to get the matter going in Chester it appears that the city council made an appropriation of $1,500 for the purpose of testing for a well. Prof. S. L. Powell made a survey and reported to council two proposed sites, one on the property of J. J. McLure, near the residence of Paul Hemphill, and the other in the eastern section of the town, in the old McCoy orchard property.

In September 1896 Perry Andrews reported to Council that he had dug a well 470 feet and wanted to know whether to continue the well beyond 500 feet. This well did not turn out satisfactorily and a second was dug 374 feet and that from 150 to 200 gallons of water per hour was secured.

Surrounding property was purchased by the city and it was decided to add sewerage, an electric light plant and a suitable water works plant. In April 1897 an estimate was prepared as to the cost of such improvements and was as follows: Water works, $29,000; sewerage, $15,000; electric lights, $6,000; total $50,000. Electric light rates were fixed at 50 cents per light per month for the first light, the second at 49 cents and for each additional light the cost dropped down one cent per light per month. All above 15 were charged 35 cents each, and the lights were for 16 candle power.

Locals got very impatient during the construction of the sewerage pipes and it is stated that Paul W. McLure went before the council asking permission to ride his bicycle on the sidewalks from his home to town, saying that it would save him considerable time and that in so riding he would not occupy the street more than 30 minutes a day.

As time went on, the West End plant was unable to supply the needed amount of water and the well was abandoned and a pumping plant erected on Sandy river.

Some 8 to 9 years later the West End plant was abandoned and a new plant erected on Sandy river at a cost of about 200 thousand dollars.

MARION BLDG

CHESTER METROPOLITAN DISTRICT

Chester officials in 1961-62 determined that the greatest need in Chester County was water. They began a long and tedious process to plan, finance and implement an adequate system.

At that time, the city of Chester had its own water system, originating in Sandy River, and a reservoir on the western side of the city. Its filter plant, built in 1927, had a capacity of two million gallons per day. One tank built in 1938 held 250,000 gallons and the other built in 1926 held 100,000 gallons. The city at that time had 2,350 water taps in the city and 150 outside the city.

Table of water usage in 1952 showed almost 353 million gallons, and in 1962 almost 385 million gallons. The three Springs Mills, Gayle, Eureka and Springsteen, used about a million and a quarter gallons per month. The system was almost up to maximum use.

Hal McLure of West End was city clerk and treasurer, overseer of water and sewer works, fire department, and other services of the city.

At end of West End was Southern Power substation where "Junebug" Leckie and Sam Cassels monitored switches. Chester at the time was known as the Power Center of the South.

MAIN STREET

Filter plant and storage tanks for Great Falls were owned and operated by Republic Mills. Raw water was taken directly from Catawba River into the filter plant which was built in 1920 and modified in 1949. The Great Falls Public Service Commission was created in 1949 in order to levy taxes to pay for improvements through issuing $400,000 in general obligation bonds.

In the summer of 1961, Chester County was designated as an economically depressed area. Unemployment and under employment reached six percent in the county according to Employment Security Commission.

Federal funds administered by Area Redevelopment Administration (ARA) were available for such areas. Chester County was invited to review the overall picture of resources, markets, and skills it had to work with in its efforts to help itself.

Local officials involved in review and planning were members of Chester County Delegation, Senator Wilbur G. Grant, Representatives L. C. Wright, Jr. and Harry R. Gardner, CCBCD Director Ed Stanfield, and the newly appointed Chester Metropolitan Commissioners, E. J. Fowler, Robert H. King and W. E. McGuinn, Jr., and Attorney David A. Gaston.

Lockwood Greene Engineers, Inc. reported that a feasibility survey showed that Chester County could solve its water shortage by tapping the Catawba River. They submitted a plan for a 30-inch pipeline to be laid along South Carolina Highway 9 about 20 miles into Chester where it would make a loop around the city. An 18-inch line would branch off at Bascomville and follow Highway 99 into Great Falls.

A raw water intake and filter plant would be located on the west bank of Catawba River near a bridge on Highway 9. The plant would process and pump nine million gallons per day and could be doubled in capacity. Cost of water to residents would remain about the same as it was in mid-1963.

Cost of constructing the water system would be about $5,225,000, the engineers reported. An application for $2,600,000 was made through Community Facilities Administration under the federal Accelerated Public Works program. The balance of $2,625,000 could be financed by selling a bond issue to the U. S. Housing and Home Finance Agency at 3½ percent interest. The bonds and interest could be amortized from water sales and the bonds retired in 30 years. The district board would have the power to sell revenue bonds.

Engineers estimated the operational cost of the water project at about $75,000 a year. This included salaries of a supervisor and nine maintenance men.

County officials envisioned a big industrial park along this route of the proposed water system. Approximately 100 square miles are contained in the boundaries of Chester Metropolitan Water District. Benefits would extend to the towns of Chester, Great Falls, Richburg and Fort Lawn.

The county's overall economic development plan was submitted to the U. S. Department of Commerce in January, 1962 and was approved October 2, 1962. Construction on the water system was started in July, 1964, and was to be completed by October 1, 1966.

Planning, getting approval and constructing CMD was not accomplished without controversy, opposition and criticism from many citizens of the county. This is clearly revealed in issues of local papers published during the five year period.

CHESTER TELEPHONE COMPANY

The first telephones in Chester were installed in 1890. The first three were on a line connecting the office of I. N. Cross to the Southern and Seaboard depots. He used the phones in connection with his drayage business.

In 1893, the first switchboard was in operation. It was located upstairs near the Wylie and Gadsden Street corner. T. E. Pryor was manager and night operator of this switchboard which had the capacity for fifty telephone lines.

In 1897, the company was incorporated by five progressive men, Augustus M. Aiken, I. N. Cross, S. M. Jones, A. W. Love and Dr. G. B. White. Authorized capital was $2,000. Each person wanting a telephone subscribed $10. Dr. G. B. White was first president of the new company that was named The Chester Telephone Company.

In 1901, there were 200 telephones. A copy of the first directory is owned by Mrs. W. O. McKeown, Route 1, Blackstock. It contains a list of subscribers, and the admonition, "Please ring off when through talking." Some of the earliest subscribers were ladies, strengthening the old adage that women love to talk. Among them were Mrs. W. H. Caldwell, Mrs. A. M. Aiken, Mrs. I. Clarence

Cross, Mrs. John Frazer, Mrs. J. T. Collins, Mrs. J. L. Hamilton, Mrs. H. S. Heyman, Mrs. J. W. Stringfellow and Mrs. Mannie Wachtel, J. M. Bell became superintendent of the company.

By 1906 there were lines to Magdalene Hospital, Kluttz's Big New Store, Patterson Library on second floor of city hall, Peoples Bank, National Exchange Bank, and Commercial Bank, also to Brainerd Institute, Masonic Temple, Hotel Nicholson, Hotel New Nicholson, Red Racket Store (W. R. Neil, owener), Lancaster Exchange (25¢ per message), Yorkville Exchange, Lowryville and Crosbyville.

In 1908, a fire destroyed the telephone exchange which was located upstairs over Hardin and Vaughn store. It was several weeks before service was restored. The local system was then connected to the outside world via long distance. L. D. Childs became president.

In 1912, the Common Battery system was installed in Chester, replacing the hand crank or magneto system. Rural population centers were encouraged and assisted in operating their own systems. These exchange centers were Armenia, Blackstock, Crosbyville, Halselville, Edgemoor, Fort Lawn, McKeown, Lowryville, Richburg, McConnellsville. Some of these were in operation from the early 1900s interconnecting Chester County. Crop failures and technical changes made the operation impractical.

A long distance line was constructed in 1920 to Great Falls connecting to a system operated by Republic Cotton Mills serving the town of Great Falls.

By 1937, there were 1,000 telephones in the system; by 1945, 2,000.

RUNYAN JEWELERS

Dial telephones came to Chester County with the establishment of the the Lewisville exchange serving the northeastern part of the county. The Lowrys exchange in 1947 and Blackstock exchange in 1948 extended service across the county. In 1951, the Great Falls exchange was converted to the dial system; in 1953 Chester was converted, completing the dial modernization program. In 1954, the entire system was linked to Nationwide Intertoll dial system.

The seven digit system was established in 1960 to simplify long distance and extended service calling.

The number of telephones has grown at the rate of 600 to 700 per year. At the beginning of 1981, there were 16,870 in service. Message volumes for the year approached the two million level for the first time. The company had 55 employees.

Presidents of The Chester Telephone Company were Dr. G. B. White (1897-1908), L. C. Childs (1908-1918), R. R. Hafner (1918-1935), John M. Bell (1935-1947), S. Lewis Bell (1947-1975), Joe McElwee. The present office at 112 York Street was built in 1953.

THEATERS

In 1936, Fred J. Powell, Sr. came to Chester from Patterson, North Carolina and bought out Joe Walters' interests in a theater on Gadsden Street. He later founded Powell Theater on Wylie Street and established the theater business known as Chester Theater, Inc. The theater on Gadsden Street was moved to a new building he had constructed at the corner of Hudson and Main Streets. It stood for many years as the town's only movie house until Powell Theater was opened.

About 1970, Chester Theater was torn down. About 1975 Chester Little Theater purchased the Powell Theater building and staged local productions there.

Cinemas I and II were constructed about 1975 at People's Plaza.

MANUFACTURERS

Chester has had her share of large and small manufacturing plants during the years. One was the firm owned by the late Mrs. John Patton who made mayonnaise.

Another was the late H. V. Knight, father of Harry Knight. Mr. Knight invented an egg substitute, which he named Eggsact, and he held a patent on the name. He manufactured the egg substitute in a small building behind his residence on Saluda Street. The item was quite popular on grocery shelves throughout the city. Many housewives used the product as a suitable substitute for eggs in the baking of cakes.

Chester also had an establishment which manufactured overalls. It was located on Gadsden Street in the building next door to Murray Lumber Co. and was owned by Mr. Barton, who resided on Hemphill Ave. The company enjoyed splended business for a number of years.

There was an ice cream manufacturing plant on Hudson Street at one time. It was owned and operated by Southern Dairies, which now sells ice cream under the Sealtest label. A candy kitchen on Gadsden Street was operated by Mrs. Myra Artemis and family.

There was a brick-making business located on Columbia Rd. near Evans, south of Chester. The company was forced to close as the type clay needed was limited and soon was exhausted.

There was a small business operated in the Halsellville section of the county which manufactured a powder used in ridding premises of roaches, and other pests. The company was operated by a Mr. Johnson and his son. One of the producer's largest users was the Greyhound Bus lines.

Chester at one time boasted of having one of the state's best marble yards. It was located in the block fronting Wylie Street between Main and McAliley streets. At first the company "engraved" markers through the use of chisles and hammers, but later converted to the use of air pressure, which was quite a progressive step.

Located on the old York Road in the present American Legion Hut building was a winery which was owned and operated legally by a Mr. Doster who later moved to California. The winery did quite well for several years.

Back in the '20's, Chester had a plant which manufactured axe handles, hatchet and shovel handles. It was located on Saluda Street on the property adjoining the Coca-Cola plant. It was known as Baldwin Tool Works and was owned by northern interests.

Chester has had her share of bottling plants, ice manufacturing plants, bakeries, grist mills, fertilizer manufacturing plants, machine shops, cotton gins and power generating plants.

In more recent years a company which made men's ties was located on Wylie Street in the building now occupied by The Little Theatre. About this same time, Chester boasted a company which made hot air balloons. It was located in the building at the corner of Main and Wylie streets across the street from the Public Library. It was owned by Tracy Barnes who is in the same type business in Charlotte.

Chester had a company on Hudson Street next door to Hall Lumber Co. which for a brief period made tops for pick-up trucks.

CHESTER COUNTY BANKS

Bank of Chester

Chester's first bank opened in 1853. In October of that year the Bank of Chester began business with a capital stock of $300,000, more than three-fourths of it subscribed and paid in by the residents of Chester County (then Chester District).

James Hemphill was president; Col. John A. Bradley, cashier, and J. Leonard Harris, teller; Paul Romare and John Beard, assistants. The bank did a large and profitable business up to the breaking out of the war.

Three ferocious bull dogs were kept in the back yard of the bank in a space enclosed by a fence. The dogs were the bank's burglary insurance.

Bank of Great Falls

The Bank of Great Falls was organized in 1917. An adjunct of the J. B. Duke interests, Duke was one of the biggest benefactors of progress and prosperity in the Carolinas and was founder of the giant Duke Power Company. The Bank of Great Falls profited from the sound judgment and mutual reliance of Duke's manufacturing and electric power industries in this section. It has been said that one outstanding quality in the generalship of James B. Duke was his uncanny ability to select the right man for the job at hand.

SOUTHERN BANK

The success and service of the bank through the years is a tribute to the judicious direction of R. C. Mullican, president; Killough H. White, vice-president and cashier of Republic Mills; and C. M. Harkey, cashier.

Directors of the bank in its early years were E. H. Hall, K. H. White, Dr. J. B. McKeown, L. M. Jordan and R. C. Mullican.

J. B. Duke was one of the original stockholders of the Bank of Great Falls. His large estate still retains its ten percent interest as a stockholder. It has been said that the Bank of Great Falls is the only bank in South Carolina Duke ever had stock in, and he was always proud of the success of this bank.

In 1964, the Bank of Great Falls merged with First Citizens Bank and Trust Company.

People's Bank

Chester's venerable octogenarian, William Andrew "Mr. Will" Corkill, is one of few individuals who held the distinction of founding a bank.

His fledgling institution, started on a shoestring in the early 1900's, became the firmly established and thriving People's National Bank in Chester, one of the area's leading banks for many years. It successfully weathered three depressions or business recessions, in its 75-year history.

During one of these, the great depression of the 1930's, People's Bank was one of only three banks in South Carolina that was permitted to open without government aid after being inspected by Federal bank examiners. This indicated a stable condition. It was during this period that many banks failed and were unable to reopen after President Franklin D. Roosevelt's five-day bank moratorium mandated an examination of all banks in the United States. This was a first step toward stabilizing the nation's shaky economy.

From his first job as collection clerk of the Exchange Bank in Chester, Will Corkill gained his knowledge on how to operate a sound and stable bank and his desire to establish a new one. His mentor was T. H. White, cashier.

In 1905, Corkill asked Dr. G. B. White, prominent Chester dentist, if he would become president of the proposed new bank. Dr. White agreed with the stipulation that his son, Henry White, be employed in the bank.

Soliciting of subscriptions for $35,000 capital investment for the new bank was begun. A state charter was applied for and received and the new bank named The People's Bank of Chester was born.

On October 12, 1905 a meeting of subscribers to the stock in the bank met for organization. Directors elected were Dr. G. B. White, D. J. Macauley, John Frazer, W. A. Corkill, John S. Stone, M. H. Wachtel and Wm. Patrick.

The board subsequently elected officers: Dr. G. B. White, president, D. J. Macauley, vice-president; W. A. Corkill, cashier, M. H. White, assistant cashier.

The bank opened its doors on Monday, October 16, 1905 in temporary quarters. Later on a building on Gadsden Street was bought from the E. C. Stahn estate through his daughter, Mrs. Bertha Stahn Knowles. The purchase price was $6,000. The bank was operated there until 1969 when it was moved to a handsome new building in People's Plaza.

Will Corkill's philosophy on banking made his venture a success: Use good judgment in making loans, always exercise kindness, courtesy and patience to customers, work hard.

"A man's character is the most important consideration in loaning him money," Corkill said. "His material assets and securities come second."

Peoples Bank merged with South Carolina National Bank in 1984.

The Commercial Bank

The Commercial Bank was organized in Chester on November 3, 1899. Application for a charter was filed at Chester County Court House on September 23, 1899, by organizers A. G. Brice, W. Holmes Hardin, Jr., M. A. Carpenter, J. L. Abell, R. B. Caldwell, A. L. Gaston and W. A. Eudy.

From its beginning this bank was recognized as one of the strongest and most liquid small banks in South Carolina. During the "Banking Holidays" following the stock market crash of 1929, the Commercial Bank was one of few banks in the State that didn't fold. It was closed only briefly when all banks in the United States were closed for inventory.

Original stock certificate ledger, now in possession of Chester County Historical Museum, records in flowing Spencerian script names of more than 250 original subscribers.

The bank's first home was in a building on top of Chester's hill. It was later moved to a building near Masonic Hall on Gadsden Street where Stone Insurance Agency is now. The walk-in vault that served the bank is still there.

The handsome red brick building with impressive Corinthian columns, was built to house the bank in 1913. It sits on the corner of Gadsden and Wylie Streets, where it has played an important role in Chester's growth for almost 90 years. Several interior renovations have been made as the years have gone by. The exterior was sandblasted and refurbished in 1983. A branch bank was built later on the corner of Saluda and Walnut Streets.

In 1971-72, a group of stockholders influenced a majority of stock holders to merge with American Bank and Trust Company of Orangeburg, South Carolina. This merger, consummated in 1972, proved to be a disastrous one. Stockholders lost considerable funds.

In 1974, the bank merged with Southern Bank and Trust Company of Greenville, South Carolina. In April 1986 it merged with First Union National Bank of South Carolina.

Presidents serving Commercial Bank were Ashbel G. Brice 1899-1918, R. B. Caldwell 1918-1941, Robert Gage 1941-1965, B. Clyde Carter 1965-1971, and John W. Simril 1971-72.

First Federal Savings and Loan Co. of South Carolina came to Chester in 1977, and built a handsome bank building on Saluda Street in 1981.

CHESTER NEWSPAPERS

Chester's newspapers, since about 1849, have been the main chroniclers and repositories of local history. They have also had colorful histories of their own.

The Chester Observer was started in 1849 by Zion Bridwell, Jr., editor and owner. After the departure of Mr. Bridwell the name of the paper was changed to The Palmetto Standard, edited by C. P. Melton. After another name change, it became the Chester Standard, owned and edited by C. Davis Melton and Samuel W. Melton, brothers and lawyers. The first issue appeared January 12, 1854.

The Standard of the 50s was a large seven-column double sheet. In the 60s during the Civil War paper was hard to get, so the size of the sheet became smaller, only a five column publication. When folded it was about the size of a man's handkerchief.

Ownership changed hands a number of times. Subsequent owners were J. B. Mickle, E. J. McDaniel, George Pitcher, E. C. McLure, J. A. Bradley, Jr. (who established it as The Chester Reporter in January, 1869), J. H. Buchanan, J. C. Hardin, then co-owners J. T. Perkins and W. J. Irwin.

Perkins and Irwin printed a semi-weekly and directed its fate for more than forty years.

By 1891, Chester had three newspapers, the Reporter, the Bulletin and the Enterprise. The Enterprise merged with the Bulletin in 1898 when editor W. P. Crawford volunteered for service in the Spanish-American War and on his return contracted a fatal illness and died. After his death the paper folded for all time.

Chester Bulletin was started in 1879 by Thomas W. Clawson and E. C. McClure. Subsequent owners were J. A. Bradley, Jr., Whitlock, F. H. Morgan, W. P. Crawford and W. A. Barber.

The Lantern, a semi-weekly, was started in 1897 by J. T. Bigham. Former editor Crawford greeted the new newspaper venture with a back-handed welcome: "A new publication appeared in town last week called The Lantern. The ink is good."

The Lantern passed through a succession of owners, W. F. Caldwell, J. Dana Jones, J. Otis Hull, C. N. Wrenshall, J. E. Nunnery, S. L. Cassells, W. W. Pegram, Sr., and W. W. Pegram, Jr. The name was changed to Chester News.

About 1945, the Reporter was sold to J. F. Tindal and W. T. Hedgepath who owned and published it until Tindal sold his interest and bought a paper in Marion, Virginia.

In 1950, the Springs Company bought the Reporter and incorporated it into Tri-County Publishing Company of Lancaster. In 1971, the same company bought the Chester News and changed the name of the semi-weekly to The News and Reporter with Don McKeown as editor and James McKeown as publisher.

Palmetto Standard

The Palmetto Standard, proudly proclaimed as a "Woman's Paper" was first published in Chester on May 28, 1895, under the management of Ladies of Presbyterian Church, Chester, S. C. Mrs. B. H. Stringfellow was editor and Mrs. Julia Campbell was "editor of Chronicles."

From its columns comes a kaleidoscope of life in Chester in 1895:

The Chester public is indebted to the Musical Association for "Olivette" gotten up by Mrs. A. M. Aiken, ably assisted by Miss Mamie Lindsay. Cast of characters:

Olivette — Mrs. A. M. Aiken
Duke des Ifs — Mr. J. H. Marion
Captain — Mr. T. E. White
Valentia — Mrs. A. M. White

Signs of improvements are all around. Col. Atkinson's handsome house on Saluda Street is nearing completion. Mr. J. D. Mean's house on West Main when completed will be one of the handsomest homes in Chester.

Our city is proud of the work of her contractors and builders. Witness the handsome residence of Rev. S. W. Pryor built by the experienced hands and watchful eye of Mr. J. R. Simril, the Atkinson house, the skillful work of Messrs. Carpenter Bros. — the artistic residence of J. W. Means, Esq. as done by the faithful, firm hand of Mr. George Albright.

Personal News

Paul Hardin of Wofford College is home for a few days on account of sickness. He will return to Spartanburg for Commencement; he is one of the Junior debaters.

Mr. Porter Hollis of Chester will graduate at Wofford in June.

Mrs. Margaret Gaston returned from Montgomery, Ala. last week where she has been for a month visiting her son, Dr. Lucius Gaston.

The Chester Sanitarium under Dr. Davega's skillful management is a happy retreat for poor suffering humanity.

B. M. Spratt & Co. turn out first class work at their mill, they make as handsome doors and mantels as can be found in the State.

Our honored ex-congressman, Hon. J. J. Hemphill, has been at home for a few days, he returned to Washington Friday night.

The Cistern in front of the A.R.P. Church has been jugged over by Mr. M. A. Carpenter, his work is always well done.

College Street is being macademized.

The ladies will find at Mr. John Blake's as beautiful bread as any housekeeper could wish, made of the finest flour and no alum to injure the health.

Mr. J. M. Jones has sold 5,000 yards of gingham since January.

Advertisements:

Hardin and James, fire insurance agents

Joseph Lindsay & Co., dealers in fine groceries

Davidson College, beginning its 59th year on September 1, 1895 with nine instructors

John Frazer, manufacturer of wagons and buggies

Joseph W. Wylie & Company, groceries, hardware, dry goods and clothing (members of the firm listed were Joseph Wylie, William Lindsay, T. B. Woods, John G. White)

The New York Racket of Chester termed "the biggest store in the state," advertised these prices:

Gent's light color suit clothes, only $2.95

Calico, 2 1-2 cents a yard

Pure black silk umbrellas, 50 cents

Arbuckle's Ariaso Parched Coffee, 22 cents a pound

Suit clothes for the dear boy, 50 cents

Pure Castile Soap, 2 cents a cake

Ladies' and Gents' Shoes, 75 cents a pair

Needles, pins and Hair Pins, 1 cent a paper

Straw hats, 5 cents each

Lace effect black Dress Lawn, 7 1-2 cents a yard

One Advertiser Resorted to Poetry:

> Thermometers will have their day
> Though things seem out of tune;
> We used six tons of coal in May,
> But fire'll be free in June.
> And you can get your printing done
> And none can do it finer
> Than the said Richard C. Wilson
> In Clinton, South Carolina.

HOSPITALS OF CHESTER

(Lecture by Dr. Wm. R. Wallace Dec. 3, 1969)

Prior to 1900's, the practice of medicine was little of a scientific matter — doctors gave drugs as a matter of routine without any scientific reasoning. This was the way medicine was practiced. During the dark ages and the centuries that followed, no progress was made in the practice of medicine. As late as 1865, surgery was a hazardous profession. Just about that time, the idea was developed that bacteria were the cause of disease. The advances in medicine in the last 65 years were greater than the whole period before it. I don't claim any credit for this improvement. I just happened to be here when it happened. In the Civil War, Stonewall Jackson died, not from hemorrhage, but from some infection. As the knowledge of bacteria grew, surgery came into its own. Lister had the idea that he could spray the operating room and kill all the bacteria. He didn't realize that the germs were on his own hands. The surgeon's reputation was enhanced by the amount of blood encrusted on his Prince Albert coat.

Prior to hospitals, most surgery was done on the kitchen tables. I did a leg and an arm amputation on kitchen tables when I first came to Chester. Both recovered and lived long lives. One man said he wouldn't take $10,000 for this stump because it held his coat on so well.

Along in the middle 90's, Dr. Torbit Henry, who was an uncle of my associate, Dr. Henry, and a distant relative of mine, who had trained in surgery in New York, came to Chester. He and Dr. Marion, a G. P. from Richburg, built the first hospital. This building now the home of Dr. R. J. Gosh is still standing on Pinckney Street. Dr. Henry was a brilliant and successful young surgeon. He had a premature death in that he developed measles and while paying a call was caught in a snow storm and developed pneumonia and died. Dr. Marion returned to Richburg and the building was closed.

The second hospital in Chester : is still standing and is the Barron Funeral Home on Wylie Street. It was the residence of Dr. S. M. DeVaga. He had quite a reputation in that he was successful in the appendix operation. Prior to this time, perithylitis (as appendicitis was called) was considered fatal. Dr. DeVaga converted the upper floor of his building into a hospital. It could take care of 10 or 12 patients. Mrs. DeVaga served meals from the downstairs kitchen.

Before Dr. DeVaga's death, Dr. S. W. Pryor converted his home (corner of Hudson and Saluda Street) into a hospital. In the general outline, the upper floor was for patients and Mrs. Pryor supplied the food from the kitchen. I would like to pay tribute here to these two women who did such a fine job of supplying the patients' meals.

MAGDALENE HOSPITAL

Magdelene Hospital was located on Saluda Street, a frame building. At that time, the roads were in such condition that ambulances could not travel much. The hospitals drew patients from other areas because they could only be transported on the railroad. There were no hospitals between Athens, Georgia and Raleigh, N. C. on the Seaboard route except the one in Chester.

The rest of us here in Chester had no place where we could place a patient. Dr. Pryor kept the Magdelene full of surgery patients. A group of us attempted to have a general hospital, but we could get no interest from the public. You have to get the public to realize, they must realize, the hospital has done a great deal to lengthen the span of life. They did not realize Dr. Pryor's hospital was not adequate so this idea of a general hospital faded out.

In 1915, Dr. Robert E. Abell finished his residency in Baltimore. We began to build on that. Dr. Abell said that if we established a general hospital, his father would supply about one-half of the money if we would supply the rest, and we organized the Chester Sanitarium on York Street, acquiring the Child residence, with an addition for a nurses home. This organization consisted of Dr. McConnell, President, Dr. Cox, Vice President and myself as Secretary. I have a book full of minutes of every meeting. Dr. Abell was Manager. Dr. Abell had a reputation as a successful surgeon and the hospital flourished from the beginning. Although the beginning was small, we kept the bills paid. Later, Duke Hospital reported we had $25,000 in assets and $9,000 owed on old stock notes, and we gave Chester County Hospital $16,000 when we closed.

The Magdelene went up in smoke but all the patients were brought out. No lives were lost. The Chester Sanitarium took over the emergency cases. Dr. Pryor quickly converted a house he owned into a hospital and rapidly built the Pryor Hospital.

Chester Sanitarium has a very warm place in my heart. I was operated on for appendicitis in Greenwood where I had attended a medical meeting and was transported back and occupied a room in the Chester Sanitarium. I was anesthetist in those days. I never had a patient die on a table. I poured a lot of ether for Dr. Patterson and Dr. Abell. My first born, William, was born in that hospital.

Pryor Hospital was finished in 1917. It was one of the nicest hospitals in South Carolina, small, four stories high. It had an operating room and kitchen on the fourth floor. Dr. Pryor was in his prime, but during the flu epidemic, he died of flu or "flumonia" as we called it.

Dr. Abell, in the meantime, was in the draft age. He went into the Army (before being drafted) so that he would be in the Surgical Department. We went to sign up — he thought he would be a Captain because he was a surgeon — but he was made a Lieutenant. But, on account of my age, they gave me a Captaincy. They said they would call me later but I never did serve. Two or three weeks later, they sent me a letter that so many doctors had come from Chester County, I was needed more at home.

Drs. Abell, Ross, Love, Malone and McLurkin had volunteered. I had a hard time with about one-third of the practice of Chester on my hands. The Armistice came along and Dr. Abell was

PRYOR HOSPITAL

relieved from service immediately and in a matter of days, he was back in Chester.

Dr. Pryor had left in his will that Dr. McFadden, his son-in-law, or Dr. Malone and Dr. Thomas would be in charge of the Pryor Hospital and on his deathbed he said, "There will always be a Pryor Hospital in Chester."

For a while, Dr. Bost of Charlotte, Dr. Coleman and Dr. Rakestraw were surgeons in Chester, but Dr. Abell was too much of a competitor, so the Pryor Hospital gradually became weaker and we decided to amalgamate the two, but it wouldn't work. Mrs. Sigmon, one of the best head nurses, and Dr. McFadden just couldn't get along.

In 1926, the Pryor Hospital was closed and Chester Sanitarium rented it. The rent was $275 per month. The Pryor Hospital served a good purpose, however, there was a fire and we had to do so much repair because of the smoke damage, our rent was reduced from $275 to $175. We continued to pay bills and kept our heads above water.

Dr. Abell became incapacitated with ruptured diverticulitis and a disability in his hand due to arthritis. In 1940, we found Dr. Patterson, a retired missionary from China and he served here since 1940. With Dr. Patterson as General Manager, I remained as Secretary and we operated the hospital.

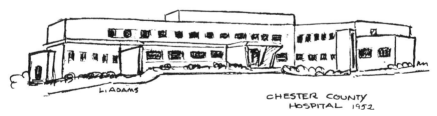

L. ADAMS

CHESTER COUNTY
HOSPITAL 1952

In 1947, we realized that the Pryor Hospital had become obsolete (we were not allowed to bring patients on the fourth floor), so we decided the time had come when the taxpayers of Chester County should assume their rightful obligation and so we had a contract in which we turned the hospital with its assets (new x-ray equipment, etc.), over to the county. All we owed was $9,000 on old stock notes, so we made a deal with Senator Grant that if he would give us $9,000 we would turn over the hospital to Chester County. We had an understanding with Senator Grant that he would be ready with a bond issue to build this hospital, so in 1952 this hospital was built with Hill-Burton funds and Chester County Funds.

The Nursing Center was built with the aid of Hill-Burton money and was opened to receive patients on July 1, 1969. The hospital was enlarged from 74 beds to 119 beds in 1963.

Doctors

Records show that Dr. William M. Love came in 1765 to Fishing Creek area. He is one of the earliest physicians known to practice in Chester District. His son, Dr. Samuel Glenn Love graduated in medicine in 1881, 32 years after his father. He practiced in McConnells 1881-1910, then came to Chester.

During the Colonial and Revolutionary periods the most feared diseases were smallpox, scarlet fever, influenza, and the fevers — typhoid, yellow, and malaria. A visitor to the state said that "Carolina was in the spring a paradise, in the summer a hell, and in the autumn a hospital."

About 1900, Judge Hudson lists Chester physicians: Dr. Moffitt (died of consumption), Dr. A. P. Wylie, Dr. Reedy, Dr. J. B. Jennings, Dr. William Wylie, Dr. Stringfellow.

Dr. Walker Gill Wylie

Dr. Walker Gill Wylie was born in Chester September 2, 1948, son of Alexander Pearson Wylie and Juliet Agnes Gill Wylie. His grandfather was Peter Kelso Wylie, probate judge in Chester for 40 years, and his father was a leading physician and surgeon of the same city for nearly half a century.

He entered the service of the Confederate Army as a lieutenant when he was 16 years old. During the winter of 1864-65 he commanded a company of boys in active service under Hardee and Johnson in front of Sherman's army as it passed through South Carolina on its march to the sea.

Dr. Wylie was graduated at the University of South Carolina in 1868 in all scientific subjects including civil engineering. Upon going to New York, he was persuaded by Dr. J. Marion Sims, famous South Carolina physician and surgeon, to study medicine and surgery.

He entered Bellevue Medical College in New York in the same year, and received his M.D. degree in 1871. In the fall of 1870, he succeeded, by competitive examination, in securing the position as surgical intern in Bellevue Hospital, and served there 18 months. In 1872, by the same competitive process, he became surgical intern in the Woman's Hospital of the State of New York and served there 18 months.

In 1872, Dr. Wylie went abroad to study hospital conditions and the system of trained nursing, especially the Florence Nightingale system. He assisted in establishing the first training school for nurses in this country, organized at Bellevue Hospital in New York in 1873. In the same year he began private practice in New York. He was widely known as a skillful and successful operator in abdominal surgery, and his practice was among the largest in the United States.

Dr. Wylie was visiting gynecologist to Bellevue Hospital for 25 years, and after his resignation was appointed consulting surgeon to the hospital. He was professor of gynecology in the New York Polyclinic School of Medicine for Post Graduates. After lecturing for 25 years on gynecology and abdominal surgery, he retired as professor emeritus.

The Boylston prize of Harvard University was awarded to Dr. Wylie in 1876, and he was awarded the McMaster gold medal by the University of South Carolina, given to the alumnus who had done the most for humanity.

Dr. Wylie from time to time contributed to medical literature essays and articles, notably in the fields of gynecology and surgery. Many of these articles are considered the best works of their kind in medical literature.

Dr. Wylie attributed his success as a surgeon to his practical mechanical training, applying the laws of mechanics, mathematics, and physics to his practical work as a surgeon, thus becoming a pioneer of modern surgery.

Dr. Wylie was also a pioneer in the field of hydro-electric development in the South.

Dr. James Woods Babcock

Dr. James Woods Babcock, a native of Chester, was a highly qualified psychiatrist who graduated from Harvard Medical School in 1886. He determined that corn was the dominent culprit in a serious diet deficiency which results in the disease pellegra, a source that caused skin sores, intestinal inflammation and insanity.

In 1907, Dr. Babcock presented a detailed and convincing argument to the S. C. Board of Health contending that not only was pellegra widespread in South Carolina but it was a major cause of insanity among the patients at the State Lunatic Asylum where he was superintendent.

A careful search of the Asylum records by Dr. Babcock showed that pellegra had been identified there as early as 1834 by Dr. James Davis, then superintendent. Other studies showed a high incidence of pellegra in Civil War Prison camps.

In 1910, Dr. Babcock and Dr. D. H. Levinder of the U. S. Public Health Service collaborated in writing and publishing the first comprehensive book on pellegra. The same year Dr. Babcock called a National Conference on Pellegra in Columbia which was attended by a majority of South Carolina's doctors, and 120 doctors from other states. Dr. Babcock's research and work received national attention.

In spite of advances made in diagnosis and treatment of pellegra, it was not until 1949 that the state Legislature came to grips with the dominant culprit, corn. The Legislature made it illegal to sell or trade corn products unless the additives, Vitamin D and calcium, niacin, riboflavin and thiamine were added.

Anyone buying cornmeal or grits in South Carolina since 1949, buys the "enriched" product, thanks to an early Chester physician. James Woods Babcock's medical research and chronicles rank him as one of the great pioneers in South Carolina medical history.

Later Chester County Physicians

Dr. William J. Henry (deceased)
Dr. George A. Hennies (deceased)
Dr. William R. Wallace (deceased)
Dr. John Newton Gaston
Dr. Charles W. Brice, Jr.
Dr. Malcolm L. Marion
Dr. Malcolm L. Marion, III
Dr. Halstead M. Stone
Dr. Samuel R. Stone
Dr. V. P. Patterson (deceased)
Dr. Robert E. Abell (deceased)
Dr. Pratibha P. Raut
Dr. Premanand S. Raut
Dr. Richard Hughes
Dr. Madison Ross (deceased)
Dr. Sarah Taylor Morrow (moved)
Dr. Lacy Morrow (deceased)
Dr. Gregory L. Phelps
Dr. Corey Evans (moved)
Dr. Al Jones (moved)
Dr. David Keely (in school)
Dr. Douglas Marion
Dr. Frederic W. Brown
Dr. Weston Cook (deceased)
Dr. Kamran Borhanian
Dr. Eugene Crisler
Dr. Carl Simkins
Dr. Edwin C. Hentz
Dr. J. S. Neviaser
Dr. William J. Westerkam

Great Falls Physicians

Dr. Carl H. Jones III
Dr. L. W. Fort

Dentists

Dr. Morris Ehrlich
Dr. Conrad Nichols (deceased)
Dr. Hamilton (deceased)
Dr. John D. Sherer
Dr. Robert E. Shannon
Dr. Joel Johnson
Dr. Mary S. Johnson
Dr. J. W. Crowder (deceased)
Dr. J. D. Rucker, Jr.

Chiropractors

Dr. R. J. Gosh
Dr. Douglas B. Hughes

Veterinarians

Dr. James T. Anderson
Dr. "Rummy" McGill (deceased)
Dr. M. D. Culpepper
Dr. Richard Crisler
Dr. W. J. Lazenby
Dr. Linda Weatherell

Buildings on Hill Destroyed by Fire

XXII DISASTERS

CYCLONE, EARTHQUAKE, DROUGHT

On February 19, 1884, Chester was visited by a disastrous cyclone that damaged quite a number of buildings and completely demolished the Baptist Church. Everything that could be lifted went flying that night and strong new homes rocked.

Two years later, in 1886, Chester experienced the most severe earthquake that ever hit the State. Considerable damage was done to Charleston, Columbia and other places. Many people thought the world was coming to an end and they flocked to churches and prayed as never before.

The Great Drought of 1845 was the severest that befell the State during the last century. From the last week in March to first week in July, no rain fell in Chester district and in the State generally.

Owing to the absence of railroads and other facilities of transportation, the distress of the people was extreme. Man and beast suffered intensely for necessary food and water.

The only supply of corn came from across the mountains of North Carolina and Tennessee, transported in wagons sent by farmers to obtain and bring it.

Meal, rationed out in small quantities from wagons on the streets of Chester, sold for two dollars a bushel, and at this price, not more than a half bushel would be sold to a single family, and only a peck unless the family was large. These were home wagons, sent by benevolent people to bring bread to keep the masses of people from starving.

Farmers, to supply forage for fall and winter use, cut down and cured the sassafras and other green bushes growing in the fields and fence corners. To feed man and beast large quantities of fast growing turnip seed were sown.

In spite of the drought and suffering, the people assembled on

248

July 4th as was customary to celebrate the nation's birthday. On that morning it became cloudy and before nightfall began to rain. It rained for twenty-four hours, steadily but gently.

Had Chester been blessed with railroad transportation, there would have been little, if any real suffering.

CHESTER FIRES

Chester had four major fires: 1869, 1872, 1929 and 1942. From area newspapers is an account of the 1929 fire.

"At three o'clock when *The Reporter* went to press, the City Hall was a seething mass of flames, and the conflagration was extended to all parts of the structure. Originating in the rear of the building, the fire made rapid progress with the old stage scenery and other combustible materials stored in the rear. By the time the alarm had sounded, and the crowd was on the scene, the fire had jumped entirely to the front of the building, and the flames were shooting out at various cracks and crevices, and great masses of black smoke were rolling up to the skies.

City Hall, or Administrative Building, housed the City Clerk and Treasurer's office, Police Court, Fire Department, Public Library, Armory, besides the auditorium which was extensively used for shows, plays and operas.

At 3:15 p.m. the blaze was burning as fiercely as ever, and the fire fighters, though well organized and desperately struggling were making little headway. It looked like the blaze might leap across the street and reach the adjoining buildings.

At 3:30 p.m. the fire was still burning furiously, though the blaze seemed to be under control so far as adjacent buildings were concerned. One of the features of the fire was the cracking of cartridges at intermissions in the Armory, which resembled a sham battle. The big tower on the north corner of the building soon fell to the flames, as the wind was blowing toward the north. The fire siren, which was installed about two months earlier, was completely destroyed. It was feared that the tower and some of the walls might fall. Volunteer brigades helped to carry out as much of the office effects as was possible to get out.

For a considerable time the Library seemed to be safe; but the blaze finally penetrated to that part of the building, and thousands of valuable books and records, many expensive paintings and documents rich in local history were burned.

Some of the fixtures and appurtenances in the City Clerk's office were burned.

In another fire, the Baptist Church burned February 20, 1884. The new one was built and opened March 15, 1885. Dedicated on

September 20, 1885, it cost $6,387.05.

On January 15, 1942, Chester suffered its worst fire in history. The fire, "on the hill," destroyed several businesses including Belk-Hudson Company and People's Furniture Company owned by A. J. Hellman.

Duke Power Company not only lost all of its office equipment but also a large inventory of electrical supplies and appliances. Dr. George A. Hennies lost all his office equipment and medical instruments. Chester Masonic Lodge and Rathbone Lodge, Knights of Pythias, both of whom had meeting rooms on the top floor of Belk-Hudson building lost furniture and equipment. Other offices destroyed were those of Rock Hill Production Credit Corporation, Chester Radio Service, District Farm Security Administration, Miss Mabel Johnson's Insurance Company, J. C. Cornwell Insurance Office, F. A. Triplett Contractor's Office, Soil Conservation Office, Civilian Defense Office, Red Cross Office, and a ready-to-wear shop owned by Miss Alice Bradley.

Fire departments from Winnsboro and Rock Hill came to help fight the fire. Much apprehension was felt concerning Hotel Chester adjoining the burning People's Furniture Company building. If the hotel caught fire there would be no chance of keeping the fire from spreading through two more buildings and on to the Court House.

Some citizens were concerned about the city's water supply since 20 streams were turned on the blaze for many hours. But the city had two elevated tanks, one on West End with a storage capacity of 250,000 gallons, one on Loomis Street with 150,000 gallons, and about half a million gallons in a reservoir at the pumping station on Pinckney Road.

Losses from the fire were estimated between $250,000 and $300,000. A news article about the fire stated that the ruins were still smouldering a week after the fire. Chester firemen Ed Porter and White Brice were injured while fighting the fire.

HURRICANE AND FLOOD

On July 5, 1916, a hurricane with winds reaching over 100 miles per hour hit Mobile, Alabama, stalled in the Appalachian mountains for eight days and dropped 32 inches of rain in a 24-hour period.

On July 14, another storm came up the South Carolina Pee Dee basin and collided with the Alabama hurricane. The result was one of the most devastating floods in the Carolinas' history. Eighty lives were lost. Property damage was over $20 million. Transportation and communication were disrupted for weeks.

The Catawba River drops 2,325 feet from its headwaters to

Camden, South Carolina, a distance of about 200 miles. This drop created a run-off of such tremendous power that great waterspouts erupted and everything in its path was swept away.

The river crested above 50 feet as it rushed through Belmont, N. C. down to Rock Hill and into Chester County. On July 16 and 17, every highway bridge and all nine railway trestles on the Catawba were swept away.

Flood waters demolished barns and houses, uprooted trees, swept away bales of cotton, goods stored in warehouses, livestock, fowl, snakes and watermelons. River bottom crops were destroyed and rich topsoil washed away. Deep gullies, often measuring 15 to 20 feet, cut through fertile farmlands along the river. Crop losses covered thousands of acres in York, Chester, Kershaw, Clarendon, Williamsburg, Florence and Calhoun counties.

Water-powered grist mills and cotton mills up and down the river were destroyed along with grain and cotton crops. Several people were drowned trying to salvage personal property.

While the bridges were being rebuilt, Catawba Indians led by John Brown and Jim Sanders, a Carlisle College graduate, operating small row boats, or bateaus, established a ferry service to carry mail, passengers and essential goods back and forth from Chester, York and Lancaster counties.

TWISTERS STRIKE THE CAROLINAS — 1984

The winds of Wednesday, March 28, 1984 are imprinted forever in the history of Carolinas disasters. Along a 300-mile arc through the Carolinas some two dozen tornadoes touched down during a six-hour period. Winds frequently reaching hurricane velocity up to 70 m.p.h. leveled houses, stores, churches and barns and tossed tractor-trailers through the air like children's toys. Half a mile wide swath near Winnsboro looked like a landfill — a trash heap that hadn't been covered by dirt. Chester County was on the edge of the storm path and suffered minor damage around Great Falls and in West Chester.

By week's end 60 lifeless bodies had been pulled from the wreckage of small towns long the storm's path. Hardest hit were neighboring Fairfield County and the town of Winnsboro, Newberry County and the towns of Newberry, McColl and Bennettsville in South Carolina, and Maxton, Red Springs, Mount Olive and Greenville in North Carolina. The tornadoes between 4:30 and 10:50 p.m. dissipated over the Atlantic after touching the tip of Virginia.

According to U. S. Weather Service the storm raced into the Carolinas fed by an unusual set of factors that often exist over the tornado prone Plains and Midwest: dry air from the Southwest, moist air from the Gulf and rapidly moving jet stream air at 18,000 feet and up.

The hot, dry air began sucking moisture into the atmosphere, increasing the buoyancy of the air near the earth. Far overhead, the jet stream rushed across Eastern North Carolina at 135 to 150 m.p.h. Like a fan, it accelerated the upward rush of the moist air.

The unstable air rose to form thunderstorms that flung off tornadoes as they marched through the Carolinas. At least 33 times the air rose rapidly enough to generate a tornado, a powerful, twisting windstorm that travels in a funnel-shaped cloud with the roar of a freight train.

The death toll from tornadoes was the highest in the U. S. since April 1974 when 300 people were killed in the South and Midwest. At least 1,050 people were injured on March 28 and perhaps 3,000 more were left homeless. Property damage totaled at least $109 million.

The Carolina twisters skipped along erratically, touching here and there, missing big cities by pure chance but devastating small towns and farming areas. The first tornado touched down in Newberry, South Carolina at 5:15 p.m. Peggy Wilson, owner of the Wilson Dance Academy on Main Street, was giving a lesson to seven children when, she recalls, the sky took on an eerie greenish hue. "A few seconds later I heard what sounded like a million trains coming. The children ran to us and grabbed us aroung the legs and started screaming 'I don't want to die.' " Wilson and her sister Linda Busby herded the children under a staircase, where they survived as the academy exploded in a hail of broken brick. Said Busby: "The pressure was so strong from the wind that my eyelids were peeled away from my eyes."

Truck Driver Norwood McClain, 41, pulled into a truck stop to phone his home near Winnsboro. His son Jeromy, 14, answered and suddenly shouted, "Daddy, the house is shaking!" Said McClain: "I told him to get out fast." Jeromy turned up in a hospital in critical condition with broken back, arms and ribs. On Thursday his father poked through the rubble of his home, too heartbroken to pick up some family pictures he found. Said McClain, pointing to an area 30 yards away: "I lost my 2½ year old son over there. They found him in a ditch."

These are examples of many macabre scenes left behind by the twisters. In some rural areas the dead bodies of cows were found hanging from trees. Great oak trees with root systems 8 feet wide were knocked over like ten pins. Near by, all that remained of what had been a section of small frame houses was a field of splintered wood, with undamaged household articles sticking out incongruously. In the one wall remaining of a brick house, the window sill with the lady's diamond ring on the rim was left intact.

The disaster, covered in great detail by all the national media, brought out the darker side of human as well as physical nature. Cleanup efforts on Thursday were hindered by traffic jams that backed up on all roads leading to the stricken areas. The cars, many from Chester toward Winnsboro were packed with families out for some ghoulish sightseeing.

But the savage storm left something in its wake besides devastation. From the rubble arose a sometimes-exhilarating vein of camaraderie, people rushing forward to donate clothing or food or to offer shelter or help in removing rubble. Looters were scarcely to be seen. Although it was late Friday before President Reagan officially declared the two states a federal disaster area, Carolinians came to their own reckoning of need within hours.

Churches set up food banks. Service organizations established aid stations. A bottling company donated gallons of juice. Chester joined in an unprecedented outpouring of labor, cash and services to neighboring Fairfield County.

In the minds and hearts of thousands who survived, devastation brought with it a kiss of God's deliverance. Seldom is seen such a brutal, awesome and devastating exhibition of nature's power.

Chester's Hill District

Gadsden St. in Chester's Valley.

COUNTRY STORE AT BLACKSTOCK

XXIII *ROARING TWENTIES*

PRE-DEPRESSION DAYS

Chester County, as did most of South Carolina, in the 1920s remained basically agricultural and suffered thereby because poverty was the most obvious trait of the rural scene. Many people continue to insist on recalling the Roaring Twenties as a prosperity decade, but there was precious little roaring for most Chester Countians; they could not afford it. There was prosperity for some, but definitely it was not to be found amid agriculture and textiles.

Lewis P. Jones writes that by 1921, the bottom dropped out of the Utopia of "forty cent cotton" leaving behind debts accrued during that brief agricultural fling. Granges in 1930 were reorganized. Efforts were made to get the federal government to take action on this problem but little success was achieved.

In addition, cotton growers, the bulk of Carolina farmers, confronted a new and lively problem in the 1920s. The Goliath among crops was suddenly humbled by a Lilliputian enemy: the tiny boll weevil which scampered in about 1917 and by 1922 was decimating production, in some years destroying almost half the cotton crop and causing even human migration. Many Negroes, uprooted and impoverished by cotton problems, were leaving the area and going "up the road."

Cotton farmers suffered under the triple blows of low prices, boll weevils and soil erosion. New Deal measures that took land out of production did nothing for the large number of displaced tenants and sharecroppers. "Home" to these unfortunates meant a dilapidated shack, leaning out of plumb, leaking water in the rain and cold air in the winter, crowded by too many people living amid too much dirt. Poverty, disease and illiteracy were abundant in a drab scene, described by Lewis P. Jones as "marked by meat, meal, molasses, mules and monotony."

254

When the mechanical cotton picker arrived in 1935 it caused the eventual extinction of three-fourths of the labor on cotton farms.

THE COUNTRY STORE

One symbol of the rural South and of Chester County lingered on through the decades of the 1920s and 1930s, though likewise decaying: the country store, or crossroads store. It still provided not only year-long credit (and high prices and high interest) for the rural folk whom it "carried" but it also continued the one-crop system. On the other hand, second only to the church, it provided the chief social center of the rural area, and was perhaps its most racially integrated institution.

The country store provided almost every item of material needs, and also a game of horseshoes, a bench on which to whittle thoughtfully, a barrel on which to lay a checkerboard, a pump from which to crank the kerosene to light the house, a gasoline pump with glass reservoir from which to fill the Model-T, and a pot-bellied stove around which the rural philosophers could expectorate and pontificate to their heart's content.

A typical country store such as the Durham Mercantile Company at Blackstock was a general emporium recalled with nostalgia for its folding wooden chairs (advertising tobacco), "hoop" cheeses and pot-bellied stoves. The stock carried ranged from cradles to coffins. The cotton gin house was usually nearby, the post office in the corner, and the "hall" for a lodge or the Grange upstairs. Customers were "carried" till harvest season at an interest rate said to have "varied from 10 percent to grand larceny," according to Lewis P. Jones. The Durham Company was founded in 1894 and remained in business at the same place until 1983.

In Chester the biggest general stores were Joseph Wylie and Co. and S. M. Jones and Co., both on top of the hill. Wylie was where Kimbrell's is now and Jones was next door. Wylie first had a store at Richburg but later came to Chester.

According to Mrs. Cleo Wall Vaughn who worked there from age 16, the four floors of merchandise at Wylie & Co. included everything "from fat back to baby diapers." The company gave credit to local farmers at high interest rates and often held their chattel mortgages.

Some big Chester County farmers at that time were Dr. Pryor who ran 50 plows and John Frazer, 50. Dr. Pryor rode over his farm in a Packard automobile.

Mr. Samuel operated a store, with Mrs. Janie Hardin Murray as an expert in making hats. Mr. Schlosburg owned and Mr. Hellman operated the store which later became Hardin and Vaughn in the valley. Owners were James Hardin and William B. Vaughn. The business was opened in 1931 on the corner of Wylie and Gadsden Streets and went out of business in 1956. Mrs. Vaughn said bonuses paid to World War I veterans in 1936 put the store on its feet.

The J. T. Anderson Company included a bottling plant, a ginnery and an ice and coal company on Lancaster Street.

Chester Drug Company on the hill had "class and flash," and was the most popular gathering place in town. The Commercial Club on second floor was a place to meet friends and play cards. Across the street was a low brick wall where local "Rock Roosters" sat in the sunshine and talked. Mrs. Ola Glenn rode her beautiful sorrel horse around town, and local ladies who could afford them had velvet dresses, plumes and carriages.

Jack Simmons, a Jew who loved children, had a confectionary store where the War Memorial building is now. A popular feature was his whistling peanut machine. He is memorialized with a marker on the Court House lawn.

COMING OF THE "TIN LIZZIE"

Henry Ford's invention in 1885 and consequent development of the automobile changed the human race more radically than did fire or the wheel.

At first the automobile was a contraption that frightened horses. It evolved into a cog of our civilization as vital as the electric light, the telephone and indoor plumbing. For Americans, it had become nearly as necessary as the shoe. Not an unmixed blessing it has become by 1985 the instrument of death for 45,000 of us each year.

At the turn of the century, cars were still so rare that Barnum and Bailey Circus gave one top billing over a giant, an elephant and a fat lady.

A few cars were bought by the affluent of Chester in the early 20s. They caught the fancy of everyone, even those who predicted no useful future for the noisy contraption. Motor cars became the primary engines of war and of mercy, of commerce, romance, escape and fun. It gave speed, mobility and feelings of freedom that people 100 years ago could not imagine.

Cars altered both land and people in ways that have horrified parents and civic leaders for generations. America's first sexual revolution came in the Roaring Twenties when flappers and their beaus moved the first fumblings of love from the front porch swings to the back seats of roadsters. This provoked the International Reform Bureau to demand that Henry Ford "frame legislation that will stop the use of the car for immoral purposes."

CHESTER CHANGES

During the 20s a campaign was started by Governor John G. Richards, a former Blease supporter, to enforce the state's "Blue Laws" concerning Sabbath observance. This was closely allied to efforts to enforce the legal restrictions imposed by prohibition of the sale of alcoholic beverages. Editor Bob Gonzales of The State reflected much popular sentiment with his verse:

The grand old State
Is filled with woe;
We're headed straight
For H_2O.

One social problem the state had not been able to solve was the sale of beer, wine and whiskey. The State Dispensary system had brought with it many allied evils. In 1907 the General Assembly passed a law giving each county the right to prohibit the sale of liquor within its boundaries. Eventually all but six of the counties voted to prohibit the sale of alcoholic drinks. In 1915 the General Assembly forbade the sale of liquor anywhere in the state.

After the first World War, the United States adopted a constitutional amendment forbidding the sale of liquor. But national prohibition brought more problems than it solved. Liquor was smuggled into the country and sold illegally. The problems in Chester County and elsewhere were widespread drinking, a general disrespect for law, and lucrative "bootlegging" that made some illicit dealers rich.

Today South Carolina permits the sale of liquor and levies a heavy tax on it.

Chester shared in the explosive changes made by the development of a new state road system. Nothing has altered our pre-World War I lives as much as has the motor vehicle. Lewis P. Jones says it rearranged the economy: the malls and shopping centers, the motels, the supermarkets, the Burger Kings, the truck lines, the vacation plans and so on. The groundwork for all these mixed blessings came with the formation of the S. C. state highway system, which ranks as one of the best in the fifty states, and in which Chester County shared liberally. Highway development was funded by a gasoline tax imposed in 1922, one cent for the state and one for the county.

The number of motor vehicles began leaping forward, as Dr. Jones says, "toward the ultimate grand traffic jam." Among the early spinoffs from this was the beginning of the consolidated school to replace the one-room school, and the build up of drive-in movies and food services.

Chester County was affected by the 6-0-1 law adopted by the legislature in 1924 and designed to aid the poorer school districts. Under this equalization law, the state obligated itself to pay six months of teacher salaries; the county none; and the local district, one.

Part of Chester's and South Carolina's problem was obvious: so much of the county was engaged in agriculture, and not very prosperous agriculture at that. In addition, it was trying to support two school systems when it could hardly afford to support one. Although the blacks constituted about 45 percent of the population, the disproportion in funds for bus transportation, per pupil expenditures and teachers' salaries was less than a third for blacks.

The high school broadened its curricula markedly but still concentrated on college preparatory subjects. Interscholastic athletics flourished. Chester became well-known for its obsession with high school football and the town seemed to rotate around the locker room. The rivalry between Chester and Rock Hill was one of the state's hottest rivalries.

Because of widespread adult illiteracy, some efforts were made to cope with this liability. The State Federation of Women's Clubs asked Governor Manning to appoint a literacy commission, which he did. Wil Lou Gray, a human dynamo, in 1920 provided leadership that led to the establishment of the Opportunity School, a work-learning program for the underprivileged in the state.

In the between-wars days the major church denominations became more decorous, with even high-church Methodists supplanting the shouting Methodists. Rural camp meetings declined in fervor and frequency.

In the 1920s, traveling evangelists still attracted large crowds and much publicity. Billy Sunday in 1923 preached to throngs in Columbia, using sermons with such intriguing titles as "We're Going to Hell in Car Lots at Excursion Rates." Thousands "hit the sawdust trail" at his meetings. Another favorite on this circuit was Gypsy Smith. Such was their appeal that railroads offered excursions to the site of the "meetings," often held in tents, by the famed evangelists. Older citizens in Chester remember their fiery evangelism during revivals on the grounds of College Street School.

Health problems plagued the area in the 1920s. Poverty prevented adequate medical treatment. There was a high incidence of hookworm, a parasite whose curse debilitated its victim. Entering the system through small cuts in a region where a large part of the population went barefoot, it was devastating. Deaths from pellagra rose between 1920 and 1930, underlining the poverty and depression of the area since this malady stemmed from diet deficiencies and imbalances.

An obsession of Carolinians was health. The more affluent could take periodic trips to the mineral springs for bathing and drinking, as well as stilted but pleasant vacations. Local people went to Cleveland Springs, Cherokee Springs, Chick Springs, and Glenn

Springs "famous and popular watering places" to recuperate from illnesses.

Glenn Springs, nearest to Chester, was one of South Carolina's most popular mineral springs since 1825. It was named for former owner, John B. Glenn. It was recognized by Indians as having healing qualities. Revolutionary soldiers later claimed that bathing in its waters would cure the itch.

Many poorer people relied heavily on patent medicines so flamboyantly advertised in the press. Large displays convinced many that disease and death could be kept away from the door if readers would take such wondrous medicines as Mozley's Lemon Elixir, Dr. Thatcher's Liver and Bone Syrup, Mother's Friend, Lydia E. Pinkham's Compound, Wampole's Cod Liver Oil, and Wine of Cardui, some of them ranging up to 90 percent proof.

These elixirs were dispensed locally at T. S. Leitner's Drug Store in the valley where two eminent Chesterites got their start in the business world — South Carolina Governor Donald Russell and Dr. James Hardin Wall.

For entertainment, Chesterites turned to spectator sports. Baseball leagues flourished amid widespread interest and excitement. Railroads often provided excursion rates for fans to follow their favorites, the trains not being hard to schedule in the 1920s.

Movies were unprecedently popular and local movie houses were packed. Movie-goers flocked to see Mary Pickford, Clara Bow, Douglas Fairbanks, Fatty Arbuckle and others. Hundreds of movie-goers commiserated with "The Perils of Pauline." The industry boomed even more with the advent of "talking pictures" in 1928. Movies began to eclipse vaudeville shows such as Redpath Chatauqua's traveling shows, and minstrel shows. On October 29, 1923 "Runnin' Wild" opened on Broadway introducing the dance known as "The Charleston." It swept the country.

Early hot-rodders read ads in area newspapers and were fascinated by the advertised charms of the Chalmers Six, Overland Six, the Reo, the Ford ("Leaping Lena") and the Anderson, the latter manufactured in neighboring Rock Hill by John Gary Anderson. This was the South's most successful car to date. The strip down, four wheels with barely enough body to sit on, was popular with the young folks and was a fore-runner of "hot-rodders."

Other entertainment came from the Victrola, the Graffonola and the player piano. In the 1930s, dial tuners hunched over their radios listening with rapt attention to Amos 'n Andy, KDKA, Arthur Godfrey, and Ted Mack's Amateur Hour. President Roosevelt's Fireside Chats in the 1930s spread new hope and confidence to all Americans smarting from the Depression. Probably more Carolinians knew Grady Cole of WBT in Charlotte, N. C. and his rasping rapsology than knew the name of their governor. The Briarhoppers were a popular hillbilly group on radio.

The Briarhoppers, with Charles Crutchfield as master of cere-
monies, extolled the restorative powers of "Peruna," a tonic, and
"Crazy Water Crystals," another product that did deliver action.
Their favorites for banjo picking and singing were "You Are My
Sunshine," "Wabash Cannonball" and "Yellow Rose of Texas."

Industrial growth in the 1920s and 1930s was heavily concentrated in cotton mills, not themselves in robust economic health at
the time. Some optimistic local capital was lured into other optimistic ventures, and all the investors got was a "front row seat at a
factory funeral," according to Lewis Jones.

The leading counties in the textile industry in 1925, based on
value of product (in order) were Spartanburg, Greenville, Anderson,
York, Greenwood, Union and Chester. Factory hours were lowered
by state law to a maximum of 55 hours per week in 1921. After 1917,
children under 14 could not legally work in the mills. Workers were
better paid, better housed and better educated than their counterparts of 1890. The old factory towns, such as Chester, where "the
companies owned everything from the grocery store to the graveyard" were less numerous and conspicuous.

CATALOGUE KALEIDOSCOPE

A complete and realistic view of the "Roaring Twenties" can be
obtained by browsing through the 2,000 pages of the 1927 Sears,
Roebuck and Company Catalogue. This well-thumbed mail order
book was in many Chester homes. Those who could not afford to
shop in the World's Largest Store, found other uses for its crushable
pages.

Out of its pages steps the flapper in all her glory replete with the
fashion frills of the day, her flat chest and her bobbed hair. And out
of Sears' pages steps her male companion with his full-cut trousers
and handsome new "clover leaf" lapels, their children, and all the
family's belongings, necessities and material desires.

One Chester mother who will remain anonymous found a
unique way to measure her 12-year-old son for a "Sunday" suit. She
had him lie down on newspaper sheets, drew his outline in bold
black crayon and mailed the paper to Sears. The order was filled.
The suit fit.

1927 was the heyday of that era. It marked the peak between the
depression of 1921-22 and the Great Depression that followed the
stock market crash in 1929. America's habits were changing, less
time was being devoted to home dressmaking and as usual Sears
Catalogue was reflecting the change. Ready made clothes were hot
items.

Most Chester ladies up to this time either made their own clothes or had local seamstresses make them. Several hat makers were also busy in town. Fake furs called Siberian Fur Cloth made into ladies' coats retailed for $14.98.

Between 1920-29 the auto industry underwent a period of marked expansion. Ford with his black Model T dominated the industry, but Chevrolet was beginning to challenge that dominance.

Nineteen twenty-seven was the year of Lindbergh's solo flight to Paris, the year Babe Ruth hit sixty homers in a single season. Interest in sports soared as evidenced by the tremendous array of sporting goods Sears offered in the catalogue's pages. Toy airplanes were also a hot item.

The phonograph was obviously enjoying great popularity in 1927. Among the top selling discs were "Baby Face," "Ain't She Sweet" and "Bye Bye Blackbird." These tunes and others floated from open parlor windows in Chester in the early evenings as elders rocked on front piazzas and fanned themselves (the 1920s air conditioning).

Sears recognized that all Americans were not completely up-to-the-minute in their living habits. Many frugal Chesterites refused to adapt to "new fangled" offerings. A surprising number of old-fashioned items was still offered for sale. Buggies, once the proudest offering of early Sears Catalogues still found space in 1927, as did all the harness the well-dressed horse or mule would wear.

The items in the 1927 Sears Roebuck Catalogue reflected the wants of almost everyone, and so preserved for us a most vivid portrait of that period. Here we have before us the merchandise, the styles, the prices, to reflect the twenties for those who arrived too late and to refresh the memories of those who were there.

Old Carolina Hotel, Main Street

XXIV GREAT DEPRESSION

NEW DEAL IN CHESTER COUNTY

Prosperity was the keynote when Herbert Hoover entered the White House in 1929. The optimism of the twenties promised more and better for everyone, but within a year the nation had plunged into the greatest depression in its history. The Wall Street crash October 29, 1929 resounded in every city and town in America. Bankruptcies, unemployment and insecurity were rampant. Private or municipal "bread lines" proliferated when no program of social security or relief existed. Families who could not keep up rent or mortgage payments were forced to shift into shantytowns of "Hoovervilles" for shelter.

A popular ditty of the times went:

Mellon pulled the whistle
Hoover rang the bell
Wall Street gave the signal
And the country went to hell.

The 1932 election of Franklin D. Roosevelt was America's reaction to adversity. The anger and frustration of an energetic people forced into idleness and poverty by the Great Depression turned the Republican Party out of power and elected Democrat Roosevelt by a landslide.

Many Chesterites remember his inaugural address beamed across the nation by radio calling for faith in America's future. "The only thing we have to fear is fear itself," he boldly declared as he introduced the New Deal.

A new era began under Roosevelt's New Deal. In his first one hundred days, major laws and new government agencies approved were: (1) the Agricultural Adjustment Administration (AAA) to increase farm prices and pay benefits to farmers in exchange for reduction of acreage; (2) the Civilian Conservation Corps (CCC) which hired young men to plant trees, fight forest fires, and do conservation work in the national parks; (3) the Emergency Relief Administration (ERA) which gave federal money to the states for direct relief of the unemployed, and which — particularly as the Works Progress Administration (WPA) which replaced the ERA in 1935 — administered the biggest relief program in U. S. history; (4) the Federal Deposit Insurance Corporation (FDIC) under which member banks had their deposits insured.

Roosevelt explained and sold his innovative programs through the press and radio and his now famous "fireside chats."

CIVILIAN CONSERVATION CORPS

The Civilian Conservation Corps (CCC) was the most widely used and productive of all agencies created by the New Deal. It was enacted under the Unemployment Relief Act of March, 1933.

The program was set up for unemployed males aged 17 to 25. They could sign up in the CCC for six months at a time, for a total of not more than two years. More than 80,000 young men applied during the first month and about 3,500 were put to work at $30 a month. The employee could keep $8 of his pay, and $22 was sent to his family. It was a lifeline thrown to families suffering from the stock market crash of 1929, and the Great Depression that preceded it in the early 1920's.

CCC volunteers were not only clothed and fed in the camps, but were trained in work skills, physical fitness and educational fields. The War Department furnished the leaders in the public works programs.

Programs were to construct CCC barracks in state and national forests where the work was largely to be done. Since South Carolina had no state forests or parks at that time, state legislators asked President Roosevelt to intervene and formulate plans in which CCC workers could stay at home rather than be sent to another state.

As a result of the President's executive order, about 17 CC-Camps were set up in South Carolina on private land. Chester's was established on the property of W. Carlisle White on what is now Chester State Park off Highway 72 South. Many of these sites including the ones in Chester County were later incorporated into South Carolina's excellent park system.

CCCs were phased out in July 1938.

WORKS PROGRESS ADMINISTRATION

Chester County also benefitted from Works Progress Administration (WPA) statewide library project. Ida Bell Entreken (now

Mrs. Ambrose Wylie of Chester) planned, organized and got the program started. She established an office, made necessary contacts and had programs going by January 1, 1936. WPA furnished assistance with personnel, equipment, supplies and books.

Objectives of WPA Library was to extend library service to the entire state with the hope that this service would be continued with local support at the close of the project.

The depression years that began in 1929 brought difficulties for public libraries. Budgets were cut and services curtailed. But they also brought new demands for library service for the unemployed who desired to improve their job skills and education, and who simply wanted popular reading matter for their enforced leisure.

The project had district and area supervisors in all counties of the states in a training program to prepare employees for library work. Paid from federal funds, employees mended school books, mounted pictures, and copied public and private records such as wills, deeds and manuscripts.

Under the program, an equipped bookmobile was put on the roads in Chester County in 1938. The project closed in 1943 and the country took it over.

Chester City Hall Before Bell Tower was Destroyed by Fire.

Former Office of Hemphill and Hemphill, Attorneys

XXV *FAMOUS TRIALS*

DeGRAFFENREID

Judge J. Hillary Hudson tells of the arrest, trial, conviction and execution of three slaves for the murder of Allen DeGraffenreid.

DeGraffenreid was a wealthy planter residing in the western part of Chester District. He lived alone since his wife had died and his children had married and moved away.

A slave of his, called "Yellow John" was a "runaway." He knew his master kept large sums of money at home, and was familiar with the arrangements of the house and grounds.

Enlisting the aid of two other slaves on the plantation, Yellow John stealthily and in the dark of night entered the house, murdered his master, robbed the house and fled. The three culprits were captured, tried and convicted by a court of magistrates and free-holders, and were hanged on gallows erected about a mile east of the village of Chester which was known as the "hanging old field."

Their bodies were taken charge of by local physicians and carried a mile or more west of the village to a spring branch rising in a ravine in the woods. For days the work of dissecting the bodies progressed.

The place was religiously avoided by the negro, the small boy, and most whites, all of whom fully believed the place to be haunted by the ghosts of the murderers.

The bones of the dead were placed in a box to dry. The box was nailed to a tree about fifteen feet from the ground to be safe from the ravages of hogs and varmints.

When winter, came, a negro man, Hannibal Brawley, was out 'possum hunting. His dog treed and he went to capture the opossum, unaware that his walk through the woods had brought him to the haunted spot. Looking up in the tree in search of the opossum, his eyes caught sight of the box of bones. Dropping his axe, he fled in

265

terror to his home. His face, hands and arms long bore the marks of the briars and bushes through which he ran.

RAFE KING TRIAL

The famous Rafe King murder trial, growing out of the death of his pretty wife, Mrs. Faye Wilson King, in Rock Hill in 1929, attracted the attention of the entire South and especially Chester County. Many Chester residents may recall the details of the trial of Rafe King in Chester and the second trial in Lancaster. It is best remembered as one of the state's most sensational courtroom trials.

It was a bleak January morning when a pretty young Sharon teacher gave her husband two sleeping tablets, kissed him goodbye and went next door for milk. Her husband heard her return but went back to sleep. She was due at Sharon High School at noon to teach two French classes.

But her body was found about 7:30 that night lying on a pile of walnuts in the smokehouse behind their home. There was evidence of a blow on the head. Blood matted her hair, but there was none on her face. There was blood on both hands, scratches around her throat. Her lips and throat were burned as if by acid. The body lay on its back with arms outstretched. The clothes were in perfect order.

The 25-year-old Faye Wilson King was buried the next day, January 26, 1929, in Kings Mountain, "apparently the victim of suicide by taking poison."

There was some talk of foul play.

Nine days later, a warrant was issued charging that "one Rafe King did kill and murder his wife, Mrs. Faye Wilson King, by striking her on the head and by administering poison to her with intent to kill."

One month later a flood of curiosity seekers paid 25 cents admission to the King home, rented by C. E. McGurkin. As many as 2,000 poured in on Sundays from the Carolinas, Virginia, Maryland and as far away as New Jersey. Many came from Shelby, N. C., the former home of King, and from Kings Mountain, the home of Mrs. King since she moved away from Sharon as a child with her parents.

Many climbed through an inside closet to the dark attic and stumbled along under the eaves of the porch where one of the most damaging pieces of evidence had come to light.

Trial

On July 1, 1929, Rafe King's trial began in Chester. The change of venue was obtained because King's attorneys contended he couldn't obtain a fair and impartial trial in York.

The Chester courthouse was so jammed with people overflowing in a solid mass into the halls that King had to enter the court room by a ladder. The hundreds in the room were sitting as close as they could squeeze together on the benches. At least 100 pushed in through one of the side doors into the space reserved for the bar.

The majority came from Broad River and Bullock Creek Township and from York and Bethesda. Those who didn't come to Chester before daylight didn't get any closer to the trial than the courthouse doors.

Those inside were told in moving language by King's lawyers of the wrongs he had suffered, that he had no criminal record and was not an outcast but a husband who had lived in happiness with his wife and was being hounded by his enemies and the State of South Carolina. Here, they said, was a persecuted man deserving freedom and a full measure of public sympathy.

The prosecution assailed King in language that scorched and seared, branding him as a heartless killer and a despoiler of women. The red-handed murderer deserved the electric chair, they declared.

King sat through the trial mum.

The hot, sweltering crowd, made up mostly of women, listened intently to the testimony.

The state charged King with strangling Mrs. King to death by use of "his hands and arms, and with cords, wires, ropes, and belts placed upon, about and around the neck and throat of her."

The contention of the defense was that Mrs. King had committed suicide by taking poison.

Her burned mouth, coupled with the statement by King that his wife had been threatening to take her own life, caused the examining physician and most of the neighbors to conclude that it was a case of suicide.

The next day, however, suspicions having been aroused, Sheriff F. E. Quinn of York was asked to make an investigation. An autopsy was conducted by Drs. J. H. Saye and C. O. Burriss of Sharon. Before the inquest was held, Sheriff Quinn and other officers searched the house for clues and found what appeared to be blood stains in the kitchen.

At the inquest, Drs. Saye and Burriss said that when they performed the autopsy they thought they detected traces of poison in the stomach. King himself took the witness stand, his one and only public appearance, told of his wife's threats of taking her life and said she was despondent because she was in delicate health and dreaded giving birth to a child; also that she disliked the idea of moving to their farm outside of Sharon.

The verdict of the coroner's jury was that Mrs. King came to her death from poison administered by hands unknown to the jury. A warrant was sworn out at the direction of Solicitor J. Lyles Glenn of

Chester, who attended the inquest and examined the witness.

The body of Mrs. King was exhumed at Kings Mountain, after it had lain in the grave two weeks, and a more thorough autopsy made. This revealed, among other things, that Mrs. King was not an expectant mother, that her throat had been severely bruised, the veins were ruptured and that there were bruises on both elbows and knees.

A part of her stomach was sent to Dr. B. F. Robinson at Clemson College for analysis. He testified that, in his opinion, Mrs. King did not die from poisoning.

Dr. R. E. Abell of Chester, who did the dissecting at the second autopsy, expressed the opinion that Mrs. King died of strangulation. This was also the opinion of Dr. J. C. Caldwell of Chester and Drs. Saye and Burriss, all present at the autopsy. Dr. S. S. Royster of Shelby, who was also present, testified that, in his opinion, the autopsy was not thorough enough to determine whether strangulation was the cause of death.

Dr. John A. Kolmer, professor of pathology at the University of Pennsylvania, and authority of worldwide reputation on blood stains, testified that numerous specimens of stains found in the kitchen and elsewhere in the King home were made by human blood.

The grim tragedy was discussed from coast to coast. Metropolitan dailies and obscure county weeklies devoted column after column to the eight-day trial. It certainly overshadowed all other topics in this area for months.

Much was made over King's saying that he had slept until 2 o'clock January 25, and was sick because of salmon he had eaten the night before. He called a colored boy and sent for Dr. Burriss who came around 4 and stayed for an hour. He also sent for the Rev. Carl McCully, Presbyterian minister, and discussed with him his fear of Faye's committing suicide. He told him she had threatened to drink Lysol but was afraid it would cause her to turn black.

The Rev. E. B. Hunter, pastor of Sharon A.R.P. Church, was called "that tobacco-chewing" preacher when on the stand. He accidentally discovered live coals in the kitchen fireplace the night of the murder by spitting in the fire. And yet nobody, presumably, had replenished the fire since early morning. King had said he was in bed all day until he began searching for his wife.

The trial produced some of the most plain and frank testimony heard in court in regards to sexual facts. A social disease contracted by King before marriage played a big part in the case.

It was brought out that Faye was aware of King's affliction before they were married Thanksgiving Day 1927. Because of her having contracted it, she was forced to resign from her teaching position in Shelby in 1928.

A coat wrapped in a shirt, both splattered with blood, and discovered under the eave of the King porch by Chief of Police J. Frank Faulkner, were prize pieces of state's evidence. There was also a bloodstained suit of underwear which had been found stuffed away in the bottom of a trunk. These damaging articles of clothing were the property of Rafe King.

A total of 68 witnesses were presented.

Defense lawyers included Thomas F. McDow, chief council, and Robert W. Shand of York; Clyde Hoey, one of the foremost criminal lawyers of North Carolina and later a senator from that state and B. T. Falls of Shelby, and Paul Hemphill and James H. Glenn of Chester.

State lawyers included Solicitor Harry Hines (Glenn had been made a federal judge), John A. Marion and W. Gist Finley of York; Arthur L. Gaston, David Hamilton and Augus H. Macauley of Chester.

King was convicted on circumstantial evidence of first degree murder. His death in the electric chair was slated for September 20, 1929. He was 38 years old.

He was taken to Columbia and immediately returned to Chester. Even though he had been officially sentenced by Judge J. K. Henry, the law stated that no prisoner could be lodged in the penitentiary until 20 days before execution.

An appeal taken to the Supreme Court resulted in a second trial in Lancaster. It began May 4, 1931.

No new evidence was presented, although Judge C. C. Feathersonne refused to allow introduction of evidence that King was afflicted with a social disease. King again failed to take the stand. He again showed inflexible composure throughout the testimony.

King's lawyers were Williams and Stewart, Gregory and Gregory of Lancaster, Raymond B. Hildebrand, and the brilliant and aggressive McDow of York; the eloquent Hoey of Shelby and Falls.

The new state solicitor at the time was W. Gist of York who was assisted by Arthur S. Gaston, Hamilton, Macauley and the law firm of Sapp and Sapp of Columbia.

When the verdict was to be returned about 7:30 the night of May 7th, at least 700 rushed into the Lancaster courthouse, which had a seating capacity of 350. Some climbed to the second story window to peep in.

This time the verdict read guilty, with a recommendation of mercy. He drew a life sentence. When Rafe King was sitting in his penitentiary cell two days later, he expressed the hope that he would "get outside" again before his death.

He never did. He died in prison in 1950.

XXVI *AARON BURR ROCK*

FORMER VICE-PRESIDENT APPEALED FOR AID

For over forty years, a unique rock monument has attracted attention and interest on the top of Chester's hill. It bears the inscription "Aaron Burr Rock... Erected by Mary Adair Chapter DAR ... 1938." The rock memorializes a significant bit of Chester history.

Aaron Burr was an ambitious political figure of the time, a U. S. Senator from New York state who went on to become Vice-President of the United States. He was popular in South Carolina where he was a frequent visitor after his beloved daughter, Theodosia, became the wife of S. C. Governor Alston.

It was on July 11, 1804, during the time when duels were used to settle grievances, that Burr and Alexander Hamilton, former Secretary of the Treasury, fought a duel on the Hudson Palisades at Weehawken, New Jersey. Hamilton allegedly fired into the air, but Burr was on target and killed his opponent.

This act tarnished Burr's name. However, a major stigma came in 1807 when he was arrested in Mississippi on a federal charge of treason. On the return trip to Richmond, Virginia, where he was to stand trial, six guards headed by Officer Perkins, escorted him in handcuffs. The march was carefully planned to bypass the larger settlements where Burr had influential friends.

The party reached the district of Chester, which was only one day's march from North Carolina. As he approached the principal village of the district, Perkins halted the party and changed the order of their march, placing two men in front of the prisoner, two more behind, and one at each side of him. In this manner they proceeded without incident until they passed near a Chesterville tavern before which a considerable number of persons were standing while music and dancing were heard from within. Burr threw himself from his horse and exclaimed in a loud voice,

270

"I am Aaron Burr, under military arrest, and claim the protection of the civil authorities."

Perkins snatched his pistols from his holster, sprang to the ground, and in an instant was at the side of his prisoner. With a pistol in each hand, he sternly ordered him to remount.

"I will not!" shouted Burr in his most defiant manner.

Perkins, unwilling to shed blood, but resolute to execute the commission intrusted to him, threw his pistols upon the ground, caught the prisoner round the waist with the resistless grasp of a frontiersman and threw him into the saddle. One of the guards seizing the bridle of Burr's horse, led him rapidly away. The whole party swept through the small village of Chesterville and disappeared before the group of spectators had recovered from their astonishment at the scene.

A mile or two beyond the village, Perkins halted the party to consult with his comrades. Burr was wild with excitement. The indifference of the people, the personal indignity he had suffered, the thought of his innocence of any violation of the law, the triumph his enemies were about to have over him, all rushed upon his mind and, for minutes, unmanned him.

Perkins used to say, according to James Parton's *Life and Times of Aaron Burr,* that when the party halted, he found his prisoner in a flood of tears, and that the man who led his horse, touched by the spectacle of fallen greatness, was also crying. In the depths of his mortification, Burr, for an instant, lost that amazing self-command which he exhibited all through his misfortunes.

After conversing with his men, Perkins sent them forward with the prisoner, under the command of his lieutenant, and returned himself to Chesterville where he bought a gig and rejoined the party before night. After spending the night at Lewis Inn where Burr reportedly slept on a bench, he was carried in the gig on to Richmond.

On August 3, 1807, Burr was put on trial for high treason in Richmond, having been accused of organizing an expedition of 100 men who embarked on flatboats on the Ohio River, journeyed to New Orleans and planned to establish an empire that was to comprise the Louisiana Territory. His empire was to include the vast territory of what is now the Western States and Mexico. Burr was suspected of an ambition to set himself up as emperor and carry certain of the southwestern states with him out of the Union.

After a sensational trial in which President Thomas Jefferson was summoned as a witness (he refused), Burr, on September 1, was found by a jury to be "not guilty under the indictment by evidence submitted to us."

The Aaron Burr Rock on Chester's hill is a reminder that Burr drove away into history: accused, acquitted, but not cleared.

XXVII *HISTORY OF GREAT FALLS*

TOWN THAT DUKE BUILT

Great Falls, first known as Catawba Falls, is an area that capsulates a river's majestic grandeur, Indian lore and history, heroism and horrors of two wars, and development of one of the nation's greatest power companies. Lack of one vote in Congress kept it from being chosen as the site of the country's military academy that went to West Point, New York.

Great Falls is a river town of 2,700 population. Its winding streets, modest houses, churches and stores sit among enormous rock outcroppings, unexpected pockets of coolness, a gathering stillness as you near the river, and steep damp banks under leafy canopies.

Dr. David M. Ramsay, historian, first described the falls. "Nothing in South Carolina is equal to the Catawba falls," he wrote. "They are situated above Rocky Mount. Hills confine the descending stream as it approaches to them. When it advances it is narrowed on both sides by high rocks piled up like a wall. The Catawba river, from a width of 180 yards, is straitened into a channel about one-third of the extent, and from confinement is forced down into the narrowest part of the river called the Gulph. Thus pent upon all sides but one, it rushes over the large masses of stone and is precipitated down the falls.

"Its troubled waters are dashed from rock to rock, and foam from one shore to another. They rush with noisy impetuosity — over twenty falls in eight miles to a depth of 178 feet. The scenery is sufficiently grand and curious to attract the visits of the most distant inhabitants of Carolina."

Earliest known inhabitants of the area were Catawba Indians who lived, hunted and fished along the river. The abundance of arrow points and other artifacts collected from the river bottoms attest that the villages were large.

Perhaps the first Europeans to view the falls were 150 Spaniards commanded by Captain Juan Pardo. Leaving the Spanish settlement Saint Elena (Port Royal) in 1566, these armor-clad soldiers had the mission of conquering the Indian tribes and seizing the lands from the Atlantic coast to Mexico for Spain.

They traveled north and west, up the valley of the Broad river, and eventually returned, mission unaccomplished, down the Catawba-Wateree. Almost surely they saw the great falls.

Pardo does mention visiting the great town of the Guatari (Wateree) Indians on his homeward journey. This town, exact location unknown, was on the banks of the river and had "many good houses and round huts of earth." This, wrote Pardo, was "a rich land ruled by two queens."

Pardo wished to return, but Spain's deteriorating position in North America, caused by the influx of English and French, prevented it. After a time the Spanish expedition was a mere memory.

For almost two centuries after Pardo, the area was seen by few Europeans. Some came west from Charleston and the low country. Others came south from Pennsylvania, Maryland and Virginia. They were a motley lot, traders, fugitives, the lawless, the wanderers, the restless and the dispossessed.

It was bountiful country for them with towering forests along the river, grasses as tall as a man's head, and abundant variety of game and fish. They could hunt woods buffalo, deer, turkey, bear and small animals. The waters were teeming with shad, sturgeon, bass and catfish.

But these earliest trappers, hunters and traders did not have the country to themselves for long. From 1755 to 1765 the area around the falls filled with settlers from Ireland and Europe and from the New England states. By 1770, the Reverend Charles Woodmason, an Episcopal missionary, wrote about nearby Rocky Mount:

"The land is good and plowed to the summit, bringing wheat, rye, Indian corn, and all kinds of grain and fruit. This is a most delightful and healthy part of this country. It is but newly settled, but the populace is already crowded together as thick as in England."

For the next half century, the falls shared the history of the rest of the country — Regulators, Revolution and recovery. They remained a place of spectacular beauty, an excellent place to net shad, and a formidable barrier to navigation.

During the Revolutionary War, the Great Falls area was a hotbed of Tory activity, the site of three major battles and of several skirmishes. (See Chapter V.)

After the successful conclusion of the Revolution and the establishment of the American nation, ambitious men in the low country turned their interest to the State's inland waterways. With the completion of the Santee Canal in 1800 they had river traffic open from Rocky Mount down the Wateree to Columbia and Charleston.

Farmers poled their produce down to Camden in small boats, capable of carrying 50 bales of cotton. The cargo was then transferred to larger vessels to move it to Charleston.

An attempt to bypass the falls was begun in 1817 with the digging of Fishing Creek Canal. The canal was completed six years later and the event was celebrated with a picnic at Beckhamville on July 4, 1823.

Rocky Creek Canal was started in 1823 and completed in the early 1830's, but was obsolete almost from the start, for shortly thereafter, the South Carolina Railroad reached the area and the freight went to it (See Chapter on Landsford Canal).

There were many skilled stonemasons, blacksmiths and carpenters employed in the canals and locks, as well as a multitude of laborers, but when the job ended, most apparently moved on.

Some workmen of note were Nattie and Dickie Barnett, skilled boatmen. William Nichols built most of the boats and barges and a Mr. Farrar kept a warehouse below Rocky Mount. Col. Christian Senf, a Swedish engineer, designed the two canals. In 1806, he died in sight of the falls and is buried nearby in an unmarked and now lost grave. Thomas Caine, an Englishman and blacksmith, stayed and made his home in Beckhamville until he died in 1883.

Charles Boyd's survey map of 1818 reveals that most of Chester District's early development was along the Catawba. Numerous islands in the river bore the name Patton's Island, Davis's Island, Col. John Taylor's Island, Mill's Island, Allen's Island and Mountain Island. Davie's Ferry and McDonald's Ferry, Johnston's and McDonald's Fords marked the crossing points. Fisheries were listed as Luckey's and Walls.

A mill in Revolutionary days was operated on Turkey branch near the residence of W. S. Sibley. Nearby was a whiskey distillery. Both were known as Cockerell's.

A grist mill is shown on Rocky Creek on old maps of the area. It was operated by Hart, then by James Pickett. He being a wealthy planter added a cotton gin and a saw mill. Green B. Montgomery in the 1850's changed the cotton gin to a flour mill, first mill to grind wheat in the area. These mills were all washed away in the high waters of 1856. At that time they belonged to Samuel McAliley of Chester. He put in a stone dam and built a fine mill house with a stone basement, and a water wheel about twenty feet in diameter that generated power for all the machinery. His was probably the finest mill in the upcountry at that time, 1858. This mill was burned by Sherman's army in 1865.

On the west bank of the Catawba, at the foot of the falls, Captain Daniel McCullough in 1849 built the first cotton factory in the upcountry. A Northern man named Russell placed the machinery and trained slaves to do the work. Slaves operated it and it was highly successful. It only spun thread.

During the Civil War this factory was thronged with orders for thread to be used as warp in the cloth which was woven at home. This mill was also destroyed by Sherman's men.

William Lewis, Jeremiah Gaither, Green B. Montgomery, and later Hilliard J. Gayden each owned and operated a tannery.

In 1854-55, John T. Mathews manufactured buggies and carriages near Gladden's Mill. He sold the place and left the community in 1856, abandoning the factory. Sherman destroyed it in 1865.

Distilleries were numerous in these early settlements. Excessive consumption of alcohol in all its forms became a problem in the post-Revolutionary War period. Dr. Ramsay, writing in 1808, said "Drunkeness may be considered an endemic vice in Carolina."

Whiskey as an elixir was widely used on the assumption that it would kill intestinal worms and ward off malaria and other fevers. Sick horses were dosed with whiskey, and whiskey served as a pain killer and snakebite remedy for man and beast.

Historian L. M. Ford said a temperance wave struck the vicinity in the early 1850's. A chapter of the Sons of Temperance was organized as part of a national temperance movement. A club house was built for meetings and they flourished for a few years. Then the house, used as a Masonic Lodge was moved to lands near Rocky Creek belonging to T. B. Lumpkin. It was later used as a school house until it was burned by Sherman's army in 1865.

May Picnics

For almost a century and a half the Great Fall May picnic was a popular social occasion for people who lived along the Catawba River. Traditionally the picnic was held near the falls on the first Saturday in May and drew big crowds.

The picnics were held when the shad, a salt water fish, swam upstream by the thousands to spawn. Shad, obeying a primeval and timeless instinct, left the Atlantic, forced their way through a gauntlet of hostile men and animals from the mouth of the Santee, on through the Wateree, into the Catawba. The great falls was a formidable obstacle and made the shad fair game for fishermen and trappers.

Shad were sleek and silvery, the females heavy with roe and weighing as much as 14 pounds, a seasonal bounty from the sea. They were netted, first by Indians, then by early settlers in great quantities, dressed and cooked for a flavorful treat.

Tradition holds that the May picnics marked the "laying by" of farm crops and gave the Scotch-Irish pioneers an occasion to get together. They washed their buggies and wagons, greased the harness, packed food, put on their best clothes and drove to the falls. Some came the day before the picnic and some early in the morning. The road to the picnic grounds was narrow and sometimes muddy. Vehicles often had to be pushed or hoisted along.

Friendships were renewed, new friends made and romances flourished among the young. Hard liquor — vintage moonshine — oiled the amenities and livened the party.

Public gatherings of any sort — picnics, house or barn raisings, log rollings, militia muster, weddings, funerals, hangings, elections and sheriff sales days were carried out in a carnival atmosphere of tipsiness.

Two whiskey distilleries were in easy reach of the falls and every store dispensed the stuff. In addition to this, wagons from the mountains would haul it to the doors of the people and fill a three-gallon jug for one dollar or roll a 40-gallon barrel in the house for a ten dollar bill.

According to historian L. M. Ford, the usual forms of rowdiness accompanied the excesses of drinking — gambling, wrestling, fisticuffs, fist and skull fights, throwing "bullets" and horse racing. The "bullets" were small cannon balls left in the area when Mount Dearborn military establishment was abandoned. The race track was parallel with Rocky Mount Road near the residences of Robert Ford and Stark P. Martin.

The May picnics became less rowdy and more refined during the antebellum days of the big cotton planter and a flourishing economy. After the devastation of the Civil War they reverted to austerity but were continued with unabated enthusiasm.

In the 1870's shad became scarce at the falls as fishermen all along the Santee and Wateree strung gill nets almost across the streams. They left only a channel to conform to the letter of the law that the stream must not be totally obstructed. The shad could not negotiate the maze and most of them were caught.

Harnessing the river for commercial power dams brought about the final demise of both the shad run and the May picnic.

Harnessing The River

James B. Duke, tobacco baron and outstanding philanthropist, played a major role in the development of Great Falls area. His appointment with a New York doctor named Wylie led to one of the happiest events to affect the Piedmont economy in this century.

Duke's large foot felt awful and looked worse. A specialist and native of Chester, Dr. W. Gill Wylie, diagnosed erysipelas. It required rest and frequent treatment. In the course of bandaging and conversation, Dr. Wylie told Duke of his interest in water power.

A young engineer had dammed a river on Wylie's South Carolina plantation, installed a small hydroelectric plant which gave light, heat and power to the neighborhood. Wylie speculated that the many tumbling rivers of the Piedmont could supply power to support towns, cotton mills and supply other benefits such as electric lights, and streetcars as needed in the area.

Duke knew the possibilities and envisioned the benefits. He owned sites along the Catawba River and was fascinated by Wylie's working example. Eager to develop long-distance transmission of power, he wanted to meet that young man, William States Lee.

Lee presented his plans and proposal to link Great Falls and Mountain Island plants on the Catawba which would provide a continuity of service. Lee told him the operation would cost the staggering sum of $8 million. Both Duke and Dr. Wylie gave Lee a check for $50,000.00 to buy the water site.

And so began the implementation in 1904 of Southern Power Co., later Duke Power, and subsequent plants on the Catawba and other rivers.

In the summer of 1907, the first power house and dam were being completed at Great Falls. Plans were underway to build another plant at Rocky Creek. A manufacturing plant was proposed to extract nitrogen from the air to make fertilizer of which nitrate of soda is an important ingredient. The name Nitrolee was coined combining Nitrogen with that of Engineer William States Lee. The plan didn't work but the name remained and was used to designate the third power plant in the area.

There was an island several miles long in the river channeling waters to both the Lancaster and Chester sides. After the power house was completed, a diverting dam was built. Above the falls a high river bank was dynamited and all the water turned toward Chester and into the valley which is now the lake at Great Falls.

Construction continued, with the Great Falls plant completed in 1907, Rocky Creek in 1910, Nitrolee (Fishing Creek) in 1915, Dearborn in 1925 and Cedar Creek in 1926.

In 1909 with the Great Falls hydro plant in operation and the Rocky Creek plant near completion, there was no ready market for all the electricity the river could produce. This was a problem the astute Mr. Duke solved by organizing Republic Cotton Mills to manufacture cotton textiles.

Mr. Duke in the early development of the dams and mills built the Southern Power Hotel to house executives and superintendents working on the projects. He had a suite reserved for his use alone. It was said to have been well stocked with vintage wines and liqueurs. Close by were two-room "roustabout shacks" constructed of tar paper to house the 700-800 construction workers.

By 1920 water power had resulted in the establishment of more than 300 area cotton mills including the three in Great Falls. These mills kept cotton manufacturing near the cotton fields and transformed the Carolinas.

Town of Great Falls

Great Falls started as a town with the erection of the power plant and the first Republic Cotton Mill along with its village. By 1910, there were a few hundred living around the mill and the company store. All business was conducted in the building now occupied by Belk store.

Mill No. 2 and No. 3 with their villages went on line in 1917 and 1923.

During Great Falls cotton mill years a feudal and paternalistic system prevailed. The Mebanes, owners and managers, in their luxurious manor houses on elaborate grounds behind tall hedges contrasted greatly with the mill hands in mill houses. The hands traded at the company store, were policed by company police, and were subject to being expelled from the town if they incurred the displeasure of their boss man. Still, for the time, it was a benevolent feudalism, one that to this day is looked back on with nostalgia by the towns older residents.

In 1946, the Duke Foundation which owned most of the Republic Cotton Mills stock, sold the mills, business and town to J. P. Stevens and Co., Inc., the nations' oldest and second largest textile chain. George Wright, last president of Republic and resident of the luxurious house behind the hedge, departed. The hedge was cut down and the grounds and house in May 1949 became Republic Memorial Park, dedicated to those who served in time of war.

The company sold its 700 houses to employees and other citizens and cooperated with Highway Department to pave streets in the villages. In 1947, Stevens built the concrete and steel grandstand at the local ball park. In 1948, a clinic was built for doctor's offices and medical services.

Schools

Great Falls' first school was held in a small wooden building on the Southern Power Hill, later the residence of L. T. Upton, an official of the company. The school had fifteen pupils and one teacher, Mrs. B. J. Ford.

In 1911, after completion of the first cotton mill the school was expanded and moved upstairs in the Republic store, later McFadden Mercantile Company. There were three teachers, among them Mrs. J. K. Hair, principal, and Miss Ferrell.

The first school building was erected and equipped by Republic Mills in 1916 after Mill No. 2 was completed. E. H. Hall was superintendent. There were 175 pupils and eight teachers. In 1920 the Rossville and Great Falls school districts were consolidated into a high school and grammar school.

In 1924, when Mill No. 3 was completed, a third school, Mebane grammar school was built and named for the Mebanes, Republic owners and generous patrons of education. In 1928, bonds were issued to add an auditorium to the Mebane school. It was said to be one of the prettiest in South Carolina. Enrollment had reached a thousand pupils and 33 teachers and remains about the same today.

Utilities

Bank of Great Falls was organized in 1917 and a building constructed with room for post office, drug store and twelve offices. James Buchanan Duke was one of the original stockholders. It is said that Duke had stock in no other South Carolina bank. Bank officers were R. S. Mebane, president, H. B. Mebane, vice-president, R. C. Mullican, cashier.

Great Falls' first railroad was a small "dinky" used to haul rock to the dam construction sites. It was extended to Fort Lawn to make connection with Lancaster and Chester Railroad. This line was bought in 1911 by Seaboard Airline Railroad and extended to their line at Catawba Junction. Two trains per day, one north and one south, carried express, mail and passengers.

During construction of the dams and mills, the need for a post office was evident. An application was made and the name Catawba Falls submitted. The post office was approved but the name was rejected. Mr. Leland, the resident engineer, suggested the name Great Falls and it was approved.

City mail delivery wasn't started in Great Falls until February 6, 1950 when William Francis Stevenson was Congressman from Fifth Congressional District. Verlin Leonhardt and Joel Crosby were first carriers.

Great Falls operated under a Public Service Commission until May 1969 when the town was incorporated. Joe V. Pendergrass was the town's first mayor. Population at that time was about 5,000.

Economic disaster befell Great Falls on two fronts in the late 1970's. One after another the three mills were closed by J. P. Stevens Company and 1,800 workers were left without jobs. Interstate 77 bisected Chester County and diverted traffic around Great Falls, virtually closing motels and restaurants and other businesses along South Carolina Highway 21.

XXVIII *THE PACKENHAM LEGEND*

OLD PACK SOAKED IN RUM —
LEGEND OF A BRITISH GENERAL

Historian Elizabeth Reed provides this version of the Packenham legend.

On a cold and gloomy January day, a group of cronies gathered around a keg of rum at Tyre Ford's little country store in Rossville in eastern Chester County. Spirits were convivial and boisterous as the tavern keeper treated his friends, veterans of the historic battle of New Orleans in which they had fought a year before in January, 1815.

When the keg seemed empty before its time, one of the veterans seized an axe, hit the keg a mighty blow, and ripped off the head.

There sitting upright before them was the body of a man. The sight was indeed a sobering one. Peering inside, the veteran cried: "Why its old Pack, as sure as you're born."

How did the well-preserved body of a British general find its way in a cask of rum to Chester County?

General Edward Packenham commanded 8,000 smartly uniformed and expertly trained British soldiers in the latter part of the Revolutionary War. When he led them into battle against General Andrew Jackson's forces on 8 January 1815, he little dreamed that he would be routed by the rag-tag backwoodsmen pitted against him.

Snugly fortified behind bales of cotton, Jackson's men picked off 2,000 British soldiers, while losing only seven of their own.

The battle, Miss Reed said, was one of a scattered few which was decisively won after the war was officially over. The treaty of Ghent had been signed 24 December, 1814, fifteen days earlier.

After the battle, the British recovered the body of General Packenham and all agreed that it should be returned to England to be interred on British soil. They conceived a means of doing this.

They removed the internal organs, placed the body in a sitting position in a cask, filled the cask with rum, and shipped it homeward.

When the cask arrived in England it became mixed with other similar casks. Eventually it was consigned to a shipment bound for Charleston.

From Charleston by wagon train it was delivered to Tyre Ford's store. The patriotic storekeeper "rolled out the barrell" to honor the brave veterans, his friends and neighbors, who had triumphantly returned from war.

The legend persists. Old timers in that section for years pointed out the site of Tyre Ford's store. They also pointed to two large grey stones which they claimed marked the burial site of General Packenham. He was interred, still sitting upright, but minus the rum, on foreign soil where he had met defeat.

Legend or truth, the story persists.

XXIX *GRIMKEVILLE*

THE ARMORY AT ROCKY MOUNT

R ocky Mount designed to be one of the nation's three major establishments for the production and storage of military weapons promised Chester County a place in history. Prominent national figures were involved in its planning and development. Among them were Presidents George Washington and Thomas Jefferson, Secretaries of War Henry Dearborn and James McHenry, General Thomas Sumter, Engineer John Christian Senf, a German, and Eli Whitney, inventor of the cotton gin.

The armory on the Catawba river near Rocky Mount, South Carolina, was originally planned to be one of three great national armories. Its counterparts were the National Armory at Harpers Ferry on the Potomac, and the Armory at Springfield in Massachusetts, which became the most famous of the three.

During Thomas Jefferson's second administration, it was planned that those three armories would serve the New England, Middle Atlantic, and Southern states, and, in fact, the armory site in South Carolina was the only one of the three to be placed under the supervision of the Corps of Engineers.

Throughout the Revolutionary War and as late as 1794, arms and ammunition for American troops were obtained either from foreign sources or from a large number of small domestic manufacturers — gunsmiths, powder mills, and furnaces or foundries for cannon and shot.

President George Washington continued to press for a system of national arms manufactories, but not until his second term when war with Great Britain seemed about to break out again, did Congress take the first steps toward such a system. In the President's annual message to Congress 3 December 1793, he referred to the matter of arms and military stores, and voiced his thoughts on the defense of the seaboard. The House promptly formed a Committee on Arsenals and Armories, which recommended on 5 March 1794 that "in addition to the arsenal at Springfield, there ought to be erected two other arsenals, with magazines and other necessary buildings, at such place as may accommodate the Southern and Middle States." Each establishment would cost about $29,500, including $2,000 for purchase of the necessary land.

Washington authorized preliminary surveys both along the Potomac and in the north-central part of South Carolina. Two French-born engineers, Stephen Rochefontaine and John Foncin, were directed to survey the Potomac and South Carolina areas respectively.

In November 1798, Secretary of War James McHenry queried General Washington as to the best location for what he called "magazines," or arsenals. Washington then proposed a specific location for the arsenal for the South. In regard to the stations for magazines, three principal permanent stations would suffice, and these ought to be at Springfield and Harpers Ferry which were already chosen, and the vicinity of Rocky Mount on the Wateree in South Carolina.

Like the rest of the country, the state had no trained engineers, and so during the Revolutionary War, Henry Laurens, then a representative to Continental Congress, sought out a trained engineer from among the German auxiliaries. He found a qualified staff officer by the name of John Christian Senf, a 24-year-old Saxon, and arranged for Senf's appointment as a captain of South Carolina forces in 1778. Senf attached himself as engineer to the troops under Major John Faucherand Grimke, and by the time of the fall of Charleston in 1780 he was a lieutenant colonel.

After the British evacuation of Charleston, Lieutenant Colonel Senf was appointed State Engineer. He was considered available for superintending the plans and construction of the postwar canal projects. When the Santee Canal Company was chartered in 1786, Senf was hired as its engineer. He was then employed by the Catawba Navigation Company, whose president was his old commander, Major Grimke, whose immediate goal was to cut a canal to bypass the falls and shoals of the Catawba near Rocky Mount and to connect with the Wateree below the falls. The first survey of the Catawba Company was completed in March, 1788, and enclosed was a map by Christian Senf showing the proposed canal to bypass "The Shoal" of the Wateree River.

General Thomas Sumter visited President Washington several times during his term as a representative in the 1st Congress. Both Colonel Senf and General Sumter were interested in the canal project, and probably explained to the President the importance of the Catawba-Wateree route. Washington made a trip through the South in 1791, and crossed the Wateree River. He may have discussed with local dignitaries the Catawba Canal.

Washington's selection of Rocky Mount in 1798 was the basis for the future selection of that site when the Democratic-Republicans came to power. George Washington died at the end of 1798, and no further action was taken by the Federalist administration to pursue the matter of the armory at Rocky Mount.

Thomas Jefferson, winner in the election of 1800, took office in March, 1801. During 1801 and 1802 Jefferson and his Secretary of War, Henry Dearborn of Massachusetts, wisely provided for a Corps of Engineers and a Military Academy. At the same time, on Dearborn's recommendation, the President proposed to Congress on 2 February 1802, that a southern magazine finally be established in some point convenient for the States of North Carolina, South Carolina, and Georgia. He asked that Congress make some provision for preliminary site selection during the year 1802.

Dearborn mentioned this project to Senator Thomas Sumter, and Sumter volunteered his assistance.

The Secretary wrote Sumter with a definite proposal saying it was the intention of the President to commence the establishment of a magazine and armory near Rocky Mount on the Catawba River. The first preliminary step was the selection and purchase of a suitable site of 50 acres. He asked Sumter to select the site with the aid of Colonel Senf and make the purchase of the land including the water privileges.

At the same time, Dearborn wrote Colonel Senf an offer to appoint Senf superintendent of the construction of the establishment, if a mutually acceptable compensation could be agreed upon.

In July, 1802, Senator Sumter and Colonel Senf reported to the War Department the availability of a large tract of land along the Catawba just below the Great Falls. Instead of the 50 acres Secretary Dearborn had asked for. Sumter urged the purchase of from 300 to 500 acres. President Jefferson approved the acquisition. The tract of land actually purchased totaled 523 acres.

The matter of the Federal acquisition of this land was the basis for subsequent litigation which led to bad feelings between the federal and state officials, and contributed largely to the failure of the establishment. It appears, however, that a substantial part of the land sold to the government by Senator Sumter actually belonged to the Catawba Navigation Company. Both the disputed land and the role of the National Armory were to be key issues in controversies that broke out in the spring of 1803.

Meanwhile, Secretary of War Dearborn decided to employ Eli Whitney, then visiting in North Carolina, to go to Rocky Mount for the purpose of consulting with Colonel Senf on the most proper site for the proposed Armory.

Early in 1803 Eli Whitney and Colonel Senf conducted a joint survey and consultation on the proposed army site, and Whitney forwarded the results to the War Department. Secretary Dearborn wrote Colonel Senf an important letter giving the steps to be taken in constructing the Armory. For the first time, Dearborn mentioned the cooperative role that would have to be taken by the Catawba Navigation Company.

Dearborn said that the first step to be taken was that the Catawba Company cut a canal from above the Great Falls to a pond or reservoir which would provide water power for a sawmill to cut wood for the frames of the buildings, and later for operation of the machinery of the armory at the expense of said Company, and that the Company agree to open passage by the first day of October, 1803.

On 10 April 1803, Judge Grimke, president of the Catawba Navigation Company, informed the Secretary of War that the Company was pleased to find that a beginning was likely to be made in this useful work, and that they unanimously voted the sum of $500 for the purpose of opening the channel. Colonel Senf was designated as superintendent of the necessary buildings at Rocky Mount.

Early in November, 1803, Secretary Dearborn, having drawn detailed specifications for each building at Rocky Mount, decided to employ once again the expert help of Eli Whitney. Whitney, who was in close touch with the Secretary of War, advised Dearborn that he needed to travel to South Carolina to discuss with the Legislature his cotton gin rights, and the Secretary asked him to visit Rocky Mount, show Colonel Senf the specifications of the buildings, and agree with Senf on the exact site for each building. In mid-November the two men conferred at Rocky Mount.

By the end of 1803 the proposed Armory seemed to be on its way to construction. Colonel Senf was appointed as superintendent of construction, and Secretary of War Dearborn had furnished detailed plans, and all seemed to be going well except the role of the Catawba Navigation Company. The Company apparently accepted the task, but would not guarantee the deadline.

Even without the canal for the water works, construction of the buildings at Rocky Mount got under way. By the end of 1804, the Treasury had paid $11,200 to Christian Senf. "It is significant, however, that in reporting this expenditure, the War Department listed Rocky Mount under arsenals and magazines — together with Albany, West Point, Schuylkill (Philadelphia), Washington City (Greenleaf's Point), and Newport, Kentucky — while Springfield and Harpers Ferry, were categorized as Armories." This is interesting to note that the amount spent at Rocky Mount was second only to the Schuykill establishment under arsenals and magazines.

Judge Grimke professed that the entire problem was based on the fact that the works were not exactly at Rocky Mount, and he compounded this with a blunder in picking the same moment to introduce the startling fact that the Catawba Company intended to bring suit against the United States over the ownership of 200 acres of land, worth perhaps $1,500.00, included in the reservation purchased from Thomas Sumter.

Judge Grimke wrote Captain Macomb that "the Catawba Company had done what they promised to do, and if the work still continues imperfect, no blame can or ought to attach to them."

The need for a national armory on the Catawba suddenly took second place to the urgent requirement to stiffen the nation's seacoast defenses, and nowhere, except perhaps in Norfolk, was the urgency more acute than in Charleston.

When Captain Macomb returned to Mount Dearborn in September, 1807, from his visit to Charleston, he found a letter from the Company's attorney, D. R. Evans, of Winnsborough, announcing that the "President of the Company for opening the Navigation of the Catawba and Wateree Rivers has directed a suit to be instituted for the purpose of ascertaining the legal boundaries of the lands purchased by the United States, and fixing the line of division between those lands and the lands of the Company. Colonel Nunn the Sheriff of Chester District will wait upon you." The Sheriff's writ required Captain Macomb, as the agent of the United States, to appear at Chester Court House in late October.

Captain Macomb at once wrote to the United States District Attorney in Charleston to take the necessary action to defend the United States in the impending action.

Captain Macomb went to Chester, told his story to the court, and asked for a continuance. He apparently had no difficulty, for not until November of 1809, two years later, was Macomb required to attend a session of the Court in Chester.

The status of the proposed armory was unsettled during the last 15 months of Henry Dearborn's term of office.

In the fall of 1807, Captain Macomb wrote to Dearborn that little progress had been made in the works owing to sickness among the workmen.

At the end of the year 1807, Dearborn recommended to the President that several officers be promoted, and in due course the Chief Engineer was promoted to Colonel. Alexander Macomb advanced to Major and Charles Gratiot to Captain. Colonel Williams divided his officers among geographical districts to supervise seacoast fortifications construction. Under this system, Major Macomb was placed in charge of the district encompassing the coasts of the Carolinas and Georgia, with headquarters in Charleston Harbor, and Captain Gratiot was assigned to this district.

In spite of Dearborn's personal interest in the armory project, he realized that the defense of Charleston Harbor had to take priority in South Carolina, so he told Major Macomb to move the majority of the Mount Dearborn workmen to Charleston to work on the harbor fortifications.

For a few months in the summer of 1808 the work at Mount Dearborn apparently resumed, under the superintendent, Ross Bird. Then the needs of the establishment again took second place to more pressing requirements, this time augmentation of the Army.

The Act of April, 1808, authorized the raising of eight new regiments, and the new 3rd Infantry was assigned to the Carolinas and Virginia for its recruiting. Dearborn, remembered Major Macomb suggesting that Mount Dearborn would make as good recruiting place, and also Macomb's satisfaction with former Captain Bird, whom he now recommended for appointment in the 3rd Infantry. On July 18, a War Department listing of new company recruiting rendezvous showed Captain Bird's company at Rocky Mount. By the beginning of December Captain Bird had completed recruiting his company, and sent his muster roll to the War Department. It appears that Captain Bird's was the only company at Mount Dearborn, and he was the commanding officer of the military post.

As Thomas Jefferson's administration neared its end in early 1809, Dearborn resigned his War Department position in February, to accept the post of Collector of the Port of Boston.

The new President, James Madison, took office on 4 March 1809, a period of half-peace and half-war with Great Britain, until war was finally declared in June of 1812. The new Secretary of War was William Eustis, a physician and politician of Massachusetts. Secretary Eustis recognized the value of the half-completed armory in South Carolina as a recruiting place, and training site. However, he had to rely on the opinions of the officers of the Corps of Engineers, since there was no Ordinance Department prior to 1812.

Secretary Eustis directed that the troop strength at the military post at Mount Dearborn be increased. He gave instructions to the Purveyor of Public Supplies that all companies recruiting for the 3rd Infantry would be assembled at Mount Dearborn under Lieutenant Colonel John Smith, and by late fall of the year the companies of Captains Jacob J. Faust and Joseph Woodward, with a detachment under Ensign William Laval, had joined the company of Captain Ross Bird at the federal establishment.

Macomb wrote Eustis December 18, 1809, including an up-to-date report on the works at Mount Dearborn as follows:

"The Establishment at Mount Dearborn: The works at this place have been progressing slowly since its occupancy by the Troops and I am sorry to say they have not done them much good.

"The Arsenal is ready to receive any arms that may be sent there and the magazine is also finished. The quarters intended for the superintendent are not quite finished but progressing as fast as the number of hands employed will permit.

"The situation of this place-stating its advantages and disadvantages:

"The Establishment is situated in the district of Chester on the left bank of the River Catawba and is about 160 miles from Charleston. Its advantages are these — its position is central as it respects North Carolina, South Carolina, Georgia and Tennessee, and is in the vicinity of the finest iron for manufacturing small arms of any place in the United States, and when the contemplated canal is completed, a free and easy communication will be had with Charleston and the whole iron country of North Carolina by water. But the greatest misfortune at present is the difficulty of communication, both by land and water, for it is placed in the midst of all the obstructions of the Catawba, so that you can neither go up or down the River, and consequently until they are bypassed by the canal the establishment will be deprived of easy access to the iron works of the upper country as well as the free communication with the lower country.

"In point of situation for a great command of water no place can exceed it, but until the canal is cut no machinery can be put in operation at the place originally intended for the Armory. About 400 yards above there is an excellent site, where water will be found in abundance the whole year round, which on the map accompanying this report is called Gill's Mill. The country about the Establishment is so broken as to render the land carriage very difficult."

From the excellent map prepared by Macomb can be seen the actual progress at Mount Dearborn as compared to the original plan.

In November, 1809, Secretary Eustis ordered Lieutenant Colonel John Smith to remove most of the troops from Rocky Mount to Charleston Harbor, leaving twelve or eighteen men to take charge of the public buildings and property at Rocky Mount.

On the departure of Colonel Smith and his troops about the first of December, 1st Lieutenant Robert B. Moore, a South Carolinian, became the commanding officer of the post of Mount Dearborn.

Whether the establishment of Mount Dearborn continued on a caretaker status with a handful of federal troops, whether it was consigned to Civil caretakers, or whether it was abandoned to the elements and vandals either during or after the war does not appear in the War Department's records.

GRIMKEVILLE — A GHOST TOWN

Chester County has its own ghost town with a history as intriguing as any in South Carolina.

Ghost towns are often written about.

JOHNSON HOUSE RT21
1820

Most towns, however, have one thing in common — there are skeletal remains showing they once were towns. Not so with the once-thriving town of Grimkeville. It simply disappeared, leaving only one magnificent old house to mark the degree of prosperity it once enjoyed.

The site of Grimkeville is now a portion of the fields and of the forests on the western side of the Catawba River near Great Falls. Where the busy hum of activity once sounded and people ran the gamut of daily living is now the lonely haunt of the rabbit, deer, the wild birds. If there is a battered brick or rusty nail left of the once-thriving habitation or business houses, they are hidden beneath the forest floor.

Dr. David Ramsay in the early 1800's wrote:

"The situation of Grimkeville at Rocky Mt. is not only fascinating for its beauty, but eminently calculated for the enjoyment of health and transaction of business. Its summit is considerably higher than the top of lofty trees in the vicinity, and it commands a most extensive view of the surrounding country."

On the crest of this hill the town of Grimkeville was surveyed in 1792. The two main streets which ran north and south were called Washington and Pinckney. The cross streets were Blanding, Manigault, Izzard, Cripps, Barnett, Laughton, Davis, Kean, and Allen. All these streets were named in honor of prominent men of that day in the state and nation.

Among the first lot owners and probably residents were Judge J. F. Grimke, L. Smith, J. Allen Smith, Manigault, John D. Maxwell, William Houston and High McMillan.

The hill on which this town was built is the true and original Rocky Mount. It was known as Rocky Mount Proper. Lots were reserved for a seminary, parsonage, church and cemetery. The residence of the late John G. Johnston stands upon the church lot.

John Faucherand Grimke, for whom Grimkeville was named, served as a major during the Revolutionary War. After the British evacuation of Charleston, he formed the Catawba Navigation Company and turned his attention to plans and construction of postwar canal projects. His immediate goal was to cut a canal to bypass the falls and shoals of the Catawba near Rocky Mount and to connect with the Wateree below the falls. He helped to lay out the town and begin its construction.

In 1802, Secretary of War Henry Dearborn enlisted Senator Thomas Sumter of Revolutionary fame to purchase 50 acres as a suitable site for the establishment of a magazine and armory near Rocky Mount. Sumter urged the purchase of from 300 to 500 acres.

The South Carolina legislature passed an act December 18, 1817, to purchase these lands. The purchase of 523 acres was consummated May 1, 1818 at a price of $19,258. This purchase was probably made preparatory to digging the Land's Ford canal that was planned to circumvent the falls on the river.

This once populous and growing town gave promise of increasing in size, population and importance. It was situated at the head of flat boat navigation, used mainly to transport cotton down river to Charleston. The bugle blast announcing the arrival and departure of boats was often heard. A ferry was in operation to take passengers and freight across the river to Lancaster County. The town was surrounded by fields of fertile soil, cultivated by thrifty and energetic husbandmen and a considerable trade was carried on in it.

Though it had its beginnings as an enterprise of rich planters who owned lands on the Catawba, it assumed additional importance because it was near a good landing on the river from which freight boats could take cotton bales and proceed to the cotton market.

Transportation factors have always had much to do with the rise and fall of towns. This was true of Grimkeville. It was the coming of the railroads in the area providing faster and easier transportation which was one cause of its decline. Another contributing factor was the War Between the States that bankrupted the South and killed off many of its potential leaders.

General Sherman in the spring of 1865 on his March through South Carolina near the end of the war, camped with his army at Grimkeville. The troops were unable to cross the river because of high water. They remained on the site for eight days. They burned or mutilated most of Grimkeville's remaining buildings and camped in the yard of the Barclay-Johnston house. Livestock, chickens and other food items were confiscated by the soldiers from families living in Grimkeville.

The site's history antedates its 1792 surveying. Tradition is that it was first started as a trading post with the Indians.

Almost every plantation in the area had both Revolutionary War and Civil War associations. This region was the scene of continued partisan movements, skirmishes and cruelties during the last three years of the war for independence.

Near the mouth of Fishing Creek, which empties into the Catawba two miles above the Great Falls, General Sumter suffered defeat, after partial success at Rocky Mount below. Down through Chester, Fairfield and Richland, Whigs and Tories battled fearfully for territorial possession, plunder and personal revenge.

Now the historic site of Grimkeville is desolate and forsaken. No boat comes or goes on the once turbulent river that has been tamed and harnessed by Duke Power Company's huge dams and turbines. Those who walked to and fro on the streets have passed on and their habitations have moulded into dust. The streets have been obliterated by the plough share. The lowing of cattle on the hillside and the hush of bygone history take the place of the bustle and hum of business on the once crowded streets.

Only the weathered but stately Johnston house still keeps its lonely vigil on what used to be Grimkeville. The house where "refined hospitality bore rule" is beautifully situated upon an eminence overlooking the Catawba, and within a few rods of the site of the old village.

BARKLEY-JOHNSTON HOUSE

The Barkley-Johnston house was designed to be a part of the town of Grimkeville. It is built in the architectural style of the Old South, with four white columns gracing its entrance and with an unusual fan-shaped window over its double front doors. It has two and half stories.

It was in this home near the Chester-Fairfield county line that General William Tecumseh Sherman made his personal headquarters for a time during his march through the South.

History surrounds the house, and is as interesting as the reddish haired handsome general in the blue uniform of the Union Army who stopped in the early part of 1865.

That visitor, who has been roundly cursed by many a stout-hearted southerner, was found by the residents of the home to be a gentleman with a "pleasant and courteous" manner toward his men and others.

The house was built in 1830 by James Barkley, wealthy planter and slave owner, and named "Rocky Mount." The brick used in building its three large chimneys were made in England and brought to South Carolina to build Fort Dearborn, a Revolutionary War fort near Great Falls. After the fort was no longer in use, Mr. Barkley bought the brick to use in building his chimneys.

James Barkley Johnston, a grandson of James Barkley inherited the house, and he in turn left it to his daughters Kate and Gladys Johnston.

Johnston also left his story of the happenings at Rocky Mount during Sherman's visit. He was born February 23, 1857 and was eight years old when the Union troops stopped at Rocky Mount after they had been delayed in crossing the Catawba by high waters.

Mr. Johnston remembered vividly some incidents which occurred during the visit of General Sherman.

Days before the Yankees' arrival, Mr. Johnston recalled, the noise of cannon could be heard at Rocky Mount. Rumors of the cruelty and destruction of Sherman's army swept over the country, filling the people with terror.

Mr. Johnston's mother, his grandmother, Mrs. Barkley, and Miss Sarah Barkley were kept busy directing the slaves in hiding valuables and food. They carried the flat silver, weighty and burdensome though it was, in large, invisible pockets in their dresses, and it was saved. Most of the other valuables which they had hidden were found and carried off by the soldiers.

The meat was hidden between the weather boarding and ceiling of the garrett and the soldiers never found it, although there was a strong smell of smoked meat in the garrett.

When the first Yankees arrived, Mrs. Johnston thought they were some of General Joseph Wheeler's men, but in a short while swarms of soldiers wearing blue uniforms were everywhere, plundering. A silver pitcher was found in the greenhouse and the walls were soon demolished in a search for more silver. The yard fence was burned the first night, as was a large supply house full of tobacco and other stores.

The gin house full of cotton seed, the barn and the stables were in flames shortly after the arrival of the Yankees. During the eight days while the soldiers were there, Mr. Johnston said, the women lived in terror of having the house burned.

General Sherman arrived soon after February 17, 1865, and his soldiers pitched camp at Rocky Mount.

He was "striking" in appearance, tall, handsome, clean-shaven with reddish hair.

To the young Johnston boys who proudly wore brass "rebel buttons" on their jackets, Sherman's shining boots and neat uniforms were envied possessions.

Sherman stayed eight days, patiently waiting for the waters of the Catawba to drop and allow his men to pass. When he left it was on a great black horse with a Negro boy as a valet, Mr. Johnston recalled.

Sherman went into the house every day and talked with the women. Miss Sarah Barkley was "hightempered" and her eyes flashed with fire when she had hot discussions with the general. Usually Miss Sarah and Mrs. Barkley sat by the fire with large bonnets pulled down over their faces.

The officers had their quarters in the house. The first morning after they arrived, Mrs. Johnston invited several of them to breakfast. The menu included rye-coffee with no sugar, bread and meat. Later the officers showed their appreciation by preventing the soldiers from piercing the family portraits with their bayonets and breaking up the furniture. They also stopped the soldiers from tearing up the floor and using the planks to patch the pontoon bridge across the river.

The soldiers gave sugar to the little boys but they were not allowed to eat it for fear they would be poisoned.

When a soldier saw a barrel of molasses in a room, he slipped into the basement and bored a hole through the floor to try to drain out the syrup. He missed the barrel by inches. The mark is still in the floor.

Captain Isaac Withers of Winnsboro and a young man named Keller from Broad River were held prisoners by the Yankees while they were at Rocky Mount. Captain Withers came to the house for food, but stopped after the soldiers complained to their officers that "rebel" soldiers were being fed.

As the Yankees were leaving Rocky Mount, some of General Wheeler's men came up and there was a brief skirmish about the house. Wheeler warned the women and children to lie flat on the floor during the fight. The Yankees thought Wheeler's entire army was in pursuit and left hurriedly.

One of the rebels chased a Yankee through the house. The southerner's gun was cocked and fired in the hall; leaving a mark which is still to be seen. Bullet holes from the skirmish are still visible in the weather boarding of the house.

During their stay, the Yankees threw rifle pits in the garden, and breast works and rifle pits have been dug up in the old canal near the river. One bridge at the ferry was broken but the Yankees erected another at the canal. The approach which was cut for it can still be seen.

When the soldiers were gone, there was nothing left but the house and land. The place was bleak and bare. So far as the Barkleys and Johnstons were concerned the Confederacy was at its lowest ebb. The time for rebuilding had come.

Barkley Johnston caught an old crippled horse which had missed being shot. The horse, called Bill Sherman, plowed the first crop after the war. A small steel mill ground corn picked up from the camp, washed and dried for food. There was meat still in the garrett.

Mr. Johnston recounted these experiences many times and gave one of the most vivid eye-witness accounts of the fall of the Confederacy and of Sherman's infamous march through the South.

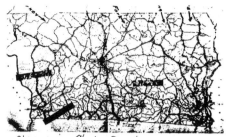
Streams in Chester County
Streams in Chester County

XXX COMMUNITIES

BATON ROUGE — CHESTER COUNTY

Everybody has heard of Baton Rouge, Louisiana. But ask someone how to get to Baton Rouge, South Carolina and they do a double take.

"Never heard of it. Are you sure?" a desk clerk at the Winthrop College Library frowned when she was questioned concerning research material on the area.

Two hours later it appeared there is no information available on the small, ill-defined community located 11 miles west of Chester.

However, one Chester County map pinpointed the general vicinity.

The Chester telephone book listed several residences in Baton Rouge, including Mr. and Mrs. Raymond McDaniel.

When Mrs. McDaniel was contacted she agreed to discuss the history of the community "if you can find us," she laughed.

"Some other people live here but they're spread out. I couldn't even guess how many . . .

"If you come, you won't see much," she warned.

Armed with a map, a notepad, and a full tank of gas, a reporter and a photographer set out for the boondocks.

Following the map, they took S. C. 9 west out of Chester, searching in vain for a smaller road to the left.

Stopping at a dilapidated country store, the friendly proprietor pointed the way to the little community located on County Road 30.

The narrow, winding road ribboned its way through gently sloping farm lands, idle fields overgrown with weeds, past tumbled-down houses and crumbling chimneys blackened by fires of long ago.

It meandered past a smattering of homes, aging barns, cattle grazing peacefully among tall trees, and ponds nestled in the valleys, banks graced by Black-eyed Susans and Queen Ann's lace.

And it was quiet, breathtakingly beautiful to city slickers who had grown up on a farm.

Passing Calvary Baptist Church and an adjoining cemetery, was an impressively large brick home at the top of a hill.

The spell was broken by two birddogs who announced visitor's arrival at the McDaniel's.

Mr. and Mrs. Raymond McDaniel invited visitors into a comfortable den scented by the faint odor of blackberry jelly bubbling on the kitchen stove.

The soft-spoken couple settled into easy chairs and told what they could remember of the history of the area, as it was passed down by relatives who had lived here for generations.

"As I get it, some Frenchmen from no telling where, laid off the streets over here and it was supposed to be a little town."

But the town never materialized. Legend has it that the name was derived from red stakes used to mark off the streets. Baton is French for stake and rouge is French for red, Mrs. McDaniel explained.

At one time there was a boarding school for girls and a public school, but the buildings burned many years ago.

Fire also leveled the post office to which mail was sent out twice a week from Chester during the 1800s.

The Seaboard Railroad used to have passenger trains coming through the nearby Sandy River Station, making four round trips a day to Chester. This service was discontinued in the early 1930s, McDaniel said.

At its peak, the community numbered about 100 persons, according to his estimate, with perhaps 75 now residing here.

Formerly a farming community, Baton Rouge is now a bedroom community for people employed in Chester.

Mrs. McDaniel, formerly a Cornwell, was born and reared in a three-storied home on the site, built in 1821. The historic landmark was destroyed by fire in the 1950s and was replaced by the present modern structure.

"They used to kill 100 to 150 hogs every year. They'd feed the slaves in the old smoke house that used to be over there," he motioned.

The well house was also destroyed by the fire. Their water is now piped from a spring, "the best there is."

"We had a dozen big oaks that must a been at least 500 years old. That one is the only one left," McDaniel pointed to a gnarled tree crippled by lightning. "Guess we ought to take it down."

Strolling down a winding path, McDaniel led the way to the foot of the hill. Carefully crossing a barbed wire fence, he parted the dense overhanging tree limbs which shelter graves of relatives buried long ago.

Some were marked with graying tombstones while most were flanked by flat dark rocks. "There must be a dozen or so," he remarked.

Mr. McDaniel spoke of the Civil War and Sherman's men marching through the area. "They tell me they stood on the hill here and looked over there and saw Columbia burning," he said.

A tour of the township revealed the woods where the school once stood, houses once filled with laughter and children, now silent as the soft breeze, and fresh deer tracks at numerous crossings. Only a few people with poignant memories remain of Baton Rouge.

BLACKSTOCK

The small town of Blackstock was named for a family of Blackstocks who settled in the area before 1850. Ned Blackstock, an Irishman, set sail from his native land and after a voyage of three months — then considered rapid transit — landed at the port of Charleston and found his way to the present site of Blackstock 12 miles south of Chester.

There was no railroad in this section of the country and the mail was carried by stagecoach. Ned Blackstock established a post office in the house now occupied by the W. W. McKown family. He became postmaster. Prior to this occupancy a family of Bells lived there.

This house was also the Wayside Inn or tavern operated by Mr. DeLaith where the stagecoach stopped overnight. The master of the house dumped out all the mail, took out those letters addressed to him and put the rest back into the bag together with letters he wished to be delivered. The postage for one letter was fifty cents.

After Ned Blackstock died, the post office was moved to a red house approximately one-half mile north of the present site of Blackstock. A man named John Strong became postmaster. The post office remained there until his death and was then moved to the home of Mrs. Bell.

At that time Frank DeBardeladen ran a store and a house of entertainment. After his death the place was bought by Mrs. Bell and continued in the family for many years.

Near the spot where the depot stood, there was a woodshop operated by Joe Fullerton. He made and repaired spinning wheels.

After the railroad was built, the town began to grow and was incorporated on February 22, 1873. DeVaga and DeGraffenreid of Chester opened a store in a wooden building where the Durham Mercantile Co. later was operated. Clerks were David Fant and Henry Pratt, who later bought the store.

Until the War Between the States they ran a dry goods and grocery store and had a flourishing business. Several other stores soon sprang up. T. M. Boulware built the first house, which was later burnt by Sherman.

A large school, Feasterville Academy, was located near Blackstock and received pupils from all over the state. It lasted until the war. One April thirty-four young men from the school departed to enlist in the Confederate Army. The school degenerated and was never revived.

Thus was the end of what was known as "First Blackstock" for Sherman soon invaded the neighborhood, leaving only destruction in his pathway.

George Hooper owned all the land near the railroad station. He opened up a barroom there near Fant and Pratt's store. This was the site of "much rowdying and fighting, as drunk men have always been the same."

Nearby, Hiram Steele built a carriage factory. He was a progressive man and built up a prosperous business. Later he moved the factory to the John Mackerall place south of Blackstock.

In 1856, George Hooper sold his real estate to T. M. Boulware who moved to Blackstock and made his home there. Soon after this, Fant and Pratt closed their store. The only things left were the railroad station and Mr. Boulware's home.

Up to this time there was neither church nor school in the little town. People of the community worshipped at Hopewell Associate Reformed Presbyterian Church which was organized in 1787, or Concord Presbyterian Church which was organized in April, 1796.

Hiram Steele who was a devout Methodist had the circuit rider of that day preach once a week at his carriage factory, generally on Wednesday evening. Mr. Steele also organized a lodge of the Sons of Temperance which somewhat counteracted the influence of Hooper's barroom.

One young man who was fond of imbibing and determined to change his manner of life joined the Sons one night. The next morning in relating his experience to a friend, remarked, "Sam, I saw the grandest sight of my life last night, fifty grown men sitting in a row with white gloves and aprons on, and all sober."

The lodge also became a victim of the war and ceased to be.

The last mention of a license to sell whiskey in the town of Blackstock was in 1883.

An interesting item appeared in Chester Lantern in 1888: Chester County had the oldest bridegroom in the world, a Negro man at Blackstock, age 123 "by his own reckoning." He was a slave.

Skelly's Folly

In the neighborhood of Blackstock there lived Alexander Skelly, school teacher, surveyor, captain of the militia company, and outstanding citizen. One of Captain Skelly's pastimes was writing poetry of all types and on all subjects. Among his queerest notions, he conceived the idea of inventing a machine with perpetual motion. For two years Skelly worked on it unceasingly. Then at last his dream seemed about to be realized. He felt that he was on the verge of completing the only machine with perpetual motion.

One day he invited all his friends and acquaintances in to witness his machine in operation. When everyone had gathered Skelly pulled the lever, the machine ran a few minutes, the band broke — and that was the end of "Skelly's Folly."

Skelly's next exploit occurred in 1883. At this time there was great agitation over negro uprisings and nullification. Skelly with his militia stood guard every night to be ready for trouble.

One night the company was on duty, stationed near the present Blackstock Baptist Church. For a long time they stood there, not hearing a sound. Suddenly they heard a great commotion in the nearby woods, sounds of shouting and crying.

The company moved forward stealthily, prepared to fire. Upon arriving in an open space they saw the cause of the excitement — a 'possum in the top of a tree, dogs barking at it while several men were cutting down the tree.

Naturally the company was very embarrassed and felt that they should do something to save themselves from being the laughing stock of the countryside. Again the company was called to attention. Each man promised that as long as two members of the company were living in Chester County, he would never disclose the happenings of that night.

And these promises were kept. Many years afterward only one member of the militia company was living in the county, an old Irishman. It was he who finally disclosed the secret.

A few years after this incident, Skelly moved to Indiana and was soon lost track of completely.

Farm products, cotton, indigo and others grown in the area were carried by wagons to Columbia or Charleston for sale. William Bonner who lived near Wateree River was the first man in the area to own a cotton gin. The farmers around Blackstock carried their cotton for miles to this gin operated on the screw press type. They were delighted if it ginned one 300-pound bale per day.

The Lathan family, it is said, still has the first gin head saw that was used in this gin. It was made by William Lathan.

There were no buggies in Blackstock until about 1850. Jeff Duffie was the proud owner of the first one. Mrs. Hemphill's carriage is said to have been the first ever driven on the grounds of Hopewell ARP Church.

In 1849-1850 the railroad was graded through Blackstock. Up to this time all the land near Blackstock was owned by Jerry Walker who sold a large portion of it to David Hemphill, father of Mrs. Margaret Gaston. It was he who donated the land to the railroad for a depot to be built. The Hemphills later sold the land to George Hooper, and by Hooper to Thomas Boulware. The contract to build the railroad was given to Dr. J. L. Douglas who did the work by slave labor from his own plantation, under Hugh Bruce as overseer. The road was completed about July 1, 1851.

When the first passenger train came through, the whole country for miles around gathered to see it. It is said that at least a thousand people were at the flagstop, later to be the site of a station, when the train rolled in. They gave it an awed inspection.

Mr. Vanderbilt was the engineer, Captain Davis, the conductor of the train. J. B. Collins was the first station agent at Blackstock.

The Post Office at Blackstock was dedicated on Sunday, November 5, 1967, with Postmaster James R. Bennett in charge. About 400 attended the exercises. Edward M. Shannon, retired educator, served as master of ceremonies. Music was furnished by Chester High School band under the direction of Robert P. Long.

Principal speaker was Congressman Tom S. Gettys of Fifth Congressional District.

Blackstock today is almost a ghost town. There are several abandoned store buildings, and a school building falling to ruin. The school was closed when county schools were consolidated in the 1950s. When S. C. Highway 321 was rerouted in the 1960s, it bypassed Blackstock. Southern Railroad bisects the little community and long freight trains blow a mournful whistle as they pass hurriedly through what used to be a busy little town.

EDGEMOOR

Edgemoor, a little town ten miles from Rock Hill, is situated on the Seaboard Air Line Railroad. It was first named Ashland, but later changed to Edgemoor. The name Edgemoor was suggested to John C. Dickey by General R. F. Hoke, president of the Seaboard Railroad.

When the railroad came to the area in 1888, only three white families lived in what is now known as Edgemoor. They were J. C. Dickey, W. D. Orr and Mrs. Nancy Robinson.

The town was incorporated in 1889. The first "City Fathers" were W. F. Adams, W. C. Woods, J. F. Chambers, R. D. Robinson and W. E. Dickey.

W. E. Dickey owned the first mercantile establishment. He also operated a gin and saw mill, and was the first postmaster. The post office was located in his store. Other merchants were Glass and Ardrey, Crawford and Ardrey, R. A. Willis, T. F. Clinton and Son, A. H. Orr, Nunnery and Orr, and W. C. Nunnery. A drug store was operated in Edgemoor for a short time.

Later merchants were W. H. Hamilton and Company (organized in 1910), H. G. Hitchcock's Estate, and George S. Glass. Mr. Glass at one time operated a garage and a grist mill. He was born n Glasgow, Scotland and came to Edgemoor in 1913. Mr. Glass was murdered in his store in 1964, and his murder has never been solved.

J. D. Glass, uncle of G. S. Glass and a prosperous farmer of Edgemoor, is also of Scottish descent. His parents were from Glasgow, Scotland, but he was born in Montreal, Canada. He came to Edgemoor in 1885.

James Shaw was the first agent for the S.A.L. Railroad in Edgemoor.

Edgemoor at one time claimed a shoemaker in the person of John Bunyan Ferguson. He was crippled, but an efficient workman.

The town and surrounding country were conveniently served by a telephone office. The stockholders were J. D. Glass, W. L. Walker and Manetta Mills.

Prior to 1883, the children of Edgemoor and surrounding communities attended school at Hefley School near Lando. Some of the teachers were Dr. Jeff Strait, Miss Cora Westbrook and Miss Anna McFadden. The parents decided this was too far for their children to walk to school, so in 1883 a school was built on Sidney Robinson's land near Edgemoor. This school was called High View.

The first teacher was Miss Alice Evans. Miss Hattie Ratterree followed her. Later this school building was torn down and rebuilt on property given to the trustees by J. C. Dickey. This was in the year 1889. In 1905, the first brick building was constructed. Dr. J. N. Gaston and J. D. Glass were the trustees.

Later Edgemoor was consolidated with Wylie's Mill and Harmony school districts. On September 3, 1925 a big picnic was held to celebrate the completion of the large brick building known as Edgemoor High School and the placing of the cornerstone of this building. The trustees at this time were L. S. Lyle, W. C. Nunnery and R. H. Westbrook.

Two school buses were secured to convey the children to school. More than a hundred pupils were enrolled in the eleven grades of this accredited school.

Through the influence of Congressman Finley, a Rural Free Delivery route was established. R. D. Robinson was appointed carrier. He served for many years and was retired on a salary. Later

Route No. 2 was established with W. C. Nunnery as carrier. Both he and Mr. Robinson used horse and buggy as a conveyance. On one occasion, W. C. Nunnery's horse ran away, threw him out of the buggy and injured him severely. R. J. White substituted for him during 1906. A. H. Orr was appointed carrier January 1, 1907 and served faithfully for more than forty years.

A memorable cyclone passed through Edgemoor on March 22, 1890. W. E. Dickey's store, the drug store, and a tenant house on John Dickey's plantation were blown down, and the depot unroofed. The Associate Reformed Presbyterian Church which was nearing completion was destroyed. Sidney Robinson's store was demolished, a Negro killed and the manager, J. M. Crawford, severely injured. Other buildings were damaged. S. C. Robinson's slogan was "never give up," so he rebuilt the store.

A few years later his gin house with many bales of cotton and hundreds of bushels of seed was destroyed by fire. This time he did not rebuild but put his entire time to his extensive farming.

Edgemoor still has an A.R.P. Church. Dr. L. A. Lummus lived in Edgemoor and served the church for over forty years. Dr. J. N. Gaston served the town and community for many years. He was the father of Dr. Frank P. Gaston of Rock Hill and Dr. J. N. Gaston, Jr. of Chester. Other doctors who served Edgemoor were Dr. W. W. Fennell and Dr. Woodham.

Edgemoor has grown from three families in 1888 to a population of about 350.

LANDO

Lando, a small town on the west bank of Fishing Creek, was settled before the Revolutionary War days and was called White's Mill for the grist mill that was situated on the creek. A family by the name of White emigrated from Pennsylvania and settled there.

After the surrender of Charleston in 1780, the British set up military posts across the Piedmont and Col. Christian Huck, with 200 British regulars, a hundred Dragoons and about 500 Tories, established a post at White's Mill. It became a traveling stop for the Britishers traveling in this area. The old-timers said that Cornwallis spent one night there. It must have been true, as the house in which he supposedly slept was thereafter referred to as "the Cornwallis house."

Eventually the British post fell to American troops and the town temporarily took the name of Eave's Mill to honor a Colonial commander.

Almost a century had passed when, in 1882, Ferguson H. Barber as president and a group of men bought the grist mill and

surrounding land to organize the Fishing Creek Manufacturing
Company. Early in 1894 this company declared bankruptcy and the
mill was put up for sale. Mr. Barber bought it and the name was
changed to Lewisville Mills. Four years later, Mr. Barber sold his
holdings to Benjamin Dawson Heath and Manetta Mills was
established.

The name Lando, given to the little town in later years, was
derived from a combination of the names of Captains Lane and
Dodson, first conductor and superintendent of the Seaboard Railroad which ran from Edgemoor to Fishing Creek. Hence the name
Lan-Do.

Just as the name Lando was coined from two names, so was
Manetta. Ben Heath's two wives were Mary and Nettie, therefore
Ma-netta.

From the time the mill was bought in 1886 it was a yarn mill
only. Then in 1904 an addition was made, looms were installed and
the first weaving of blankets began.

Since Mr. Heath was a Charlotte businessman and commuted
to Lando, it was only natural that some of the first employees of the
mill came from Union and Mecklenburg Counties in North Carolina, where he lived. As they came, additional houses were built to
accommodate them. As the mill expanded, so did the size of the
village.

In 1919, Bascom Heath succeeded his father as president of the
mill. He was responsible for additions to the mill, establishment of
the company store, building an office building and a schoolhouse.
The new school was considered one of the finest in the county.

It was also during this era the churches were expanded. The first
church at Lando was built sometime between 1882 and 1890. It was
a Presbyterian Church, but union services were held there for all the
people in the area. Eventually the Methodists took it over and used
it until they decided to dismantle the wooden structure and build a
new one in 1927. It is today the Heath Memorial Methodist Church.

The first Baptist Church (now the Church of God) was organized July 12, 1906 and the church was built in 1910. Sunday School
rooms were added in 1927. The present church was finished in 1957
and the first service held on Easter Sunday.

The story of Lando is the story of the Heath family. Gilbert
Brown Heath represented the second generation of the Heath family
as president of Manetta Mills with plants at Lando and Monroe,
North Carolina. He served in this capacity from 1932 until he
retired in 1955 to become chairman of the Board of Directors. He
was noted for his interest and contributions to civic and church
affairs.

He was succeeded by his son Harry Bascom Heath who was president until 1974 when his son Gilbert Allen Heath succeeded him.

Manetta Mills now manufactures blankets from synthetic fibers, employs about 450 people and markets its products nationwide under the Cannon brand name.

Edgemoor and Manetta Railway operated double daily passenger train service between Lando and Edgemoor, effective February 1, 1905. R. A. Willis of Lando was traffic manager.

The mill for years operated "No. 5," the little "dinky" steam locomotive which comprised the Edgemoor and Manetta Railroad, a distance of 4.6 miles. One of the last steam locos of its type, the switcher was the center of attention when photographers and railroad buffs came to town.

Another center of attention is the Lando Mercantile Co. where H. G. (Harper) Simpson ran the store for more then 43 years. He boasted that Simpsons have lived in Lando since 1866 and that his father was born in the "old Cornwallis house."

A unique feature of Lando is the enormous and mysterious pile of boulders on top of the Lando hill. Since the Ice Age glaciers never came this far south, some geologists suspect the rounded king-size rocks were shaped by waves lapping on the edge of a primeval sea.

LEWIS TURNOUT

History of the small community of Lewis, seven miles north of Chester, dates back to earliest settlements in the area. Settled about the same time as Chesterville, it served as the courthouse seat, a railroad stop, and a stagecoach inn. First settlers were Scotch-Irish migrating southward from Pennsylvania.

Its first reference as a community was as "Walkers." John Walker was a large land owner in the area, known as Craven County at that time.

In 1785, the South Carolina General Assembly moved to divide the state into 37 districts, primarily for the purpose of establishing courts of law that would be accessible to all citizens. Walkers and Chesterville were in the same district.

The Act to establish County Courts in South Carolina was passed 24 March 1775. The first court of Chester District held under this Act was organized at John Walker's house. Edward Lacy was the county sheriff and David Hopkins and James Knox "gentleman justices."

At that time, South Carolina and the rest of the colonies were beginning to recover from the horrors of war and to function as a young nation. The state had little money to spend for courthouse sites or for anything else. Walkers was chosen as the site for the first courthouse in Chester District, mainly because John Walker donated some land for its construction. Court was held there for about ten years.

Soon after the court was established, Walkers became a stagecoach stop. The line went all the way from Salisbury, North Carolina to Columbia, South Carolina. Several inns and taverns sprang up to provide travelers with lodging, meals and entertainment. Mr. Walker operated a farm and a store which was a popular place for farmers and others in the area to congregate and exchange news of the day.

In the wooded countryside around the little stagecoach stop there was an abundance of deer and other wild animals. Hunting was the general sport of the well-to-do and many people kept hounds to hunt deer. Then, as now, a hound story made good listening and was, as the proverbial fish story, never questioned.

Three of the most avid hunters were Lewis Beckham, Thomas Chisholm and James Crawford. One day while gossiping at Walker's store about their exploits, James Crawford boastingly told a tale about one of his hounds. He said while walking through his cornfield he spied a coon sitting about twenty-five feet up a post. He called his favorite hound, Jack, patted him on the head and pointed to the coon up the tree. Jack made a bound, ran up the tree, caught the coon and jumped down with it in his mouth and killed it.

In April of the following year, these three men were out deer hunting when a terrific thunderstorm came up. The hunters dismounted and stood silently holding their horses. Every moment they expected to be struck by lightning. After some time Crawford broke the silence saying, "Boys, that was all a lie — that tale about Jack killing the coon."

In 1807, as Aaron Burr was being carried through Chester District on his way to Richmond, Virginia, to face trial for treason, the little village of Walkers played a part in his journey. After coming through Chesterville where Burr pulled free, leaped onto a big rock, and pleaded for help from local citizens, the party moved on to Walker's Inn where they spent the night and ate breakfast. The tavern keeper was Abe Smith.

An owner of the Lewis tavern, Mrs. Annie (R. E.) Jones, had in her possession a bench fashioned with arms like a settee that Aaron Burr reputedly slept on. She donated it to the Chester County Historical Museum where it is on display.

The inn, later known as Lewis Inn, still stands and is now over 200 years old. The original log cabin is made of heavy handhewn logs and has the original plank floors, doors and beams.

When the Charlotte to Columbia railroad was completed about 1852, in addition to depots in the larger towns, stations or turnouts were located about every sixty miles. These were for the convenience of patrons of the road in shipping produce. The turnouts were generally designated by the name of someone living in the area or owning property where they were located.

One of these stations was named Lewis Turnout, now Lewis. It was named for John Lewis, a civil engineer for the railroad. The original name of Walkers was used no more.

Early settlers in Lewis were affiliated with Fishing Creek Presbyterian Church until this mother church organized Uriel Chapel in their community in 1888. These churches and communities have always been closely knit and are served by the same pastor. During the Revolutionary War, the ministers had a part in arousing and organizing the people, the Rev. John Simpson at Fishing Creek and the Rev. William Martin at the Covenanter Church of Beaver Dam.

During the Confederate War, the Lewis community in April, 1861, provided some of Chester County's five companies that were mustered into the Sixth Regiment, CSA. The Catawba Guards, under Captain G. Lafayette Strait, had most of the Lewis recruits who were ordered to report to Charleston on April 11, 1861.

In World Wars I and II, men of Lewis Community served bravely while the women showed themselves possessors of strong character, heroism, self-sacrifice and hard work as they manned the home front.

In February 1930, Chester County obtained the services of a Home Demonstration agent. Clubs were organized to assist families in all the best practices of farming, gardening and homemaking. Memberships were large and made a great impact, especially in rural communities such as Lewis.

The Gill house near Lewis was built on a land grant from the King of England to the Gill family. It only changed hands twice up until 1979, once by inheritance, once by purchase. Mr. and Mrs. M. P. Wooten were owners until their deaths.

The kitchen of this house had no windows, only narrow slits, to enable those inside to shoot at attacking Indians.

LOWRYS

Lowrys, formerly called Lowryville, is a quiet little town of about 275 inhabitants nestled in the northern section of Chester County.

One of the earliest settlers was Major James G. Lowry who came from Fairfield County in the 1820s and gave the community its name. A cotton farmer, he owned extensive land and many slaves. Although he was ordained in the Associate Reformed Presbyterian Church and was known as "Parson Lowry" he never preached. He supervised his extensive farming operations from a handsome white-pillared house he had built on his plantation. The house is still standing and well preserved. The Rev. Lowry was born in 1780, graduated from South Carolina College in 1808, took his ministerial training in New York and was licensed to preach in 1818.

Sometime in the late 1840s a railroad called the Carolina and Northwestern was laid in Lowryville to connect York and Chester to the main line. Construction brought a burst of activity to the area.

Robert Hope supervised the grading of the road bed that ran across the Lowry land. The work was done with wagons and mules, wheelbarrows and shovels operated by slave labor. When the trains began to run, a stop was made in front of Lowry's house. Later a small depot was built nearby. The little village was named Lowryville.

The train engines burned wood and S. W. Guy and others furnished wood by contract, piling it in cords, half-cords and quarter-cords along the tracks where it was loaded on the train by the crew.

Once the railroad line was established in the area, landowners from adjacent plantations began to build stores and open small businesses around the depot. Among these were James, William and Samuel Guy, Robert Hope, George Steele, James Darby, Joe Wilson, Robert Josh Abell and William H. Abell. A. M. Titman came from North Carolina, married a local girl, Elizabeth Guy, and settled in the village.

By that time three roads converged in the little town. In 1873, the freight depot was moved near the convergence. There was no waiting room and passengers who came to board the train waited at the home of Dr. Anderson who came to Lowryville from Baton Rouge. A local historian says "he served the people of the community, both white and colored, with very little pay, most often in homes where there was no hope of any pay. His gentle old horse, Rabbit, carrying the doctor and his flapping saddle bags was a familiar figure on the country roads."

About 1852, Lowryville got its first post office and James G. Lowry, the parson's nephew, was appointed first postmaster. The mail was dropped off by the train as it stopped in the little town. The post office was housed in first one and then the other of the stops.

There were hitching posts conveniently placed where farmers could tie their horses when they came in for mail and sat a while to discuss the news of the day. A Star Route was sent out from Lowryville to Cabal. Patrons put up wooden boxes to receive their mail. The first mail carrier was a Negro, Hardy Sanders.

Among early storekeepers were S. W. and E. W. Guy, J. S. Darby, George Steele, R. T. Sandifer, Jim Sanders and A. M. Hardee.

Dr. Stuart Pryor came to Lowryville and worked for some time with Dr. Anderson before going to Chester to earn a name for himself as a surgeon. Dr. Brawley and Dr. Johnson also began their practice in Lowryville.

A. M. Titman operated the first cotton gin. In 1898 Mr. Titman with J. L. Abell set up another gin.

Lowryville early had a school housed in a two-story frame building with a bell tower and a bell. This house was burned and another handsome one was erected in 1910 on land deeded by Mrs. Dudley Jones. It was used until 1953 when the County Unit System was set up and the children bused to Chester High and North Chester Elementary schools.

The Lowryville school was blessed with good teachers and consequently some distinguished alumnae. Among the alumnae are Dr. Dudley Jones who for 25 years taught history and philosophy at Presbyterian College; Dr. J. Sam Guy who was head of the chemistry department at Emory University, Atlanta, Georgia; General O. K. Pressley, U. S. Marine Corps; the Rev. Sam Hope, missionary to Japan; and Dr. Robert Abell, who at the time of his election was the youngest member of the American College of Surgeons.

Eli Alston Wilkes, an early teacher in Lowryville School describes the little village when he came there. "The name of most of the people was Grant. Every other man you would meet on the highway was a Grant, and if he were a young man of another name still single, the probability was that it wouldn't be long before he would marry, and she likely would be a Grant.

And a clever folk they were, the Grants, good church people, good citizens, good husbands, good wives, all contented, unpretentious and prosperous."

The town's name was shortened to Lowrys and incorporated in 1907, with J. L. Abell as first intendent. A two-story frame store building put up in 1891 was run by S. W. Guy. There were groceries on the first floor and upstairs was a hall where Sandy River Lodge, the Woodmen of the World, the Farmer's Grange and the Temperance Union held their meetings.

Some other progressive steps were: Delco lighting in 1920, electric power from Duke Power Company in 1928, the first paved road paralleling the railroad in 1935, and an automatic telephone exchange in 1947.

In 1890, Zion Presbyterian Church, organized in 1855, was moved from the outskirts to a new brick church on land donated by J. S. Guy, "a heaven-kissing hill" in the heart of the village. An educational building was added and dedicated in 1956.

Lowrys Baptist Church was organized in 1904 with 32 members. Two buildings have stood on the present site. Armenia and Capers Chapel Methodist, Mt. Pleasant and Uriel Presbyterian churches are not far away.

The Lowrys Book Club was organized in February, 1911, to provide the ladies a social, literary and cultural outlet. It was first named the Embroidery Club and members met every two weeks to chat as they did needlework,. It later became the Thursday Afternoon Book Club where literary programs and forty-two games took the places of embroidery hoops and knitting needles.

In 1949, a plot of land was bought from Mrs. Jenkins and a community health center built. Dr. Arramanus C. Lyles was in charge. He directed nurses from the County Health Department in holding clinics one day each week. In 1985, Dr. Halsted Stone and Dr. Sam Stone reactivated the center.

In 1953, L. C. Berry secured from the United States Air Force an observation tower which was set up in front of town hall. He was given the Distinguished Service Award for meritorious service and for spending 1,800 hours in the tower.

During the outbreak of World War II in 1941, Chester County was chosen as a site for military maneuvers. Khaki tents sprang up like mushrooms in the fields and woods around Lowrys. Long convoys of jeeps and trucks moved through the community and the troops in Army drab found many hearty meals, friendly faces and comfortable beds in the homes of Lowrys.

Sandy River Masonic Lodge, encompassing both Lowrys and Armenia, was organized in Armenia in August, 1880. Eastern Star, an affiliate of the Lodge, was organized later. Both are still active.

Highland Ruritan Club, with the Rev. Joe Brown as president, was organized in 1955 to provide services to the community and fellowship to its members.

As it was in the beginning, Lowrys is a rural and agricultural community with descendants from many early families still living on original farms.

RICHBURG

The region around Richburg was first settled primarily by Convenanters, as was the region around Catholic Presbyterian Church on Rocky Creek in the southeastern section of the county. It was about 1745 when the first settlers came.

During and perhaps before the Revolutionary War there was a meeting house and grog shop on the road near Richburg. Dr. Lathan says the grog shop was standing at the time of Huyck's defeat at

Brattonsville on July 12, 1780, for one of the Tories stopped for food and drink as he fled the battlefield.

Rock Creek Meeting House was standing in October of the same year. The church was built prior to 1775 but the exact date is unknown. The land on which the church stood was probably granted to Agnes Henry on May 18, 1768 who, within the year, passed it to James H. Walker.

It was from the Waxhaw settlement about 1768 that the first settlers ventured across the broad Catawba and into Chester area.

In the same year, and again in 1772, a large number of Scotch-Irish Presbyterians came into South Carolina. Some of them came to Richburg which was then only a small settlement.

The exact date of the Covenanters' coming is not known, but it was about 1745. It is highly possible that the sites for the houses of worship were selected with special reference to the accomodations to the inhabitants of the area, and that none of them were ever formally organized into congregations as they are today.

The first place of worship or "preaching point" was about two miles west of the town of Richburg. Before the Revolutionary War and for years afterward, the road leading from White's Mill on Fishing Creek did not pass where Union Church and the town of Richburg now stand. William Faden's map used by Cornwallis and Tarleton in the southern campaigns of 1780-1781, shows that the road passed west of the present town of Richburg. There was, prior to the Revolutionary War, a road leading from the Catawba River through or near the present site of Richburg into the neighborhood of General Edward Lacey, a few miles west of the present site of Chester. In the main, this last road occupies the same bed today that it did 120 years ago. These two roads crossed on the top of the hill where J. Martin McDaniel resided.

Town of Richburg Organized

Tradition has it that the section between the crossroads once known as Rich Hill was, at the close of the 18th century, settled by a religious seeking band called Millerites. They thought the end of the world was coming and they wanted to be together on a hill. They built their homes around this hill and named it Rich Hill because the people had enough goods to leave everythng behind to settle in the new location they had chosen. There was another Rich Hill in the state and the mail was getting mixed up, so the Post Office Department renamed Rich Hill "Richburg."

Among the first families to live in and around Rich Hill were the Barbers, Andersons, Kees, Wylies, Millens, Strouds, Crocketts, Hicklins, McFaddens, Drennans and Fergusons. Mrs. Alex Barber was one of the first residents of Rich Hill.

Being situate in the crossroads, Rich Hill became a meeting place for all the residents of the eastern part of the county. A large white oak tree, which stood for more than a hundred years near the crossroads, was later known as "Richburg's Tree." It was located at the intersection now known as the Charlotte-Lancaster road in the yard of the late Mr. and Mrs. Jay O. Barber. It was tree of unusual size, especially for this section of the country.

The tree had a spread of 115 feet and the body was 21 feet in circumference. Every year it was fed about a thousand pounds of fertilizer by Mr. Barber, its proud owner.

While the tree was in a private yard, it seemed to belong to everybody, for many stopped to admire it, to enjoy the shade and protection of its mighty branches, and to take its picture.

Tradition goes that Charles Cornwallis (1738-1805), Commander of the British Forces which surrendered to the Americans at Yorktown in 1781 to end the war for Independence, once camped near the tree. The story is that Lord Cornwallis tied his horse to the tree when it was just a sapling, and his horse bit the top out. It is known that he was near enough during the time his army was in upper South Carolina to have made this possible.

Another story is told that Cornwallis spent the night about four miles from the tree on Fishing Creek in a house that stood in the village of Lando until sometime in the 1930s. It is also possible he spent a night in the Echols house which stood on the same corner with the tree.

Veterans of the Spanish American War sat under the Richburg tree and related their experiences. During the years 1890-1900, political speakings and picnics were held around the big tree.

The tree also played a role in World War I and II. Mr. and Mrs. Barber entertained the veterans of World War I after their return from France. During the South Carolina maneuvers prior to World War II, Mr. and Mrs. Barber provided a rest area for the troops and gave them refreshments, magazines and papers. One of the central communication points erected by the signal corps during the mock clash between the Reds and the Blues was under this tree. The tree died of age a few years ago.

One of the first stores in Rich Hill was built by Frank Hicklin of the Bascomville Community in the late 1800s. It stood on the present site of Mrs. Alma Cauthen's home. Her father, W. H. McFadden, purchased the building from Mr. Hicklin and later remodeled it into a home. An early plat of the town made in 1876 and another one in 1878 shows the Hickin store and most of the land around it belonging to O. Barber.

The first house in Richburg was a two story dwelling owned by a Mrs. Eckles (this lot is now owned by Mrs. O. Barber). The walls were covered with imported French wall paper. Her son-in-law built the first store building which was used as a music room. Later two Jews, one named Wolfe Withowsky, opened the first store in Richburg, occupying this music room. Some years later, Captain Hugh Simpson had a furniture shop there. This property is now owned by Mrs. Laura Melton and Melton Bros. Store was built on this site.

Miss Sarah McMillan was the first postmistress. The Post Office was located in one room of her house which stood on the present site of Mrs. Eliza Wylie's house. The Wylie house is located directly opposite the Masonic Lodge. The Strouds built the house about 1840 and it was called the Stroud House for a long time. After the Strouds moved, Dr. Sam Anderson moved into this house and used one of the rooms as his office. Later, Dr. Wylie purchased the house and practiced medical surgery there. The late Dr. William DeKalb Wylie of Winston-Salem, North Carolina, was born in this house which is now owned by his sister, Mrs. Mary Wylie Carpenter.

In about 1878, the railroad came through Richburg. It was a narrow gauge connecting Chester with Lancaster. To the people of Richburg, it was a new method of transportation. Each train was met with friendly greetings for there was always someone going or coming in on it. It made as many as four trips a day, carryng passengers, mail and cotton to and from Lancaster.

An Act to incorporate the town of Richburg was made to the General Assembly on December 24, 1889.

Union A.R.P. Church was the first church erected in the community. It was organized in 1795. In 1796, it united with Hopewell and New Hope in a call to the Rev. John Hemphill. His pastorate continued until his death in 1832. The first house of worship was a log building. The present building was erected in 1848.

The Richburg Presbyterian Church was the first house of worship to be erected within the town of Richburg. The deed to the property was recorded January 8, 1883, from O. Barber. James Drennan and B. E. Fripp represented the congregation. The first pastor was the Rev. J. H. Lumpkin.

The Methodist Church at Richburg was organized Nov. 28, 1887 by Rev. G. T. Harmon. The church was begun under the ministry of Rev. J. C. Bissell in 1886.

Prior to the rise of Great Falls as a merchandising center, Richburg was the center of a widespread farm trade. This happy condition existed for many years. Great stores once graced its "main street," catering to the needs of farmers in the area. Some of the early merchants were J. B. Wylie, V. B. Millen and Drennan and Gill. The stores of that time are now gone, some having been torn down. In February 1921 a great fire destroyed Dr. Jordan's drug store, Dr. Wilkes office, Drennan's Store and warehouse, and Nelson McWatter's barn and livery stable. In 1929, the drug store was again destroyed by fire. Some of the older store buildings stand only as a reminder of the once prosperous past of the town.

As early as 1896, Richburg was the shipping point for smaller surrounding communities with merchants such as Whitesides and Reid, operators of a grist mill and cotton gin at Lewisville; Joseph G. Hollis, general merchandise at Hollis; R. H. Ferguson, merchant saw mill operator, corn and flour milling at Wylie's Mill and others. D. A. Cauthen was depot agent in 1908 and 1909. He was followed by W. D. Toms, Thompson Backstrom, Mr. Roper and J. W. Hindman. At Mr. Hindman's death, his widow became depot agent and remained until the closing of the depot in the late 50's.

The Richburg Post Office was located in a small building beside where McCain's Grocery now stands. Postmasters were W. J. Reid and Frank Gale. Blair McCrorey was postmaster for a short time, followed by Mrs. Louise Porter McCain. Mrs. McCain bought the old drug store building and remodeled it into a post office. At her death, Mrs. Claire A. Reid became post mistress. Some of the first mail carriers were C. P. Sibley, John McCrorey, D. A. Cauthen, William Russ, Claude Jordan and Macie M. Porter.

The town once had the service of several doctors: Dr. Sam Anderson and Dr. William DeKalb Wylie, who also operated a drug store together, served the town as early as 1886. Dr. J. P. Young was called to serve in the Spanish American War, so Dr. Paul Marion replaced him while he was gone. Dr. Marcus Wilkes and Dr. Septimus Jordan operated a drug store along with their practices. W. Cloud Hicklin served as druggist under Dr. Jordan.

The town and surrounding country was served by a telephone office with W. J. Reid, J. O. Barber, W. B. Gladden, and J. R. Hicklin as stock holders.

Mrs. Addie Drennan McMurray ran a boarding house in the big three story house where Mr. W. B. Gladden lived in later years. The house was destroyed by fire in 1951.

The earliest records show Richburg's first form of town government was in effect sometime before 1897. Mayors were G. W. Roddey, R. L. Hicklin, J. O. Barber, J. R. Hicklin, Francis Simpson, C. P. Hicklin, W. Cloud Hicklin, M. E. Dye, J. H. Clawson, W. B. Gladden and John Boyd McCrory, present mayor.

The first school was a little one room building (near the present site of Mrs. Joe Anderson's home) near the railroad. Some of the first teachers were R. S. Crockett and Miss Sallie Backstrom.

Francis Simpson operated a grist mill, buggy and blacksmith shop at the back of where McCain's Grocery Store is located. Alex Freeman, a colored man from Chester, later ran the mill and shop.

ROSSVILLE

Rossville, according to Mrs. Carl Gibson, was named for Brown Ross, and early settler and prominent churchman in the area. The ship on which Brown Ross's parents were sailing to Charleston was wrecked and the passengers taken to New York. Although determined to go to Charleston, they stopped in Chester, liked the place and settled there. It is reported that in the northwest corner of the road, adjoining the present community center Brown Ross built his home. He acquired a large tract of land and married Sarah Johnson.

In 1761, Governor Thomas Boone of South Carolina was authorized to grant to each settler one hundred acres of land, rent free, for ten years. The Assembly made the grant more attractive by providing funds for the passage of immigrants to the New World. The flow of immigrants greatly increased. In 1763, after the Peace of Paris, Irish immigrants arrived in such great numbers that the dominant element of the county is still Irish.

The early settlers endured many hardships on the frontiers. The houses were crude structures built of logs or rough boards. Families, with their own hands, raised the food and cattle on which their livelihood depended. Each member shared in the hard work that lasted from dawn to dusk. The farm house was a manufactory of all the articles of daily use.

From childhood, the boys learned to ride horseback, use the rifle skillfully, and to depend upon themselves. When the Revolutionary War came on and the British armies entered the up-country, the boys and young men knew what to do. They executed attacks against the enemy in their own way.

Churches were established early along with the building of homes. On Highway 97 near the R. A. Stevenson home is the site of a Covenanter Meeting House. It was erected by Rev. William Martin in 1773. In 1780, he preached a patriotic sermon which stirred the surrounding country to arms. His church and his home were burned and he was taken prisoner by the British.

Mary Adair Chapter, Daughters of the American Revolution, has placed a marker on the site.

From the first log meeting house, which developed into Catholic Presbyterian Church, sixty men with thirty-nine different family names went forth to fight in the American Revolution. Their names are engraved on a marker in the churchyard, perpetuating their memory.

Church services were faithfully attended even though the way was long and difficult. The roads were mere trails, and transportation was on foot or horseback. These devout people walked with feet bare so as to keep their shoes clean for the service. They would stop at the last creek or branch on the way to wash their feet and put on their shoes.

Mt. Zion Baptist Church was founded about 1834 in Rossville Community. There is a deed which shows that Ross Dye gave some land in 1899 which was needed for expansion. This church was later moved to Mitford.

Ebenezer Methodist Church was founded before 1850 "right in the heart of Rossville." Mrs. Dell Clarkson Stevenson recalled that the first church, of which she was a member, was built high off the ground and that the pulpit towered above the congregation. There was a slave gallery and the church faced sideways to the road.

Hebron Presbyterian Church, at first a brush arbor, was founded in 1896. It was an offspring of Catholic Church.

One of the first sawmills in the country was located in Rossville. Logs from far and near were brought to this mill, and people came to see this new-fangled circular saw Mr. Stroud had bought.

While John H. Stroud was off at war, one of Sherman's men tried to burn "Woodlawn," his home. Mrs. Stroud was able to put out the fire. When she asked the red-headed Yankee soldier if he had a mother, he began to cry. An officer asked Mrs. Stroud to point out the man who had started the blaze but she refused. Fifty-one bales of cotton were taken away as well as all the foodstuff and horses, but Woodlawn stood.

When a straggler from Sherman's camp came to the "Brown Ross Home," he heard a watch ticking behind the fine hand-carved mantle. With an axe he cut a hole and found not only the watch but the family silver, too.

Nearby Rocky Mount was so pillaged by Sherman and his men that the people almost starved. Joseph Stroud sent an oxcart regularly with meal and flour.

As time went on a bridge replaced the ford at Stroud's Mill on Big Rocky Creek. When heavy rains caused flooding, both the bridge and the mill were destroyed.

Some early businesses in Rossville were Col. Culp's store which also held the Post Office and blacksmith shop two miles from Caldwell's Crossroads. At Dewitt (now Caldwell's Crossroads) Heath Caldwell owned a general mercantile store, run by Will Morrison. James Beaty of Winnsboro built a store where the present marker for Ebenezer Methodist Church is. It was reportedly "as fashionable as those in Chester — offering imported silk and both alpaca and henrietta woolens."

The annual May picnic at Great Falls was a great occasion for the people of Chester, Lancaster and Fairfield counties. This was during the horse and buggy days, so the trip was quite a long one. The young people from two academies nearby started the picnic in the spring of 1852, on the fourth Saturday in March. After the war, the date was changed to the first Saturday in May.

Rossville Community Center was built for the grammar school in 1923 or 1924. Some of the teachers were Evans, Nealy, Aiken, Anderson, Gibson and Garrison. This school had a short life due to consolidation of area schools.

At a revival at Ebenezer Methodist Church, in the summer of 1947, plans were made from the floor to send a delegation of citizens to ask the trustees of Great Falls Schools to stop the sale of the school. Those who appeared before the trustees that morning recall the persuasive speech that Rev. Jess J. Stevenson made.

On September 2, 1947, the late Nealy Bankhead got a letter which stated that the school property would be set aside for Rossville Community Center. The letter was signed by W. M. Estridge, Townsend Freeman and J. R. Gladden.

WELLRIDGE

It is not certain where the name Wellridge originated, but it is identified as a school name. During the early 1900s Wellridge was a small one teacher school. It was located ten miles from Chester on the road between Chester and Great Falls. In 1925 it was consolidated with two other small schools in adjoining districts. Pleasant Grove district on the west, was located six miles from Chester, one quarter mile off the Chester to Great Falls road, on property owned by Pleasant Grove Presbyterian Church. Tip Top district was to the north, located near Peden's Bridge, over Rocky Creek, on a road running southeast from Chester. This road is still known as Peden's Bridge road.

There are two churches in this community. Catholic Presbyterian in the extreme eastern section and Pleasant Grove Presbyterian in the western section.

When Catholic Church's first building was erected about 1759 it was used by newly arrived Scotch-Irish groups who all held to Presbyterian beliefs and doctrines, but differed in the practice of them. So it was considered appropriate to name the church "Catholic," in the sense of the meaning of the word as universal, general, or all inclusive.

The present building was erected in 1842, is still in very good condition and is used weekly for services.

For about 10 years the people of this old congregation, who were living a considerable distance from the church, to the northwest, worshipped together in a building in their midst. Mr. Hugh White gave a small tract of land, to be used by this group on which the building for worship was erected, and was known as "Upper Catholic."

In 1847 these members in Upper Catholic organized as a separate church that was called Pleasant Grove. The present building was erected in 1888.

Following is some history of two families: The McCalla family settled in the southeastern section of the community, and the Knox family settled in the northwestern section of the community.

The "Caldwell Place," formerly known as "Hazelwood Plantation," is land that was deeded to David McCalla, Jr. by King George of England in 1760.

The farm was passed down through the McCalla family until 1835 when the father of Bertha McCalla deeded the property to her husband, William Caldwell. William Caldwell deeded it to his son, James McCalla Caldwell, who in turn deeded it to his son, James McCalla, Jr. The property remained in his estate owned by his widow, Mrs. Naomi Harmon Caldwell, and children, James M. and Nellie C. Ezell until the 1960s.

The first dwelling was located across the road from the present house, which was built in 1844.

Besides farming, William Caldwell in 1835 built a tannery, a harness shop, a machine shop, cotton ginnery, and a saw mill. The lumber in this house was grown, sawed, and kiln-dried at home.

The acreage has been reduced to the present 472 acres on which the dwelling stood.

The Knox family came from Antrim, Ireland in the year 1783. The King of England granted to Hugh Knox 100 acres of land along Bull Run Creek, 6 miles southeast from Chester, on which he built a log cabin. Hugh Knox served as a Captain in the Revolutionary War.

James Nesbit Knox, son of Hugh Knox, married Mary Dunlap, and built his home on this property. This house still stands.

Jimmie Knox of Chester, who is a great-grandson of James Nesbit Knox, has possession today of the original copy of this land grant by the King of England. Sallie Knox, daughter of James Nesbit Knox, married William Wallace. They built a house, which still stands today, near Pleasant Grove Church. This house and land on which it stands is the estate of Hugh M. Caskey, grandson of Sally Knox Wallace and is the property of Mrs. Corrine (William) Tennant and children. They are grandchildren of Mrs. Mary Bell Caskey Tennant, sister of Hugh McCaskey.

"Chiefs Park" 1985

XXXI *"CHIEFS" FILMED IN CHESTER*

The summer of 1983 will long be remembered by the people of Chester. It was the year Chester was turned into a movie lot, the year Chester mill workers and merchants and politicians began moonlighting as film extras, the year Chester was vindicated for the half century it has spent without visible progress.

This small town in the northwestern part of the state beat out sites all over the country in its bid to portray Delano, Georgia, the fictional town in which the Columbia Broadcasting System (CBS) television mini-series "Chiefs" is set. So, for the summer at least, the Masonic Temple became the Bank of Delano, Mary's Cake Box became the Delano Bakery and the Chester County Chamber of Commerce became Delano City Hall.

The transformation of Chester came about largely through the imagination of Stuart Woods, the native of a small Georgia mill town who scored a hit when *Chiefs,* his first novel, was published in 1981. The book is the riveting story of three small-town police chiefs who, over the course of 40-plus years, stumble onto the grisly murders of a mass killer living in their midst.

CBS scheduled the television adaptation to run three consecutive nights during the November 1983 ratings sweep.

Written in three parts, the story begins with the saga of the courageous first chief, Will Henry Lee (played by Wayne Rogers of *M.A.S.H.*) as he takes over the job in 1919. After his tragic death, the story takes up with the short, sadistic reign of a World War II decorated veteran (Brad Davis of *Chariots of Fire*). He, too, dies before the killer is discovered, and the story jumps to 1962 when the town gets its first black police chief (Billy Dee Williams of *The Empire Strikes Back*).

Also starring were Charlton Heston of *The Ten Commandments,* as Hugh Holmes, the town's founding father; Keith Carradine of *Nashville,* as the militaristic Foxy Funderburke; Stephen Collins of *Tales of a Gold Monkey* as Billy Lee, son of the first chief;

Tess Harper of *Tender Mercies* as Billy's mother, and Victoria Tennant of the *Winds of War* as his wife. Paul Servino of *Oh God* plays the neighboring county sheriff. Author Stuart Woods plays a cameo role.

Because of the time span of the book, the production company, Highgate Pictures, Inc., had to find a town that could be taken back to 1919, then whisked forward to the 1960s. Chester, with its original downtown architecture dating back to the mid-1800s, fit the bill.

"Chiefs" Makes Impact on Chester

In a well-orchestrated press conference held in Chester's War Memorial Building on March 24, 1983, South Carolina Governor Dick Riley came and announced that CBS-TV had selected Chester as the film site for its upcoming three-part mini-series, "Chiefs." Lt. Governor Mike Daniel and aide Bud Ferillo accompanied the governor.

"This is a great day for South Carolina and a great day for Chester," the governor announced. "Since 1980, when South Carolina's commitment to recruiting the film industry began, some $30 million in feature films, television productions and national commercials have been made here. The budget of "Chiefs" alone represents nearly one-third of these projects combined."

Indeed, the CBS mini-series — produced by Highgate Pictures, Inc. of New York City, is the largest film project in the state to date. With it came jobs for 1,000 to 2,000 local residents either as film extras or as carpenters, plumbers, electricians, drivers and the like. That was welcome news to Chester County, which had 14.4 percent unemployment rate at the time.

In addition, those outsiders involved with the filming used area hotels, homes, motels and restaurants during their stay. John Quill, Highgate producer, said he estimated that the project brought $3 million to the area.

Filming began on May 23, 1983 and ended about August 9, 1983.

Remodeling work at an old flower shop on Gadsden Street was the beginning of a transformation that made the uptown area look as it did 64 years ago. When filming began, the buildings and streets looked as they did in 1919. By early August when filming was complete, the city was redone in meticulous detail to the periods of 1945, then 1962.

"This is the biggest on-site construction project for TV in America," said production designer Charles Bennett. "This is a whole town that changes three complete times. That doesn't usually happen on TV.

"The town is as identifiable as an actor. The audience will be totally aware of how the town grows and changes."

The vacant flower shop over Terry's Taxidermy was converted to a building with a wooden facade, used as the police station. The alley beside the shop served as the fire station, complete with a vintage fire truck and a spotted dog.

Craftsmen built wooden facades or porches on about twenty buildings in the uptown area. Cloth awnings, old windows, curtains, signs and doors made other buildings fit the periods.

"There are about 72 buildings in (uptown) Chester," Bennett said. "Almost every one needed something."

Building interiors were also used in the mini-series, said Vincent Kempster, set decorator. Old items were assembled to create a town council room, drug store, police station, fire station, dress shop, newspaper office, grocery store, hardware store, telephone office, loan company, shoe repair shop and funeral home.

The streets were in for changes, too. Streets were painted red clay color to make them look like those of the early 20th Century, Bennett said. Dirt was packed on streets. For later scenes, roads were washed and black-topped.

Traffic lights were taken down and parking meter poles were sawed off at sidewalk level or changed into hitching posts for horses. Cross bars were fixed to light poles to make telephone poles. Old wooden street signs guided drivers.

The monument area on top of the hill was turned into a park with grass, dirt, trees, bushes and park benches, under the direction of Sherman Williams, assistant director. A wooden barn-front section was put up across Gadsden Street just below Wylie Street for a mule auction early in the series. Some 40 mules were rounded up — with difficulty — due to the sparse mule population of the area.

Miniseries makers looked for — and found — authentic items like old crates, cans, tools and furniture to go in businesses for inside scenes, Kempster said. They searched for old grocery store items, drug store items — especially old funeral home and doctor's office items.

The filmmakers looked for period cars in running condition, for buggies, wagons, horses and dogs. About 300 period vehicles and some 200 animals were used, Bennett said. Models needed in particular were pre-1924 panel trucks and an open touring car like the one in which President Franklin Delano Roosevelt toured the South. Work trucks and military vehicles were sought.

For the 1945 segment, "Chiefs" used a sporty 1939 convertible, several police-type vehicles, a Harley motorcycle and a late-30s model hearse. For the final segment of the story, the script called for a "new" Oldsmobile 98. Old Georgia license plates were rounded up to conform to the small fictional Georgia town of Delano.

Filming "Chiefs" on top of Chester's hill — "Chiefs Park"

Filming at St. Mark's Episcopal Church, Wylie St., Chester

L to R: Producer John Quill, Actor Charlton Heston, Actor Brad Davis (behind Heston) Actor Paul Sorvino, Actor Keith Carradine, Actress Tess Harper (back) Actress Victoria Tennant (back) Actor Steven Collins

L. Cliff Coleman, asst. director, Charles Bennett, art director for "Chiefs"

Chester was converted to a movie set

Actors Steven Collins, Billy Dee Williams on Main Street set in Chester

"Chiefs" CBS mini-series filmed in Chester in summer of 1983

Actor Wayne Rogers on set in Chester

Extras Joel Collins III, Anne Collins, Larry Freeman on the set

After visiting and photographing 60 other sites, Chester, a city of 6,820 was selected. Chester won out over Manchester, Georgia, and Albany, Arkansas because it has a more unusual character than the other towns considered for the movie-series.

The producers were taken with Chester just the way it is — rolling countryside surrounding the town's well-preserved Southern ambience, its centerpiece Confederate monument and 1914 jailhouse with cells intact. The producers were looking for a town that hadn't changed, and they found it in Chester.

The big name CBS producers "were enormously impressed with the look of Chester, its hills, curves and angles, and with the hospitality and precision of the South Carolina welcome they received. It is safe to say that Chester rang their bell," Governor Riley said.

On the Set in Chester

Swamps with snakes, cliffs, railroad tracks, farmhouses, a small airport, country churches, and homes in other sections of the county proved close enough to what the filmmakers required to allow the entire movie to be shot on location.

If the physical attributes of the town were ideal for the movie, the townspeople made it doubly inviting. Wayne Rogers, the first star to arrive on the set, told city manager Penn Colvin that "they are killing me with kindness."

The popular actor — and the host of famous faces to follow — wasn't the only thing creating good will in Chester. Highgate spread money around with abandon, and quite a few Chester residents were at the receiving end.

For instance, a scene in which Will Henry Lee is shot by a malaria-crazed black man was filmed in a kind of bottom land at the end of Mill Street, a predominantly black neighborhood. Director Jerry (Shogun) London ordered all electric lines removed, so electricity in four houses was cut. Highgate gave residents money for motel and restaurant bill, and paid for any food that spoiled in their refrigerators.

Marie Chislom moved into a very un-1920s-like trailer adjacent to the set. In blocking the trailer off with a giant wooden wall, the filmmakers also blocked the normal breeze that flowed through it. To compensate, they installed an air conditioner for Mrs. Chislom.

George and Nancy Anderson own the 1920s house on Hemphill Avenue that was selected as the Lee family's town house. A film crew moved in and painted the woodwork, repapered it, and even arranged a backyard garden by paying a neighbor $50.00 for the 12 flourishing cabbages transplanted to the Lee plot.

Other local businesses sharing in Highgate's bounty were Chester News Stand and Ward's Printing that sold hundreds of copies of *Chiefs,* Pundt's Restaurant that had the catering contract, and Joe Collins Real Estate, Inc. that located housing for most of the cast and crew, approximately 160 people.

There was money to be had for folks willing to rent out their homes for the movie people. Some families went to the beach or lake and rented their homes out for handsome fees. Charles Bennett, the movie's art director, liked the area so much he purchased a house on Woodland Drive in Chester.

The lure of easy money went a long way, but when it comes down to it, the glamour of moviemaking was more dazzling to Chester residents than anything else. Townspeople eagerly pitched in as the hunt for actors, extras, craftsmen, guards and go-fers got underway.

Those who weren't actively helping were avidly watching. The town of fewer than 7,000 swelled mightily on the weekends when tourists from all over the state and beyond flocked to watch the action of truly big time movie making.

Sites used in shooting "Chiefs" other than the downtown area were the Durham farm, Williamsville Church, the homes of Fred Lalli, Tom Triplett, Edith Coogler and Clyde White, the old city reservoir and others. Several scenes were shot in Columbia, S. C. around the State Capitol and the Governor's Mansion.

The mini-series was shown in three episodes in November 1983 and again on July 26-28, 1985 on CBS-TV network.

AN EVENING WITH CHARLTON HESTON

When Shakespeare wrote that all the world is a stage, he probably didn't have the Chester War Memorial Building in mind.

But the building became a stage Sunday evening, July 10, 1983 for Charlton Heston, Paul Sorvino, Keith Carradine and Victoria Tennant who presented dramatic readings to benefit the Chester County Library.

Heston was Chester's most famous resident during two months of filming the CBS six hour mini-series "Chiefs." When library trustees chairman Anne Collins wrote Heston asking if he would head a library benefit he was happy to oblige.

Tickets sold for $25.00 minimum donation and were limited to 150 at Heston's request. He said he preferred a smaller, more intimate group, and wanted to perform primarily for the people of Chester.

The memorial building was transformed for the occasion. Pink and green candles, framed in magnolia leaves, were placed in the windows. A harpsichord was donated for background music for the evening. Caterers provided complimentary roast beef, crudités, fresh fruit, cake and champagne from elaborately decorated circular tables.

And Anne Collins, chairman of library trustees, came up with an eight-stanza original poem to introduce the actors to the 150 who dressed in their Sunday best for the event.

"Early in the spring of 1983, stars fell on Chester to a fabulous degree," began Collins. "When Highgate Pictures of New York City, came to Chester with its site-selection committee."

"I think that's the only introduction in verse I've ever had," said Heston. "And I'm grateful for it. I'm delighted not only to be here tonight but to be in Chester."

The audience was attentive as Keith Carradine read Rudyard Kipling's "The Betrothed" from a book he borrowed from Heston. Sorvino read one of his own poems, then a scene from "Caruso" which he hopes to produce and star in on Broadway.

Victoria Tennant read two Shakespeare sonnets. And Heston, living up to his fabled stardom, read from the final chapter of "Moby Dick," acting out all the parts and shaking the audience when he bellowed, "Do you see him?" at one point.

After the performance, audience members were ecstatic as they lined up to meet and talk with the actors, and have their keepsake programs autographed. Mrs. Lydia (Charlton) Heston, actress Tess Harper and several other members of the "Chiefs" cast and staff attended. Congressman and Mrs. John Spratt were among the guests who attended the elegant Southern reception.

"An Evening With Charlton Heston" raised $3,750 for the library.

This was the second local benefit that Heston and "Chiefs" stars appeared in, the first being a softball game that raised funds for Grover Pundt Development Center, Jobs for the Jobless, and Chester County Law Enforcement Officers Club.

CHIEFS PARK

Two years after Hollywood movie makers left Chester, the drumstick-shaped park on top of Chester's hill the movie inspired was dedicated and became the centerpiece of Chester's Bicentennial celebration.

On Saturday April 19, 1985, the $15,000 "Chiefs' Park" — named for the 1983 TV movie "Chiefs" that was filmed in and around Chester — was dedicated during a bicentennial kick-off on the anniversary of the day Chester County's boundaries were drawn by S. C. map makers. S. C. Lt. Governor Mike Daniel, Mayor Willie Cranford, Rep. Paul Short and County Manager Carlisle Roddey were on hand to provide oratory for the occasion. The Chester High

School band, drill team and color guard performed. A birthday party followed at City Hall.

In the summer of 1983, when Chester became the fictional Southern town of Delano, much of Delano's activities centered on the park and its tall Confederate monument. Chester's main business district, Main and Gadsden Streets, underwent a dramatic makeover that caused Chesterites to view their town with new awareness of its uniqueness and beauty.

Since the filming, the town has won assistance for downtown development from the national Main Street program. Many shop owners have spruced up facades, City Hall was renovated, and a handsome new library built. Local residents hope this transformation of a declining city and county into a reawakening signals a viable beginning for the next century.

Chester Landmark, City Hall, Built in 1850's

XXXII

CHESTER COUNTY INDUSTRIES 1986

METRO AREA

B & H Foods
  Packaged Salads and Sandwich Spreads
Boise Cascade Corporation
  Plywood, Wood Chips, etc.
Borden Food Company
  Cremora
Campus Sweater and Sportswear
  Distribution Center
Canal Wood Corporation
  Sawlogs and Pulpwood
Rock Hill Concrete, Inc.
  Ready Mixed Concrete
Chester Foundries, Inc.
  Aluminum Plaster Cast Items
Chester Sportswear, Inc.
  Mens and Boys Shirts
Consolidated Engravers, Inc.
  Engraving for Flexographic Printing
Essex Group, Inc.
  Communication Wires and Cables
GAF Corporation
  Glass Mats
GFT Glass Fiber Technology, Inc.
  Glass Fibers
JLM, Inc.
  Ladies Blouses
MESCO Metal Buildings, Inc.
  Pre-engineered Steel Buildings

Oxford Industries of Chester
Ladies Pull-on Slacks

Palmetto Metals, Inc.
Metalwork

Perfo-Tex, Inc.
Blank Screens for Textiles

Phillips Industries, Inc.
Mobile Home Aluminum Doors and Windows

Marathon Abrasives
Abrasives

Schlegel Corporation
Buff Polishing Pads and Wire, Carrier for Auto Door Seals

Shugart Manufacturing Company, Inc.
Construction Equipment, Sectional Barges-Floating Equipment, Steel Fabrication, Textile Specialty Machinery

Springs Mills, Inc. — Textiles
Eureka Plant — Polyester-Cotton Broadcloth and Batiste, Katherine Plant — Polyester-Cotton Sheeting

Sun Chemicals
Textile Finishing Chemicals, Paper Chemicals, Graphics Resins

Textile Arts and Film
Photo Engraving for Textiles

Triplett-Ryan, Inc.
Fiberglass Products

W. R. Grace & Company
Phosphatic Fertilizers

Zenith Engraving Company
Photo Engraving

FORT LAWN AREA OF CHESTER COUNTY

Morrison Textile Machinery Company
Textile Machinery

Springs Mills, Inc. — Textiles
Elliott Plant — Polyester-Cotton Broadcloth, Frances Plant — Polyester-Cotton Sheeting, Leroy Plant — Polyester-Cotton Broadcloth, Riverlawn Plant — Pinsonic Quilted Coverlets, Draperies and Kitchen Accessories, Cotton Warehouse — Fibers Storage

GREAT FALLS AREA OF CHESTER COUNTY

Acme Nameplate Manufacturing Co., Inc.
Metal Nameplates, Metal Decorative Trim

D & D Foundry
Aluminum and Brass Foundry

Ebert Enterprises
Beach Jackets

Cinderella Knitting Mills, Inc.
Boys and Mens Undershirts and Polo Shirts

J. P. Stevens & Company, Inc.
Republic Plant No. 3 — Warping

MCM Industries
Electronic Printed Circuit Boards

LANDO AREA OF CHESTER COUNTY

Manetta Mills, Inc.
Blankets

LEEDS AREA OF CHESTER COUNTY

Klapat Textiles, Inc.
Hammocks

Virginia Chemicals, Inc. of S. C.
Sodium Hydrosulfite

RICHBURG AREA OF CHESTER COUNTY

LRC Truck Lines
Groceries and Perishables Distribution Center

National Steel Company
Cold Rolled Steel, Hot Rolled Steel

Agurs Building on Top of Hill

EPILOGUE

Chester Countians are proud of their county and of themselves. Sometimes they wear that pride like a chip on the shoulder and with a swagger and a smile, dare anyone to knock it off. They like a fight — always have. Many hardly admit yet that we lost the Civil War.

They like themselves as they are, — and are not surprised when "emigrants" from Ohio, New Jersey, Wisconsin or even Canada come look Chester County over and decide to stay. They soon become partisan and prideful. There is no zeal like that of a convert.

For example, a retired officer from Canadian Army, Col. Laurie Schmidlin, after looking the country over, decided to retire in the pleasant countryside near Richburg in Chester County. He liked the climate, he liked the people and soon became a red hot Clemson Tiger football fan. We welcomed him, as we have welcomed many others, not ostentatiously, but with a neighborly visit on his porch of an evening and a swapping of yarns. Even neighbors of Carolina Gamecock persuasion came and visited — though they winced at the tiger paws on the Colonel's clothes and cars.

Chester County has managed to retain its rural state, although some industries are springing up around Chester's Bypass and along the South Carolina Highway 9 corridor to Interstate 77. Industry is transforming our economy and culture since the county was caught in the crucible of changes during the period 1940-1980.

The great Twentieth Century industrial revolution brought an improved standard of living for most and made it possible to afford changes in schools, homes, roads, and health care. It accelerated the trend away from agriculture and toward urbanization, providing jobs and steady income. Federal wage and hour laws jacked up the floor under personal income, as did Social Security and unemployment insurance.

Between 1959-1972, the number of manufacturing plants in South Carolina increased by 177 percent. "Like two buckets on a well chain agriculture was going in the opposite direction," says Dr. Lewis P. Jones. Farms declined 71 percent and population on farms 88 percent. These changes were evident in Chester County.

A discovery by a Georgia chemist, Dr. Charles Herty, during the depression of the 'thirties had a tremendous impact upon South Carolina and Chester County agriculture. Dr. Herty invented a process for making paper out of loblolly pines, the commonest, quickest-growing pines in the Up-Country. According to historian Lewis B. Wright, profits from wild stands of pines induced farmers to plant worn-out cotton land in seedlings supplied by nurseries established by the State Commission on Forestry. During the next two decades, millions of pines were planted, and the work still goes on. Chester County from the air looks like a pine forest interspersed with greedy and galloping kudzu vines. Few red hills are any longer visible and soil erosion cutting the land into gullied scars has been halted.

Despite changes, town and country have compatibly fused in Chester County. The urban employee often lives in the country where he has his own garden and fish pond and drives his pickup truck to work in Rock Hill or Charlotte.

Chester County still has several cotton gins, even the skeleton of an old-timey "screw press" on the Rodgers Reid farm, that testify to the departure of the old monarch. The leading money crops in the county are pulpwood, soybeans, corn, cotton, vegetables and hay. A few dairy farms and pastures remain.

Chester County does not face the waning quadrant of the Twentieth Century on the upbeat. A report from Catawba Regional Planning Council made on April 18, 1985, predicts slow growth for Chester County in the next 15 years while neighboring York and Lancaster Counties will burgeon about 50% each. Managerial jobs will rise 13.8%, labor jobs will decline 12.2%, farming jobs will decline 41.7% while sales jobs will increase 55% in Chester, 97.7% in Lancaster and 131.6% in York.

The most dramatic potential for change in Chester County is the completion of I-77 from Columbia to Charlotte. The county expects to see most of its growth along the interstate corridor near Richburg where industrial recruiters have been getting utilities on line to draw businesses.

There will be little population growth elsewhere in Chester County through 2000, the study says. The 1980 census reports the population at 30,148 and predicts a 2.3% annual growth rate.

Chester County is working diligently to attract new industry, to diversify, to share some of the growth burgeoning in neighboring Charlotte, North Carolina, Rock Hill and the Piedmont Crescent.

Accompanying this push for industrial metamorphosis has been the mushrooming of technical education. Students attend York Tech and other tech schools in growing numbers. Slide rules and pocket calculators protrude from many plaid shirt and blue jean pockets. Industrial arts, computer sciences and auto mechanics are popular courses of study.

Chester County has 16,870 telephones, proving that we talk too much, 17,958 vehicles, proving we match the national average in the number of wheels per capita.

A heap of country clings like kudzu vines to Chester. Most of the population was built up of people with a rural background. More people than ever are going for country things like chopping wood, joining the homemade biscuit binge at Hardees, and planting gardens. Country music is now the top seller in America. Guitar picking and mouth organs are popular. The Circling Squares attest to the lively revival of square dancing. All the real "laid back" guys are wearing cowboy hats adorned with feathers and geegaws, and blue jeans. The country has never left town.

Chester is full of good ol' country boys underneath the coat-and-tie professions of doctors, merchants, lawyers, bankers and businessmen. There has even been a revival of tobacco "chawin" shared by all ages from teenagers to grandpas. The younger generation hankers for motorcycles, boats and pickup trucks, and a place on the river.

Chesterites, most of them, retain the "all wool and a yard wide" character traits taught in rural homes and rural churches and brought to town with them. Religion, brainpower, thrift, honesty, minding their own business, and other Scotch-Irish virtues are their heritage.

A pithy observation is made by Van Woodward in his essay, *Search for a Southern Identity.* "In this fast-changing world," he states, "the South still has one distinctive trait setting it apart: its history, the collective experience of the Southern people who have had a unique historic experience as Americans." In this heritage, not yet obliterated is that intriguing something described always as the "Southern way of life."

Add an admonition by Atlanta Journalist Ralph McGill who says, "Gone are the myths of white pillared mansions and a magnolia-scented civilization. After the ravages of war, reconstruction, economic revolution, and depression — we can, for the first time, see the cotton South plain."

Maybe, he adds, we who are so in love with our fantasied history need to be careful that we "see it plain." Certainly that is the beginning of wisdom — and a purpose in looking at history especially if after having looked, we then look about ourselves at our own day, learning something about a keen eye as a way of developing conscience.

BIBLIOGRAPHY

Adair, James: *History of American Indians*
American Legion in South Carolina: the First Thirty Years
Banks, Rev. William: *Catholic Church, An Historic Discourse*
Barrett, John G.: *Sherman's March Through the Carolinas*
Bierer, Bert W.: *Discovery of South Carolina*
Bradford, W. R.: *The Catawba Indians of South Carolina*
Brown: *The Catawba Indians*
Brown, Richard Maxwell: *The South Carolina Regulators*
Biographical Directory of the South Carolina House of Representatives Vols. I and
    II
Cash, W. J.: *Mind of the South*
Files of Charlotte Observer
Chepesiuk, Ron and Pettus, Louise: *The Making of a State*
Chester County, Center of Carolina's Back Country
Charleston News and Courier: 1772-1773
Chester News
Chester News and Reporter
Chester Reporter
Chestnut: *A Diary of Dixie*
Collins, Anne P. and Knox, Louise G.: *Chester County Heritage History*
Columbia Register
Cooper, Wm. J.: *The Conservative Regime in S. C.*
Cornwell, Arthur and Gaston, David A.: *Chester County Economic and Social*
Daniels, Jonathan: *A Southerner Discovers the South*
Davidson, Dr. Chalmers G.: *The Life and Times of General William Lee Davidson*
Davidson, Dr. Chalmers G.: *The Colonial Scotch-Irish of the Carolina Piedmont*
Dickson, R. J.: *Ulster Emigration to Colonial America 1718-1785*
Drayton, John: *A View of South Carolina*
Dublin Weekly Journal 7 June 1729
DuBois, W. E. B.: *The Gift of Black Folk*
Evening Herald, Rock Hill, S. C.
Ellett: *Women of the Revolution, Vol. III*
The Farmer's Alliance
Ford, L. M.: *Memories, Traditions and History of Rocky Mount and Vicinity*
Faris, Rev. D. D.: *Reminiscences of the Reformed Church in South Carolina*
Fiske, J.: *Old Virginia and Her Neighbors*
Gent, John Lawson: *History of North Carolina*
Glasgow, W. Melanchton: *History of the Reformed Presbyterian Church in America*
Gordon, Asa H.: *Negro Life and History in South Carolina*
Hemphill, J. C.: *Men of Mark in South Carolina*
Hilliard, Samuel Bowers: *Hogmeat and Hoecake*
Hudson, Joshua Hillary: *Sketches and Reminiscences*
Johnson, Elmer D.: *A History of Libraries in the Western World*
Jones, Dudley: *History of Purity Presbyterian Church*
Jones, Katherine M.: *The Plantation South*
Jones, Lewis P.: *South Carolina, A Synoptic History for Laymen*
Kratt, Mary Norton: Articles in Charlotte Observer
Kohn, August: *The Cotton Mills of South Carolina*
Lauder, Ernest M.: *A History of South Carolina*
Lawson, John: *History of North Carolina*
Logan: *History of the Upper Country of South Carolina*
Lathan, Rev. Robert: *A Historical Sketch of Union A. R. P. Church*

Lathan, S. B.: Chester Reporter July 19, 1921 and Lathan Papers
May, John A. and Faunt, Joan Reynolds: *South Carolina Secedes*
McCallum, Butler: *Early History of Four Families* (unpublished)
McCrady, E.: *History of S. C. Under Royal Government*
McGehee, Larry: *Southern Scene*
McKeown, Mrs. W. W.: Papers
Miller, Kelley: *These Colored United States — South Carolina*
Mills, Robert: *Statistics of South Carolina 1826*
Mirken, Allen: *Sears*
Moore, M. A., Sr., M.D.: *The Life of General Edward Lacy*
Morrison, Joshua: *W. J. Cash, Southern Prophet*
New York Messenger: December 1925
Nunnery, Jimmie E.: *Dissertation on Farmer's Movement in South Carolina*
Oliphant, Mary Sims: *History of South Carolina*
Pamphlets: South Carolina Wildlife and Marine Resources, State Parks, Department of Parks, Recreation and Tourism
Parton, James: *Life and Times of Aaron Burr*
Ramsay, David, M.D.: *History of South Carolina, Vol. I*
Recollections of Chester County Schools
Records of General Synod, Presbyterian Church
Reid, J. S.: *History of Presbyterian Church in Ireland*
Revolutionary Soldiers of Catholic Church
Robertson, Ben: *Red Hills and Cotton*
Roddey, Wade B.: Papers
Rogers, George C., Jr.: *A South Carolina Chronology 1497-1970*
Sandlapper
Simkins and Woody: *South Carolina During Reconstruction*
Sinclair, W. A.: *The Aftermath of Slavery*
Smythe, J.: *Sketch of Ecclesiastical History*
Snowden, Yates, L.L.D.: *History of South Carolina, Vol. 1-5*
Springs, Elliott White: *Clothes Make the Man*
Stadiem: *A Class By Themselves*
State Newspaper files
Stephenson, Jean: *Scotch-Irish Migrations to South Carolina 1772*
Stinson, Daniel Green: Papers
Swanton, John R.: *The Indian Tribes of North America*
Trelease, Allen W.: *White Terror*
Wallace: *Short History of South Carolina*
Wallace, D. D.: *History of South Carolina, Vol. I*
Watson, J. F.: *Annals of Philadelphia and Pennsylvania*
White: *The Making of South Carolina*
White, Mrs. John G.: *Old Homes of Chester, South Carolina*
Williams, Jack Kenny: *Vogues in Villany*
Wilkes, Eli Alston: *Echoes and Etchings*
Woodmason, Rev. Charles: *Diary*
WPA Writer's Program 1941: Palmetto Place Names
Wright, Louis B.: *South Carolina*

Credits:

Dr. William R. Wallace
Mrs. Eliza Walker Welborn
Miss Corinne Miller
William A. Corkill
John H. Hill, II

William D. Breedin
Ward W. Pegram, Jr.
Dr. R. W. Sanders
Wm. Randolph Sims
W. J. Irwin
Mrs. W. J. Irwin
Lucille and John Bramlett
Robert D. Knox
Louise Gill Knox
Mrs. Cleo Wall Vaughn
Mrs. Margaret Powell Ehrlich
H. Phelps Brooks, Jr.
Dr. James Hardin Wall
Charles Bell
Nancy Collins Anderson
Mrs. Jean Nichols
Mrs. Ethel Ayers Davis
J. Edward Davis
James Gaston, Jr.
L. W. Pittman
Herbert B. Tibbs
Doris B. Schumacher
George B. Anderson and First Federal of S. C.

INDEX

335

INDEX (Continued)

INDEX (Continued)

INDEX (Continued)

INDEX (Continued)

INDEX (Continued)

INDEX (Continued)

INDEX (Continued)

INDEX (Continued)

INDEX (Continued)

INDEX (Continued)

INDEX (Continued)

INDEX (Continued)

INDEX (Continued)

INDEX (Continued)

INDEX (Continued)

INDEX (Continued)

INDEX (Continued)

INDEX (Continued)

INDEX (Continued)

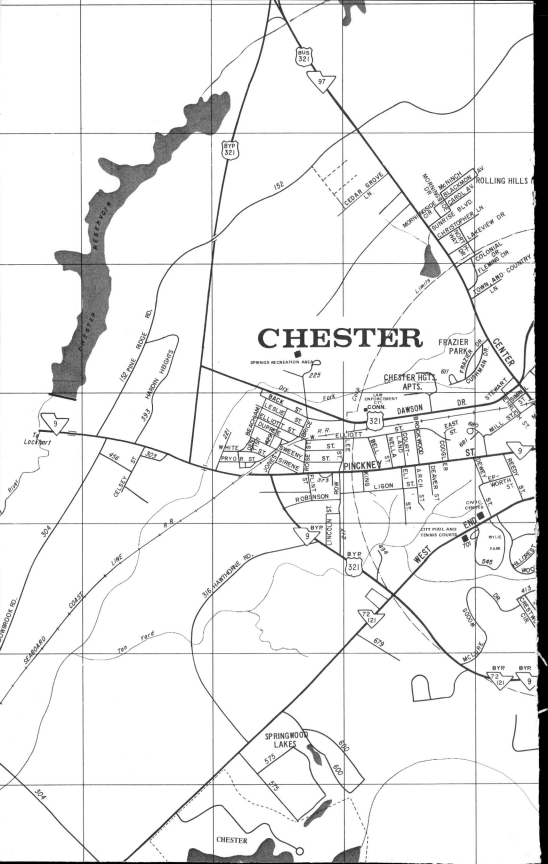

CHESTER